SCORPIONS' DANCE

ALSO BY JEFFERSON MORLEY

The Ghost

Snow-Storm in August

Our Man in Mexico

SCORPIONS' DANCE

THE PRESIDENT, THE SPYMASTER,
AND WATERGATE

Jefferson Morley

ST. MARTIN'S PRESS
NEW YORK

First published in the United States by St. Martin's Press, an imprint of St. Martin's Publishing Group

SCORPIONS' DANCE. Copyright © 2022 by Jefferson Morley. All rights reserved. Printed in the United States of America. For information, address St. Martin's Publishing Group, 120 Broadway, New York, NY 10271.

Designed by Omar Chapa

www.stmartins.com

Library of Congress Cataloging-in-Publication Data

Names: Morley, Jefferson, author.
Title: Scorpions' dance : the president, the spymaster, and Watergate / Jefferson Morley.
Description: First edition. | New York : St. Martin's Press, 2022. | Includes bibliographical references and index.
Identifiers: LCCN 2022002311 | ISBN 9781250275837 (hardcover) | ISBN 9781250275844 (ebook)
Subjects: LCSH: Watergate Affair, 1972–1974. | Helms, Richard. | Nixon, Richard M. (Richard Milhous), 1913–1994—Friends and associates. | United States—Politics and government—1969–1974. | United States. Central Intelligence Agency. | Intelligence service—United States.
Classification: LCC E860 .M67 2022 | DDC 973.924—dc23/eng/20220121
LC record available at https://lccn.loc.gov/2022002311

Our books may be purchased in bulk for promotional, educational, or business use. Please contact your local bookseller or the Macmillan Corporate and Premium Sales Department at 1-800-221-7945, extension 5442, or by email at MacmillanSpecialMarkets@macmillan.com.

First Edition: 2022

10 9 8 7 6 5 4 3 2 1

CONTENTS

Introduction   *1*

1   Arriba   9
2   Defeated   19
3   The Black World   26
4   Monster of Self-Possession   35
5   Martyrs of Tomorrow   43
6   Freedom of Action   53
7   The Shadow   62
8   Women   71
9   The Silent Service   83
10 Honeymoon   94
11 Flattery   100
12 Madman Theory   109
13 Public Relations Job   115
14 Sledgehammer   127
15 Blackmail   134
16 The "Who Shot John?" Angle   146
17 Our Side   156
18 The Sorest Spot   169

19   The Ruse   181
20   Precipice   192
21   Escape   206
22   The Witness   215
23   Magnificent   223
24   Ghastly   231
25   Interrogation   241
26   The Puritan Ethic   247
27   Judgment   257

      Epilogue   264
      Acknowledgments   269
      Notes   271
      Source Material   309
      Bibliography   311
      Index   317

"Hell is empty and all the devils are here."

THE TEMPEST, WILLIAM SHAKESPEARE

SCORPIONS' DANCE

INTRODUCTION

"The CIA had no involvement in the break-in," declared the duly sworn witness, Richard Helms, former director of the Central Intelligence Agency, his voice starting to rise. Helms spoke to seven U.S. senators seated at the desks not ten feet in front of him. "No involvement whatever," Helms emphasized with a broadside of rattling consonants. "And it was my preoccupation, consistently from then to this time, to make this point and to be sure that everybody understands it."

Helms, a saturnine scion of Philadelphia's Main Line, sixty years of age, sat forward at the wooden witness table. His long, slate-gray hair curled over the collar of his silk suit jacket. Filaments of silver glistened on his temples in the glare of white TV lights. His jaw was firm and active. He was surrounded by hundreds of spectators crowded into Room 318 of the Russell Senate Office Building in Washington, D.C. The televised hearings of the Senate Watergate Committee (formally known as the Select Committee on Presidential Campaign Activities in 1972) were high political theater in America that summer, though not quite the hot ticket they had been a few months before. When the TV camera swung his way, Helms bared his teeth in a grin.

Anticipation accompanied the witness. Richard Helms had served as director of Central Intelligence for almost seven years, from June 1966 until January 1973, when President Richard Nixon named him U.S. ambassador to Iran. He was making his fifth appearance before a congressional committee, but this was his first full public accounting of the Agency's role in the scandal that had already forced the resignation of Nixon's chief of staff, H. R. Haldeman, and his chief domestic policy adviser, John Ehrlichman. Despite a year of intensive news coverage, first by the *Washington Post* and then by the rest of the Washington press corps, the role of America's clandestine service in the Watergate burglary was still murky. CIA directors never testified in open session, much less about a domestic political crime committed by former Agency employees.

The witness caught the crowd by surprise. With one hand, he clasped the microphone at its base. With the other, he chopped the table with his neatly aligned fingers, and his voice rose still further.

"It doesn't seem to get across very well for some reason but the agency [*thump*] had nothing [*thump*] to do [*thump*] with the Watergate break-in!" he shouted. The murmur of talk in the far reaches of the hearing room was stilled as his words resounded to the high ceiling. *No involvement whatever.* Helms surveyed the faces around him. "I hope all the newsmen in the room hear me clearly now."[1]

They did. The *CBS Evening News* and ABC *News* both led their coverage of the hearing with footage of Helms's bravura outburst.[2] A front-page story in the *New York Times* declared "Helms Says He Resisted Pressure by White House for CIA Cover-up Aid."[3] The *Washington Post* lauded his appearance with the headline "Helms Displays His Old Skills as a Diplomat." Senior *Post* reporter Lou Cannon wrote that the "quiet and aristocratic professional" who ran the CIA during President Nixon's first term displayed a "strange sadness" about pressure from the White House.[4] That was a story many people wanted to believe as the Watergate affair consumed Washington: the law-abiding CIA director as an innocent bystander to a lawless president.

Empirically speaking, Helms's claim that the Agency had no involvement in the break-in was dubious. Four of the seven men arrested at the Watergate office complex in the early hours of June 17, 1972, had worked on or collaborated with CIA operations to overthrow the government of Cuba. A fifth burglar had held a senior position in the Agency's internal police force, the Office of Security.

"No involvement" implied no connection or association with the burglary. Yet two of the burglars, Howard Hunt and James McCord, had retired from the Agency two years before and gone into business with Helms's personal blessing and CIA institutional support. The Agency's statement, reported as fact, that Hunt and McCord "were former employees with whom we have had no dealings since their retirement" was simply false.[5] A month before his arrest, McCord bought electronic gear with Agency help. In retirement Hunt continued to meet with his longtime case officer, Tom Karamessines, the deputy director of operations and one of Helms's closest confidantes.[6]

A third burglar, Rolando Martínez, was known in the Langley cable traffic as AMSNAP-3. He had worked for the Agency as a full-time boat captain from 1963 to 1971, running[7] hundreds of sabotage, infiltration, and terrorism missions into Cuba.[8] Then he was kept on as an informant.

A fourth burglar, Bernard "Macho" Barker, was a police captain in Havana who had become a CIA source in the 1950s. Known by the code name AMC-LATTER-1, Barker recruited "a number of valuable agents" in Cuba, according to one classified memo.[9] He went on to serve as deputy to Hunt in Operation Zapata, the CIA's failed attempt to rout Fidel Castro's socialist government in April 1961. As a prelude to the landing of the CIA-trained brigade at the Bay of Pigs, Hunt and his men planned to assassinate Castro, but Cuban security forces broke up the plot and several of Hunt's men went to prison.[10]

A fifth burglar, Frank Sturgis, had briefly served in Castro's government and then joined the exiles in Miami, where he cultivated a reputation for violence.[11] If Helms had checked the file—and he usually did—he knew that Sturgis had once participated in a plot to kill Castro, which the Miami station considered and rejected.[12] No one in the Senate Caucus Room would have guessed that the Watergate crew included three aspiring assassins, and Helms didn't leave them any wiser.

It was true that the CIA, as an organization, did not select the target for the break-in. But Hunt, the former undercover man working in the Nixon White House, had brought the four Cubans into the operation. Without Hunt there would have been no team of burglars at the Watergate. And unbeknownst to senators and spectators, Hunt was a longtime personal friend of Helms, whom the director had groomed for fame. At the witness table, Helms transmuted tacit involvement into total innocence.

In ninety minutes of testimony, the former director recounted how President Nixon's Praetorian Guard, namely the vigilant Haldeman and Ehrlichman, had pressured him at a meeting on June 23, six days after the break-in. He said they practically ordered him to tell L. Patrick Gray, the acting FBI director, that further investigation of the burglars would compromise a CIA operation. He refused, he claimed. He had stood up to presidential pressure from the start, he declared, which had the virtue of being almost true.

Fred Thompson, counsel for the Republican minority on the committee, took over the questioning. An incisive lawyer with a head of hair that would take him far in Hollywood and Washington, Thompson noted that Helms had testified, under oath, just ten weeks before, that the subject of Watergate never came up at the June 23 meeting. Helms's colleague, deputy CIA director Vernon Walters, had stated, under oath, that it did. Thompson read back to Helms his earlier statement. He asked if he stood by it.

It was the first tough query Helms had fielded all day. Helms hedged, saying, come to think of it, Walters was probably right, that Watergate had been discussed at the meeting. "Mr. Helms," Thompson asked, "are you basing your testimony now on your own memory or on Mr. Walters's memory?" The agile Helms squirmed out of Thompson's clinch like the lithe long-distance runner that he was. "It was a combination of the two," he explained gaily.[13]

To the Capitol Hill crowd and a TV audience of millions, Helms dissembled with evident sincerity. He allowed that he knew Mr. Hunt. "A bit of a romantic," he sniffed. Couldn't remember a single operation he had participated in, Helms added, an audacious lie affably expressed. Helms knew the operational details of Hunt's political action and propaganda work over two decades, including his involvement in the Guatemala operation, his role as producer of the animated version of George Orwell's *Animal Farm*, his divisive leadership in the Bay of Pigs operation, and his ghostwriting stints for a *New York Times* columnist who liked to lunch with Helms. On more than one occasion, Helms had extricated Hunt from trouble with more straightlaced (and competent) colleagues. No one in the Senate Caucus Room guessed that story either. Not even Bob Woodward and Carl Bernstein, the Pulitzer Prize–winning *Washington Post* reporters, quite grasped the buddy-buddy friendship of the raffish burglar and the gentlemanly director.

Did the witness know Mr. McCord? asked Senator Joseph Montoya of New Mexico. The spectators in the quiet vastness of the Senate Caucus Room listened attentively and knew not what they heard.

"It is hard to tell you when I might have first met him," Helms sighed.[14] It was hard because the answer was twenty years before, in November 1953, at the latest. That's when McCord, working in the Office of Security, helped Helms clean up the story of Frank Olson, a U.S. Army scientist who fell (or, more likely, was thrown) from the window of a New York City hotel room that he shared with an Agency psychologist. Olson was considered a security risk because of his qualms about mind control experiments conducted on humans. McCord backstopped the psychologist's cover story, and the New York City cops were none the wiser about the presence of Agency personnel at the crime scene.[15] Helms tidied up the file in Langley, and the unpleasant business of Frank Olson was soon forgotten. McCord also proved helpful on a Cuban prison break operation and the hardening of Agency facilities against attack by armed radicals.

"Mr. McCord was in my office on two or three occasions on various matters," Helms allowed.[16]

It was Senator Baker's turn. Howard Henry Baker Jr. was the ranking Republican on the Watergate Committee, a well-barbered dealmaker from Nashville who strutted in three-piece pinstripes, an avatar of Tennessee's reputation as the home of shrewd operators. Was Mr. McCord an expert wiretapper? he inquired gently. He was all that and more, as Helms knew well. The former director pivoted around the well-laid perjury trap with the deft two-step of a seasoned ballroom dancer, which he was. "I do not remember," he pleaded. "If there is a document to that effect, I have no reason to question it."[17]

While courteously aggressive, Helms knew how to charm and disarm.

"I was told by some gentleman this morning that people seem to have a good forgettery when they get into this chair," he said, early on. "I do not pretend to be any better or any worse than anyone else, and my memory is fallible from time to time, but I am doing my very best at all of these hearings to tell you what I remembered at the time." Who in the Senate Caucus Room or the nationwide TV audience knew the dictionary definition of the unusual term "forgettery"? A facility for forgetting. No one in the room had more such facility than Helms himself.[18]

Senator Sam Ervin, Democrat of North Carolina, believed Helms and believed in the CIA. Ever since the Senate Select Committee launched its televised hearings two months before, the garrulous chairman had hammed it up for the TV cameras. With his Deep South drawl, the pro-war, race-baiting country lawyer from North Carolina became an improbable liberal hero in the summer of 1973. At his best, Ervin dilated on the meaning of the Constitution for evasive White House witnesses. As time went on and the TV ratings declined, Ervin reverted to habit, currying favor with the powerful, not that Dick Helms minded.

To Ervin's left sat Baker, the poker-faced vice chairman, looking chilly as a vanilla ice cream cone in his seersucker suit. Baker didn't quite believe the duly sworn witness. To Baker, the CIA seemed ever present yet never quite visible in the Watergate story. The more he heard, the more he wanted to investigate. "There are animals crashing around in the forest," Baker observed cryptically. "I can hear them but I can't see them."[19]

Helms's appearance in the Senate Caucus Room catalyzed the partisan tensions that suffused the Watergate Committee and staff. For the first time, Ervin and Baker, the two ranking senators, expressed disagreement in public on a central issue not obvious to the spectators or even the reporters in the Senate hearing room. They differed on Richard Helms's credibility. The Democrats on the committee knew that Baker was communicating, if not coordinating, with Nixon's aides in the White House. Baker and his lieutenants denied that. They saw the Democrats and the press making Nixon a scapegoat and going easy on the CIA, a secretive, sometimes sinister, organization with its own agenda, whose operatives had been caught in flagrante. Helms thought Baker was looking for somebody, anybody, to blame besides the president.

Howard Baker was indeed a partisan; and rather more conservative than the liberal majority of the committee. But he would go on to serve as Senate majority leader and White House chief of staff, the only man to ever hold both jobs. His acumen about the workings of American power could be underestimated but not doubted. Baker had sufficient reason to squint at Helms's protestations of innocence. He understood that the scorpions' dance of Richard Nixon and Richard Helms, two devious—and, at times, dangerous—men, was key to understanding the events of Watergate.

"Helms and Nixon have so much on each other," Baker muttered, "neither of them can breathe."[20]

Scorpions' Dance is about what Helms and Nixon had on each other, the secrets they kept and the secrets they shared. The burden of the argument is that the Watergate affair originated in the clandestine collaborative relationship of Richard Milhous Nixon, the thirty-seventh president of the United States, and Richard McGarrah Helms, the eighth director of the Central Intelligence Agency. The narrative is informed by nine recorded conversations between Helms and Nixon that took place between February 1971 and June 1972. These tapes, collected by Professor Luke Nichter of Texas A&M University, bring to life the edgy rapport of a paranoid president and a supple spymaster. In their words, we hear voices of power, intimations of intrigue, reverberations of history.

Scorpions' Dance posits that the Watergate events were shaped by the fraught, labyrinthine relationship of these two canny power brokers, as it deepened during the U.S. government's Cold War confrontation with the Soviet Union, secret war in Cuba, and land war in Vietnam. These two Machiavellians rose in the heyday of what they proudly called the Free World, America's postwar empire (which included more than a few unfree countries), and achieved positions of supreme power in 1966 and 1968, respectively. They expanded the unwinnable war in Vietnam into Cambodia and Laos, raining death on once peaceful countries and triggering unprecedented social convulsions at home. With Helms's support, Nixon escalated war, entered into the first strategic arms negotiations with the Soviet Union, assassinated a top general in Chile, and opened diplomatic relations with China. Their fates, like their policies, were intertwined.

As a biography of power, *Scorpions' Dance* aspires to inform, not rebut, other interpretations of the Watergate story. As told by the *Washington Post* and the film *All the President's Men*, Watergate is the tale of a lawless president brought to justice by an independent press. The reports of the Senate Watergate Committee and the House Judiciary Committee wove narratives of impeachable offenses committed by a president who had abused his powers, both at home and abroad. Nixon's defenders depict a flawed conservative innovator vanquished by the entrenched liberal elites that he battled his whole career. Revisionist journalists adduce new facts showing the Watergate affair involved secret agendas of blackmail and manipulation that the other Watergate narratives missed or avoided.

Whatever the merit of these interpretations (and they all have some, I think), *Scorpions' Dance* widens the lens to view the Watergate affair not merely as a chapter in the history of the Nixon presidency but also as a chapter in the history of the Central Intelligence Agency. The president's paranoia, the Agency's impunity, and the covert politics of assassination culminated in a crime spree that ended disastrously for the country, and for Nixon and Helms personally. Nixon was disgraced, his landslide victory undone. Helms became the first CIA director convicted of a crime. Their fall from power was followed by defeat in Southeast Asia, the imposition of congressional and judicial oversight on the CIA, and the reopening of the investigation of the assassination of President Kennedy. Watergate did not end well for them.

While Helms liked to depict himself as Nixon's antagonist, the declassified record and White House tapes that have emerged over the years show he just as often served as Nixon's ally in expanding the war in Southeast Asia and enhancing the government's powers of surveillance at home, as well as lending discreet support to the president's burglars. Helms was, as Bob Woodward put it, "the perfect Watergate enabler."[21]

Without Helms, Nixon would not have had his burglars. Without Nixon, Helms would not have occupied the director's suite in Langley for nearly seven years. Without these two men, the Watergate affair would never have happened, prompting two questions: When did it all begin? And how the hell did Dick Helms (almost) get away with it?

1

ARRIBA

Rolando and Juan Pedro slid through the glass doors of the Montmartre in the early hours of Sunday morning, pistols in their pockets. A balmy breeze blew in from the Malecon esplanade outside. It was October 28, 1956. La Rampa, the street passing the white neon sign of the Havana cabaret, was thronged as the two men plunged into the glittering, purring, tinkling confines of what the guide-books called "America's most luxurious nightclub," where the "the golden hours go by more smoothly." They were looking for a man in a white linen suit.

Rolando, twenty-three years old, not quite six feet tall, had a petulant mouth and intense brown eyes a little small for his face.[1] Juan Pedro was taller, broad-shouldered, and fair-skinned with frame glasses and a dark blue sports coat. They edged their way into the lounge. Ladies in gowns, necklaces glittering around bare throats, were talking to men in silk suits who lit cigarettes amid faux French furnishings, the air thick with cigar smoke, Spanish and English, jazz and cha cha cha. The duo passed under the raised hoofs of a massive white marble statue of a vaulting stallion ridden by a bare-breasted Joan of Arc. They searched for the cold visage of Esteban Ventura, captain of the Fifth Precinct of the Havana police, a man known for issuing orders to kill and torture with the blank chill of a bureaucrat. Ventura often gambled at the Montmartre, flanked by bodyguards. He wore only the finest English cloth.[2]

Sidling into the bar, Rolando recognized another leader of the regime,

Colonel Antonio Blanco Rico, the chief of the Servicio Inteligencia de Militaria, SIM.[3] He was sitting, in uniform, with two other officers and their wives, laughing and smoking as they talked about a friend's twentieth wedding anniversary. Just thirty-six years old, Colonel Blanco Rico was already trusted by dictator Fulgencio Batista as well as by the Americans. After Vice President Richard Nixon visited Havana in February 1955, he sent Colonel Blanco Rico a letter of thanks.[4]

If Ventura didn't show up, Blanco Rico would suit their purposes just as well. He was said to be the rare commander in Batista's regime who did not resort to torture during interrogation.[5] Nonetheless, the SIM had a reputation as one of the bloodiest of the government's repressive organs.[6] In the den of corruption, any henchman would serve as an exemplary target for patriotic Cuban youth.

Rolando Cubela was the son of a tailor in the town of Placetas in central Cuba. His parents sent him to a well-regarded private secondary school in Cárdenas, the port city eighty miles east of Havana.[7] With his friend and classmate José Antonio Echeverría, he went on to the University of Havana, where they joined the Federación de Estudiantil Universitaria, or FEU, in 1950.[8] Echeverría, an architecture student, soon gained a reputation for passionate eloquence in denouncing President Fulgencio Batista, who had taken power in a bloodless coup in March 1952.[9] Elected president of the FEU in 1955, Echeverría and friends secretly formed the Directorio Revolucionario, a group of like-minded young men and women pledged to take armed action against the dictatorship that controlled the island.

Echeverría conceived a strategy of tyrannicide.[10] The Directorio would lead a national rebellion by assassinating prominent figures in the government and working their way up to Batista himself. Echeverría's only rival, in terms of energy and eloquence, was Fidel Castro, a tall, rangy lawyer who graduated from the gangster politics of the university to found the 26th of July movement, a coalition of leftist and labor groups that had also taken up arms against Batista.[11]

Why did these boys from good families turn into *pistoleros*? The University of Havana had long been a rough place, where an election for law school or business school representative to the FEU might be settled by a gun battle, because those positions usually led to real jobs in the government or business. Now, the government was just another racket controlled by the dictator, his accomplices, and his paymasters who owned the casinos and hotels sprouting up in Vedado, near the university campus. Chief among them was Meyer Lansky, a five-foot-four accountant from Brooklyn, known as "The Little Man."

Lansky had come to Havana in the thirties while handling the finances of Charles "Lucky" Luciano, the boss of New York City who unified disparate Italian crime syndicates into the loose-knit federation known as the Mafia.[12] Batista, the son of a cane cutter, had emerged from a 1933 student-led revolution to become president. Lansky cut his new friend in on the revenue from his casino the Nacional, the grandest hotel on the Malecon. When Batista returned himself to power in 1952 the Little Man persuaded him to implement a new law that made casino licenses available for $25,000 and exempted hotels from paying corporate taxes. In return, Lansky's courier delivered a suitcase groaning with greenbacks to the side door of the Presidential Palace every month.[13]

Lansky imported the classiest and sexiest American and European musical acts to the Montmartre. With the spread of commercial jet travel, tourists from North America and Europe started to stream into La Habana for the legal gambling and uninhibited nightlife. Yet not far from the opulent pleasure dome swarming with white North Americans was Las Yaguas, a sprawling district of rundown houses and open sewers. Thousands of poor people, many of African descent, lived in the filth of the *solares*, densely packed neighborhoods that the tourists never saw. The rich thrived while the middle class was throttled and the poor forgotten. Cuba had a proud past, a decadent present, and a humiliating future.

Colonel Blanco Rico and his friends paid their check and strolled to the elevators. Marta Poli de Tabernilla was talking to Colonel Blanco Rico as she pushed the down button. Looking over his shoulder, she was astonished to see two men extract pistols from their jackets, raise them, and aim. An explosion jolted the colonel in the back, near his upper right shoulder. Another shot punctured his lower back, a third quivered in his chest, a fourth thudded into his thigh. Senora Tabernilla's vision went blank as panicky ladies careened into mirrors, thinking they offered escape from the gunfire.[14]

Colonel Blanco Rico, now crumpled on the plush carpet, looked up at Rolando and smiled. Perhaps the dying man understood why a young patriot would raise a pistol. Rolando stared. The colonel's smile froze.[15] Juan Pedro pulled at Rolando's elbow. They tucked away their guns, ducked down the service stairs, burst out onto the cobblestones of Humboldt Street, and joined the stragglers heading home into the night.

Even as the shock of Colonel Blanco Rico's killing subsided, nothing much changed. Batista's men went on a killing spree of their own, gunning down ten students who had taken refuge in the Haitian Embassy. With the leaders of the

Directorio in hiding and Fidel Castro criticizing the attack from exile,[16] Batista had never been more secure in his power. The American ambassador paid a sympathetic visit to the Presidential Palace. The Little Man's suitcase arrived punctually. Nat King Cole crooned at the Tropicana. The good life in Havana rolled on. The bloodshed of the regime no longer shocked. After the assassination at the Montmartre, the joke went around, *"Que era mejor ser un negro pobre, que un blanco rico."* Better to be a poor Black man than Blanco Rico (a rich white man).[17]

A revolution was coming.

BRIEFING

The vice president extended a limp paw. The CIA man shook it firmly. Richard Nixon knew the type, another snobbish Georgetown liberal, no doubt. Dick Helms introduced himself as the assistant deputy director, standing in for his boss, Frank Wisner, who was traveling in Europe. The two men sat in Nixon's quiet office in the Senate Office Building on Capitol Hill. Nixon's secretary Rose Mary Woods, a trim redhead, toiled at a typewriter outside the office door.

Nixon and Helms were the same age, though Helms, two months younger, wore his forty-three years rather less anxiously. As Nixon digressed on the tragedy of Hungary, Helms flicked a match to light a Chesterfield. His smile did not always include his eyes.[18]

The news of December 1956 was dispiriting. The front-page headline in the morning *Post* shouted, "General Strike Grips Rebellious Hungary; Police, Crowds Clash." Both men knew the U.S. response would be muted. Two months before, Hungarian student demonstrators attracted enough popular support to force the replacement of the widely despised first secretary of the Communist Party. The antigovernment crowds burgeoned, and Hungarian military units began turning on their Soviet comrades. The Hungarian communists, previously deferential to Moscow, turned over the government to Imre Nagy, a reformer in their ranks.

The dream of "rolling back" the Soviets' postwar empire in Eastern Europe had animated the Agency ever since its founding nine years before. In the dumpy buildings along the Reflecting Pool that housed the clandestine service, "rollback" was more than mere aspiration—it was a mission, a way of life. Suddenly it seemed possible.

As the Hungarian uprising gained strength, Britain, France, and Israel seized the moment to launch a surprise attack on Egypt designed to oust nationalist president Gamal Abdel Nasser and replace him with someone more compliant to their interests. The aggressors laid their plans well, neglecting only to inform the retired general who lived in the White House. President Dwight Eisenhower, recovering from a heart attack and cruising to reelection, didn't care for this colonialist adventure and refused to support it. The gambit collapsed, and Nasser emerged a hero to the non-aligned nations of the world.

Soviet premier Nikita Khrushchev, fearing the appearance of weakness in the face of Western aggression, sent elite Red Army combat forces into Budapest. With the Soviet Union's massive superiority of forces in Central Europe, Eisenhower knew when to do nothing. The fighting continued for weeks, but the rebels were doomed. Tens of thousands of Hungarians fled the country. The dream of "rollback" died under the treads of the Red Army tanks.[19]

Nixon asked for the briefing because he was going to Austria, a pilgrimage of penance. He had questions for the CIA. With Wisner frantically touring Europe, Helms was delegated to answer the vice president's questions. How many refugees were there? Where were they staying? How many would other countries take? As Helms replied, Nixon took notes on a yellow legal pad.

The two men had little in common. Nixon, the son of an ineffectual grocer father and a Quaker mother, grew up attending public school in a small town in southern California. Helms, the son of a district manager for the Aluminum Company of America, grew up on Philadelphia's Main Line and went to Le Rosey, a boarding school in Switzerland.[20] They both felt the effects of the Great Depression, albeit in very different ways.

Helms's father lost his job and Helms had to finish his secondary education at a public high school in Germany. Nixon went to hometown Whittier College, while Helms matriculated at Williams, a selective liberal arts college in western Massachusetts. Nixon, weighing all of 150 pounds, went out for the football team and rode the bench. Helms, standing six foot two, already fluent in French and German, was a big man on the Williams campus, as editor of the college newspaper. With his excellent grades, Nixon was admitted to Harvard Law School but didn't have the money to pay for it. He settled for Duke.

Helms, on the strength of his father's connections, landed a job straight out of college as a foreign correspondent for the United Press wire service in Germany. While Nixon was grinding through his law books, Helms was reporting on Adolf Hitler's Germany. Helms returned to America and settled in Indianapolis, where he planned to pursue his ambition to become a newspaper publisher. He married Julia Shields, a wealthy divorcée with two children. Nixon settled in Whittier, married his college sweetheart Pat Ryan, and started practicing law.

The two men shared wartime service in the navy. After the Japanese attack on Pearl Harbor, the lanky Helms signed up for the naval reserves and wound up plotting the position of Allied ships dodging German submarine attacks. In 1943 his language skills won him a transfer to the Office of Strategic Services, America's newly created wartime intelligence service. He was sent to OSS training school, where he learned to handle a lockpick, tune a shortwave radio, and thrust a bayonet. In May 1945, he was assigned to Germany where his supervisor was Allen W. Dulles, an amoral, pipe-smoking Wall Street lawyer who had spent the war in Switzerland running agents in the business elite of Europe and plotting with "good Germans" to overthrow Hitler.

The pugnacious Nixon did a none-too-hazardous stint in the South Pacific where he played endless poker and lightened the wallets of his fellow servicemen. Duty in wartime made for a good talking point when he returned stateside and ran for U.S. Congress in Orange County, California, in 1946. Helms's dull dream of becoming a publisher evaporated in the OSS. "Very early in my career," he later wrote, "I realized that secret intelligence is not for the fainthearted. From the mortal peril of organizing resistance and stealing secrets in police states, to dealing with one's own government, secret intelligence can be a lethal version of a rugged contact sport."[21] It was a game he loved.

When the war was over, both men had a calling. Southern California Republican voters liked Nixon's earnest manner and slashing style, electing him to Congress twice and then the U.S. Senate in 1950. In 1952, Republican nominee Eisenhower heeded pressure from the party's conservatives and named Nixon as his vice presidential running mate. By then Helms was running the foreign intelligence desk of the newly created CIA. Allen Dulles, now director of the Agency, appreciated his discretion and efficiency. No one doubted his ambition. During a CIA background check, a college classmate predicted Helms would one day become secretary of state, which wasn't far wrong.[22]

Both knew the clandestine ways of powerful men. When Roger Hollis, chief of Britain's MI5 domestic intelligence service, paid a visit to Washington in 1956, Helms took him around to his meetings. To make small talk, he asked, "Who's this writer Ian Fleming?" The former British intelligence officer had recently published a novel, *Live and Let Die*, about a secret agent named James Bond. "Don't know," shrugged Hollis, a self-regarding intellectual. A few days later, Helms read that Prime Minister Anthony Eden had flown to Jamaica to spend some time at Fleming's Goldeneye beach house. As chief of MI5, Hollis had to approve the security arrangements wherever the British prime minister went. "Hollis must have cleared the prime minister to stay with Fleming," Helms deduced. "Hell," he thought. "The man lied."[23]

Nixon too was getting a taste for covert action. When President Eisenhower and executives of the Seven Sisters, the seven largest oil companies in America, grew concerned in 1954 that Greek shipping magnate Aristotle Onassis was on the verge of gaining a monopoly on oil shipments from Saudi Arabia, Nixon led a CIA-organized initiative to block him. The Agency contracted with a former FBI agent turned public relations man named Robert Maheu to discredit Onassis in the press, antagonize his partners, and disrupt his incipient monopoly.

Maheu swaggered with American style. He dressed like a French banker and consorted with crime bosses. As a brash young FBI agent, he impressd J. Edgar Hoover until he went into business for himself. With a monthly retainer from the CIA, his firm of Robert A. Maheu and Associates offered "private investigations," meaning a host of shadowy services ranging from procuring women to wiretapping to, as some alleged, murder.

Two years before Nixon had summoned Maheu to the same office where he and Helms now sat. "I know you'll be careful," Nixon said, "but you have to understand that while this is a national security mission of terrific importance, we can't acknowledge you in any way if anything should go wrong." Maheu knew the realities of his trade and went to work. Onassis soon found himself plagued with lawsuits, negative newspaper stories and charges of bribery, which led the Saudis to cancel his contract.[24] A spook with solid gold cuff links, Bob Maheu had a knack for blackmail that would bedevil Nixon and Helms for a decade.[25]

Both Nixon and Helms had absorbed the lesson that the path to the top begins with serving the needs of the boss. As Nixon served President Eisenhower and the White House, so Helms served Director Allen Dulles and the Agency. Helms left the meeting in December 1956 thinking the vice president did his homework but lacked charm.[26] Nixon forgot about Helms altogether.

ARRIBA

Havana beckoned. "It was a rip-roaring city—a Mafia-riddled, spy-infested, booze-addled, women-crazy city with the world's best night-life," said Everette Howard Hunt, a brash OSS veteran who worked in the CIA's Directorate of Plans. Hunt sauntered into the Cuban capital over New Year's 1957 for the annual conference of Western Hemisphere station chiefs. It was there in fervid Havana that his enduring friendship with Dick Helms began.

Like Helms, Hunt had the erudition of an Ivy League education but lacked the ineffable gloss of old money that elevated the Harvard, Yale, and Princeton men who dominated the Agency. Hunt came from the town of Hamburg in up-state New York with a chip on his shoulder. He graduated from Brown, went into the navy and then OSS training camp, where he received training in martial arts, knives, lockpicks, and cryptology. He was deployed to Yenan province in China, where he boasted of "dynamiting convoys and bridges, infiltrating agents into coastal cities and recovering and returning Allied pilots shot down on the main-land."[27] Action was his instinct.

Yet his ambition was literary. When the war ended, Hunt shunned intelligence work for the writing life. In 1948 he won a Guggenheim Fellowship, much to the envy of two young novelists named Gore Vidal and Truman Capote, whose appli-cations were turned down.[28] When he couldn't make a living as a screenwriter in Hollywood, Hunt took a job in the Economic Cooperation Administration, which administered Secretary of State George Marshall's plan for rebuilding Europe. In the office, he noticed an attractive woman with dark hair and high cheekbones. He asked her out on a date. Dorothy Wetzel de Goutiere was in the process of divorcing her dissolute husband. Hunt found her witty, sexy, intelligent and conservative in her politics. They were proud to call themselves the only non-leftists in the Marshall Plan office. They made plans to meet again in Paris where he was assigned to work. When Dorothy's divorce came through, they married.

In 1950, Hunt jumped to the Central Intelligence Agency. He volunteered to open the Agency's first station in Mexico City, where he hired young William F. Buckley, a recent Yale graduate and the author of a best-selling polemic about his alma mater. Buckley was precocious, frightfully articulate, and often oblivious to the dandruff on his shoulders. Buckley absorbed the basics of espionage, while Hunt ran the station. He funded anticommunist front organizations, recruited local journalists, burglarized the Guatemalan Embassy, and infiltrated the Com-munist Party of Mexico. Hunt and Buckley bonded over secret intelligence work and became friends (and correspondents) for the rest of their lives.

Hunt proved an imaginative Cold Warrior. He surreptitiously obtained the film rights to *Animal Farm*, George Orwell's parable about the dangers of to-talitarian government, and produced an animated version "carefully tweaked to heighten the anti-Communist message," he said.[29] Four years later, the film was a critical and box office success, and virtually no one knew it was a CIA production. Dick Helms, now serving as Frank Wisner's chief of operations for the Directorate of Plans, took note of Hunt's creativity.

In his spare time, Hunt wrote several more novels, while Dorothy raised their children: daughter Lisa, born in 1950, daughter Kevan, born in 1952, and son, St. John, born in 1954.[30] Hunt asked Bill Buckley, who had traded espionage for opinion journalism, to be the godfather to his daughters, and Buckley accepted.

Hunt was the sort of man who enjoyed baiting his wife with racist comments. Dorothy, who claimed to have Native American ancestors, was conservative but not bigoted. She took vocal exception, and people noticed. The Office of Security notified Hunt that his wife "held left-wing views regarding certain minority groups." Hunt explained his wife was "one of those individuals who carries the torch for minority groups and always been too ready to take up the battle when any derogatory remarks are made." When he realized how strongly Dorothy felt, Howard ceased his race-baiting but remained a racist all of his life, according to son St. John.[31]

In 1954, Hunt was recruited for an operation to overthrow the government of President Jacobo Arbenz of Guatemala, who had offended the powerful United Fruit Company with modest plans for land reform. President Eisenhower and Vice President Nixon had approved the operation, known by the code name Success.

"While I did not enjoy thinking of myself as United Fruit's lapdog," Hunt wrote, "the bigger picture of stopping communism had to be considered."[32] After several months of diplomatic attacks and psychological warfare, Arbenz panicked and fled. As a bloody military dictatorship took over in Guatemala, Hunt's star rose in the CIA's Western Hemisphere Division. He was promoted to station chief in Uruguay.

When the station chiefs assembled in January 1957 at the new embassy building on the Malecon, Helms was glad to see former OSS men around the table. While Helms thought the World War II exploits of the OSS were often romanticized, the OSS men did have the attitude the chief of operations wanted. They had been trained to wage a holy war against the Nazis. "They learned how you did the meanest thing to kill that other guy that you could think of," Helms said. "The Russians, who likewise are a pretty rough lot, had to be fought in the gutter. It was a perfectly natural thing to do. If you've got to fight a guy, you fight him, and you fight to win, you don't fight to lose. There are no good losers. Losers are dead people."[33] That was Dick Helms's credo.

During this working vacation, Helms and wife Julia stayed at the home of their friends Dick and Nancy Cushing. Dick Cushing served as the press attaché at the embassy; Nancy Cushing, like Julia, was an artist.[34] On New Year's Eve the

Cushings threw a large party in their small house, and Helms relaxed in a way he rarely did in buttoned-up Washington.

As Helms mingled and bantered with a flute of champagne in hand, his friend and colleague David Phillips noticed he was having a thoroughly good time. Phillips was a former expat newspaper publisher in Chile, turned undercover officer with a specialty in "psychological warfare." Like Hunt, he had won a medal in the Guatemala operation.

As the volume of the party grew, a guest explained to Helms the versatility of the Spanish word *arriba*, meaning "up" or "onward" in the sense of moving ahead decisively or charging into military action.

"Helms was fascinated by the word," Phillips recalled, "especially in the latter meaning. He repeated it over and over as the party went into the early hours."

"Where is the action in Havana now?" Helms asked his hosts.

The Montmartre had been shuttered since the assassination of Blanco Rico.[35] "There's always a blast at the Country Club," Cushing shrugged, "but for members only." He looked around at the half dozen guests still at the party. "None of us qualify."

"Arriba," Helms cried. "Let's go. They'll let us in."

Despite protests from the Cushings, who knew how snobbish the Havana Country Club truly was, Helms insisted.

"I'm afraid that only members are allowed," said the maître d' who intercepted them at the entrance to the club.

"But I am a member," Helms said.

"Your name please?"

"Oliver Cromwell," replied Helms.

"Cromwell? The maître d' opened a huge black book of the club's membership, flipping the pages to the C's. "Cromwell?" He ran his finger down the page. "Ah yes, Mr. Cromwell. Of course, go right in, sir."

"Arriba," said Helms, ushering his party forth.[36] David Phillips, thoroughly impressed, stepped in behind his boss. He and Howard Hunt would follow Helms into action for the next seventeen years.

2

DEFEATED

In CIA cables, Dick Helms was known by the cryptonym "Fletcher Knight," and it is fair to say he saw himself as a knight of the Free World. In the course of 1958 he and Nixon were tested and forged. What they had in common was tenacity.

Nixon survived a mob. In May 1958, the vice president traveled to the capitals of South America on a goodwill tour. One of his first stops was Uruguay, where station chief Howard Hunt served as his translator. Hunt reminded Nixon they had met once before, by chance in Washington's Mayflower Hotel, where Hunt had congratulated him for exposing former State Department official Alger Hiss as a communist. Nixon went on to Peru where he was jeered by university students, and Venezuela, where Jake Esterline, chief of the Caracas station, frantically warned that he should stay away. Washington's resolute support of recently deposed dictator Marcos Pérez Jiménez was deeply resented in Venezuela, and not just by communists. Jiménez had wielded absolute power for ten years during which time Eisenhower had bestowed a medal on him for "exceptionally meritorious conduct." When he was driven from power, the United States gave Pérez Jiménez safe haven in Florida, an insult that had not been forgotten.[1] A crowd organized by the Venezuelan Communist Party greeted Nixon by hurling garbage, mobbing his motorcade, and smashing the windows of his limousine. Nixon and his entourage barely escaped to safety.

Back in the United States, Nixon's ordeal elicited sympathy, even in the often-hostile liberal press.[2] When he returned to Washington, he was greeted by a cheering crowd of nearly ten thousand people at National Airport, including President Eisenhower himself.[3] The old general wanted to get in the picture with his vice president, a gratifying reversal of their usual roles. Caracas was Nixon's Calvary, an ordeal that tested his faith, a test he did not fail. Most Americans did not know or care that the Eisenhower administration had embraced a hated dictator, who tortured and killed with impunity. Nixon risked his life in defense of an America that was both imperious and ignorant, which paid off politically. And he had mustered physical courage amid the chaos. For an insecure man who was awkward and often clumsy, Caracas was a revelation. Mortal danger? Dick Nixon could handle it.

Helms endured a snub. In October 1958, his mentor and friend Allen Dulles informed him over a sandwich lunch that he was going to name Richard Bissell as the next deputy director of plans, the formal title for the job of running the clandestine service. Frank Wisner, energetic scion of a Mississippi family who had held the job since 1947, had resigned at the urging of family and friends. Ever since the crushing of the Hungarian rebellion in 1956, Wisner suffered from increasingly frequent bouts of incomprehensible volubility followed by episodes of catatonic sadness—what a later generation would diagnose as bipolar disorder.[4]

Helms was stunned. Bissell, an economist from MIT who wrote the first draft of the Marshall Plan to rebuild Western Europe, was a newcomer to the CIA. Best known for the creation of the U-2 spy plane, a technological marvel that transformed U.S. understanding of the Soviet armed forces, Bissell was brilliant but had scant experience in covert operations. Of the top one hundred rated operations officers in the CIA, Bissell knew perhaps twenty. Helms knew them all.

"No matter how gracefully Dulles presented his decision, this apparent vote of no confidence was reason enough to consider leaving the agency," Helms later wrote. He rejected an overseas assignment out of professional principle. "It would almost certainly be read as an agency decision to emphasize covert action over the traditional responsibility for espionage and counterintelligence abroad."[5]

Helms smothered his pride and soldiered on. In the nuclear standoff of the Cold War, he understood the CIA was central to American power. "The wiggle room between a diplomatic standoff and a military confrontation," he later observed, "seemed most likely to be dominated by the nation with the wisest foreign policy and the best intelligence service." He decided to stay on as assistant deputy director. Like Nixon, Helms kept his eye on the top job.

What brought them together again was revolution in Cuba.

VENCER O MORIR

The end came quickly for the seemingly invincible Batista regime. After returning from Mexican exile in December 1956, Fidel Castro and his guerrilla army had strained and drained government forces across the island. In March 1957, José Antonio Echeverría and the Directorio launched an attack on Batista in the Presidential Palace that the wily dictator foiled. Echeverría was killed outside the radio station he tried to commandeer. Twenty-five-year-old Rolando Cubela inherited leadership of the decimated group. He was haunted by dreams in which Colonel Blanco Rico smiled and spoke to him. He suffered a nervous breakdown. He recovered in a Miami motel owned by a wealthy friend.[6]

In February 1958, determined to return to the armed struggle, Cubela led a boatload of Directorio fighters from Miami to a remote landing spot on the north coast of Cuba with a pledge to take the fight to the dictatorship. In December, he agreed to join forces with the 26th of July movement, led by Castro's lieutenant, Ernesto "Che" Guevara. After conferring in a small-town hotel room he and Guevara planned the final assault on the provincial capital of Santa Clara. They issued a joint war declaration on behalf of the Directorate and the 26th of July movement: "Unir es la palabra de orden . . . vencer o morir." *Unity is the word of the day . . . victory or death!*[7]

The Directorio's target was the headquarters of Squadron 31, an elite unit of Batista's armed forces. As Cubela led a caravan of trucks and jeeps on the highway to Santa Clara, American-made B-26 planes came roaring overhead with machine guns spitting fire. "A rain of lead," he called it.[8] The men dove out of their vehicles and hid until the planes passed. They resumed their march into the city where they laid siege to the government cuartel. A burst of machine gun fire blasted a wall next to Cubela, knocking him through the door of a house. He was not shot but he could not find his right arm. It was completely twisted around the back of his body and badly fractured. He was evacuated to a clinic where the broken bone was reset. He returned to the battlefront, arm in a sling.

On December 31, 1958, Cubela met Guevara again. He told him Squadron 31 was close to surrender. Guevara gave him the bigger news. Batista had packed his bags and flown to the Dominican Republic. The dictatorship was done. All the rebel forces headed for Havana, believing that whoever controlled the city would rule the nation. Cubela and the Directorio fighters laid claim to the University of Havana campus and the Presidential Palace.[9] Cubela received a hero's welcome. Basking in the glory of victory, he saluted comrade Che Guevara's "stupendous initiative and firm decision-making."[10] Castro marched into Havana on January 1, 1959, and assumed leadership of the Cuban nation by acclamation. Cubela and the Directorio reluctantly agreed to disarm. The revolutionary government was standing up.

With the flight of Batista, the gangsters of Havana had lost their patron and protectors. Lansky's dream of making Havana the Monte Carlo of the Caribbean evaporated. The Little Man decamped for Israel. The American gangsters who had dominated the city for a decade stayed away, as the Cuban people exacted their revenge. Men with sledgehammers smashed the plate glass windows of the Sevilla Biltmore Hotel. A crowd swarmed inside and tore up the lobby and casino. A few blocks away another crowd broke into the casino at the Plaza. Gaming tables, roulette wheels, and slot machines were dragged into the street and set on fire. Menacing throngs were turned away from the Nacional and the Capri. In all, seven of thirteen casinos in the city suffered major damage.[11]

Castro announced the nationalization of all large businesses and landholdings. Guevara, a medical doctor, took over the Central Bank. Cubela accepted a diplomatic post in Spain. The mayor of Havana announced the construction of fifteen new schools, with plans for thirty-seven more.[12] Castro promised elections, a free press, and an end to the reign of organized crime. "If I'm in this office I'm going to run all these gangsters, all these crime people out of Cuba," he told Frank Sturgis, an American soldier of fortune who had supplied the 26th of July movement with weapons. "Which he did," Sturgis added.

Born in the United States as Frank Fiorini, Sturgis adopted the surname of his stepfather as a young man. He served in the marines in World War II and moved to Havana in 1956, attracted by Castro and the fight against Batista. The 26th of July movement needed guns and Sturgis delivered them by the planeload. Fidel Castro and his brother Raul came to trust him. Not long after taking power in 1959, the Cuban leader put Sturgis in charge of Havana's gambling houses.

"He gave me orders and I did close up the gambling casinos for ten days in Cuba," Sturgis later told investigators.[13] Castro soon reopened the casinos on a limited basis to preserve jobs and tourism. As he and Guevara steered the national rebellion toward socialist revolution, Sturgis felt betrayed. He helped the chief of the Cuban Air Force defect, a propaganda coup for Washington. Sturgis wound up in Miami where he joined the ranks of Castro's foes as a soldier of fortune. He fed information to the FBI and became a source for the CIA's Miami station.[14] His winding road to Watergate had begun.

ACTION OFFICER

Nixon and Helms both responded to the Cuban revolution, albeit in different ways. While preparing to run for president in 1960, Nixon cast himself as the action officer on U.S. policy toward Castro.[15] "Mr. Nixon was gearing up and getting ready to run for president," recalled General Robert Cushman, his assistant for military affairs, "an operation which, at least in concept and for planning, had been approved by the President and the CIA, was proceeding full speed ahead. . . . And I was told by the Vice President to monitor it and keep him informed."[16]

The CIA's concept for overthrowing Castro was, in Dave Phillips's words, "the Guatemala scenario." As in Guatemala in 1954, the United States would isolate the government diplomatically, then launch radio propaganda operations to discredit the regime and divide the population. The application of paramilitary pressure, including covert U.S. air support if needed, would create an untenable atmosphere of insecurity. Castro, like Jacobo Arbenz, would either flee or surrender power to a leadership group friendly to the United States. They called it Operation Zapata.

Nixon took measure of Castro in person. Invited to Washington in April 1960 by the American Society of Newspaper Editors, the Cuban leader agreed to a meeting with the vice president. They spoke for three hours in Nixon's Capitol Hill office. Castro found Nixon surprisingly young, "a teenager, not in appearance but in behavior . . . a bit superficial." Nixon thought Castro was "either incredibly naïve about communism or under Communist discipline.[17] In fact, Castro was a communist and not under anyone's discipline but his own.

Helms shared Nixon's view of Castro, but when it came to Operation Zapata, the CIA's plan to overthrow his government, the assistant deputy director abstained. In one meeting Phillips noticed Helms, his idol, inspecting his carefully manicured fingernails and saying nothing.[18] The Zapata plan reprised "what were perceived by some to have been the successful tactics in Iran and Guatemala," Helms said later. "The perception was often an illusion to the experienced eye."

Howard Hunt was more enthusiastic. As one of the top-rated officers in the Western Hemisphere division, he was sent to Havana to assess the revolutionary situation. He returned with four recommendations, the first of which was to assassinate Castro. The idea was not the subject of much debate in the offices of the CIA along the National Mall. Having seen Adolf Hitler in the flesh, Dick Helms would never rule out assassination as a moral policy choice. Nixon would deny that he ever participated in assassination discussions, but his military assistant, General Cushman, met often with Hunt, and even gave him his private phone number.[19]

Cushman was not the only Nixon associate talking assassination. When the CIA men decided to act on Hunt's recommendation, the first person they turned to was Bob Maheu, the private investigator who had done the Onassis job under Nixon's guidance.[20] Maheu arranged a meeting with Johnny Rosselli, former manager at the now-closed Sans Souci nightclub in Havana, which had been controlled by Sam Giancana, the Mafia boss of Chicago.[21]

Rosselli, born Filippo Sacco, grew up in Boston. He was believed to have killed his first man at age seventeen. He moved to Los Angeles, took on his new name, and became an executioner for the Mafia. In 1943 he was indicted on charges of conspiring to extort money from the Columbia Pictures studio in Hollywood. He was convicted, sentenced to ten years in jail, and then mysteriously paroled after just three years. A witness in his extortion trial was killed by a car bomb. Two other co-defendants died in gangland slayings.[22] His murderous reputation was attractive to the CIA men who wanted to kill Castro.

Rosselli introduced them to his capo de capo, Giancana, who disdained gunplay for the job. He asked for "some type of potent pill that could be placed in Castro's food or drink."

The CIA obliged. Dr. Edward Gunn, a wizard of the Agency's Technical Services Division, developed an untraceable lethal pill with rapid solubility. The pills were turned over to several intermediaries who claimed to have access to Castro, including a young German woman named Marita Lorenz who was briefly Castro's girlfriend in 1960. In her memoir Lorenz said her friend Frank Sturgis introduced her to Maheu and to Rosselli (whom she called "Mr. Hollywood") in a Miami hotel room where they gave her two poison pills and urged her to "change history." Lorenz, barely out of her teens, couldn't bring herself to poison her lover.[23] The CIA men waited for Castro to drop dead. They would wait in vain.

Helms knew nothing of this scheme at the time, though he would soon be cleared into the program.

Vice President Nixon, running hard for the top job, was not detained by the details of the Cuba operation either. If elected, he would see Zapata through to the overthrow of Castro and the installation of a pro-American government. But as a candidate, Nixon felt he had to preserve the secrecy around Zapata, which put him in a delicate position with the CIA. His White House bid might depend on it.

Nixon's opponent, Senator John F. Kennedy, forty-three years of age, was one of the youngest men ever to run for president. The son of Joseph Kennedy, a bootlegger turned liquor importer, movie producer, and ambassador, JFK was ambitious and cautious. In eight years in the Senate, he had compiled a modest legislative record and rankled liberals by avoiding taking a stand on Senator Joe McCarthy, the Wisconsin Republican who charged that the U.S. government was infiltrated by communists.

Kennedy cited Cuba when indicting the Eisenhower administration for passivity. "We never were on the side of freedom," he charged in his second TV debate with Nixon. "We never used our influence when we could have used it most effectively and today Cuba is lost to freedom. I hope someday it will rise, but I don't think it will rise if we continue the same policies toward Cuba that we did in recent years."[24]

Nixon felt he had been set up. The CIA had briefed candidate Kennedy on Cuba in July. Nixon suspected "JFK's" friends in the Agency had told him about Zapata. He concluded Kennedy had spouted a tough line on Cuba, knowing Nixon couldn't take credit for the administration's secret policy.[25] With his knack for self-punishment, Nixon felt obliged to go further. "I had no choice but take a completely opposite stand and attack Kennedy's advocacy of open intervention in Cuba," Nixon said later. It was, he added, "the most uncomfortable and ironic duty I have ever had to perform."[26]

Nixon's message about Kennedy took on a personal edge. He was annoyed when CBS News correspondent Eric Sevareid declared the two candidates "cool cats," meaning "men devoid of deep passion or strong convictions." They were both "sharp, ambitious, opportunistic, with no commitments except to personal advancement."[27] Nixon preferred the praise of a conservative friend who lauded his "continual slashing at Kennedy as reckless, irresponsible, dangerously impulsive, immature, obsessed with fear, a breast-beating imitator of Adlai Stevenson, a distorter of facts helpful to communist propagandists, putting politics above relief of misery, a downgrader of America, confused, uncertain, imperiling the cause of peace, a planner of inflation, a blundering advocate of retreat and defeat, et cetera."[28] That was how Dick Nixon wanted to be seen.

The mean streak almost worked. When the votes were counted on Election Day, Nixon narrowly lost to Kennedy. Suspecting vote fraud in Illinois, he considered demanding a recount and reluctantly decided he could not do so without harming the country. Nixon chose to be bitter. "The mark of a good loser," his college football coach had taught him, "is that he takes out his anger on himself and not on his victorious opponents or on his teammates."[29]

Nixon took out his loss in the 1960 election on himself. He sometimes attributed his defeat to Kennedy's opportunism on Cuba. His grudge against the CIA deepened. As Kennedy prepared to take office, the Agency's Zapata operation continued to develop, delivering the new president into disaster.

3

THE BLACK WORLD

One day in early 1961, Dick Helms ran into his new boss Richard Bissell and McGeorge Bundy, the Harvard professor whom the newly inaugurated President Kennedy had brought in as his national security adviser. They were speaking in the corridor of a CIA office on the Mall. "I sensed an almost conspiratorial air in their head-to-head conversation," Helms later recalled. "It was my guess at the time, which was subsequently proved to be correct, that Dick was 'selling' the new special assistant to the president for national security affairs on the operation to unseat Castro and change the nature of the Cuban government."[1]

The work of spies had taken on a certain glamour. President Kennedy had been introduced to Ian Fleming, author of the James Bond spy novels, at a dinner party in 1960. Kennedy asked him how he would get rid of Castro, and Fleming answered facetiously. One man who knew them both said Kennedy was fascinated "by the line dividing Ian's real life from the fantasy life that went into his books." When Kennedy listed Fleming's *From Russia with Love* as one of his ten favorite books for 1961, sales of the Bond books boomed. The fantasy of espionage achieved a new degree of reality in the culture of Washington.[2]

Operation Zapata gained momentum. The Agency was training fifteen hundred Cubans at a camp in Guatemala to serve as the invasion force. In Washington, David Phillips had pulled together the Frente Revolucionario Democrático, a coalition of groups opposed to Castro, most of them dependent on CIA funding.

In Miami, Hunt recruited expatriate Cubans with counterrevolutionary fervor, including Manuel Artime, a psychiatrist who ran an organization called the Movimiento de Recuperación Revolucionaria (Movement for the Recovery of the Revolution, MRR). Hunt thought Artime "exuded the intangible charisma of leadership." Manolo, as he was known, became CIA agent AMBIDDY-1 and a close friend.[3]

To evade the eyes of the press and FBI in Miami, Hunt summoned the Cubans to Mexico City to build the counterrevolution. And there he made a big mistake. A former Agency officer, hired by Hunt, left two briefcases filled with classified information in his car, while he made a brief stop at his office. When he returned the briefcases were gone. A damage assessment found the stolen papers contained the real names of eleven CIA officers in the country (including Hunt), confirmed the identities of dozen Mexican agents who assisted the Mexico City station, and the details of an unknown number of covert operations. Despite a panicky search, the suitcases were never found. The Agency concluded they had been taken by common criminals and were never obtained by any intelligence service. "The loss was caused by lamentably poor security practices," the Agency concluded, not for the last time, about Hunt's tradecraft.[4]

In Washington, Helms avoided the meetings on Zapata, which didn't go unnoticed. The operations chief telegraphed his misgivings without ever expressing an opinion. Privately, Helms thought the plan was likely to fail, and failure could be a career killer. At the same time, he made it his business to learn broad outlines and specific details of the operation—"by osmosis," he said. That was a spy's nomenclature for absorbing office gossip, which Helms loved. Helms also kept current on the office politics of the White House. He judged Kennedy's foreign policy team was "very strong" but noted that early in a presidential term was "not the most propitious time to risk radical foreign policy undertakings," which overthrowing a popular sovereign government most certainly was.

Zapata was, as Helms sensed, poorly conceived and sloppily executed. After months of training with ill-concealed stealth in Guatemala, the CIA-trained 2506 Brigade landed at the Bay of Pigs on April 17, 1961, full of bravado and wishful thinking. Castro's army met the invaders with heavy artillery fire, pinning them to the beach. The brigade had its own air force. The United States supplied planes with Cuban pilots disguised as defectors from the regime. In the first air strike, they suffered ten fatalities and failed to get control of Cuban airspace. Kennedy suddenly faced the same choice Eisenhower had in Guatemala in 1954. The Zapata plan called for air strikes to enable the rebels to establish a beachhead where they

could announce a government-in-exile and appeal for overt U.S. support. In Guatemala, Eisenhower had approved air support, and the rebels prevailed. Helms and
others assumed JFK would do the same. "In for a dime. In for a dollar," as Helms
put it.[5] But Kennedy, who had been assured air strikes would not be necessary,
refused. He didn't want to take the United States into a land war in an unimportant country on behalf of the remnants of a hated regime. That was not how he
wanted to launch his presidency.

Kennedy's decision enraged the men who wanted to retake Cuba by whatever
means necessary. When Admiral Arleigh Burke, the hawkish naval chief of staff,
arrived at the Pentagon situation room early the next morning, he was horrified.
How could Kennedy "pull the strings out of an operation at the last minute?" he
roared. In a CIA office in downtown Washington, Howard Hunt, Dave Phillips,
and other CIA officers erupted in anger at acting director Charles Cabell. "Goddamn it, this is criminal negligence!" one shouted.

The men on the beachhead were pinned down and the Americans were not
coming to the rescue. When a brigade leader radioed a final bitter message, "I
have nothing to fight with. Am taking to the woods. I cannot wait for you," Hunt
started to weep. "Never before had I seen a room filled with men in tears," he wrote
in his memoir of the operation. "I was sure Artime and all the others were dead,
and I blamed myself for being party to their betrayal."[6] Over the next two days, 119
brigade fighters died on the beach. A few escaped. Most were captured. Hunt and
Phillips, among many other CIA men, never forgave the president.

The president took full responsibility for the debacle. "There's an old saying
that victory has a hundred fathers and defeat is an orphan," he said at his next
press conference.[7] In Havana, Castro exulted, a tropical David who had defeated
the American Goliath. He put the captured Brigadistas in front of the TV cameras
where they explained they had been recruited by an American named "Eduardo,"
namely Howard Hunt. The CIA men felt like they had been stripped naked in
public, and Kennedy let it happen.

The Kennedy administration was simply inexperienced, said Helms. "In their
haste to rid Washington of the old and to substitute a shiny new penny, the transi-
tion teams tend to concentrate on personnel appointments and new organizational
concepts," he wrote in his memoir. "This is particularly true in the 'black world'
of clandestine operations and secret weapons developments. The new players have
much to learn about how things in this strange new universe actually work."[8]

The "black world" had its own rules and realities in Helms's view. When the
moment of decision came, Helms thought John Kennedy simply lacked the will to

win. "Great actions require great determination. . . ." he said, quoting Allen Dulles's unpublished post-mortem on the Bay of Pigs. "One never succeeds unless there is a determination to succeed, a willingness to risk some unpleasant political repercussions, and a willingness to provide the basic military necessities. At the decisive moment in the Bay of Pigs operation, all three of these were lacking."[9]

The result was the greatest defeat in the fourteen-year history of the CIA, a failure that stoked contempt for John F. Kennedy in the ranks of the clandestine service.

THE DDP

In the fall of 1961, the Agency moved from its shabby scattered offices in Foggy Bottom to a gleaming seven-story office block tucked in the woods of suburban Langley, Virginia, five miles northwest of the White House. It was one of the largest office buildings in the country, a keystone of America's imperial ambitions as memories of World War II faded and the president proclaimed a New Frontier. The new headquarters signaled the Agency's ascendancy in the structure of national power. Yet the modernist gleaming architecture could not erase the existential humiliation of the Bay of Pigs defeat.

After a decent interval of seven months, Kennedy eased Dulles and Bissell out of their jobs. To replace Dulles as director of Central Intelligence, Kennedy named John McCone, a curmudgeonly corporate executive and Republican then serving as chairman of the Atomic Energy Commission.

The Bay of Pigs debacle vindicated Helms's prudence and ensured his promotion to the job he thought he should have gotten three years before. After fifteen years of running secret operations, Helms was the consensus choice to replace Bissell as the DDP, deputy director of plans. (Inside the Agency the initials could refer either to the Directorate, which consisted of five regional divisions with desks for every significant country in the world, or to the man who headed it.)

The Bay of Pigs debacle vindicated Helms's operational prudence and insured his promotion to the job he thought he should have gotten three years before. On Helms's first day as DDP, McCone told him he was in charge of Cuba. "Yes, sir," said Helms.[10] As a dutiful civil servant, he often presented himself as a veritable butler of espionage who served up whatever information or action his political masters called for.

Helms was also a man of action. Three Agency operatives had been arrested in Havana in September 1960, while mounting an audio operation against the offices of the Chinese news service.[11] They were sentenced to ten years in jail, though not identified as CIA agents. Helms asked John Mertz, deputy chief of the Counter-intelligence Staff, to come up with a plan to free the prisoners. Mertz consulted with his boss, James Angleton, counterintelligence chief, who supplied him with some "underworld" connections in Havana.[12] Mertz then tasked James McCord, deputy chief of the Security Research Staff in the Office of Security, to scope out the prison and execute the escape. As McCord later explained, his agents "gained entry to the prisons" and returned to the United States "with data acquired," but the captured men were freed in a prisoner exchange before any rescue operation could be mounted. McCord was credited with being "an actual case officer for Cuban agents" from 1960 to 1962.[13] Helms surely knew of his work, at least in passing. McCord's road to Watergate had begun.

Helms's greatest challenge in his new job was serving the two very different brothers in the White House, John and Robert Kennedy.

"John Kennedy was urbane, objective, analytical, controlled, contained, mas-terful, a man of perspective," wrote historian Arthur Schlesinger, an OSS veteran and friend of Helms, who worked in the White House. "Robert, while very bright and increasingly reflective, was more open, exposed, emotional, subjective, intense, a man of commitment."[14] Novelist Gore Vidal, a friend of First Lady Jacqueline Kennedy, was less charitable. Bob Kennedy's "obvious characteristics are energy, vindictiveness, and a simplemindedness about human motives which may yet bring him down," Vidal wrote. "To Bobby the world is black or white. Them and Us. He has none of his brother's human ease; or charity."[15]

Personally, Helms preferred the president. JFK's dry wit and detached style were closer to his own. Professionally, he had to deal with Bob much more often, because of president had made his brother the point man for his post–Bay of Pigs Cuba policy. Helms appreciated Bob's anticommunism which liberals like Vidal found simplistic. What bothered the deputy director was Bob's naivete.

"Within a few weeks of Bob Kennedy hammering on us for results, I realized he had but a slight idea of what was involved in organizing a secret intelligence operation," Helms wrote in his memoir. "He appeared to equate the director of the Central Intelligence position with that of the chief of the General Staff."[16] Helms thought RFK something of a fool, but he kept his opinion to himself until late in life.

Meanwhile, at his Tudor-style home in Wesley Heights in northwest Washing-ton, Nixon brooded and scrawled on his legal pads. He conferred with Kennedy after the humiliation of the Bay of Pigs and urged him to invade Cuba, "to find a proper legal cover" and "go in," advice that JFK spurned.[17] He called friends and drank and brooded some more. Nixon couldn't bear the thought of practicing law, which was the most common advice he heard after leaving the vice presidency. Instead, he conceived of a plan to return to California. He would write a short accessible political testament like JFK's *Profiles in Courage*. Then he would run for governor of California, where he had already won three elections. Then he would have a rematch with JFK in 1964, and the Bay of Pigs would help him make his case.

Pat Nixon thought she would have more time with her husband after he left the vice presidency. Daughters Julie and Tricia thought they would see more of their father. They saw less. "As usual, the ones who suffered most and most silently were my family," he wrote.[18]

It was his secretary Rose Mary Woods, more than anyone, who sustained Nixon's enormous ambition. Like many young women, Woods moved to Washington during World War II to get a good job. As a secretary to the Select House Committee on Foreign Aid in 1948, she had been impressed by the precision of Congressman Nixon's expense accounts. When he was elected to the Senate in 1950, she accepted an offer to become his secretary.

Nixon felt lucky. "Next to a man's wife, his secretary is the most important person in his career . . . ," Nixon said of Woods. "She has to be flawlessly proficient at shorthand and typing. She has to have the quite different skill of making hundreds of decisions a day for her employer, and she has to know just what decisions not to make as well. . . . She is the balance wheel of the whole office."[19]

From the start, Woods saved Nixon from his self-defeating instincts. In 1952, when Eisenhower chose Nixon to be his running mate on the Republican ticket, he was hit with a newspaper story reporting that his supporters in California had put aside money for his personal use, a "slush fund" in the lingo of headlines. The story was essentially accurate. Nixon, a man of modest means, liked having money, and his backers kept him flush. To save his candidacy, Nixon gave a speech, broadcast on the radio and the increasingly popular medium of television. His self-pitying performance, complete with reference to the family dog, Checkers, was a hit with Republican voters. When Eisenhower responded favorably but did not commit to keeping Nixon on the ticket, the sulking candidate wrote a telegram of resignation. Woods knew better than to send it.[20]

With Woods's constant assistance, Nixon was both running for governor and writing the memoir that would become the best-selling book *Six Crises*. He yearned—burned to return to power. He moved his family to swank Bel Air, California, in the foothills of the Santa Monica Mountains. He began meeting with a ghostwriter every morning. One day a brushfire swept through the neighborhood, forcing Nixon to scurry to his car while carrying framed photographs, his precious memories in danger.[21] He was a witness to conflagrations, a man close to the flames.

UNCORKED

Helms was a manager, a man with a neat desk. He cleaned house in the Cuban operation, relying on his trusted deputy, Tom Karamessines, to execute his every order. Tom K., as he was known, came from Bridgeport, Connecticut, attended Columbia University in New York, and graduated from the law school in 1941. In the war, he joined the OSS and opened its station in Athens. A taciturn pipe smoker, Tom K. was renowned for his covert skills. "On such matters as letter drops, cutouts, safe houses, two-time codes, 'magic,' and other tricks and treats of the espionage trade," one journalist wrote, "Karamessines is said to have no peer."[22] Tom K. would serve quietly at Helms's elbow for the next decade.

Helms relieved Jake Esterline, chief of the Cuba task force. He replaced him with Bill Harvey, the chief of the Berlin base, whom Helms regarded as perhaps the finest operations officer in the DDP. He brought in Ted Shackley, a brusque deputy of Harvey's, to run the Miami station. He sent his energetic protégé David Phillips to Mexico City to wreak havoc on the Cuban embassy, Castro's first intelligence outpost in the western hemisphere. Helms had bad news for Howard Hunt. "It was made abundantly clear to me in a very pleasant way that I was to have nothing further to do with Cuba operations," Hunt recalled.[23]

Helms conferred a consolation prize on Hunt more appropriate for his literary talents. He assigned him to serve as covert action chief in the newly created Domestic Contacts Division, where he supervised what a later generation would call "soft power" activities. Hunt later testified that he took over the Agency's relationship with Frederick Praeger Publishing Company, which published books that aligned with the Agency's interests but were not "economically feasible." With subsidies from Langley, Praeger generated books that advanced the Agency's mission. In this domestic propaganda operation, Hunt reported to Karamessines.[24] Helms took care of his pal.

The deputy director had to deal with the mess left by the inexperienced Dick Bissell. Bob Maheu might have been the right man to introduce Agency officers to organized crime figures. But telling the amoral ex-FBI agent the specific and lethal nature of their interest was a mistake for which the Agency soon paid. As Maheu's friend, Johnny Rosselli, put it, "If somebody gets in trouble and they want a favor from the G [meaning the U.S. government] we can get it for them. You understand.

We have the government by the ass."[25] Bob Maheu—no surprise—had a feel for blackmail.

Helms knew this terrain better than most gentlemen.

"Let's leave aside the notion of theology and the morality of all good men for just a moment," he dilated for TV talk show host David Frost. "If you hire someone to kill somebody else, you are immediately subject to blackmail, and that includes individuals as well as governments."[26] As Helms knew full well, Maheu was one of those individuals. Maheu had a problem, and he wanted the CIA to fix it.

It seems that Sam Giancana, while negotiating with the Agency about the Castro hit, expressed concern that his girlfriend, pop singer Phyllis McGuire, was getting "too much attention" from comedian Dan Rowan, who was performing in Las Vegas. Giancana asked Maheu to bug Rowan's hotel room to determine "the extent of his intimacy with Miss McGuire," as the CIA inspector general chastely put it. Maheu hired an experienced "wire man" to plant the bug, but the man wasn't experienced enough. Hotel security officers nabbed him in the act. When he called Maheu for help, the FBI was listening in. The Bureau decided to charge both men with violating federal wiretapping statutes. Maheu let his friends at the CIA know that, if prosecuted, he would start talking about the Agency's scheme to kill Castro. The charges were soon dropped. Blackmail worked.[27]

The CIA men had to explain the story to Attorney General Bob Kennedy in all of its tawdry detail. Kennedy listened impassively, irked by the means, not the ends. He needed the Agency to avenge the Bay of Pigs, the biggest blot on his brother's record, in time for the 1964 campaign. He expressed no view on the killing of Castro, but loathed the choice of assassins. "I trust that if you ever try to do business with organized crime again—with gangsters—you will let the Attorney General know," he said.[28]

Dick Helms had other plans. He put Bill Harvey, former chief of the Berlin base, in charge of ZR/RIFLE, the Agency's new assassination program. William King Harvey, a former FBI agent from Indiana, was fat, brilliant, and dangerous. Some called him America's James Bond, though he was hardly handsome or debonair. His biographer dubbed him a "flawed patriot."[29] His longtime colleague, John Whitten, chief of the Mexico desk, called him a "gun fanatic" and a "thug."[30] Helms thought him indispensable. "He was much more than heavyset," Helms wrote in his memoir. "A more pertinent description would have concentrated on his phenomenal memory, aggressive approach to business, and knowledge of Soviet espionage in the United States."[31]

Helms authorized Harvey to provide a trailer full of weapons to Johnny

Rosselli for the purpose of killing Castro. Harvey, a savvy bureaucratic operator when sober, asked if he should inform director John McCone about the mission. Now a man of considerable guile, Helms said no. Nor did Helms tell Bob Kennedy that Harvey was plotting with Rosselli.[32] In his memoir, the older and presumably wiser Helms wrote, "In peacetime the assassination of troublesome persons is morally and operationally indefensible. There are invariably other solutions, not the least of which is time—time for the immediate and sometimes fierce tactical pressure to subside or for the problem to be reevaluated or another solution found."[33] Helms would assure interviewer David Frost, "I have never believed in assassination."[34]

In 1962 and 1963 at least, Helms believed, as he himself conceded. "We were under great pressure to make contacts in Cuba," he told Frost. "I let the pressure to do something—because we didn't have very many contacts—overwhelm my judgment. We never should have gone forward the second time with that Rosselli thing. When I found out about it, I should have corked it."[35]

Instead, he uncorked it—he authorized Harvey to work with the gangster Rosselli and he didn't bother to tell Bob Kennedy, who had made clear he wanted to know if the CIA was relying on organized crime figures. Helms later said he didn't feel the need to tell RFK about his assassination activities because he viewed his job as serving as "a secret screen between overt officialdom and some of the more dubious, or self-serving, denizens of the nether depths."[36] Helms, it seems, didn't want to burden the attorney general with the unseemly details of how he defied his order. It was a matter of protecting the White House, he said. As novelist Thomas Mallon observed, Helms was slippery, even for a spy.[37]

4

MONSTER OF SELF-POSSESSION

Nixon drove himself deeper into the political wilderness. In the fall of 1962, his campaign for governor of California sputtered. Voters could sense he didn't really want the job, which he later admitted was true. He was trailing Democratic incumbent Pat Brown in the polls when President Kennedy went on TV to announce that the Soviet Union had secretly installed nuclear missiles in Cuba and that he was demanding their removal on threat of war. To Rose Woods, Nixon dictated a statement endorsing Kennedy's actions. Privately he wrote, "I knew any chance I had of narrowing Brown's lead in the polls was gone."[1]

The threat of imminent nuclear war gripped Washington. In what Arthur Schlesinger called "the most dangerous moment in the history of the world," Kennedy resisted the advice of his generals, who unanimously recommended air strikes to destroy the missile bases and an amphibious invasion to remove Castro's government. On the island, Castro mobilized the population to prepare for the U.S. invasion he had been expecting for months. Soviet forces on the island received permission from Moscow to use tactical nuclear weapons if attacked. A nuclear war that might incinerate millions of Americans was suddenly possible. After a week full of dread, opaque statements, TV speculation about annihilation, elementary school safety drills, and blunt back-channel communications, Khrushchev agreed to remove the missiles. Kennedy kept the peace and soared in the polls, while the generals of Joint Chiefs of Staff fumed at what they saw as his weakness.

Helms professed to admire Kennedy's management of the crisis. In his memoir, he praised JFK for showing "considerable wisdom." Kennedy, he wrote, "balanced sage advice against various hotheaded or weak-kneed proposals and navigated a steady course to the best possible result."[2]

On Election Day, Nixon lost his bid to become governor by a wide margin. At a press conference, he announced his retirement from politics, famously declaring that reporters wouldn't "have Nixon to kick around anymore."

Defeat punished Nixon in all his insecurities. Not only had he lost another election, his rival Kennedy was now portrayed as a statesman. Kennedy's journalist friends Stewart Alsop and Charles Bartlett, recipients of selective leaks from the White House, wrote a glowing account of Kennedy's handling of the crisis for the *Saturday Evening Post*. They depicted Kennedy as a level-headed statesman who prevailed over the Russians by staring them down.[3] As the Washington press corps picked up on the White House narrative that "Khrushchev blinked," the Republican advantage on the Cuba issue vanished. Most galling of all to Nixon, the Bay of Pigs debacle had been entirely forgotten.

MISSILES IN CAVES

In taking over the DDP, Helms made a point of distinguishing between intelligence—the government's information and analysis—and policy—the government's plan of action. As an intelligence officer, he insisted that he didn't do policy. And indeed, Helms usually refrained from offering policy opinions. But the canny deputy director had other ways of exercising invisible influence in visible ways.

"Exiles Tell of Missiles Hidden in Cuban Caves," declared the front-page headline in the *Washington Star* on Tuesday, November 5, Election Day. The story began ominously: "Soviet missiles in Cuba have been placed in seven caves and other underground installations in sufficient number to destroy half the American continent since the Kennedy-Khrushchev agreement to dismantle the open missile sites, a Cuban exile leader said today."

The story was written by reporter Jerry O'Leary, a CIA asset who happened to be a good friend with Dave Phillips, now a senior Cuba operations officer.[4] O'Leary quoted a spokesman for the Directorio Revolucionario Estudiantil (DRE), a CIA-funded student group, saying the group had forwarded the information to "our contacts" in the U.S. government. "The CIA, which masterminded the Bay of Pigs invasion, remains active among Cuban exile groups," O'Leary reported, "and is believed to provide financial support for some of them, including DRE." That was true. The Agency provided $51,000 a month to the Cuban students under a program codenamed AMSPELL that was run by Phillips.[5] The funds paid for the DRE's propaganda, political action, and intelligence collection, as well as a network of delegations throughout North and South America.

The "missiles in caves" story can be fairly described as a CIA gambit, condoned by Helms, to influence Kennedy's policy. As intelligence, it would never rise above uncorroborated hearsay. As psychological warfare, the story had a precise point: to create pressure on the president for a more aggressive Cuba policy.

President Kennedy intuited that the story emanated from Langley. In a meeting the next day, he asked McCone where the story came from. "We need to persuade responsible editors to check such stories with the government before they print them," he said.[6] That didn't happen.

A week later, Luis Fernandez Rocha, a twenty-four-year-old medical student and secretary general of the DRE, appeared on the nationally televised *Today Show* to repeat the allegation of Soviet missiles in Cuban caves. The show, one of the most popular daytime television programs in America, was seen across the country. Unbeknownst to the TV network and the viewing public, Rocha was a paid CIA agent with "provisional operational approval" to participate in covert activities. In CIA files he was identified by the cryptonym AMHINT-53.

Decades later in an interview, Rocha, a retired doctor in Miami, recalled speaking to *Today Show* host Hugh Downs and an audience of millions.

"I told him very simple and very straight, that we had information about the missiles that [was] passed to the government as early as late September," Rocha said.[7] He said offensive missiles had been buried in Cuba and not all of them had been shipped back to Russia as Khrushchev promised.[8]

Kennedy was watching and grew furious. "As for that fellow on the TV *Today* show," Kennedy snapped in the Oval Office later that day, "I want our officials to interrogate every Cuban refugee who is making statements about arms going to Cuba within twenty four hours. The refugees are naturally trying to build up their story in an effort to get us to invade. We must get to the people the fact that the refugees have no evidence which we do not have. Such refugee statements, if they continue, could make the problem almost unmanageable."[9]

McCone passed the president's order to Helms. The deputy director wasted no time summoning Rocha to Washington. The next day Rocha was ushered into Helms's office in the Langley headquarters. "They wanted the DRE for one simple reason," Rocha said. "We had the best organization in Latin America that they had ever seen."[10]

It was unusual, to say the least, for the deputy director to meet face-to-face with a working agent, but the president had spoken. With trusted aide Nestor Sanchez taking notes, Helms grilled Rocha about the missiles and the caves where they might be found. The information was far from solid, Rocha admitted. In closing, Helms told Rocha that he was assigning a new contact in Miami who would report personally to him. "I can assure you of my continuing personal interest in this relationship," Helms promised.[11] Rocha said he was as good as his word. "After our conversation with Helms our level of communication with the Agency was put up several notches," Rocha recalled.[12]

Helms had fulfilled the letter of the president's order. He had called the Cuban students on the proverbial carpet, checked their story, and demanded they clear future public statements with their new case officer. The spirit of JFK's order was another matter. If the president expected the CIA to curb the students for making unsupported inflammatory claims in a time of crisis, Helms evaded the chore. In his meeting with Rocha, Helms mentioned but did not reduce the group's monthly subsidy. The CIA continued funding the DRE's so-called Military Section, whose members had made headlines (and embarrassed the White House) back in August with a maritime cannon attack on a seaside hotel in Havana that Castro denounced as international piracy. Helms avowed his "continuing personal interest" in the group, a virtual invitation to continue pressuring Kennedy.[13] He brought George Joannides, an up-and-coming officer from the Athens station, to keep the AMSPELL boys under control.[14]

Helms was mastering the art of faithfully serving a president while discreetly exercising the Agency's operational freedom. Nixon was rethinking his path to power.

MONSTER OF SELF-POSSESSION

In his season of defeat, Nixon took to quoting Honoré de Balzac, who described politicians as "monsters of self-possession." To which Nixon added, "Yet while we may show this veneer on the outside, coming inside the turmoil becomes almost unbearable."[15] Retiring to southern California, Nixon summoned the monstrous self-possession that enabled him to shed his sore-loser attitude, shake off rejection by the voters of California, disregard the mockery of the liberals, requite the undeserved suffering of his family, and come up with a plan—a solid plan, he assured himself—not only to make a six-figure salary, and make Pat and the girls happy, but also to come back and do what most everyone thought was all but impossible: win the presidency of the United States of America in 1964.

In his turmoil, he found solace in the memoirs of Charles de Gaulle, who had returned from a political exile to achieve supreme power. He underlined one of the French president's aperçus, which he strove to master. "Great men of action have without exception, possessed in a very high degree the faculty of withdrawing into themselves."[16] As 1962 turned into 1963, the injured Nixon withdrew and reinvented himself.

Go east, he decided. He would leave California behind. He would go to New York, to the heart of the Eastern Establishment that he had long scorned as a bastion of liberal elitism. Nixon let a longtime supporter, Elmer Bobst, chairman of the Warner-Lambert pharmaceutical company, know he was interested in becoming a public partner at a big New York law firm. The public partner role, perfected by Thomas Dewey, former governor of New York, would allow him to travel and give speeches while his reputation as a man of power would attract new clients to the firm.[17]

Nixon returned to politics in March 1963. He warmed up with an appearance on the *Jack Paar Show*, the popular late-night talk show, where he played the piano, accompanied "by fifteen Democratic violinists," Paar quipped. The same day the show aired Nixon held his first press conference since November. The genial piano player turned partisan slasher attacking Kennedy for the Bay of Pigs, accusing the president of "not seeing it through and finishing the job." He called for a "political, diplomatic, economic and military quarantine" of communist Cuba, a virtual declaration of war.[18]

Kennedy preferred to defuse the Cuba issue. At the end of March, he disregarded McCone's advice. Attorney General Bob Kennedy ordered a crackdown on Cuban exiles in Miami who were launching unauthorized attacks on Cuba-bound ships.[19] A score of militant Cubans on the CIA's payroll, including Luis Fernandez Rocha and Manuel Salvat of the DRE, received letters instructing them not to leave Miami without permission. Kennedy's name became anathema, both among the CIA men and their agents. "Why is this SOB going against the anti-Castro Cubans?" Dave Phillips fumed to his agent Antonio Veciana, AMSHALE-14, whose Alpha 66 terror group was behind some of the maritime attacks.[20]

Nixon escalated his criticism of Kennedy. In a speech to the American Society of Newspaper Editors, he called for a "freedom policy" to liberate Cuba from communism. "In Cuba we have goofed an invasion, paid tribute to Castro for the prisoners, then gave the Soviets squatters rights in our backyard," Nixon scoffed.

"We have courageously dared a blockade to keep the peace, withdrew the blockade to avoid war." After the missile crisis ended, JFK had pulled "defeat out of the jaws of victory." Nixon stopped short of endorsing a naval blockade or invasion, insisting that only a "minimum" of U.S. power needed to be applied.[21]

At his next news conference, Kennedy challenged Nixon to say if he was advocating an invasion of Cuba. "Now we're coming down to the question which is rather side-stepped," the president said. "That is, if the United States should go to war in order to remove Castro. That nettle is not grasped."[22]

ENGINEERED PROVOCATION

Helms believed the nettle had to be grasped. Without a willingness to commit U.S. troops, the president's policy of overthrowing was unrealistic, the deputy director thought. "A year hence, (barring Castro's death or some decisive U.S. intervention in the situation)," said the Agency's latest estimate, "the Castro regime is likely to be more firmly established than ever. The mere passage of time tends to favor Castro as the Cubans and others become more accustomed to the idea that he is here to stay . . ."[23]

Worse yet, from Helms's point of view, Castro now perceived that Kennedy might be willing to do the unthinkable: normalize relations between the two countries. On May 1 the deputy director delivered a three-page memo to McCone, summarizing what the Agency learned in debriefing Lisa Howard, an ABC News correspondent who had just returned from an extended interview with Castro in Havana. "It appears that Fidel Castro is looking for a way to reach a rapprochement with the United State government," Helms wrote. Castro told Howard that "he considered the U.S. limitation on exile raids to be a proper step toward accommodation."[24] Helms and the CIA men worried the president might be interested.

The struggle for control of U.S. Cuba policy deepened. That same day, the Joint Chiefs of Staff met in the Pentagon to adopt unanimously a daring alternative to JFK's passive policy. The generals approved—or rather revived—the solution of a pretext operation, what military planners call a "contrived provocation." The concept, first developed by the JCS in March 1962, called for orchestrating an outrageous attack on an American target and arranging for the blame to fall on Castro's government so as to put the U.S. government "in the apparent position of suffering defensible grievances from a rash and irresponsible government." The deception would create a "justification for U.S. intervention in Cuba." They called it Operation Northwoods.[25]

"We could develop a Communist Cuban terror campaign in the Miami area, in other Florida cities, and even in Washington," wrote one planner. Another

Northwoods scheme envisioned faking the shooting down of a U.S. airplane and manufacturing "evidence" that Castro's government was responsible. A third scenario involved faking the hijacking of a civilian airliner, taking the passengers hostage, and making it look like Cuba was responsible. A fourth called for sinking a boatload of Cuban refugees, "real or imagined," and implicating Castro in the atrocity. The planners contrasted the Northwoods approach with the White House policy of supporting Cubans who wanted to overthrow Castro from within. "Engineered provocations would provide greater advantages in control, timing, simplicity and security than would a fomented revolt," the chiefs concluded.

The Northwoods concept amounted to hijacking American democracy in service of a military goal, as the generals recognized. Pretext operations "are inherently extremely risky in our democratic system in which security can be maintained, after the fact, with very great difficulty," the Northwoods planners noted. "If the decision should be made to set up a contrived situation, it should be one in which participation by U.S. personnel is limited only to the most highly trusted covert personnel." Operation Northwoods was approved without dissent, according to the available record, and would remain secret for another three decades.

Northwoods was never implemented, asserted David Robarge, the CIA's in-house historian, in a 2017 blog post. He presented no evidence to support the claim.[26] The Northwoods plans, not declassified until 1997, show only that the concept was approved in May 1963. The available record does not show whether preparations for a "contrived situation" were formally rejected by the White House or terminated by the chiefs. In any case, there is no doubt that the idea of staging a spectacular crime and blaming it on Cuba as a way of overthrowing Castro appealed to the highest echelons of the Pentagon and CIA in mid-1963. All the while dissension about Kennedy's policy simmered.

Dissension about Kennedy's policy bred desperation. The Agency was willing to support almost any plan to turn U.S. public opinion against Castro. In the summer of 1963, William Pawley, owner of Civil Air Transport, a CIA proprietary company, wanted to jump-start Kennedy's Cuba policy. Pawley was a millionaire businessman, adventurer, and personal friend of Allen Dulles. He agreed to fund a team of commandos for a daring mission: to capture four Russian military technicians said to be working a Cuban missile site.[27] Richard Billings, chief of *Life* magazine's Miami bureau, would accompany the men. The raiders would bring the technicians back to the United States; *Life* would hold a press conference proclaiming they had living proof that Soviet missiles were still in Cuba. Then, Pawley figured, JFK would have to order an invasion.[28] Also participating, according to a declassified CIA memo, were the ubiquitous Frank Sturgis and another man destined to wind up at the Watergate, boat captain Rolando Martínez.[29]

In the waters off Cuba, the commando team (not including Sturgis or Martínez) boarded a small, high-speed boat owned by Pawley's company. As the men waded ashore, they drew fire from Cuban security forces. Two were killed and the rest were never heard from again.[30]

With U.S. policy divided and adrift, Helms decided to act. In June 1963, he approved renewal of contacts with Rolando Cubela, the assassin of the Montmartre, the hero of Santa Clara, the haunted man they dubbed AMLASH. Dave Phillips said that those who thought Helms operationally timid didn't know the man. He recalled Helms approving one risky operation with the injunction that "in espionage anything less than controlled boldness would minimize the chance of success."[31]

The AMLASH operation exemplified controlled boldness. Helms might yet save the day for Kennedy's policy with a closely held operation. The deputy director felt no need to tell the president. Besides, what options did he have? Bob Kennedy playing case officer for Hunt's friend Manolo Artime wasn't going to achieve anything. The Northwoods approach was a non-starter with the president. If the pretext for a U.S. invasion could not be generated by engineered provocation, Castro's elimination might achieve the same goal more efficiently. And so the gentlemanly planner of assassinations went to work.

5

Dick Helms always insisted that the AMLASH operation was a not, repeat not, an assassination conspiracy. He denied it, under oath, to Senate and House investigators. He repeated the claim in his memoir. "The AMLASH operation was a political action operation to get a political grouping together to unseat Castro," he said. "It was not an assassination operation. It was not designed for that purpose. I think I do know what I'm talking about here."[1]

Helms certainly did know what he was talking about, he just wasn't sharing all that he knew. By the summer of 1963, the deputy director was well briefed on AMLASH. He knew about Cubela, the assassination of Colonel Blanco Rico, and the battle of Santa Clara. The Agency knew of Cubela's passionate defense of the revolution while serving as president of the student body at the University of Havana, the same position once held by his martyred friend José Antonio Echeverría. Cubela's leadership gave the government de facto control of a campus that had traditionally been autonomous and a hotbed of antigovernment activism.[2]

As a hero of the revolution, Cubela was an attractive target for recruitment. He told friends that he loathed what Castro's government was doing to Cuba. The CIA men knew he wasn't a communist. They just didn't know how to approach him. Tony Sforza, a deep-cover agent, recommended contacting Carlos Tepedino, a jeweler in Havana, who had given Sforza safe haven while he was being hunted by Castro's security forces. Tepedino had also given money to the Revolutionary Directorate in the fight against Batista, and was personally close to Cubela.

"In view of the many years of friendship we have had with Subject's [Tepedino's] family," one station asset wrote, "we can his assure that his family [is] absolutely trustworthy and are willing to give any type of help." Sforza's suggestion paid off. When contacted, Tepedino agreed to arrange a meeting with Cubela in Helsinki, Finland, where they were attending an international youth conference.[3]

In the dim confines of a Helsinki restaurant called the White Lady, Cubela told the visiting CIA officer, "If he could do something really significant for the creation of a new Cuba, he was interested in returning to carry on the fight there." And what did "really significant" mean? the CIA man asked. "To eliminate Fidel, by execution if necessary," Cubela replied.

That's why Helms regarded Cubela as the best hope for getting rid of Castro. "Given the relentless blistering heat from the White House," he explained in his memoir, "I was scarcely of a mind to drop anyone whom we were satisfied had a reasonable access to Castro and who was apparently determined to turn him out of office."[4]

Helms's determination to kill Castro was tested in August 1963 when the story of the now-abandoned Mafia plots emerged for the first time. The *Chicago Sun-Times* published a story under the headline: "CIA Sought Giancana for Cuba Spying."[5] The story detailed contacts between CIA officers and the Chicago crime boss Sam Giancana in the fall of 1960. It did not mention the poison pills or assassination, but given Giancana's murderous reputation, the implication was there.

McCone called Helms. "What's this about?"

The deputy director brought McCone a memorandum for the record about the CIA's meeting with Attorney General Bob Kennedy in May 1962. It memorialized the story of how the Agency approached Giancana with poison pills, how Bob Maheu blackmailed the government into dropping charges against him, and how Bob Kennedy reacted.[6] McCone scanned the memo rather quickly, Helms observed. This was a sensitive subject. McCone was a devout Catholic who abhorred the idea of assassination, at least on Sundays. It was a Friday, so he chose not to make an issue of it. "This did not happen on my tenure," McCone said, looking up.

Helms took advantage of his forbearance with a dose of guile. "There's only one copy of this memorandum in the building," he said. "I don't think it should be in your office. I would like to take it with me."[7] Helms took the incriminating paper and exited.

There was a method to his neatness. Helms and his CIA colleagues understood and emphasized the importance of the historical record, observed Thomas Powers, Helms's biographer. They had a sure answer to the philosopher's query, if a tree falls in the woods without a witness, does it make any sound? "The CIA would say no," Powers observed. "It would agree with historian David Hackett Fischer. History is not what happened but what the surviving evidence says happened. If you can hide the evidence and keep the secrets, then you can write the history."[8] Helms didn't merely believe that. He lived it.

A few days later, Helms sent a copy of the *Sun-Times* article to Bob Kennedy with a cover note saying the piece "was brought to my attention today for the first time, so I was unaware of its appearance when I talked with you Monday afternoon." That sounded true but was not. Helms had discussed the article with McCone the day it came out. That was three days before he shared it with RFK. Helms's fib fit his method. *If you can hide the evidence and keep the secrets, then you can write the history.*

The AMLASH conspiracy proceeded. The partisan politics of the Cuba issue had quieted since the missile crisis. The talk of war in Cuba, prevalent in the fall of 1962, was muted after the dreadful scare of the October crisis. The president wanted calm. The chief voice for Cuba action in the White House, Bob Kennedy, was preoccupied with bitter resistance to court-ordered desegregation of the Jim Crow South. While the Pentagon and the CIA wanted action in Cuba, Kennedy wanted quiet. He kept open the option of negotiating with Castro, a disturbing development to the Cuba hawks.

Helms nurtured his plan to eliminate Castro. In September 1963, he sent Nestor Sanchez to meet Cubela on the sidelines of a sports festival in Brazil. As a representative of the Cuban government, he was a well-known figure. His first-person account of the Battle of Santa Clara had just been published as a cover story in *Bohemia*, Cuba's leading news magazine. On the fourth anniversary of the revolution, he and Guevara were depicted as comrades in arms. Yet Cubela was so disillusioned he continued talking to the enemy, the CIA.

Sanchez got right to the point. If Cubela wanted to move against Castro, he could offer U.S. support. Cubela reiterated that he would only act on behalf of the most serious effort. They agreed to meet again. Ten days later, Cubela turned up in Paris with a severe case of cold feet.[9] Helms sent Sanchez to buck him up. Cubela responded by saying he wanted to meet a senior U.S. official, preferably Robert Kennedy, to confirm Washington's support as he risked his life for their cause.

Cubela's request bothered Harold Swenson, the top counterintelligence officer in the Cuba operation. Swenson was a former FBI agent who devoted hours to studying the personnel and methods of Castro's spy service. "I felt first that we were dealing with people whose bona fides were subject to question," he said.[10] He thought they should cut off contact with AMLASH. Helms overruled Swenson. He sent his top Cuba deputy, Desmond FitzGerald, to Paris to meet with Cubela. FitzGerald introduced himself as "James Clark," the personal emissary of Robert Kennedy, which wasn't true. In another display of guile, Helms had asked Fitz-Gerald not to disclose the mission to RFK.

It is a tribute to Helms's immense charm that, in the face of a paper trail studded with words like "eliminate" and "execution," punctuated by the delivery of two weapons to a man who would later be convicted of an assassination conspiracy, and corroborated by sworn testimony of CIA officers, Helms still managed to convince two competent biographers and his worldly wife that AMLASH was not really an assassination operation.

"When people wanted to invade Cuba or kill Castro, his attitude was, 'Oh, God,'" Helms biographer Thomas Powers told Chris Whipple, author of a laudatory book about CIA directors. "He just was so against it all," said Cynthia Helms of the plots to kill Castro. "He said to me one day, 'I was never going to do it. We were never going to do it.' But they made his life miserable over it."[11]

The CIA's files betray no trace of Helms's putative resistance to the lure of assassination. In August 1962 the Agency's reporting on Cubela in Helsinki made it clear AMLASH was serious about assassination. In July 1963 Helms approved renewed contact. In August 1963, he chose not to disclose the operation to Mc-Cone, a man with moral objections to assassination. The next month he selected the trusted Nestor Sanchez to handle AMLASH. When Cubela lost his nerve in Paris, Helms sent Sanchez to hold his hand. When Cubela wanted to meet a senior American official, Helms dispatched FitzGerald. And when Swenson questioned Cubela's bona fides, Helms dismissed his concerns and delivered a lethal weapon. In this chain of events, no one but Dick Helms was in charge, and his purpose was plain: assassinating Fidel Castro.

FAST TRACK

Nixon, out of politics and far from the policy action, was pursuing his intricately plotted route back to the White House. In May 1963, he agreed to join the Mudge Rose law firm in New York in a public partner position that would allow him to combine legal work with politicking.[12] Before starting his new job, he and his family left for a long-planned tour of Europe. In Paris, Nixon arranged a lunch with President de Gaulle, whose career now served as a template for the down-and-out former vice president.[13] De Gaulle had led the French nation through World War II and then was sidelined by lesser politicians. Nixon had risen to great heights in the Eisenhower administration and then been cheated, or so he believed, by the Kennedys and their establishment allies. In political exile, de Gaulle cultivated his contacts and sharpened his message until the force of his ideas returned him to power. Nixon planned to do the same.

Upon his return Nixon took up the life of a working attorney, dutiful dad, and doting husband. Each day his driver and house servant, Manolo Sanchez, delivered him to the law firm offices at 20 Broad Street by eight thirty in the morning. Nixon found New York exciting and cutthroat. "Any person tends to vegetate unless he is moving on a fast track," he explained to a reporter. "You have to bone up to keep alive in the competition here."[14]

Nixon simplified his life. He dissolved his political office, sending his chief of staff Bob Haldeman back to California while retaining Rose Woods as his secretary. Now a face in the Gotham crowd, Nixon dedicated himself to business and the law. Journalist Theodore White thought he looked wiser. "The lines on his face from nose to chin, the cheek folds themselves, were deeper, more furrowed," White wrote. "Yet the more mature man seemed more attractive, less harsh than the man of 1960."[15]

Nixon did not—could not—abstain from politics. In October 1963, he returned from an overseas trip and unburdened himself to reporters about President Kennedy's much-touted "image," which had him riding high in the polls and low in Nixon's estimation. "I have never been abroad when American prestige was lower than it is now," he said.[16] Even in retirement, he was ready with a barb, alert for an opportunity to score points. And when events in Southeast Asia gave him an opening, he attacked Kennedy again.

DOROTHY AND DIEM

Dick Helms was a man of many meetings—about budgets, personnel, and operations—where he dealt with questions, large and small. He paid attention to personalities, collected intelligence voraciously, and kept the interests of the president in mind. When Howard Hunt wanted to bring wife Dorothy into the spying profession, the deputy director liked the idea. Dorothy, working as a translator for the Spanish ambassador in Washington, was well positioned to learn about Spain's intentions toward the United States. Hunt proposed that Dorothy be hired as a contract employee. The Office of Security objected. Hunt "has been a continuing security problem due to disregard for regulations and established procedures," one official warned.

Dorothy spied anyway. In February 1963, she filched a letter from the

ambassador to a friend of First Lady Jacqueline Kennedy, asking for help in secur-
ing a presidential visit to Spain. The ambassador wanted to talk about U.S. policy
in Latin America with Kennedy. Howard passed his wife's report to the chief of
foreign intelligence, who showed it to the deputy director. Helms thought the
information worthy of White House attention.

"Mrs. Hunt is engaging in intelligence collection in the United States—without
any official sanction for such activity," complained another official. Helms dismissed
the objection via his deputy. "We believe that there is sufficient gain from the contact
and certain pieces of information to take the calculated risk," Karamessines told the
Office of Security. Dorothy continued to spy on the Spanish ambassador until June
1963, when she gave birth to the Hunts' fourth child, David. Helms, the manager,
showed a deft touch. He took care of his pal's wife.[17]

Punctual and attentive, Helms sat through many country briefings. On the
analytical side he presided over the editing of formal National Intelligence Estimates that the White House and the National Security Council constantly demanded. Operationally, he administered an annual budget of a billion dollars,
employing some 15,000 people. He kept current on covert activities in some eighty
countries. Which minister was on the payroll? Whose phone was tapped? Who
could be blackmailed? Who could help with a break-in? Who could make a communist disappear? Helms presided over a vast empire of coercion and deception
in service of the Free World.

The deputy director scheduled the most time for meetings on the secret wars in
Cuba, Laos, and increasingly South Vietnam, where communist forces were gaining
on the government of President Ngo Dinh Diem. After he and Julia visited Saigon
on a trip in 1962, Helms came away favoring expanded covert operations and en-
hanced military assistance. He envisioned the CIA serving as the cutting edge of
U.S. forces fighting a land war against a totalitarian power, like the OSS did in
World War II. When Julia met Madame Nhu, wife of Diem's interior minister and
de facto First Lady of South Vietnam, she was struck by Nhu's disdain for her own
country.[18] Helms sensed Diem's independence was a problem.

Diem had been elected president of South Vietnam in 1956 in an election in
which all opposition candidates were banned. His political strength derived from
his resistance to the Japanese occupation during World War II and his refusal to
collaborate with the French colonialists afterward. He embodied a Vietnamese
nationalism that was not communist, so the U.S. government held him up as
an exemplar of the Free World. Diem also enjoyed the support of the Catholic

Church in the United States, not the least because his government favored the country's Catholic minority over the Buddhist majority.[19]

"It became apparent irrespective of U.S. counsel and support, Diem was determined to go his own way," Helms wrote in his memoir. In May the Diem government ordered Buddhist flags celebrating the upcoming birthday of the Buddha to be taken down. Only religious institutions could have flags, the government said, and Buddhism was a religion, not an institution. When the Buddhists protested. Diem's brother, Interior Minister Ngo Dinh Nhu, violently suppressed their demonstrations. One Buddhist monk responded by burning himself to death on a busy Saigon street, and the ghastly photograph was seen around the world. By the end of the summer, six more monks had immolated themselves in protest.[20] Nhu's beautiful and imperious wife, who served as a First Lady for the bachelor president, blurted out that she would "clap for another monk's barbecue," ensuring her reputation as a twentieth-century Marie Antoinette.[21] As an ally, Diem had disappointed Kennedy too many times.

In August 1963, Kennedy came around to the idea of letting Diem's rivals in Saigon know that Washington would not object to a coup. He approved the idea in a conversation with Henry Cabot Lodge, the former senator and Nixon's running mate in 1960, whom he had just appointed ambassador in Saigon. "The time may come, though, we've got to just have to do something about Diem," Kennedy said in a White House tape recording first made public in 2020, "and I think that's going to be an awfully critical period." Warned that Diem and Nhu might well be killed in a coup. Kennedy was more concerned that they be replaced. "It may be they ought to go," he said, "but it's just a question of how quickly that's done and if you get the right fellow."[22]

The president polled his advisers to weigh in. The CIA's chief of station in Saigon opposed the idea of a coup, saying Diem should be given time. The newly married John McCone was on his honeymoon, so Helms was called at his home on Fessenden Street in northwest Washington. He supported Kennedy's decision. "It's about time we bit that bullet," he said, according to journalist David Halberstam.[23] The coup plotters held off, fearing Diem might be laying a trap. Under pressure to increase U.S. military support for the embattled regime, Kennedy resisted sending more troops while signaling again in late October that he would welcome a new government.

JFK got what he wished for. On November 1, a cabal of generals in the Armed Forces of South Vietnam, led by Duong Van Minh, known as Big Minh, decided

Diem had to go. Minh's troops besieged the presidential palace in Saigon. Diem and Nhu tried and failed to rally their supporters in the armed forces. Finding none willing to act, they slipped out of the palace and took refuge in a nearby church. They sent word to Minh they were ready to surrender in exchange for safe passage out of the country. Minh ordered his men to pick up Diem and Nhu and deliver them to the U.S. military headquarters, where the CIA was arranging a flight out of the country.

One of Minh's lieutenants, Captain Thung, took Diem and Nhu into custody, handcuffed them, and secured them in an army personnel carrier. En route to the American headquarters, the captain stopped the truck and flung open the doors to the vehicle in a rage. He started slashing the handcuffed Diem and Nhu with his bayonet. While they were still alive, he cut open their stomachs and extracted their gall bladders, considered trophies of war. With his bloody victory in hand, Thung pulled out his pistol and shot both men dead.[24]

Back in Washington, Kennedy blanched when he heard the news in a meeting with his national security advisers. Diem was a friend of his father's, a gentle man he'd known all his adult life. Kennedy jumped up and left the room. "I've never seen him more upset," said Defense Secretary Robert McNamara.[25] Helms was not impressed. The coup was Kennedy's idea. What did he expect? JFK had "never quite hoisted this operation aboard," he said, meaning he had never taken full responsibility for his own policy. In Helms's view, Kennedy wasn't quite in charge.

Nixon thought worse, that Kennedy had blundered badly, again, and he relished the opportunity for attack politics. Diem's fate could serve as ammunition in the 1964 campaign. Nixon sent a note to Henry Cabot Lodge in Saigon. Lodge epitomized the Eastern Establishment that Nixon envied and challenged and hoped to join.[26] To address Lodge was to address American power itself.

"I could tell from news reports how frustrated you must have been by the obstinacy of Diem, his brother, Madame Nhu and their associates," Nixon wrote. "But the heavy-handed participation of the United States in the coup which lead inevitably to the charge that we were either partially responsible for, or at the very least, condoned the murder of Diem and his brother, has left a bad taste in the mouths of many Americans . . ."

Nixon's relentless intelligence homed in on the opportunity to blame Kennedy for the deaths of Diem and Nhu. As in the Bay of Pigs operation, the president had demonized and abandoned an American ally. That was a message that could get through to voters everywhere and put him in the White House. "This may not seem important now," Nixon told Lodge, "but I don't need to tell you, the villains of today may become the martyrs of tomorrow."[27]

GUN

For Helms the news from Cuba was no better than it was from Vietnam. On November 6, the deputy director reported to the 303 Committee, the interagency group that reviewed covert operations. A recent sabotage mission on the island had proved a total failure, he said. Cuban security anticipated the raid and routed the attackers. Castro was growing stronger, U.S. policy more ineffectual. At the next week's meeting, on November 13, Helms was pleased to hear the discussion come around to Castro's support for revolutionaries throughout the hemisphere. The sense of the meeting was that something had to be done to generate support for a more aggressive policy. "The CIA, in connection with Department of Defense, should concentrate on attempting to catch Castro red-handed delivering arms to communist groups in Latin American countries," said the minutes of the meeting.[28]

That was a request Helms could fulfill in short order. The CIA had been monitoring Havana's support for revolutionaries in Venezuela, he claimed in his memoir. "An agent informed us that Castro operatives were about to land some three tons of small arms, ammunition, and mortars on the Venezuelan coast," he wrote in his memoir.[29] The Agency, it seems, had caught the Cubans "red-handed."

Or did they? Six months earlier, the Agency had developed a deception operation to fake a communist arms shipment. The plan, according to a May 1963 memo, involved "the laying down of an arms cache containing Soviet, Czech, and ChiCom [Chinese Communist] arms in selected Latin America areas, ostensibly proving the arms were smuggled from Cuba." When the 303 Committee resolved to find an arms cache, Helms provided one within the week. Historian David Kaiser suggested "the cache may have been a plant, the execution of a long discussed plan," a disinformation operation against the president himself to create pressure for a tougher Cuba policy.[30]

The Cuba issue was deeply felt by the CIA men. Helms, often reluctant to express policy views, did not hesitate on Cuba. He was an adamant advocate. Kennedy needed to act. Now.

"Castro's scheme was a clear violation of the policy agreement that followed the missile crisis," Helms wrote, "and came almost exactly a year after the press conference in which President Kennedy had pledged peace in the Caribbean, if all offensive weapons were removed from Cuba, *and* (emphasis in original) if Cuba ceased attempting to export its aggressive communist objectives."

Helms felt so strongly about the issue that he went to Bob Kennedy's office at the Justice Department to make his case, bringing with him one of the guns the Agency had supposedly seized. The impulsive attorney general, feeling guilty that he hadn't done enough on Cuba, said they should tell the president right away. Half an hour later, JFK was looking at a gun in the Oval Office.

Helms thought the scene worth recording in all its chilly detail.

"When the meeting ended, the President arose from his rocking chair and stood beside the coffee table looking toward the Rose Garden," he recalled. "I leaned over and took the submachine gun from the coffee table and slipped it back into the canvas airline travel bag in which we carried it—unchallenged—from the parking lot to the President's office. As the President turned to shake hands, I said, 'I'm sure glad the Secret Service didn't catch us bringing this gun in here.'"

Helms was a subtle man making a pitiless point. Did Kennedy, in his last days of life, appreciate that his Cuba policy was a matter of life and death? Apparently not. "The President's expression brightened," Helms recalled. "He grinned, shook his head slightly, and said, 'Yes, it gives me a feeling of confidence.'"[31]

The deputy director worked in a deadly milieu. The next day, Helms received the latest report from Nestor Sanchez on AMLASH. Cubela was satisfied by his recent meeting with Des FitzGerald but "could not understand why he was denied certain small pieces of equipment, which promised a final solution to the problem."[32] Helms promptly fulfilled Cubela's request. He called on Dr. Edward Gunn, the chemist who concocted the poison pills for Castro's consumption. On short order, Gunn manufactured a hypodermic syringe disguised as a fountain pen that could be loaded with poison. Helms sent the lethal device to Sanchez in Paris.

On November 22, 1963, Sanchez welcomed Cubela into the secure apartment of a CIA colleague in Paris. Cubela said he was returning to Cuba fully determined to initiate a coup against AMTHUG [the CIA's unsubtle codename for Castro]. He named ten government officials who could be trusted to join the plot, and another five military commanders who would "fall in line" once the coup was successful. Sanchez was encouraged. He thought Cubela's operational thinking "appeared much less foggy than before." When Sanchez handed over Dr. Gunn's lethal writing instrument, Cubela returned it, saying it was useless. Cubela demanded a cache of heavy weaponry, including hand grenades and high-powered Belgian-made FAL rifles with scopes.

Helms had to forever deny the lethal nature of the AMLASH operation because of another event that day. When Cubela and Sanchez emerged from the meeting in the early evening, a passerby asked them if they had heard the news from Dallas.[33]

6

FREEDOM OF ACTION

President Kennedy's motorcade flowed past friendly crowds along Main Street in downtown Dallas and took a careful right turn at Dealey Plaza. The lead limousine, carrying the president, First Lady Jacqueline Kennedy, Texas governor John Connally, and his wife, Nellie, proceeded one block to Elm Street, and then turned left. Shots like a string of firecrackers rang out. A bullet struck Kennedy in the back, another hit Connally, a third missed and ricocheted off the curb. As the limousine slowed and the onlookers recoiled in the hail of bullets, another shot blasted out the back of Kennedy's head, spattering his brains and blood all over the first lady. The Secret Service driver of the limousine raced to the nearest hospital with the press car in pursuit. As orderlies rushed the grievously wounded president into the trauma room of Parkland Hospital, Merriman Smith, a veteran reporter for United Press International wire service, jumped out to question Secret Service agents about what had happened. Less than an hour later, he dictated the first draft of the story that would win him a Pulitzer Prize.

"A single shot through the right temple took the life of the 46-year-old Chief Executive," Smith reported. "Some of the Secret Service agents thought the gunfire was from an automatic weapon fired to the right rear of the president's car, probably from a grassy knoll to which police rushed."[1]

As medical personnel sought to stabilize the dying president, Dr. Robert Mc-Clelland, one of the senior attending physicians, saw the president's shattered skull and knew he would not live. McClelland, who observed the head wound from less than eighteen inches away, later concluded the fatal shot had come from the front.[2]

Kennedy was declared dead a few minutes later. The news spread instantly around the world via radio and television. By coincidence, Nixon had been in Dallas the day before, attending a meeting of the PepsiCo board. In the morning he caught a flight to New York. As the taxi pulled up to his Fifth Avenue address, the doorman rushed up. "Oh, no, Mr. Nixon," he cried, tears streaming down his face. "Have you heard, sir? It's just terrible they've killed President Kennedy."[3]

Nixon went up to his apartment. His first phone call went to FBI director J. Edgar Hoover.

"What happened?" Nixon asked. "Was it one of the right-wing nuts?"

"No," Hoover replied, "it was a communist."[4]

AMSPELL

Dick Helms was having a sandwich lunch with John McCone in the director's suite on the seventh floor of the CIA building when an aide burst into the room. "The president's been shot!" he cried.[5] McCone turned on a television and watched the news bulletins from Dallas. Then, Helms recalled, the director "clapped his hat on his head and left to meet Bob Kennedy at his home at Hickory Hill, not far from the agency Headquarters."

In his memoir, Helms chose not to mention Bob Kennedy's first question to McCone when he arrived. Helms knew the story because his friend Arthur Schlesinger recounted it in his biography of RFK. Stunned by the news of his brother's assassination, Kennedy voiced his gut suspicion. "I asked McCone . . . if they"—referring to the CIA—"had killed my brother," Kennedy said, "and I asked him in a way that he couldn't lie to me and they hadn't." But Bob Kennedy was not convinced—not that day and not ever—by the denials of the CIA men. He would always believe his brother had been killed by some combination of anti-Castro Cubans, renegade CIA officers, and Mafia bosses.[6]

Helms rushed to his office and sent a "book message," a cable communication to every CIA office in the world, calling for "any bit of information conceivably pointing to a plot involving any foreign power."

Within ninety minutes, a suspect in Dallas had been arrested. By four o'clock Eastern time, radio stations reported a man named Lee Harvey Oswald was being held in a Dallas jail on suspicion of killing a police officer. Within minutes a search of the Agency's Central File Registry turned up a personality file, also known as a 201 file, for Oswald, which contained a handful of documents, indicating that

Oswald was a twenty-four-year-old ex-marine who had defected to the Soviet Union in October 1959 and returned in June 1962. The Agency, it seemed, had received no information about him since then. That was the first story the CIA told about the Oswald file. It was far from the whole story.

"Tragic death of President Kennedy requires all of us to look for any unusual intelligence developments," Helms said in his message. "Although we have no reason to expect anything of a military nature, all hands should be on the quick alert for the next few days while new president takes reins."[7]

At ten past six that evening, Miami station chief Ted Shackley sent a cable to Desmond FitzGerald with a copy going to Helms's office. The station had heard from Luis Fernandez Rocha, the secretary general of the Cuban Student Directorate, whom Helms had grilled in his office almost exactly one year before. The AMSPELL agents said they knew all about the suspected assassin.

Jose Antonio Lanuza, a twenty-four-year-old law student and spokesman for the group, recognized the name "Oswald." He remembered that one of the group's North American delegations had a run-in with an American named Oswald a few months before. He checked his files and found that Carlos Bringuier, the Directorate's delegate in New Orleans, had a series of encounters with Oswald over the summer culminating in a debate on a local radio program. The file included Bringuier's letters about Oswald and Oswald's pamphlets from the pro-Castro Fair Play for Cuba Committee. Within hours of the gunfire in Dallas, the AMSPELL network delivered an intelligence coup: Kennedy's killer was a Castro supporter.

Lanuza went on to become a businessman and then a schoolteacher in Miami. In retirement, he and Luis Fernandez Rocha spoke freely about the DRE, the CIA, and their actions on the night of November 22, 1963.

"I went to Luis, and said, 'We've got the guy.'" Lanuza recalled in an interview. "Luis talked to Salvat." Juan Manuel Salvat, cofounder of the DRE, was also a CIA asset, code-named AMHINT-2. "He said, 'We have to tell our friends at the CIA.' Luis made the phone call."[8]

Rocha said he did not recall the conversation but agreed with Lanuza that he made the call. The DRE's friend at the CIA was "Howard," the alias for George Joannides, the case officer whom Helms assigned to run the group after the "missiles in caves" story. "If somebody called Howard it was me," Rocha said.[9]

The CIA man told them to wait an hour, Lanuza said. Joannides then passed the DRE's information to Miami station chief Shackley, who relayed the news to Langley.

"AMHINT-53 reports AMSPELL delegate had radio debate with Lee H

Oswald of Fair Play for Cuba Committee sometime in August 63 on New Orleans station WDSU," Shackley wrote. "According [to] AMSPELL files, Oswald former US Marine had traveled Moscow [19]59 at which time renounced American citizenship and turned passport over to American consulate. Alleged Lee H. Oswald lived in home Sov[iet] Foreign Minister for two months. In course [of] radio debate subj. confessed he [was a] Marxist."

The DRE was remarkably well informed about the suspected assassin, who had been in custody for barely two hours. Oswald never lived in the home of the Soviet foreign minister, but Rocha's information was otherwise accurate. Shackley cabled that he was not passing the report to the FBI or Secret Service because the AMSPELL boys were planning their own release to news organizations that evening. A CIA propaganda operation was unfolding.

"I waited fifty minutes," Lanuza recalled. "Then I started to call my list." Decades later he could still rattle off the reporters' names and publications from memory. "I called Hal Hendrix. He was the most important person in Miami News." (Hendrix, who won a Pulitzer Prize for his coverage of the 1962 missile crisis, was one of the Agency's "most valuable personal relationships" in the U.S. press corps, according to Carl Bernstein, the Watergate reporter who later investigated the CIA's ties to news organizations.[10]) Lanuza called Mary Louise Wilkinson, a sympathetic reporter at the *Miami News*.[11] He called John Dille, a writer at *Life* magazine who had written a laudatory cover story on the DRE.[12]

The DRE's story of the suspected assassin's support for Castro had credibility, thanks to the group's record of activism. It was corroborated by a tape of the WDSU radio debate, made by an anticommunist organization called the Information Council of the Americas, which specialized in publishing "truth tapes" about the spread of Castroite communism. The group's vice president, Ed Butler, sent the tape to NBC, which played it on the air on November 22. INCA, as it was known, would go on to establish a collaborative relationship, according to declassified memos. Butler was "our contact," said one CIA memo.[13] Thanks to the DRE and INCA, Oswald's association with the pro-Castro Fair Play for Cuba Committee became headline news all over the country and the world within twenty-four hours. No one outside of Langley knew both groups were CIA propaganda assets.

The DRE/AMSPELL-generated message about Oswald was more than influential. It was defining.

"Oswald Tried to Spy on Anti-Castro Exile Group," said the front-page story in the *Miami Herald* the next day. In Texas, the *Austin American-Statesman* blared

"Pro-Castroite Seized as Suspect in Killing." In upstate New York, the *Rochester Democrat-Chronicle* reported, "Pro-Castro Gunman Charged in Assassination of Kennedy." The *New York Times* reported Oswald "tried to infiltrate the Cuban Student Directorate seeking to overthrow Cuban Premier Fidel Castro, according to Cuban exiles in New Orleans and Miami."

Of course, Helms recognized the name of the Cuban Student Directorate. He knew its cryptonym, AMSPELL. He had assigned their case officer, George Joannides, and met their secretary general, Luis Rocha. And he knew the Agency was still funding the group. In all of his testimony to JFK investigators, Helms never mentioned his case officer's paid assets were the first to identify Oswald as a Castro supporter.

The day after the assassination, the pandemonium in Langley headquarters subsided, replaced by frantic energy. In a cable from Mexico City, station chief Win Scott said he had asked local authorities to detain a Mexican woman, Silvia Duran, who worked at the Cuban Embassy. Audio surveillance indicated that Oswald had made contact with her in late September, apparently while he was seeking a visa to travel to Cuba.

At four fifteen that afternoon, Helms's top deputy, Tom Karamessines, responded forcefully on his boss's behalf. He told John Whitten, a senior official on the Mexico desk, to order Scott to call off the arrest of Duran. Whitten made the call, but Scott told him it was too late. The Mexicans had already picked her up. Karamessines followed up with a FLASH cable to Scott—FLASH indicating the highest degree of urgency.

Duran's arrest "is extremely serious matter which could prejudice [U.S. government] freedom of action on entire question of [Cuban] responsibility," he wrote. He asked Scott to "ensure that her arrest is kept absolutely secret, that no information from her is published or leaked, that all such info is cabled to us, and the fact of her arrest and statements are not spread to leftist or disloyal circles in the Mexican government."

When he was first asked by Senate investigators about the FLASH cable thirteen years later, Karamessines had no recollection. "Are you sure I ordered him to call off the arrest?" he asked. "Maybe somebody else did. I don't recall any such thing." When shown a copy of the cable, Karamessines's memory started to improve. Did he talk to Helms about this exchange, he was asked?

"I couldn't possibly answer that question," he replied, which wasn't exactly responsive.[14] In fact, it would have been highly unusual for the loyal, low-key Karamessines to send a FLASH cable without his boss's approval. ("The greatest adventure Karamessines could imagine," said one CIA officer who knew him well, "was staying out of trouble."[15])

The phrasing of the memo was curious to the Senate investigator. The president had been killed barely more than twenty-four hours before. Why was Karamessines more worried about "freedom of action as opposed to finding out what happened?"

Karamessines unwrapped his calculation with care.

"Let us assume that Silvia Duran is hauled in by the Mexicans," he began, "and she says, 'Fellows, it is very simple I know, because [this] ex-Marine was actually hired by the Soviet Government with the assistance of Cuban intelligence to kill President Kennedy.' And you get a real hot little Mexican counterintelligence guy, and he says, I have got the scoop of the century. And he calls his newspaper guys in, and he says, 'This is the information fellows. This is what the witness has said.' And the next morning the world is reading: Soviets and Cuba planned assassination of President Kennedy."

In other words, Karamessines explained, the CIA wanted to preserve President Johnson's options. "Now you are sitting downtown in the White House or in the State Department, and you are wondering, where do we go next?" he asked. "Declare war on the Soviets and the Cubans? Where do we go?" If Duran "had that kind of dynamite information," he went on, "then we would've been in a much better position, our government, the president, and the State Department would've been in a much better position . . . to blame Cuba or not."

This was the "black world" of clandestine operations in which Dick Helms thrived. He knew better than anyone how things in this strange universe actually worked.[16] The chilly truth was that Kennedy's assassination presented opportunities for the CIA men: the opportunity to blame Castro for a heinous crime, to raise the specter of Cuban responsibility, to increase the pressure on the government in Havana so as to bring about its destruction and to implicate Cold War rival, the Soviet Union, for good measure.

Helms disliked the term "spymaster," but no other word captures his extraordinary—and invisible—position in the wake of Kennedy's assassination. The deputy director had one handpicked case officer in Miami, George Joannides, running the AMSPELL network, which was generating headlines that Kennedy had been killed by a communist. He had another handpicked case officer in Paris, Nestor Sanchez, who was advancing the AMLASH operation to assassinate Castro and mount a military coup. And in Langley, his top aide fought to preserve "freedom of action" on "the question of Cuban responsibility" for Kennedy's murder.

For the very few people in Washington who knew about Operation Northwoods, the plan approved by the joint chiefs back in May, the scenario had familiar contours: a spectacular crime against a U.S. target had taken place, and CIA assets were seeking to lay the blame on Cuba.

In time, Helms worried, on the record, that CIA people might have been involved in the Dallas ambush. In 1992, he told CBS News program *48 Hours* that the Agency had "made sure we had no one in Dallas on that particular day." "Why did you do that?" asked correspondent Richard Schlesinger. "Had anybody accused the CIA at that time?"

Helms was at a rare loss for words. He knew of Castro assassination plots and Pentagon-engineered provocations, but he couldn't talk about any of that.

"The place was in an uproar," he finally said. ". . . There was great concern this might have been a foreign doing of some kind."

Did someone ask you to check on your agents in Dallas, Schlesinger persisted?

"I just thought it was a wise thing to do . . ." Helms finished. "I did not think anybody [from the CIA was involved] and don't try and make me say it."[17]

In fact, as Helms knew full well, the Agency did have someone in Dallas on that day, a veteran operations officer named J. Walton Moore. He ran the local office of the Agency's Domestic Contacts Division (DCD). Moore not only knew that Oswald was living in Dallas after his return from Russia in June 1962, he had actually recommended the communist ex-marine to a Russian-speaking friend, George de Mohrenschildt, an itinerant geologist on good terms with the Agency. Helms would make sure the American people did not learn about the CIA's man in Dallas.[18]

The day after the assassination, he assigned counterintelligence chief James Angleton to maintain liaisons with the FBI. He asked John Whitten, a veteran counterespionage investigator, to serve as the focal point for the incoming reports from stations around the world.[19] He wanted senior officers to sift all incoming reports, worried that "junior people in isolated posts" might pass on "manifestly lunatic rumors or allegations." Once transmitted, he explained, "any urgent message of such a sensitive subject would perforce be immediately disseminated in Washington and would forever remain a part of the permanent record."[20]

That was Dick Helms, consummate bureaucrat. From the moment he heard the news out of Dallas, he sought to control the historical record as found in the Agency's files. And there were certain sensitive subjects—not "lunatic rumors" but authorized clandestine activities like AMLASH and AMSPELL and Tom

Karamessines's FLASH cable—that the deputy director would seek, not always successfully, to keep out of the record of JFK's assassination.

Saturday, November 23, dragged on wet, gray, and miserable in the nation's capital. "A shroud of rain fell over Washington yesterday," wrote reporter George Lardner in the *Post*. "It took up where tears had stopped."[21]

At his home on Fessenden Street in northwest Washington, Helms did what a gentleman would do under the circumstances. He penned a condolence note to Bob Kennedy.

> *Dear Mr. Attorney General*
>   *When you sent me to see the president on Tuesday afternoon, he never seemed more confident or in control of the crushing forces around him. Friday struck me personally.*
>
> *Sadly and respectfully, Dick Helms*

Bob Kennedy never trusted Helms again. Mere politesse could not erase his abiding suspicion that CIA personnel connived in the murder of his brother.

Nixon too composed a condolence letter. Sitting up late in the library of his Fifth Avenue apartment, he wrote to Jacqueline Kennedy, the now-former first lady.

"Dear Jackie," Nixon began. "In this tragic hour Pat and I want you to know our thoughts and prayers are with you. While the hand of fate made Jack and me political opponents, I always cherished the fact that we were personal friends from the time we came to the Congress together in 1947 . . ."

Nixon had cherished the friendship rather more than Jack, but no matter.

"You brought to the White House, charm, beauty and elegance as the official hostess for America," Nixon wrote, "and the mystique of the young at heart which was uniquely yours made an indelible impression on the American consciousness."[22]

The condolences suited the consolers. Helms wrote to Bob Kennedy about JFK's confidence and *the crushing forces around him*. Nixon commended Jackie for her style and *the mystique of the young at heart*. Both prized the sort of intuitive and nuanced personal understanding that Helms called "human intelligence," and which Nixon knew as "charisma" in the political arena. Both paid tribute to the now-extinct power of Kennedys, but mourning was not Dick Helms's mode.

There are no good losers, he liked to say. *Losers are dead people*.[23] And Jack Kennedy was going to be buried on Monday.

At a chaotic late-night press conference in the Dallas jail, Oswald denied that he had shot Kennedy. "I'm just a patsy," he said. The next morning, he was shot dead on national TV by Jack Ruby, a nightclub owner with friends in the Mafia and the Dallas police department. The surreal assassination of the alleged assassin, seen by tens of millions of people at the same time, unified the country in shock while triggering an explosion of speculation about the forces behind Kennedy's assassination, even among senior CIA hands. Desmond FitzGerald, chief of Cuba operations, who was watching TV at his home in Georgetown, broke down in tears, the first and last time his wife saw him cry. "Now we'll never know," FitzGerald moaned.[24]

Reality had been rearranged by Dallas. Nixon had a new opponent in 1964. Helms had a new boss in the White House. The vice president–turned–Wall Street lawyer had a lot to learn. The deputy director had a lot to hide.

7

THE SHADOW

"I think it has become necessary to take another look at the purpose and operations of our Central Intelligence Agency," wrote former president Harry Truman in the *Washington Post* on December 22, 1963, exactly one month after Kennedy's assassination. At his home in Missouri, Truman had been thinking about Dallas, about Oswald, about the strange story of his defection to the Soviet Union and his return to the United States, his denial that he killed Kennedy, his astonishing execution on live television, and the speculation in the international press that Kennedy had been killed by enemies within his own government. Truman always had misgivings about the CIA. After Kennedy's murder, they returned.

Truman was not a revered statesman. When he left the White House in 1952, he was widely unpopular. He had little clout in the Democratic Party of John Kennedy and Lyndon Johnson. But few people in Washington knew the realities of the CIA better than Truman. When World War II ended, he abolished the Office of Strategic Services without delay, saying he did not want to risk creating an "American Gestapo." Two years later, as the Cold War confrontation with the Soviet Union deepened, Truman reversed himself and signed the National Security Act, creating the Central Intelligence Agency.

"I wanted and needed the information," Truman wrote in the *Post*. "But the most important thing about this move [to create the CIA] was to guard against the chance of intelligence being used to influence or lead the President into unwise decisions and I thought it was necessary that the President do his own thinking and evaluating."[1] That was a veiled allusion to the Bay of Pigs, where Truman thought the Agency had led JFK into an unwise decision.

The Agency, he went on, had become "an operational and at times a policy-making arm of the Government." He added, "I never had any thought that when I set up the CIA that it would be injected into peacetime cloak and dagger operations."

This was no impulsive stand. In extended interviews with biographer Merle Miller after the Bay of Pigs, Truman expressed regret about creating the Agency. "I think it was a mistake," he said, "And if I had known what was going to happen, I never would have done it . . . [Eisenhower] never paid any attention to it, and it got out of hand . . . It's become a government all of its own and all secret."[2]

No names were mentioned, but there was no mistaking that Truman was talking about the clandestine service, the DDP, as run by Dick Helms. "This quiet intelligence arm of the President has become so removed from its intended role that it is being interpreted as symbol for sinister and mysterious foreign intrigue— and a subject for cold war enemy propaganda," Truman lamented.

In a season of grief, Truman wanted to face a hard truth.

"There are searching questions that need to be answered," he said. "I therefore would like to see the CIA restored to its original assignment as the intelligence arm of the president . . . and that its operational duties be terminated or properly used elsewhere."

Truman couched his proposal in language complimentary to the Agency. He praised past directors, including Dulles, as "men of the highest character, patriotism and integrity—and I assume this is true of all those who continue in charge," which could only be a reference to McCone and Helms. Nonetheless, Truman said, it was time to abolish the CIA.

Truman never said that Kennedy's assassination caused his change of heart about the Agency, but there seems to be no other explanation. The records of the Truman Library show that the former president started composing his column on December 9, three days after the FBI report on Dallas came out. In the wake of Kennedy's murder, Truman saw the clandestine service as a threat to America's democracy.

"We were all stunned," Helms recalled.[3] The CIA men parleyed about how to respond. Dulles took the lead, writing to Truman to say he was "deeply disturbed" by the *Post* piece. The former president refused to disavow his views. In a measure of his seriousness, Dulles decided to go to Missouri to speak with Truman in person.[4]

COVER-UP

The protection of CIA interests related to Kennedy's assassination began around five o'clock in the evening of November 24, when President Lyndon Johnson conferred by phone with J. Edgar Hoover. He assigned the FBI to investigate the crime, even though the murder of a president was not a federal offense. He approved Hoover's suggestion that the Bureau quickly produce a report "showing the evidence conclusively tying Oswald in as the assailant of President Kennedy."[5] The next day Nicholas Katzenbach, deputy assistant attorney general, laid down Johnson's command for Press Secretary Bill Moyers.

"The public must be satisfied that Oswald was the assassin, that he did not have confederates who are still at large. . . . Speculation about Oswald's motivation ought to be cut off, and we should have some basis for rebutting the thought that this was. . . . a Communist conspiracy or (as the Iron Curtain press is saying) a right-wing conspiracy to blame it on the Communists."[6] Johnson had not yet appointed the Warren Commission to investigate the crime and he already had the conclusion that he and Hoover wanted: one man alone was responsible.

Helms was not unaware of the new president's thinking. He did not meet with Johnson in the weeks after JFK's assassination, but John McCone did.[7] According to CIA historian David Robarge, McCone "shared the administration's interest in avoiding disclosures about covert actions that would circumstantially implicate CIA in conspiracy theories . . . If the commission did not know to ask about covert operations against Cuba, he was not going to give them any suggestions about where to look."[8]

Helms did the same. He knew the Agency's vulnerabilities better than anyone.

When the Agency finally declassified all of Oswald's pre-assassination file in the early 2000s, the contents confirmed that the Warren Commission's description of Oswald as a marginal man of merely "routine" interest who had never attracted sustained attention was factually false. In truth, the Counterintelligence Staff, led by Helms's friend Jim Angleton, had monitored Oswald for four years prior to the assassination. Helms's equivocal claim that the Agency's pre-assassination knowledge of Oswald was "probably minimal" was definitely false.

The first Oswald file was opened in November 1959 by Angleton's mole-hunters, who worked in a secret office called the Special Investigations Group, known as CI/SIG. Over the next four years, Angleton's staff received more than forty different reports on Oswald from other CIA components, the FBI, the Office of Naval Intelligence, and the Department of State. The Counterintelligence Staff never lost track of Oswald, nor lost interest in him.

If Helms didn't know the details, it was because he left such matters to Angleton. When Oswald returned to the United States in the summer of 1962 with his Russian wife, an FBI agent in Dallas interviewed him and sent his report to Washington. Hoover passed it to Angleton's office with a note, "this item will be of interest to Mrs. Egerter, CI/SIG." Betty Egerter was the chief file clerk for the office.[9] When Oswald showed up at the Soviet and Cuban diplomatic offices in Mexico City fifteen months later, Angleton's staff was notified within days.

This paper trail, extracted from the CIA filing system, was not something Helms cared to share with the Warren Commission, the panel of seven eminent men—including Dulles—appointed by President Johnson to investigate the assassination. The reason was that the five documents found in Oswald's 201 file in the afternoon of November 22 were only part of the story.[10] The rest of Oswald's 201 file, containing three dozen more documents, had been held and controlled separately by Angleton's people, which was not disclosed to the Warren Commission for ten weeks after Kennedy's death.[11] When the commission's lawyers came calling about this belated discovery, Angleton relayed word to Helms that he wanted to "wait out" the investigators.[12]

Of course, Angleton was interested in Oswald because of his defection to the Soviet Union and his return. Perhaps not even Helms knew how tightly the file on the thoroughly obscure Oswald had been held. CI/SIG was, in Egerter's words, the "office that spied on spies." The restricted access to the full Oswald file was "a monitoring device," she explained to congressional investigators.[13] "If new information came in, by restricting it I would have a better chance of seeing the information . . . (for) tighter control." Contrary to the complacent faith of Agency apologists, the Oswald file was not lost or ignored or scattered between 1959 and 1963. "It was under my control," said Egerter,[14] which is to say Jim Angleton was reading about Lee and Marina Oswald well before Lee became world-famous.

Nothing in the file indicated that Oswald might pose a threat to the president. But the contents refuted Helms's sworn testimony to the Warren Commission that "we had known very little about him" before November 22. In fact, Angleton's staff had received nine CIA and FBI reports on Oswald in the ten weeks before Kennedy was killed.[15] The Agency had taken no action in response, except to inaccurately tell the Mexico City station on October 10, 1963, that the "latest HQS info" on Oswald was seventeen months old.[16]

That was erroneous, if not misleading. The latest report on Oswald concerned his clash with the DRE in New Orleans, and it was only two weeks old, as Jane Roman, Angleton's liaison officer, later admitted in an interview. William Hood, who ran Western Hemisphere operations for Helms in 1963, also signed off on the October 10 cable. Hood went on to write several well-received books about the CIA and to co-author Helms's posthumous memoir. In an interview, Hood denied that the CIA was running an operation involving Oswald but could not explain why he, as chief of operations, had to sign the cable. "It's perfectly perfunctory," he said. "I don't think there's anything smelly about it."[17]

By Helms's exacting standard the Agency's performance stunk. The assassination of the president was a catastrophic counterintelligence failure. Helms defined counterintelligence as "information gathered and activities conducted to protect against espionage, other intelligence activities, sabotage, or *assassinations* [emphasis added] conducted for, or on behalf of, foreign powers, organizations, persons or terrorist activities."[18] By this definition, the Counterintelligence Staff conceivably bore some responsibility for November 22. The information about Oswald gathered by Angleton and his people had not protected Kennedy from assassination.

Helms thought his friend Jim Angleton was a genius whose sources and methods around Oswald could not be acknowledged, much less discussed. Asked by Congressman Christopher Dodd if he ever viewed JFK's assassination as a counterintelligence matter, Helms dodged the question. "It was not perceived in any specific terms at all that I recollect," he said. "It was perceived as a great national tragedy, and I think the feeling in the Agency was that anything it or its personnel could do to help resolve the questions that prevailed at the time, we would try to do."[19]

In time, the Agency itself would refute Helms's self-serving account. Under McCone's and Helms's direction, CIA support for the Warren Commission could best be described as "passive, reactive, and selective," wrote house historian Robarge. Helms admitted that he did not volunteer information about the events leading to Kennedy's death. "I was instructed to reply to inquiries from the Warren Commission for information from the Agency," he told investigators. "I was not asked to initiate any particular thing." Helms was frank in his belief that he had no obligation to disclose material facts in the case of the murdered president. When queried, "[I]n other words. if you weren't asked for it, you didn't give it?" he replied, "That's right."[20]

Dick Helms was not a sentimental man, least of all about the deceased liberal president to whom he had shown a gun three days earlier and joked about his porous Secret Service protection. The CIA existed to serve the president, and the president was named Lyndon Johnson. If Johnson wanted to blame Cuba, the CIA had shown its readiness to enhance his "freedom of action." Congress was picking up the theme. Five days after the assassination, the staff of the House Un-American Activities Committee (HUAC) scheduled executive session testimony from three DRE leaders. They were invited to talk about Oswald in New Orleans.[21] The story of the pro-Castro assassin could be developed if that's what the president wanted.

Johnson, however, feared blaming Castro might lead to a wider conflict. He strong-armed a reluctant Chief Justice Earl Warren into heading the assassination investigation, saying that if rumors weren't put to rest there might be a nuclear war.[22] The HUAC appearance was cancelled. AMSPELL case officer George Joannides hustled the DRE leaders out of the country and reported nothing on their contacts with the alleged pro-Castro assassin.

In 1976 the Senate Select Committee on Intelligence INSE Activities, chaired by Senator Frank Church, concluded that the Agency's response to Kennedy's assassination was "deficient." While finding no evidence of conspiracy, the Church Committee "developed evidence which impeaches the process by which the intelligence agencies arrived at their own conclusions about the assassination." The committee's final report stated that "facts which might have substantially affected the course of the [JFK] investigation were not provided the Warren Commission or those individuals within the F.B.I. and C.I.A., was well as other agencies of the government, who were charged with investigation the assassination."[23] That conclusion impeached no one more than Dick Helms.

Kennedy's death may have been a great national tragedy in Helms's view, but it was not an urgent investigative priority for a man who intended to keep his job. If LBJ wanted the Agency's seal of approval on Hoover's lone gunman scenario, who was the deputy director to say no to Higher Authority? "You go with the president," Helms observed, "or you get out of government."[24]

RANSOM

Nixon's job was still running for president in 1964, only now he was running against Lyndon Johnson. Unproven and unpopular with the liberals who martyrized the fallen president, Nixon felt sure LBJ could be beaten. His plans were intact. He pulled in a six-figure income from the law firm and book royalties. Julie was a freshman at Smith College, Tricia a senior at Manhattan's exclusive Chapin School. He was a provider for his family, and he was proud. "After all the frugal years in Washington, I felt that Pat and the girls deserved the best," he recalled.[25]

Nixon cultivated his corporate connections."[26] He arranged another grueling foreign trip, this one to the Middle East and Asia. In March 1964, he traveled with Donald Kendall, the Pepsi CEO who had brought the company's legal work to Nixon's law firm. In Beirut, Nixon toured a Pepsi plant, attended a reception, filmed a TV commercial, and paid a visit to the country's president—all in just seven hours. In Taiwan he had a warm reunion with General Chiang Kai-shek, the exiled leader of the Chinese nationalists. "It would be disastrous to the cause of freedom for the United States to recognize Red China or accept its admission into the United Nations," he declared in Taipei.

In Vietnam, a country at war, Nixon's visit was more low-key, less commercial. Indeed, Nixon had a secret mission: to ransom five captured U.S. soldiers from communist forces. On his second day in Saigon, Nixon dressed in army fatigues and climbed aboard a helicopter with a sergeant and a crew of four. They flew to a village northwest of the capital, where they met with Father Nguyen Loc Hoa, a legendary Catholic priest whose black cassock was usually cinched with a web ammo belt and a pair of holstered .45s. Hoa was a symbol of militant anticommunism in South Vietnam.[27] He was the go-between who arranged the ransoming of the U.S. prisoners. The following day, Nixon and his party departed for An Loc, a nearby village. Nixon met with a Viet Cong lieutenant who established a price for the return of the prisoners.

Nixon went back to Saigon and the crew flew to a village across the border in Cambodia with a box of gold bars so heavy it took three men to lift it. At the exchange point, the five U.S. servicemen were rustled out of the jungle, and the ransom was handed over to the Viet Cong.[28]

Nixon not only had a taste for secret operations, he wanted allies in South Vietnam who were serious about winning the war. Father Hoa needed a prominent American to assure the Viet Cong that the deal had U.S. blessing. There is no record of U.S. prisoners of war being released in April 1964, suggesting that the men Nixon ransomed were Special Forces or CIA operatives.[29] No armchair warrior, Nixon saw himself on the battlefield. He went to Caracas. He went to An Loc. He went to war.

"PROBABLY MINIMAL"

On May 7, 1964, Dick Helms and John McCone traveled together to the offices of the Warren Commission on Capitol Hill. The meeting was friendly and private. Chief Justice Earl Warren was there, along with Allen Dulles.

Helms was sworn in to explain CIA procedures regarding agents and informers, and his old friend Dulles took over the questioning. The former director started with a leading query suggesting the State Department had not kept the Agency informed about Oswald's defection, his life in the Soviet Union, and his return. "Well, I am not sure that we got full information, Mr. Dulles," McCone agreed. "The fact is we had very little information in our files."

"It was probably minimal," Helms added.[30]

Minimal? The Counterintelligence Staff had collected forty-two documents concerning Oswald before Kennedy was killed. They abounded with details about his travels, foreign contacts, politics, and personal life. Angleton's staff was so interested in Oswald, they opened and read his mail for six months in 1959–60 and for ten months in 1961–62.[31] When asked if the Agency had learned about Oswald's defection to the Soviet Union and return and his subsequent travels to New Orleans and Mexico City in real time, Helms pushed the envelope of truth. "It is my impression that we were not informed step by step." That was simply not true. The Counterintelligence Staff was informed about every change of Oswald's residence, every stop on his foreign travels.

The Warren Commission, seeking to confirm Oswald's sole guilt, never questioned the CIA's handling of the Oswald file. And Helms never let on that he was plotting to kill Castro on the day a pro-Castro marksman supposedly shot Kennedy. The deputy director truly had a lot to hide. In 1978 Rep. Christopher Dodd, a member of the House Select Committee on Assassinations (HSCA), waxed incredulous about Helms's failure to disclose his actions.

"In light of the obvious interest and emphasis that the entire U.S. Government had on the possible activities of the Cuban Government," Dodd asked, "and in light of that you knew that Lee Harvey Oswald had engaged in these activities, why didn't you tell the Warren Commission about the efforts to get rid of Fidel Castro or to overthrow the Cuban Government?"

Few things offended Helms more than impudent questions about JFK's death.

"All kinds of people knew about these operations high up in the Government," Helms protested. "Why am I singled out as the fellow who should have gone up and identified a Government operation to get rid of Castro?"

Dodd asked about the poison pen given to Rolando Cubela on November 22.

"I'm sorry he didn't give him a pistol," Helms snapped, "because it would have made the whole thing simpler and less exotic."

"Well, whether it is a pistol or a needle, if AMLASH is a political plot to destabilize the government," Dodd asked, "what in the blazes are we doing giving an agent a device to kill Castro for, if it is not an assassination plot?"

"If you want to have it that way," Helms barked, "why don't you just have it that way?"[32]

Helms had to deny that AMLASH was an assassination operation for an understandable reason: to head off a counterintelligence investigation that might have cost him his job, said his colleague John Whitten. A former Army officer, Whitten had investigated the defection of West German intelligence chief Ofto John in 1954. He was more candid than most CIA men.

Helms's failure to inform the Warren Commission about the Castro plots was "a morally highly reprehensible act, which he cannot possibly justify under his oath of office," he told congressional investigators in closed-door testimony years later.[33] "If Helms had disclosed the Cuban assassination plots, we would have gone at that hot and heavy," he explained. "We would have queried the agents about it in great detail. I would have polygraphed the best operatives security had to see if [Cubela] was a double agent informing Castro about the poison pen things and so on."[34]

Helms and the CIA would not have survived the disclosure of the AMLASH plot in 1964, Whitten said. "I think that Helms withheld the information [about AMLASH] because he realized it would have cost him his job and would have precipitated a crisis for the Agency, which could have very adverse effects on the Agency."[35]

When it came to JFK's assassination, Helms maintained "plausible deniability," which is to say, as long as the Oswald file remained classified, he could plausibly deny that the CIA had any operational interest in him. That was good enough for the Warren Commission and the Washington press corps. It wasn't good enough for Harry Truman.

On April 17 Dulles met with the former president at his home and urged him to repudiate his *Post* column calling for abolition of the Agency. Truman rebuffed him and stubbornly reiterated his opinion. "The CIA was set up by me for the sole purpose of getting all the available information to the President," he told a reporter soon after. "It was not intended to operate as an international agency engaged in strange activities."[36] He was sticking with the ominous thesis of his *Post* piece: "There is something about the way the CIA has been functioning that is casting a shadow over our historic position, and I feel we need to correct it."[37]

The former president was ignored. Faith in the veracity of the U.S. government was high. The CIA's reputation was sterling. So was Dick Helms's. But Harry Truman, the man who authorized the creation of the CIA, understood better than anyone that the actions of the clandestine service in November 1963 cast a shadow over the U.S. government. The shadow of JFK's assassination lingered as a vulnerability for Helms, a weakness that Richard Nixon, as the thirty-seventh president, would intuit and exploit.

8

WOMEN

Between 1964 and 1968, Dick Nixon and Dick Helms fulfilled their lifelong ambitions. Helms was energized by a new love as Nixon was sustained by the fierce loyalty of Rose Mary Woods. Cuba faded as an issue, and Vietnam exploded. As Nixon slashed away at LBJ's war policy, Helms implemented it with growing reservations. Nixon remade himself as the epitome of Republican unity. Helms became America's top spy.

Nixon's energy was agile. He bowed out of the 1964 race just as it became apparent that conservative voters favored Barry Goldwater as the Republican nominee. Lyndon Johnson's landslide victory in November propelled Nixon's ambitions. The party lost badly at every level, and the most committed Republicans—local party chairmen, aspiring candidates, and conservative intellectuals—flocked to Nixon as a man with a plan to rebuild. The volume of mail, phone calls, comments, and speaking requests coming into Nixon's office surged. "Rose was working 12 and 14 hours a day. Pat came to pitch in," Nixon recalled. "By the end of the year, it was clear I would have to begin building a personal staff not just for the 1966 campaign, but with an eye to be ready for 1968."[1]

Rose Woods became the channel through which the world communicated with Nixon. She was, in the words of journalist Garry Wills, the "heroine of a thousand crises that flare up and are extinguished around a public man, who cannot be distracted by them." She was also "villainess to many disgruntled veterans of these crises." She was protective, devoted, and inclined to hold a grudge.[2]

Nixon was growing fervent about Southeast Asia.

"It is dangerous and foolhardy to try and gloss over the truth as to what the war in Vietnam really involves," he declared in a speech to the Sales Executive Club in New York in January 1965. He was talking to a banquet hall of advertising men about a country that few in the room, save himself, had ever visited. "I urge that we take the war to North Vietnam," he railed, "by naval and air bombing of the communist supply routes in South Vietnam and by destroying the Viet Cong staging areas in North Vietnam and Laos."[3]

The soldiers of Madison Avenue cheered Nixon's bombast and went back to their accounts. Nixon went right on agitating for escalation, domination, and victory. His vehemence about Vietnam replaced his passion for Cuba. President Johnson pursued the very course that Nixon recommended (and Kennedy had resisted), He committed two hundred thousand men to South Vietnam, including combat troops for the first time. The United States launched a massive bombing campaign against North Vietnam, with B-52s disgorging ten-thousand-pound bombs from the sky, annihilating military bases, rail depots, airfields, and many of the people in them, whether civilians or armed combatants.

The realities of the war soon reached America. In August 1965, U.S. Marines torched a peasant village near Da Nang as CBS correspondent Morley Safer and millions of viewers looked on in horror. That month, one hundred seventy-nine Americans were killed in Vietnam. Seventy-six died in aircraft or helicopter crashes. Twenty-eight were officers. Three were named Johnson. Their average age was twenty-three years old. U.S. generals expected to break the enemy's will in a year.[4]

Nixon, while a good study, overestimated his allies and underestimated the enemy. The Vietnamese communists fighting the government in Saigon drew on the nationalist tradition that resisted French colonialism, Japanese occupation during World War II, and Chinese incursions from time immemorial. Ho Chi Minh, who studied Marxism in Paris and spent time in the United States, had updated national feeling with a Marxist analysis of imperialism to forge an independence movement that took power in the northern part of the country. The South Vietnamese government, rooted in the more superficial soil of Saigonese pride and French influence, had no such compelling cause. Nixon assumed that America's firepower and ideology would inevitably prove superior, a colonialist mentality updated as a defense of the Free World.

But it was China that began to occupy pride of place in Nixon's geopolitical imagination. Under communist rule, the world's largest country shunned foreign trade and contacts while pursuing a vast project of collective development under Mao Zedong. Nixon envisioned the United States prevailing in Vietnam and making peace with China. "We simply cannot afford to leave China forever outside the family of nations, there to nurture its fantasies, cherish its hates and threaten its neighbors," he wrote in *Foreign Affairs*, house organ of the American policymaking class, in October 1967.[5] The ambitions of this dogged man from Whittier—and the violence of his statecraft—almost defied reason. Nixon was "defined by the quality of absolute tirelessness wrapped around total determination," said columnist William White.[6] Waging war in Vietnam had become essential to the country's future—and his.

"MAGNIFICENT OPPORTUNITY"

In 1965, Helms's ambitions were deferred once again, though not fatally. Johnson had become disenchanted with John McCone, who wanted to brief the president every day. Johnson, Helms said, "finally got bored, closed the door, and that was the end. He just didn't want to do it anymore. You couldn't make him do it anymore." For the ambitious Helms, the lesson was obvious: "You either adjust your production to the man you have in office or you're going to miss the train."[7]

The proud McCone, who could not stand being ignored, announced his resignation. President Johnson, like Kennedy before him, wanted an outsider to run the Agency. He appointed navy admiral William Raborn as the next director, but he made a point of asking Helms to stay on, attend NSC meetings, and cultivate the Agency's contacts on Capitol Hill. "Now you get yourself known around town," LBJ advised.[8] The message was implicit: Stick around. Helms called 1965 his "training period."[9]

Helms didn't share his good news with many people, but he did tell his friend Howard Hunt. The two men lunched between three and six times a year in Hunt's estimation. In between, they talked on the phone.[10] Helms confided to Hunt that he had just returned from LBJ's ranch in Texas, where he spent a wild weekend speeding around in a jeep with the president. Johnson had told him he was keeping him on as deputy director, with the implication that if he maintained good relations with key senators, he would become director someday. "So far as I know," Hunt said, "I was the first person he told about such an important event in his life."[11]

Helms attended to the image of the Agency by cultivating sympathetic journalists. He lunched with Hugh Sidey of *Time* magazine and Cyrus Sulzberger, a *New York Times* columnist. He befriended Katharine Graham, who had taken over as publisher of the *Washington Post* after the suicide of her husband Phil in 1963. He befriended Richard Russell of Georgia, the ancient segregationist chairman of the Senate Armed Services Committee, and bantered with Eugene McCarthy, a witty liberal maverick from Minnesota.

Helms didn't countenance criticism of his Agency. In the spring of 1964 he sought to block Random House from publishing a book by journalists David Wise and Thomas Ross, which depicted the Agency as "The Invisible Government" that made its own policies and bungled major operations. The book became a bestseller, which bothered Hunt even more than it bothered Helms. Hunt drafted a negative review for his old friend Bill Buckley, now publisher of the *National Review* and a syndicated columnist. Buckley trimmed Hunt's prose and published it under his own byline in seventy-five newspapers around the country.[12]

Amid the new questioning of the Agency, Helms conceived a new assignment for his restless friend Hunt. In early 1965, he transferred him from the Domestic Contacts Division to a unit called the Operations Group, where he could focus on what he did best: write. His mission: to become the Ian Fleming of the American clandestine service. Fleming's best-selling James Bond novels, and the movies based on them—*Dr. No, From Russia with Love,* and *Goldfinger*—had glamourized the British secret service in the eyes of the world. Why not do the same for the CIA?

Victor Weybright, editor of the chief of the New American Library, a paperback publishing house, had approached Hunt with the idea of developing an American counterpart to the James Bond series. "As you may imagine this is plenty delicate," Hunt wrote to Buckley, "since no matter how popular the series might become, I need certain guarantees that are, up to now, unique in publishing," presumably a reference to keeping his true identity secret.[13] Hunt submitted the idea to Helms, "who agreed this was a magnificent opportunity to boost the image of the CIA. Of course," Hunt told Buckley "the editor had no idea that he was working with a current CIA officer who had an ulterior motive to write the books."[14]

Hunt was a plausible candidate for the job, at least to Helms. For much of his career, Hunt devoted himself to writing novels, possibly more than he devoted himself to spying. "He wrote between four and eight hours a day during the week and all day every day on the weekend," said daughter Lisa.[15] By the summer of 1965 he had finished *On Hazardous Duty*, a thriller introducing Peter Ward, a natty, pipe-smoking, world-weary CIA officer, and magnet for women, doing battle with international communism. Writing under the pseudonym "David St. John," Hunt intended Peter Ward to become the American 007.

Hunt knew the world of which he wrote. *On Hazardous Duty* opened with a burglary, a black-bag job, with a team of crack operatives reporting to Peter Ward in a nearby command post, much as Hunt would direct the Watergate burglars seven years in the future. In Hunt's tale, however, the burglars managed not to get caught.[16]

Hunt's plots unfolded in exotic locales lovingly described. A Tokyo brothel. A Hong Kong music studio. A Phnom Penh tea house. In the Peter Ward books that followed, a fetching woman inevitably appeared at some point, seductive and treacherous, or loving and generous. The communists could be counted on to kill the liberals who fell for their propaganda. And all the while Peter Ward took orders from an imposing deputy director back at CIA headquarters named Avery Thorne. Save the color of his hair, Thorne resembled no one so much as Hunt's great good friend Dick Helms.

"The deputy director was a tall, spare man, dressed conservatively with fine entirely white hair, and an ageless face that had a touch of asceticism," Hunt wrote. "A highly controlled man, not given to emotional extremes, Thorne's eyes had narrowed as he gazed towards the sunlit glass wall, and [Peter Ward] remembered that he had earned his spurs in Berlin against the Russians and stayed on to begin the endless secret fight."

Avery Thorne was a superior man. "Thorne resembled a broker or financier rather than spymaster. His manners were somewhat elegant, and he could don the air of affability for the Hill, but professionally, he was as single minded as a monk on hazardous duty."[17]

Helms was flattered. No literary snob, he liked Fleming's *From Russia with Love*, and he rather liked *On Hazardous Duty*. Perhaps Helms imagined the suave Avery Thorne on the big screen, an American version of "M," as James Bond's MI6 boss was known in the 007 movies. Helms's colleague, Walter Pforzheimer, was less impressed. Pforzheimer was a career analyst and a bibliophile with his own private library of espionage books filling an entire apartment in the new Watergate complex in Foggy Bottom. Curious about the identity of the author "David St. John," he obtained the copyright application for *On Hazardous Duty*, which included Hunt's home address. Not for the first time, Hunt's tradecraft was sloppy.

Pforzheimer reported his finding to Tom Karamessines. "If the agency is involved in this thing," Pforzheimer huffed, "why not see that Hunt leaves his address off the copyright application in the future?" Five minutes after he left Karamessines's office, Pforzheimer got a scorching call from Helms.

"For Christ's sake, Walter," Helms barked, "this is the first book to come along and say something good about the Agency. Why not leave the goddamn thing alone?"[18]

Only Helms and Karamessines had known the identity of Peter Ward's creator, which is to say Pforzheimer had a point. Hunt's name might become public. Helms put out the word that Hunt was retiring, while switching him to a one-year contract working in Spain.[19] Few in the Langley headquarters believed the retirement story. In fact, Hunt was going on a taxpayer-funded vacation to concoct the further adventures of Peter Ward.[20] "I wanted to get out of Washington," Hunt said, "I thought it was a great idea to get to Spain."[21]

In July 1965, Howard and Dorothy Hunt, with their four children, Lisa, St. John, Kevan, and David, boarded the S.S. *Covadonga*, a freighter and passenger ship that operated between New York and Spain.[22] Adventure was calling, and the Hunts were willing. Howard had few operational duties, only an opportunity to write books glorifying the clandestine service he loved. The Hunts settled in a suburb of Madrid, where Howard retreated into the world of Peter Ward, poking away at his typewriter, or leaving for unexplained trips. "Even when he was around, he wasn't around much," recalled son St. John.[23] All of his communications with the Agency were handled by Tom Karamessines, Hunt told Senate investigators. "This was a project that had been laid on by Dick Helms."[24]

Hunt's next Peter Ward adventure, *Festival for Spies*, opened with a scene perhaps too obviously written for the movies, with nautical details supplied by yachtsman Bill Buckley.[25] Peter Ward is captaining a sailboat in the Newport-to-Bermuda yacht race when a helicopter appears overhead and drops a message from—who else?—Avery Thorne. He orders Peter to quit the race and leave for a secret mission to Cambodia, where Ward falls for the sex-starved wife of a cabinet minister, thwarts her blackmail scheme, and fortifies a government struggling to resist communism.

Hunt's jaunty style concealed real pain. He had a duodenal ulcer that hemorrhaged and fits of depression that recurred. When he learned that Frank Wisner, the former deputy director who hired him in 1950, had shot himself to death at his country home on Maryland's Eastern Shore, he wondered "how much longer I could take the work myself if this Gibraltar of a figure had succumbed to the pressure?"[26] In January 1966, Hunt's mother died in upstate New York. He returned to Albany for her funeral and then went on to Washington to talk to Helms. Hunt's youngest son David was mysteriously ill, and he wanted advice. "[Helms] agreed that the welfare of my son was paramount," Hunt said, "and left in my hands the decision whether to remain in Spain or return to the United States undercover."[27] Hunt decided to stay in Spain.[28]

Hunt finished three more Peter Ward books in the course of the year, *Festival for Spies*, *The Venus Probe*, and *The Towers of Silence*. None of the manuscripts had been submitted for review as required by Agency regulations;[29] all were published by New American Library in paperback.[30] To lend his hero the savoir faire of Bond, Hunt made Peter Ward a master of menus and wardrobe, a gourmand with a gun. In Hong Kong's Parisian Grill ("P.G." to those in the know), Ward "began with Malossol caviar on Melba rounds, a brace of dry martinis, soupe a l'oignon, tiny French lambchops with a crisp green salad, and for dessert a frozen mousse with crushed fruit and liqueur known as plombieres."[31] Espionage, it seems, was delicious.

All the while the booze flowed. Peter Ward often took refuge in a bottle of Canadian Club, nothing unusual in hard-boiled fiction but not necessarily endearing. After reading through Hunt's collected oeuvre, Gore Vidal picked up on the increasingly "obsessive need for the juice to counteract the melancholy of middle age. The hangovers, as described, get a lot worse, too."[32]

CYNTHIA

In the spring of 1966, Dick Helms planted himself by the piano at a reception in the Lebanese Embassy in Washington. He noticed a brown-haired woman about his age enter the salon, and she noticed him. He winked. She wasn't expecting a flirt. "By chance, we sat next to each other at dinner," recalled Cynthia McKelvie. "We hit it off and had an immensely good time talking. His wife, Julia, and I were members of a group of women called, 'the Minnows,' who swam together."[33]

McKelvie, an English expatriate and mother of four, was ending a loveless twenty-five-year marriage. Helms had grown apart from Julia, "and it was probably my fault," he confided in his memoir.[34] He and McKelvie had more than a few things in common. One was the shared experience of England during the war. While he worked for the OSS in London, she had served in the Wrens, the female contingent of the British armed forces. Helms liked to banter and gossip, and so did she. She was a docent at the Smithsonian, curious, artistic, and vivacious. When they were alone, he liked to listen to classical music and play the conductor, waving his arms to bring in the violins, pointing a finger to cue the brass section. Cynthia bought him a baton.[35]

Helms moved out of his house and moved into guest quarters at the Chevy Chase Country Club, where he was a member. Hunt was among the few who knew he was getting divorced. At the office, colleagues saw the same man: a crisp and efficient boss, loyal to competent underlings, stringent about standards, and tight with the budgetary dollar.

Helms became known for his managerial aphorisms. Dave Phillips, now stationed in the Dominican Republic, recalled the deputy director's routine when sending a station chief out to some foreign capital. After a few minutes of laconic conversation, "Helms would deliver one of his famous one-liners," Phillips wrote. "One might be, 'Ring the gong for me,' meaning he wanted to know in advance of a coup or other rapid change of government. Or it might be, 'Teach those people how to run an intelligence service.' Or 'See what you can do to bring the Ambassador around,' meaning he wanted good relations restored where a Station Chief and an Ambassador had been feuding." And sometimes his advice was nothing more profound than "Get along with the FBI."[36]

Helms paid attention to the bureaucratic breezes. Frances FitzGerald, daughter of Desmond FitzGerald, now Far East division chief, overheard Helms talking to her father at their country house in Virginia. "Helms was always checking with the higher ups, . . . saying, you know, 'stay within these lines,'" she recalled in an interview. ". . . He was always looking up as opposed to down."[37]

He devoted ever more time to Vietnam. LBJ's escalating war demanded the Agency's support, both in analyzing the strength of the enemy and conducting secret operations in country. Johnson and his generals assumed that killing more people would force the North Vietnamese to negotiate. The Agency's operational officers thought the key was killing the right people—the cadre of the Viet Cong. The pessimistic estimates from the Directorate of Intelligence found little evidence that either strategy was winning the war. "At no time was the institutional dichotomy between the operational and the analytical components more stark," Helms wrote.[38]

In March 1966, 563 Americans died in Vietnam. Only thirty-six had been drafted. Four were named Johnson. Their average age was twenty-four years old.[39] Many thousands more Vietnamese were killed for which there was no statistical accounting. The brutality of the war was obvious. The futility was unexpected.

"NOT INVOLVED"

On the morning of March 7, 1966, Helms dictated a memo to Secretary of State Dean Rusk. He wanted to correct news reports about the arrest of two men in

Havana, Rolando Cubela and Ramon Guin Diaz, for allegedly plotting with CIA agents. "The Agency was not involved with either of these two men in a plot to assassinate Fidel Castro," Helms wrote, ". . . nor did it ever encourage either of these two persons to attempt such an act."[40]

The memo was, in Helms's ineffable style, partially true and wholly misleading. It was true that case officer Nestor Sanchez did not incite Cubela to kill Castro in any of their five clandestine meetings in Brazil and France in late 1963. But Helms knew Cubela had been recruited precisely because he had a record of armed action. The purpose of Helms's memo, however, was not veracity but plausible deniability. The secretary of state could now plausibly deny to the world (and himself and his wife and his friends) that the U.S. government was not involved in political murder. After all, his esteemed intelligence chief had told him so.

One of the last living participants in the AMLASH operation scoffed at Helms's claim. Carl Jenkins, a ninety-four-year-old retired CIA trainer, recalled many details of the operation in an interview for this book. Jenkins trained counterinsurgency teams in Cold War battlegrounds from Indonesia to Cuba to Laos. His role in the conspiracy only emerged with the declassification of AMLASH files in 2017. They told the story that Helms preferred to obfuscate. Asked if assassination was the goal of the AMLASH operation, Jenkins didn't hesitate. "Of course," he said.

In 1964 Jenkins was reporting to Henry Heckscher, a veteran officer whom Helms had assigned to handle Bob Kennedy's Cuba projects under a program called AMWORLD. After the still-grieving RFK quit as attorney general and LBJ scaled back Cuba operations in 1964, Helms used AMWORLD to support the Cubans still fighting Castro. Jenkins said he became "great friends" with Nestor Sanchez, Helms's aide who had stayed in touch with Cubela after Kennedy's assassination. In the cable traffic, Jenkins was known by a string of acronyms that denoted his position: WH/SA/SO/HH. That meant Jenkins worked in the Agency's Western Hemisphere (WH) division. He was involved in Special Affairs (SA), meaning Cuba. He was responsible for Special Operations (SO), secret missions. And he acted on behalf of Henry Heckscher (HH). In other words, it was Jenkins's job to implement orders handed down by headquarters through four layers of bureaucracy.

Jenkins wrote five memos to Heckscher about the AMLASH project in the fall of 1964, in which he recounted meetings with Cubans who supported Cubela's plans to eliminate Castro. One of the plotters was Manolo Artime, the chameleonic doctor known inside the CIA by the cryptonym AMBIDDY-1 who was now godfather to Hunt's infant son David. Artime had replaced Nestor Sanchez as the Agency's contact with Cubela. When Artime and Cubela met in Madrid in December 1964, Cubela reiterated his demand for a weapon, specifically a Belgian-made FAL rifle.

"The FAL was the NATO rifle," Jenkins explained. "It was easy to get ammunition for it. That was something I could do." Thanks to Jenkins's arrangements, Artime delivered the weapon to Cubela. Jenkins's account extinguishes Helms's claim that AMLASH was not an assassination conspiracy. Cubela was arrested fourteen months later.

"Just another busted operation," Jenkins shrugged. As for Helms, "he was an asshole as far as I'm concerned," the old soldier growled. "My recollection is that he made a point to get just close enough to try to influence things—and just far away enough to not get his hands dirty and get caught."[41]

The same day that Helms wrote his memo to Rusk, the chastened Rolando Cubela took the stand in La Causa 108 (Court Case 108), heard in a Havana courtroom. His bushy beard and revolutionary bravado were gone, replaced by a playboy's pencil-thin mustache and the contrition of a convict. He wanted to explain his guilt, not excuse it.

"I was carrying around a series of preoccupations and contradictions, the product of long struggle after the triumph of the Revolution," he said, perhaps alluding to his nightmares about the smiling Colonel Blanco Rico. "They made me fall into a disorderly life, a life of parties, cabarets, a completely insane life. I was decomposing and deteriorating."[42]

Some press accounts assumed Cubela's contrition was coerced. *Time* magazine said he was drugged.[43] "The clear, precise, careful, educated statements he made throughout the trial do not bear this comment out to any degree," wrote the CIA analyst who covered the trial via translations from the Agency's Foreign Broadcast Information Service. Cubela, in fact, was a cagey witness who knew how to present the image he wanted. "He has some skill in adjusting his style to the people he is talking to. While he can be rather eloquent, he is not likely to divulge anything which should be kept secret."[44]

On the stand, Cubela confessed his playboy lifestyle got the better of him. "I was losing the demanding principles of the revolution . . . relaxing, accommodating myself to a life that was completely disorganized and that produced in me a pretty big emotional imbalance." He admitted plotting "against the integrity and the stability of the nation." Indeed, he said he had planned the "physical elimina-tion" of his former comrade Castro.[45] He admitted what Helms denied.

Because no one knew the scope of the busted operation, much less Helms's leading role in it, the deputy director was free to minimize the Agency's relation-ship with Cubela. "These contacts," he assured Secretary Rusk, "were restricted to obtaining intelligence."[46]

After Cubela was sentenced to death by firing squad, Castro sent a letter to the court saying he did not favor capital punishment in La Causa 108. Against the treacherous nature of Cubela's actions, Castro cited the noble impulses that prompted him to take up arms against Batista. Cubela had fought shoulder to shoulder with Che in Santa Clara and defended the revolution on campus. "Among revolutionary men," Castro wrote, "nothing can replace the bond of the beginning." The court reduced Cubela's sentence to twenty-five years in La Ca-bana, a fort and prison overlooking Havana harbor, where Cubela served as a doctor for his fellow prisoners.

"He was a very attractive guy," recalled Santiago Morales, a young man from Havana arrested in Castro's post–Bay of Pigs crackdown. Morales met Cubela when his tonsils became infected. Cubela arranged for an operation, and they became close friends. "Everybody liked him," Morales said in an interview. "He had no special privileges. We talked a lot but, as a rule never got into details of our reasons for being there. . . . He told me . . . about being interviewed by Raul Castro while he was in prison." Cubela believed it was Raul who prevailed on Fidel to spare his life.

Cubela spoke only in passing about his execution of Colonel Blanco Rico in the Montmartre, Morales said. It was a painful subject. "It's one thing to kill not knowing who you're killing," Morales said, "but when there's a name and a family and a pleasant human being—and they say he [Colonel Rico] was a pleasant hu-man being—it hurts. And it didn't lead to a happy ending."[47]

Three months after Cubela's conviction, Helms achieved his dream. On June 18, 1966, he received a phone call from the White House. He was told that President Johnson was holding a press conference later that day to announce his appoint-ment as director of Central Intelligence. Twenty-three years after joining the OSS, Helms assumed control of the global U.S. intelligence service. "He loves power," said his soon to be ex-wife Julia, "and must have it."[48] At long last, he did.

The following month Richard Nixon embarked on yet another foreign trip seeking to meet world leaders, keep his name in the news, and open doors for his law firm. With Pat and Rose Woods, he traversed Europe and Asia. He claimed he wouldn't attack the Democrats or President Johnson while overseas, and then proceeded to do just that. Along the way he called for increasing the number of U.S. troops in Vietnam from less than three hundred thousand to more than five hundred thousand.[49]

In the fall Nixon campaigned for both liberal and conservative Republicans across the country. His message on the war was simple: "Let's get it over with and get the boys home," he declared in Ohio. "Let's end it without escalation of ground warfare or appeasement." One reporter found Nixon tanned, relaxed, friendly, and articulate as he posed for pictures "with possible winners and born losers."[50] "Skillful tactician or fanatical opportunist?" another reporter wondered.

In November 1966, Nixon was a winner. In the mid-term elections, Republicans picked up forty-seven seats in the House, three in the Senate, and eight governorships.[51] Polls showed Nixon was the party's favorite candidate for 1968.

What makes you run, a reporter asked?

"Sometimes I wonder myself," Nixon replied. "I started in this thing when I was thirty-two. Now, I'm not an extrovert. I like people but I don't love the adulation of the crowd and all that stuff. But I'm one who believes that you pass this way only once. When great decisions are made, you want to be in on them."[52]

The greatest decision was Vietnam. Six hundred forty-one Americans died in fighting that month. Five hundred sixty-one were white, seventy-three were African American, and seven were Asian or Native American. They hailed from forty-five states, Puerto Rico, and the District of Columbia.[53] The Joint Chiefs' predicted victory was less than two years away.

9

THE SILENT SERVICE

In February 1967, Dick Helms became a public figure. He graced the cover of *Time* magazine. The artist's rendition for the popular newsweekly gave his profile the cast of a Roman nobleman looking over his shoulder.[1] The statuesque visage suited a laudatory story on "The Silent Service" and its latest public relations ordeal. *Ramparts*, a left-wing monthly, had published an exposé of the CIA's covert funding of the supposedly independent National Student Association, which represented U.S. universities at international conferences. The Agency had been secretly funding the group for years through phony foundations set up by Cord Meyer, chief of the International Organizations division. Helms said the *Ramparts* story was "cockeyed," though he could not dispute its accuracy.

With protests against the war in Vietnam spreading on college campuses everywhere, student leaders were not happy to learn they had been fronting for the Agency. Their elders felt used too. "It is a poisonous business," said Harvard College dean John Monro. "Something very important in our national life, the real independence and freedom of our institutions, has been brought into question." Helms's friend Senator Eugene McCarthy said, "Where do you draw the line? Is it all right for the CIA to tell us that 'everything goes'?"

The editors of *Time* lionized Helms in response. He was "an intense, controlled, self-effacing professional," said to exemplify Allen Dulles's ideal of a secret service run by an elite corps of men with "a passion for anonymity and a willingness to stick at that particular job." Helms was no spook, *Time* proclaimed, more like an open-minded civil servant with a knack for espionage. "The CIA is only an arm—and a well-regulated one—of the U.S. Government," *Time* concluded. "It does not, and cannot, manipulate American policies. It can only serve them."[2]

Two weeks later, Drew Pearson, one of nation's leading syndicated columnists, published a story in the *Washington Post* indicating the CIA was anything but well regulated.

BLACKMAIL II

"President Johnson is sitting on a political H-Bomb," Pearson wrote in his March 3 column, "an unconfirmed report that Senator Robert Kennedy may have approved an assassination plot which then possibly backfired against his brother." Pearson's "Washington Merry-Go-Round" column, published in hundreds of newspapers across the country, was read by millions of Americans. While reliably liberal in his politics, Pearson was no partisan. He was known to stretch the facts, but nobody knew more people of consequence in Washington.[3]

One story circulating among "top officials," Pearson reported, was that "underworld figures actually were recruited to carry out the plot" against the Cuban leader. By "top officials," he meant President Johnson and Chief Justice Warren, with whom he had shared the story before publishing his column. Pearson added that "the rumor persists, whispered by people in a position to know, that Castro did become aware of an American plot of his life and decided to retaliate against President Kennedy."

The evidence for the Castro-done-it theory was scant indeed, but Pearson heard the story from a reliable source, Edward Morgan, a prominent criminal defense lawyer. Morgan had served as chief counsel to the congressional committee that investigated the Pearl Harbor attack and worked for seven years as chief inspector of the FBI.[4] He did not speak idly. Morgan told Pearson he had a client who feared being called to testify before Congress. He said the client had been approached by the CIA in the early 1960s to help out with a plan concocted by Bobby Kennedy to assassinate Castro. His client—described only as a hoodlum—said he hired two gunmen with experience in Havana who spent six months preparing to kill Castro. "They were even given pills to take in a hurry if they were captured," Morgan said. His client said the two men were apprehended, tortured, and executed, but not before confessing they were put up to the job by Kennedy. Castro retaliated by recruiting Oswald to kill JFK. Or so the story went.

Morgan's client was none other than Johnny Rosselli, the middleman in the failed plan to kill Castro, who remained a crime boss in Las Vegas. Rossellli told the story to Morgan because he didn't want to appear before Senator Edward Long's committee, which was investigating the growing business of electronic wiretapping.

When Pearson shared Morgan's story with the president and the chief justice, Warren lamented the growing public doubts about his commission's lone gunman finding. Johnson listened carefully and made no comment. "There wasn't much he could say," Pearson observed in his diary.[5] The U.S. government was getting blackmailed by a Mafia boss.

Johnson called Helms for an explanation.[6] Helms said the events in question had taken place before he became director and he would have to look into the matter. He knew the blackmail threat was real. As the CIA's inspector general later concluded, much of Pearson's scoop was verifiably true. For the new director the shadow of JFK's assassination had returned.

The story also disturbed Robert Kennedy, now a senator from New York, by raising questions that he was not ready to answer in public. In the fall of 1964, RFK had endorsed the Warren Commission's report, even though he did not believe it. He still suspected the plot emanated from right-wing enemies of Jack's Cuba policy.[7]

That same day Kennedy's secretary called Helms's office and asked for a copy of the Agency's memorandum for the record of Kennedy's meeting with CIA officials on May 7, 1962, where RFK learned that the CIA men had enlisted the Mafia to kill Castro. Helms parried the request by inviting Kennedy for lunch.

The bad news kept coming. The next day, New Orleans district attorney Jim Garrison charged businessman Clay Shaw with conspiring to assassinate President Kennedy. Shaw, former managing director of the International Trade Mart in New Orleans, scoffed at the charges and pled not guilty. Garrison claimed that Shaw worked for the CIA in 1963. Helms and staff put out the word to Washington editors and reporters, off the record, that Shaw was merely an unpaid source of the Domestic Contacts Division, a businessman who volunteered information about what he learned from his overseas travels, nothing more. In fact, the Agency was dissembling. When the Agency's in-house historian J. Kenneth McDonald reviewed Shaw's file many years later, he stated in a memo for the record that while there was no evidence Shaw was involved in JFK's assassination, he was "a highly paid contract agent until 1956."[8]

Helms felt the pressures of power. He needed to placate the sitting president. He needed to satisfy the brother of the slain president. He needed to protect the

Agency's "sources and methods" around Oswald, and he needed to deflect un-precedented criticism of the Agency in the press. A less skillful civil servant might have cracked or lashed out, denied, decried, or quit. Helms's response was more than adroit. With firm control of the Agency's apparatus and extensive contacts in Washington, Helms managed to accomplish most of what he needed to do. The spymaster not only knew how to steal and keep secrets. He also knew how to manage perceptions.

"FRIENDLY ELITE CONTACTS"

Helms never lost sight of the need to control the record. For his lunch with Senator Kennedy, he brought a copy of the memo that RFK had requested and allowed Kennedy to read it, but did not leave him a copy, giving Helms the upper hand. The director had proof that RFK had sanctioned the Castro assassination plots; RFK did not have proof that he had rejected the recruitment of gangsters. The two men, "had a barely restrained loathing for one another," wrote RFK biographer David Talbot, "and a tense understanding of some sort was certainly hammered out."[9]

As for Pearson's column, Helms asked the Agency's Inspector General John Earman to review the files and interview everyone involved in the Castro plots. Given what Helms knew about the Castro plots, he was effectively having himself investigated. It was the gambit of a confident bureaucrat.

At the same time, Helms acted on the Agency's JFK problem, launching a covert global campaign to defend the Warren Commission and to impugn its critics without revealing the Agency's hidden hand. Bill Broe, chief of Western Hemisphere Division, drafted a six-page memo titled "Countering Critics of the Warren Commission," which Helms approved. The classified memo, with nine attachments, was sent to selected CIA offices around the world on April 1, 1967.

Helms wanted respect. Growing skepticism about the official story of JFK's murder "is a matter of concern to the U.S. government including our organiza-tion," the memo began. "The members of the Warren Commission were naturally chosen for their integrity, experience and prominence. Just because of the standing of the Commissioners, efforts to impugn their rectitude and wisdom tend to cast doubt on the whole leadership of American society."

He felt threatened. "Our organization itself is directly involved," the dispatch pleaded. "Among other facts, we contributed information to the investigation. Con-spiracy theories have frequently thrown suspicion on our organization."

"We do not recommend the discussion of the assassination be initiated where it is not already taking place," the dispatch advised. With "friendly elite contacts, (especially politicians and editors)," CIA personnel should point out that "the Warren Commission made as thorough an investigation as humanly possible, that the charges of the critics are without serious foundation, and that further speculative discussion only plays into the hands of the opposition. . . . The conspiracy talk appeared to be deliberately generated by Communist propagandists."[10]

The dispatch provided arguments for Agency personnel to use in conversation with skeptics based on information the Agency knew was false. Oswald was described as "an unknown quantity to any professional intelligence service," which sounded plausible but wasn't true. The KGB had monitored Oswald closely when he lived in the Soviet Union and the CIA's own Counterintelligence Staff had tracked his movements and political activities for four years.

The good men (and few women) of the Washington corps simply accepted the official story. Senior editors and reporters in Washington and New York could not imagine the CIA, run by gentlemanly Dick Helms, might conceal material evidence in the murder of an American president, although that is exactly what happened. But President Johnson had his suspicions. Assistant FBI director Cartha DeLoach received a call from Marvin Watson, an aide to Johnson, who said the President had told him "in an off moment that he was now convinced there was a plot in connection with the assassination." DeLoach added, "Mr. Watson stated that the President felt that the CIA had something to do with this plot."[11]

Less than a year into the job, Helms's position was precarious. As Inspector General Earman delivered his report in installments to Helms over the next few weeks, the director's reaction "could only have been one of queasy horror," said biographer Thomas Powers.[12] In 144 typed pages, Earman laid out in lawyerly detail the story of the Mafia plots and the AMLASH operation. The inspector general underscored the fact that Nestor Sanchez was delivering the poison pen device to Rolando Cubela on November 22, 1963. "[I]t is likely that at the very moment President Kennedy was shot, a CIA officer was meeting with a Cuban agent in Paris and giving him an assassination device for use against Castro."[13]

The unflappable Helms took a draft of Earman's report to lunch at the White House on May 10, 1967. It was among the better moves he ever made. The inspector general's account lucidly explained the whole story of multiple plots involving a rotating cast of killers, blackmailers, and spooks trying and failing to murder Castro. The account did not scant Helms's role in the Agency's schemes. Nearly a quarter of Earman's report was dedicated to the AMLASH operation.

Johnson skimmed the report. He came away thinking Kennedy had run "a

goddamn Murder Incorporated in the Caribbean."[14] (Murder, Inc. was the nickname for the Chicago Mafia, under the bloody leadership of Al Capone and Sam
Giancana.) Johnson also came away impressed by Helms's direct approach. *Here's
what we did and why we did it, warts and all,* a declaration that the Agency couldn't
be blackmailed by the likes of Johnny Rosselli.

Johnson handed the report back to Helms—it was the only copy in existence—
and invited him to come to lunch the next day. "During this meeting the President
invited Dir. Helms to lunch in the mansion tomorrow at 1:30 pm," read a note
in Johnson's desk diary. That was Thursday, May 11. LBJ then invited Helms to
attend his weekly Tuesday lunch with top advisers on May 16 and May 23.

Helms would tell biographer Powers that he won Johnson's confidence with
an accurate forecast about the Six-Day War between Egypt and Israel in June
1967.[15]

The Six-Day War began on June 5. The Agency's accurate forecast about its
outcome might have helped, but Helms had already won the president's confidence
three weeks before the war started.[16]

Candor about the business of assassination earned Helms a seat at LBJ's table. Serving the president in lethal matters was crucial, a lesson Helms would not
forget with Richard Nixon.

"IMPLICATIONS OF AN UNFAVORABLE OUTCOME"

Helms commuted daily from the Bradley House residence on the grounds of the
Chevy Chase Country Club, across the Chain Bridge over the Potomac, and on
to the Langley headquarters where he served as chief clandestine officer of the
American empire. He embodied the Free World.

From his seventh-floor office, he waged war in Vietnam. His analysts waxed
pessimistic about the prospects of defeating the Viet Cong while his operation
officers, led by Far East division chief William Colby, were stepping up the "paci-
fication" program in the countryside, featuring a state-of-the-art counterterror
campaign known as the Phoenix Program, which relied on summary execution
and torture to disrupt the communist cadre. The Phoenix bird was a predator,
riddled with corruption but brutally effective. "Thousands died or vanished into
Saigon's prisons," wrote journalist Neil Sheehan, ". . . the guerrillas were forced
into a period of relative quiescence."[17]

That didn't mean the United States was winning the war. Helms felt constant pressure from the president. As antiwar demonstrations grew and race riots
spread in the summer of 1967, Johnson demanded to know who was behind it

all. "LBJ simply could not believe that American youth would on their own be moved to riot in protest against U.S. foreign policy," Helms recalled. LBJ's complaint wasn't an order, but Helms took it as one. He called in Richard Ober, a senior counterintelligence officer, and put him in charge of Operation CHAOS, an undercover campaign to infiltrate the antiwar movement in search of foreign sponsors. Helms didn't view this as a violation of the Agency's charter forbidding domestic operations. CHAOS, he claimed, "lay within the Agency's responsibility to determine if and how foreign powers might be provoking and funding antiwar and political dissidence in the United States."[18]

Helms activated a complementary project, dubbed MERRIMAC, "to provide timely advance notice of impending demonstrations in order to protect CIA assets and installations." Howard Osborn, chief of the Office of Security, turned to the chief of the Physical Security Division, James McCord. He had returned from a temporary duty assignment at the Air War College to a senior management position, supervising a staff of seventy people charged with protecting Agency offices from "unauthorized physical penetration." McCord expanded the Agency's Security Command Center, which protected its facilities in times of demonstrations, riots, and civil disturbance.[19]

Helms's private doubts about the war led him to ask his staff to examine what might happen if the U.S. acknowledged that the war was lost and simply withdrew its troops. The resulting thirty-three-page memorandum, titled "Implications of an Unfavorable Outcome in Vietnam," concluded that the region might become "turbulent and regressive . . . but we think would not bring any major threats to U.S. security."[20]

Helms knew that conclusion, in a written memo, would be explosive if it ever became public. It was November 1967—1,132 Americans died in Vietnam that month, ten times the monthly death toll of just three years before.[21] As for Vietnamese casualties, one "extremely conservative" estimate of Vietnamese deaths found them proportionally a hundred times greater than those suffered by the United States."[22] Yet the Americans were still not winning.

Opposition to the war was burgeoning on college campuses and simmering in Congress. "A new generation of the American young had come along different from five previous generations of the middle class," wrote Norman Mailer after the October 1967 March on the Pentagon. "The new generation believed in technology more than any before it, but the generation also believed in LSD, witches, in tribal knowledge, in orgy and revolution. It had no respect for the unassailable logic of the next step."[23]

Helms, career civil servant, had no other logic, and he was confounded. Contrary to the administration's public statements, his own analysts said the war was not going well, militarily or politically. In the March on the Pentagon, an unprecedented crowd of 50,000 demonstrators had demanded an end to the war. The protesters put flowers in the barrels of the paratroopers standing guard. When the demonstrators refused to disperse, U.S. marshals waded into the crowd, beating the protesters, especially the women, and dragging them away.[24] Almost seven hundred people were arrested. Forty-seven people—demonstrators, soldiers, and marshals—were injured.[25]

"The burning of villages by napalm," wrote Mailer, "was the index of our instability."[26]

Helms ordered tighter security at the Agency and infiltration of antiwar organizations. He wondered if the war was necessary. Cynthia Helms recalled her husband's trepidation. "He told me that he was going to stay behind after the Tuesday lunch and talk to Johnson, and give him the memo," she said. "He said it's a little risky because I shouldn't really be doing that. But he really felt so involved in LBJ's trauma. He really thought that Johnson should get out of Vietnam." Helms gave Johnson the memo in a sealed envelope. The president never responded. The director never brought up the memo again.[27]

Helms listened to his son, Dennis, now a student at Princeton, a campus that had matriculated Allen Dulles, Bill Colby, and many other spies. "Dad, you must know that most of my friends loathe this war and hate the prospect of being drafted," Dennis said. "In the long run, this will affect their attitude toward the government."

"I know Dennis," Helms replied glumly. "Believe me, I know."[28]

AVERY THORNE

In the fall of 1966, Dorothy and Howard Hunt and family returned to Washington. They bought a sprawling horse ranch they called Witches Island in suburban Maryland, a twenty-minute drive from the Langley headquarters. Assigned to the Western European division, Hunt was looking to move on from the Agency. He joined the Brown University Club of Washington, where he met other alumni, among them a former Marine turned lawyer named Charles Colson.

Hunt's passion remained literary. His friend Bill Buckley rather liked the idea of Peter Ward as the American 007. So did Helms, who touted Hunt's spy tales to his friend Jack Valenti, the head of the Motion Picture Association of America (MPAA), the political arm of Hollywood in Washington. Valenti was a pal of President Johnson's and the industry's ambassador in the nation's capital. Valenti promised to pass Hunt's books to the head of the Paramount Pictures studio. Few spy novelists came so well recommended.[29]

His family, alas, was plagued with misfortune. Hunt's daughters, Lisa and Kevan, were badly injured in a car crash. Hunt turned to Helms for help, and his friend did not fail him. "Helms made the agency's resources freely available to me," Hunt recalled, "and they included legal and psychiatric counseling, plus no-interest loans from a special employee fund."[30] While Dorothy and the doctors nursed Lisa and Kevan back to health, Hunt began writing a memoir of the Bay of Pigs operation "to distract my mind from the unhappiness into which Lisa's tragedy had plunged my family." In the book, he wanted to tell his children why he had been so frequently absent during their youth. The answer was Cuba.

The result was "Give Us This Day," a passionate unpublished diatribe that was more convincing than any Peter Ward fiction, if only for its authentic anger and reactionary fervor. From its opening words to its bitter conclusion, Hunt believed the manifest destiny of the United States as the leader of the Free World was derailed on that distant beach, and the late unlamented Jack Kennedy was to blame. Hunt could not forgive or forget the Bay of Pigs.

"No event since the communization of China in 1949 has had such a profound effect on the United States and its allies as the defeat of the US-trained Cuban invasion brigade," he wrote. "Out of that humiliation grew the Berlin Wall, the missile crisis, guerrilla warfare throughout Latin America and Africa, and our Dominican Republic intervention. Castro's beachhead triumph opened a bottomless Pandora's box of difficulties."[31]

Hunt was especially caustic about JFK. Responsibility for the Bay of Pigs failure had been obscured by the "folklore" that Kennedy was "mislead by CIA, State, and Defense advisers . . . and that when the ill-conceived expedition seemed on the point of failure he judiciously refused to increase the stake lest he plunge the world into World War III."

Hunt's polemic was characteristically careless. No one in the Kennedy White House ever said or thought the Bay of Pigs invasion would lead to World War III. That was a figment of Hunt's ideological imagination. Hunt was conflating his outrage over the handling of the Bay of Pigs with his irritation about Kennedy's peaceful resolution of the missile crisis (where World War III was a very real danger) to indict Kennedy's Cuba policy generally.

His point—and he was not shy about saying it publicly—was that Kennedy's Cuba policy cost him his life. "Let it not be forgotten Lee Harvey Oswald was a partisan of Fidel Castro who made desperate attempts to join the Red

Revolution in Havana," Hunt wrote in his introduction. "In the end, he was an activist for the Fair Play for Cuba Committee. But for Castro and the Bay of Pigs disaster there would have been no such 'committee.' And perhaps no assassin named Lee Harvey Oswald." JFK's assassination was no tragedy for Hunt. It was poetic justice.[32]

Hunt wanted to take on Senator Robert Kennedy, who had just announced he was running for the Democratic presidential nomination. "Do you know a publisher who could be trusted to give my memoirs a pseudonymous reading in total confidence," Hunt wrote to Buckley in April 1968. "With RFK coming on strong, I'd like to rattle coffins from the past if it could be managed discretely." Buckley replied he would show the manuscript to a senior editor at the Henry Holt publishing house.[33]

While Hunt wanted to influence politics, Helms wanted to feed the press. "I've got a couple of files," the director told Hunt one day in 1968. "I want you to do a story about eight hundred words, and I'll try it out on Cy Sulzberger." Sulzberger, columnist for the *New York Times* and scion of the family that owned the paper, was a regular luncheon companion of Helms. The files came from Howard Osborn, chief of the Office of Security, whom Hunt had known since they attended the same high school in Hamburg, New York.[34] He delivered his copy to Helms on a tight deadline. A few days later, Sulzberger's column in the *Times* asserted that more than a hundred Soviet intelligence agents had been uncovered posing as journalists, diplomats, and commercial agents between March 1966 and April 1967. Hunt said Sulzberger's column was "75 percent unchanged" from what he wrote.[35]

In turn, Helms took care of his pal. In July 1968, he named Hunt as chief of covert action for the European Division. His job was to monitor Communist Party operations and counter Soviet political action gambits, but Hunt's heart wasn't in the work. The division's chief of operations praised him as "a very competent tough-minded senior professional." The deputy chief observed that "a series of personal and taxing problems, beyond his control, have tended to dull his cutting edge just enough to be noticeable."[36]

Dull was the word for Peter Ward, according to Jack Valenti. In September 1968, he sent Helms Paramount's assessment of Hunt's books. It was dismal.

"While the David St. John paperbacks may be quite acceptable to readers of this sort of international intrigue action melodrama," the studio review said, "they are indifferent screen material. Both books have plot and substance for a single TV episode; neither has enough of a feature length picture. The emphasis is not on people or action, for all that the books are filled with murder, bloodshed, and casual sex. All these values are handled in pretty cliche terms. . . . Peter Ward does seem pretty dull—and he has no one to talk to . . . a loner without humor and with little or no personal life or personal charm is not a character to win an audience easily."[37]

Thus spake Hollywood: Peter Ward was no James Bond. Howard Hunt was no Ian Fleming. But Helms persisted. When Paul Gaynor, a senior official in the Office of Security, complained that Hunt's spy books had not been cleared with the Agency, he was told by higher-ups, "Keep your stinking nose out of this business." Gaynor said he was "led to believe that Mr. Helms desired to improve the image of the intelligence service and that Hunt's books were part of the program to do so."[38]

As for Hunt himself, his prospects grew hazier. In his thriller *Festival for Spies*, Hunt had voiced Peter Ward's doubts about the CIA life.

"Sitting on the edge of his bed, he sipped a Canadian Club nightcap, gazed around the empty room, and felt old, tired, and disillusioned. For more than a decade, he had been an officer of the Clandestine Services—a CIA agent, in journalism's inexact phrase—losing a wife as a direct consequence of his work and following a career that in the last few years had become increasingly disjointed. True, his assignments came from the top level of the Agency, but they seem to be conditioned by the fact he was single. Lifting his glass, he drank and reflected that he did not want to become simply an odd-job man for Avery Thorne."[39]

But that's what happened, and he would lose his wife in the process. Hunt was a spy and a hack—and a prophet too.

10

HONEYMOON

As the carnage in Vietnam mounted, Nixon's all-consuming ambition collided with Helms's dutiful service to Lyndon Johnson. In January 1968, one thousand five hundred and forty-five Americans died in Vietnam. Four hundred sixty-seven had been drafted. One hundred died in helicopter crashes. Six of the dead came from the District of Columbia. There were three homicides and two suicides.[1] North Vietnam's demand for complete U.S. withdrawal remained unchanged.

Nixon couldn't depend on the Johnson administration's overoptimistic statements. He distrusted the reports of Saigon correspondents in the major newspapers, who had long since soured on the war. After the Tet Offensive in late January 1968, when the Viet Cong fought their way onto the grounds of the U.S. Embassy in Saigon, even CBS News anchor Walter Cronkite questioned the war.

Nixon no longer talked about the "aggressor." He talked about peace. "I wanted the war to end but in a manner that would save the South Vietnamese people from defeat," Nixon wrote in his memoir. "I felt there were a number of unexplored avenues to probe in finding a way to end the war."[2]

One place where Nixon probed was among the South Vietnamese themselves. He renewed his friendship with Anna Chennault, the Chinese-born wife of World War II hero General Claire Chennault and an outspoken supporter of Nationalist China. Nixon had first met the Chennaults in Chiang Kai-shek's palace in Taiwan in 1955. When her husband died in 1958, Anna was touched by

Nixon's condolence letter. They kept in touch about Asia and Asian communism, for which, she noted, "he showed a certain fascination."[3]

In 1967 Chennault moved to Washington and lived with her two daughters in a penthouse apartment in the Watergate complex. She became a fundraiser for the Republican Party. Her thronged soirees attracted politicians, donors, diplomats, and CIA hands. Helms did not know Anna Chennault personally, but he certainly knew who she was. Her late husband was a founder of an air freight company that had supplied the OSS in Asia and serviced U.S. military bases throughout the region ever since. She was friends with Helms's colleague Ray Cline, who had served as station chief in Taiwan in the early 1960s. Cline, now deputy director of intelligence, made a point of conferring with Chennault every six weeks or so because of her superb range of contacts, "to exchange ideas and interpretations, not information," he said.[4]

One of Chennault's "very close personal friends" was South Vietnam's ambassador to Washington, Bui Diem, with whom President Johnson met with before traveling to Saigon in March 1968. LBJ returned home and stunned the country by announcing a pause in the bombing of North Vietnam, the opening of peace talks, and his decision not to run for reelection in 1968. Ambassador Diem became the South Vietnamese observer to the talks. Johnson knew the South Vietnamese had little interest in facilitating negotiations they feared would strengthen the communists, and he suspected Bui Diem might be in touch with Nixon's people.

Helms, the butler of espionage, responded to the president's needs. CIA agents "reported regularly" on the activities of Bui Diem, wrote Thomas Powers. The Agency bugged the Washington office of South Vietnamese president Nguyen Van Thieu as the National Security Agency intercepted and deciphered radio transmissions from South Vietnam's embassy in Washington. As director of Central Intelligence Helms delivered the full take to the Oval Office.

Johnson was convinced the former vice president was encouraging the South Vietnamese to resist his terms. Nixon feared the peace talks were designed to help elect Vice President Hubert Humphrey, who announced his candidacy after Johnson bowed out. For his part, Helms was under no illusion the war could be won. After the Tet Offensive, he convened a panel of Agency analysts to assess its impact. They concluded that the Saigon government lacked key attributes of nationhood. It could not defend its frontiers, lacked resolution to fight the communists, and resisted reforms to win public support.[5] Helms conveyed this dismal conclusion to the president, knowing he did not want to hear it.

Helms feared for his country. After the assassination of Martin Luther King on April 4, 1968, looting and rioting raged in the heart of the capital. "To get home after a meeting with the President I had to pass through military check-points in place along the route from the White House . . ." Helms later recalled. He found his emotions "roiled by the realization that half a million troops were at risk in Vietnam, a country many Americans might have trouble finding on a map," while "a semblance of martial law was in effect in Washington; and carnage and arson had erupted across the country."[6]

Helms's tenure as director depended on the results of the 1968 presidential campaign now upended by Johnson's decision not to run. In June, Robert Kennedy emerged as the front-runner for the Democratic nomination, before he was shot and killed in the kitchen of the Ambassador Hotel in Los Angeles on the night he won the California primary. In August, Nixon secured the Republican presidential nomination by positioning himself between New York governor Nelson Rockefeller, the favorite of the Eastern Establishment, and California governor Ronald Reagan, the new darling of conservatives. When the divided Democrats nominated Humphrey in Chicago as police mauled antiwar protesters and innocent bystanders, Nixon adopted a supporter's plaintive plea, "Bring Us Together," as a campaign slogan. He offered himself, improbably but effectively, as a healer.

Under orders from Johnson, Helms stayed current on Nixon's Vietnam contacts, either through a campaign spy or the NSA wiretaps or both. He went along with LBJ's command, he told aide George Carver, because, as he never tired of saying, "I only work for one president at a time."[7]

SOCK IT TO ME?

Dan Rowan had come a long way since 1960 when his affection for singer Phyllis McGuire drew the ominous attention of Sam Giancana. In 1967, he and his partner in comedy, Dick Martin, put together a new TV variety show for NBC called *Laugh-In*. CBS had scored a hit with *The Smothers Brothers Comedy Hour*, a variety show that featured antiwar musicians such as Harry Belafonte, Joan Baez, and Pete Seeger, which was daring for a prime-time show. *Laugh-In* mostly avoided the war while cultivating a youthful aesthetic with quick-cutting skits and sexual innuendo packed into punchlines like, "You can bet your sweet bippy," and "Sock it to me, baby." *Laugh-In* was, in many ways, an establishment show, the commercial, rather than the cutting, edge of the cultural change sweeping America.[8] It was also the most popular TV program in the country.

Laugh-In was, in the lingo of the day, a "rip-off." Here was a national television network co-opting the moral justice of the sit-ins to desegregate Jim Crow lunch counters and the campus teach-ins to protest the war in order to make jokes and sell advertising. *Laugh-In* was a case study in what Herbert Marcuse, the popular New Left philosopher, called "repressive tolerance," namely the ability of a capitalist society to defuse dissent by commodifying it. *Laugh-In* was also sixty minutes of fast, funny comic relief for millions of Americans traumatized by Vietnam, riots, assassinations, and the draft.

Nixon intuited its possibilities. When *Laugh-In* writer Paul Keyes proposed an appearance on the show, Nixon agreed. Keyes, a rare conservative among TV jokesters, rehearsed Nixon to deliver the program's signature punchline. After several takes, they came up with a bit that was broadcast on the premiere of the show's second season in September 1968.[9] With his recognizable bulbous nose in profile, Nixon slowly turned to the camera and converted the punchline into a question, "Sock it to *me*?"[10] It was deft and self-deprecating, unexpected, and amusing. Nixon's men underscored the message with campaign ads during the show.[11]

Marcuse's analysis was eclipsed by Nixon's performance. The canny candidate had applied the reactionary genius of repressive tolerance to the needs of retail politics. "It elected Richard Nixon," claimed George Schlatter, the show's creator.[12] Hollywood hype aside, *Laugh-In* made Nixon seem normal, no small feat.

"GO SEE HELMS"

Nixon heard the disturbing news from Henry Kissinger, former adviser to Nelson Rockefeller, now angling for a job in the administration. Kissinger said he'd heard from Democratic friends that Johnson was planning to drop his conditions for peace talks in order to jump-start negotiations with the North Vietnamese. Nixon felt it was a craven move, abandoning a firm U.S. negotiating position to buck up Humphrey's lagging campaign.[13]

On October 16, Johnson called Nixon and briefed him on his plans for an imminent halt to the bombing. While Nixon listened in sullen silence, LBJ urged him to be discreet in his public statements. When Anna Chennault heard the news, she wrote a note of protest to Nixon, and then flew to Kansas City where Nixon was campaigning. She brought with her a written presentation that deplored the idea of a bombing halt and recommended a long-term approach to the war.

That same day, Nixon's running mate, Maryland governor Spiro "Ted" Agnew, received a briefing on Johnson's plans. The NSA intercepted a call from Chennault to President Thieu, telling him to "stand fast," reject LBJ's deal, and wait for Nixon to take office. According to biographer Powers, Chennault's intercepted conversations were written up in the office of Tom Karamessines, now the deputy director of plans. Helms gave them to Walt Rostow, Johnson's national security adviser, and Rostow shared them with the president.[14]

Nixon wanted to know what Helms knew about LBJ's intentions. On October 22, he decided he could pressure the CIA director into disclosing the White House plan, but he didn't want to do it himself. He ordered Haldeman to tell Agnew to "go see Helms." The message was simple and brutal: "Tell him we want the truth [about Johnson's plans for a bombing halt]—or he hasn't got the job," meaning he wouldn't be retained as CIA director.[15] Haldeman knew when to ignore a Nixon order, and this was one of those times. Agnew never called Helms.

On October 31 Nixon was preparing to address a nationally televised rally at Madison Square Garden when he got another phone call from Johnson. There had been a breakthrough in Paris, the president said. After wide consultations among his advisers, he had decided to call a total bombing halt over North Vietnam. He would make the announcement in two hours.

"Whatever this meant to North Vietnam," Nixon confided to his diary, "he had just dropped a pretty good bomb in the middle of my campaign." Nixon suppressed his anger and thanked the president for the call.[16] "I had done all this work and come all this way," he complained to himself, "only to be undermined by the powers of an incumbent who had decided against seeking reelection."[17] Johnson told aides he thought Nixon was sabotaging his peace initiative. Nixon called the president back to assure him he would never do such a thing. LBJ didn't believe him.

On Tuesday, November 5, seventy-two million Americans voted. When the ballots were counted, Nixon had narrowly defeated Humphrey to win the presidency. The Go East strategy that Nixon crafted after his defeat in the California governor's race had finally succeeded. His mastery of business, the law, and American politics had been vindicated. Nixon gave a victory speech to supporters in the ballroom of the Waldorf Astoria Hotel in New York, then went home to the Fifth Avenue apartment to have a meal with his family. He ended the day by retreating alone to the privacy of his library where he put one of his favorite albums on the turntable, Richard Rodgers's musical score for a World War II documentary, *Victory at Sea*. He turned the volume all the way up.[18]

Richard Helms saw the realities of American power like few others. Not just the shattered consensus and growing recriminations among U.S. policymakers. Not just the divided Congress and the alienated youth. Not just the elusive enemy and the unwinnable war but the raw struggle for power at the very top: the wrathful Johnson, deploying all instruments of national intelligence to contain a rival for power; the crafty Nixon, using Anna Chennault to thwart the diplomacy of his own president in a successful bid to win the White House.

Helms's directorship hung in the balance. A week after the election, he and other top national security officials briefed Johnson and the president-elect in the Oval Office. In his memoirs, Nixon said he found them all capable men but "very nearly worn out" and devoid of new ideas.[19] After the meeting broke up, Johnson pulled Helms aside. He said Nixon had asked, for a second time, if he should keep him on as director of Central Intelligence. Johnson said he told Nixon, "I've no idea how he [Helms] voted in any election and have never asked what his political views are. He's always been correct with me and has done a good job as director. I commend him to you."

Four days later, the president-elect summoned Helms to a hotel suite in New York. Helms was greeted by Bob Haldeman, the advertising executive now serving as Nixon's chief of staff. The two men took an instant dislike to each other. Nixon told Helms he was retaining him as director because he wanted to keep the CIA "out of the political arena." Helms hastened to agree. They shook hands. Helms exited by a freight elevator to avoid the reporters lurking in the lobby.[20]

HONEYMOON

Three days later, Richard Helms and Cynthia McKelvie were married in a Presbyterian ceremony at his brother's home in South Orange, New Jersey, not far from where he grew up. McKelvie was amused to be described in *Time* as "a divorcée," which she said "made me sound far more glamorous than I was in reality."[21]

Howard Hunt sent congratulations and a couple of presents. "Having some experience with the institution of divorce," Hunt wrote, "I know how rewarding and fulfilling another marriage can be." Helms replied with his thanks for his intrepid pal. "I must confess I am awed by your ability to produce these goodies," he wrote, "but then I remember that you have never failed to extricate your heroes from impossible situations."[22]

Mr. and Mrs. Helms flew off to Jamaica as the guests of Lord Ronald Graham, an old friend and classmate of Helms's at the Swiss boarding school La Rosey. Graham, once notorious for his youthful pro-Nazi views, lent them a cottage on the grounds of his estate in Ocho Rios, high on a hill overlooking the Caribbean.[23] Twenty-two years before, Lord Graham had arranged the sale of a nearby property to Ian Fleming, the former MI6 man turned novelist, who built the estate he called Goldeneye. It was there Fleming had conjured up the adventures of James Bond.[24]

It was just the neighborhood for Dick Helms's honeymoon, which was soon over.

11

FLATTERY

Twelve years after their first forgettable meeting, Dick Nixon and Dick Helms became improbable partners in power. In disparate ways, they embodied the American power elite after World War II. One a gentleman, the other a self-made man. One a master of office politics, the other of attack politics. While sympathetic in their anticommunism, each was jealous of his power and zealous in defending it. In America's most turbulent days since the Civil War, the new president and the incumbent spymaster needed each other: to defend the country and deter threats, to wage war and win peace, to manage dissent and master enemies. Yet their mutual mistrust ran deep. Helms, the patrician, could not help but condescend to Nixon, the striver, who could not help but put the spymaster in his place.

Helms endured the first insult even before Nixon had taken the oath of office. The president-elect had brought on Kissinger as his national security adviser, and it was Kissinger who delivered the slight. He told Helms that the president wanted to run the meetings of the National Security Council in a different way. Helms would open the NSC meetings with the Agency's intelligence briefing but then leave before the NSC debated the policy issues. Helms didn't care for the role of delivery boy, but he was too astute to object. "Helms accepted this directive with slightly raised eyebrows," Kissinger observed.

"Actually, it was my idea," said Morton Halperin, Kissinger's staff director in 1969. Halperin was one those defense intellectuals like Paul Wolfowitz and

Richard Holbrooke who came into the federal government during the Vietnam War. With a PhD in international relations from Yale, Halperin was an assistant professor at Harvard, where he met Kissinger. In 1966, McNamara brought him on as deputy assistant secretary of defense, with responsibility for political-military planning and arms control. Under Nixon, Halperin became Kissinger's point man on the NSC.

"My view," Halperin said in an interview, "was the interagency process was distorted by having the CIA participate, pretending they were an analytic organization, but [were] actually bringing to bear their views about policy. I wrote the memo that Kissinger sent to Nixon creating the NSC system. . . . I thought that was the right thing to do [to exclude the CIA director]. So, I put it in [the memo]. And to my surprise, Nixon approved the document virtually verbatim."[1]

Kissinger allowed that Helms's position in the new administration was "delicate." The president, he wrote in the foreword to Helms's memoir, "regarded Helms as a member of the 'Georgetown social set,' which Nixon believed—not incorrectly—to be more sympathetic to Democratic administrations than to his own."[2] This was not quite fair to Helms, who attended his share of parties in Georgetown but never lived there or identified himself as a Democrat or a liberal. Nixon's antenna for enemies in the CIA was sensitive. He still believed Agency leaks to JFK in 1960 had forced him to argue publicly against the Bay of Pigs operation that he actually supported. He wanted revenge.

Helms wanted relevance. Well versed in bureaucratic power plays, he appealed to his friend, Melvin Laird, the Wisconsin congressman whom Nixon had just named secretary of defense. Laird told Nixon that excluding Helms was a bad idea and wouldn't help on Capitol Hill, where the director had friends.[3] Nixon relented. The CIA kept its seat at the policymaking table.

By the time Nixon took the oath of office as the thirty-seventh president of the United States on January 20, 1969, the peace talks undermined by Anna Chennault were deadlocked and the opposition to the war still growing. Protest at presidential inaugurations was not unknown, but for the first time since 1861 when Confederate sympathizers attended the swearing in of Abraham Lincoln, the capital city was thronged with Americans who wanted to see the new president defeated on the field of battle. Some of the antiwar protesters wore Nixon masks, crinkly white disguises with the undeniable nose.

As the presidential motorcade came up Pennsylvania Avenue, with Dick and Pat smiling and waving, a crowd of young people surged down 12th Street toward the parade throwing rocks and chanting "Ho, Ho, Ho Chi Minh, NLF is gonna win." Nixon was infuriated by their contempt and heartened to see the protesters outnumbered by well-wishers. But when Nixon mounted the reviewing stand, observed Garry Wills, "his faced bunched up in its instant toothed smile, so circumspect, so vulnerable." He had one thing in common with the kids jeering him, Wills noted. "He wore a Nixon mask."[4]

Underneath Nixon's masks were his multiple personas, crafted and displayed to the American people over the years, sometimes inadvertently. He was, alternately, a Red baiter, Ike's understudy, a civil rights supporter, a sore loser, a Wall Street lawyer, and now a president who said, "Bring Us Together." Two of the Nixons within the new president, however, were as yet mostly unseen: Nixon, the intellectual with ambitions to reshape geopolitics, and Nixon, the paranoiac willing to break the law to defeat his enemies. As CIA director, Helms would enable both.

In late January, Helms came to the White House for his first briefing with the president. He brought along two top lieutenants, Tom Karamessines and Cord Meyer. "We gave the President an overview of our most productive operations and closed with a discussion of more risky activity," Helms said. He found Nixon affable and quick with pertinent questions. Helms invited the president to pay a visit to the Langley headquarters. "As we gathered up our papers and were making our way from the office," Helms recalled, "the President—in what I later realized was a rare jovial moment—called out, 'But don't get caught.'"[5]

SECOND WIFE

Rose Mary Woods had long worked right outside Nixon's office, controlling access to the man she called "the boss," but when Nixon moved into the Oval Office, Bob Haldeman claimed Woods's territory. Haldeman, jealous of Woods's influence, stripped her of job responsibilities and sought to move her out of the Executive Office Building altogether. Nixon refused. He let Haldeman prevail in practice, but he wanted to take care of Woods.

"She knew who everyone was, what their relationship to the President was, all the secrets of the past," one former Nixon aide told Judy Bachrach, *Washington Post* columnist. "Who contributes ideas? Who contributes money? Who makes a big noise and couldn't be counted on? And to have somebody like that when you're not very good at it yourself is invaluable. And Nixon wasn't very good at that."[6]

Not long after taking office, Nixon gave three favored friends a present. Woods, speechwriter Pat Buchanan, and valet Manolo Sanchez received options to buy stock for a Miami real estate development in which Nixon had invested.

Woods exercised the option to buy ten thousand shares at a dollar apiece and immediately sold them for two dollars each, netting ten thousand dollars.[7]

Woods had arrived in life. Born in a small town in northeastern Ohio, she now reigned in Washington. She moved into a two-bedroom apartment on the seventh floor of the Watergate complex. When she traveled with Nixon on his first trip as president, she returned to find that her apartment had been burglarized. The thieves took twenty-seven pieces of jewelry valued in excess of $5,000, including a pearl brooch with diamonds, three rings, four watches, and a diamond campaign pin emblazoned "N 68."[8] A few months later, Woods bought the apartment.

Woods was a woman out of style. At a time when birth control and feminism were redefining the lives of women, Woods occupied the most of traditional roles. She was a queen of the capital, at least among Republicans, but for those who didn't like Nixon, she was just one more reason not to. She was selfless and seemingly subservient to a man at a time when more and more women wanted to be anything but.

Still, she knew Nixon best, better than Haldeman, who served his boss for a decade without ever really becoming friends with him. Woods knew the man. When Anna Chennault sought a cultural affairs job in the State Department, Woods scotched the idea. "This would be a disaster," she told another Nixon aide. "The sooner we can keep her as far away as possible from the Administration—the better."[9]

More than a secretary, Woods had become a kind of second wife to Nixon—"as protective as the second Mrs. Wilson," wrote Garry Wills, referring to Edith Wilson, who controlled access to her husband President Woodrow Wilson after he suffered a crippling stroke in 1919.[10] The comparison to an incapacitated president would prove prescient.

MR. AND MRS.

Cynthia Helms found a new home for herself and her husband, a two-bedroom apartment in the Irene, a charmless, ten-story apartment block in suburban Bethesda, Maryland. The members of the Georgetown social set that Nixon so resented might have dropped their troubled teenage children to see a psychiatrist in the Irene, but they never, ever would have lived there.

Mr. and Mrs. Helms felt right at home. "It suited our immediate needs as well as our tight budget," Cynthia wrote in her memoir. Like Helms, she had come of age in the Depression and World War II and abhorred profligacy. They fit together like a pair of old shoes, she said. Helms had a reputation for being taciturn. Not with Cynthia.

"We talked endlessly about the news, friends and our mutual interests and my specific interests," she said in her memoir. "We had mock debates about who had the more interesting day. He taught me to read a newspaper in a more discerning way and to question where the story was coming from." She especially appreciated his thoughtfulness. Not long after they married, he asked, "What would you like to do today?" "I was dumbstruck," she said. "I hadn't been asked that in 25 years."

Helms had his shortcomings as a husband, she admitted. He was useless in the kitchen, lousy at cards, and a menace to all peace-loving plants in the garden. Her teenage daughters thought he was a hilarious fuddy-duddy for shooing dinner guests out the door before the clock struck ten. "Don't you people have a home?" he would cavil at friends who wanted to linger over dessert.[11]

In his long days at the office, Helms had to grapple with a daunting new reality. There were no more Tuesday lunches with the boss. His path to the Oval Office was blocked by the Praetorian Guard in the White House. "I was not a man for Haldeman and Ehrlichman," Helms rued.[12] He dubbed them "the Germans," and it wasn't a compliment.

Haldeman sensed an unspoken feud between the president and the director: "Helms, the aloof, aristocratic, Eastern elitist, and Nixon the poor boy (he never let you forget it) from a small California town." But if there was a feud, it was mostly Nixon's doing. In their infrequent encounters, Helms didn't fight with the president. He ingratiated.

Politically, the two men were more compatible than Nixon assumed. When Allen Dulles died in January 1969, Helms escorted his widow, Clover, to the funeral service in Georgetown. Nixon sent a tribute: "He was a man who brought civility, intelligence and great dedication to everything he did," the president eulogized. "In the nature of his task, his achievements were known to only a few. But, because of him, the world is a safer place."[13] Helms might have uttered the words himself.

Helms's briefings to the National Security Council impressed Nixon, according to Kissinger. The president wanted to hear Helms's policy views—or at least the CIA's assessment of the consequences of various policy options. After one NSC briefing in early 1969, Nixon invited Helms to join him for lunch. "From that point on Dick Helms was an integral member of the NSC team," Kissinger said.[14]

But the NSC team was not where Dick Helms cared to play. That meant

Kissinger, not Helms, met regularly with Nixon, and for Helms personal meetings with the president were the coin of his realm. In the new administration, the national security adviser, not the director of Central Intelligence, served as president's senior intelligence adviser.[15] While professing admiration for Helms, Kissinger had effectively demoted the Agency from its traditional position as the president's source for objective reporting and analysis on international affairs.

A more egotistical man might have objected. Helms went along, eyebrows barely raised. He used every means, no matter how humbling, to exercise influence. He fed Kissinger intelligence reports that he felt contained especially pertinent information, with notes politely suggesting they be passed to the president.[16]

"He was strong, and he was wary," observed Kissinger. "His urbanity was coupled with extraordinary tenacity. He had seen administrations come and go and he understood that in Washington, knowledge was power. He was presumed to know a lot and never disabused people of that belief." At the same time, Kissinger added, "I never knew him to misuse his knowledge or power."[17]

When Nixon named General Robert Cushman, his longtime military adviser, as deputy director of the CIA, news reports quoted unnamed sources saying the president wanted a spy in Langley. Unfazed, Helms welcomed Cushman. The Agency was running a massive paramilitary operation in Laos, the remote landlocked country west of North Vietnam. Much to Helms's chagrin, some congressmen were calling Laos "the CIA's war," as if the Agency wasn't there on presidential orders. "I'm glad to see a military man here," Helms told Cushman. "We've got a war in Laos and you're in charge of it starting now."[18]

The president demanded Helms focus on Vietnam. "Nixon would say, look don't talk to me about this that and the other thing," he recalled. In an early meeting of the interagency committee reviewing all CIA covert operations, Helms warned that if the United States wanted to head off a leftist victory in Chile's 1970 presidential election, they had to come up with a plan soon.[19] The president wasn't interested. "There's only one problem these days in the United States," Nixon said, "and that's in Vietnam."[20]

Helms found Nixon difficult, if not damaged.

"He seemed to dislike and distrust persons who he supposed might not put personal loyalty to him above all other responsibilities," Helms wrote in his memoir. "This obsession sometimes seemed combined with deep suspicion of people Nixon thought might consider themselves his social superior. Nixon never seemed to have shaken his early impression that the Agency was exclusively staffed by uppity Ivy Leaguers, most of whom lived in Georgetown and spent every evening gossiping about him at cocktail parties. The explanations for these attitudes, which in some cases seemed to blind his judgment, is best left to board-certified medical specialists."[21]

Nixon returned Helms's disdain with his own.

"At NSC meetings, he interrupted Helms frequently—sometimes gratuitously, often correcting him on some niggling point of fact or geography," said author Chris Whipple. Nixon's low opinion of the CIA's workforce was also on display. "What are those idiots out in Maclean doing?" Nixon wondered aloud. "There are forty thousand people out there, reading newspapers."[22]

"MY DEAR MR. PRESIDENT"

Helms remained true to his OSS origins. He was first and foremost an intelligence collector, a role that Nixon could appreciate. With secrets, Helms had the means to win White House favor. The process began almost imperceptibly. In February 1969, Helms sent Kissinger an updated version of "Restless Youth," a secret report on the antiwar movement that he had given LBJ in November 1967.

"In an effort to round out our discussion of this subject we have included a section on American students," Helms wrote. "This is an area not within the charter of this agency, so I need not emphasize how extremely sensitive this makes the paper. Should anyone learn of its existence it would prove most embarrassing for all concerned."[23]

In addition to domestic spying, Helms offered flattery. When Nixon returned from his foreign trip in March, Helms wrote him a little note varnished with admiration.

"My dear Mr. President: After hearing you this morning and reading incoming reports from Western Europe, may I say what a remarkable personal tour de force you achieved on your trip. . . . I feel compelled to tell you that your approach to the real world is a most reassuring one. I do not mean to sound gratuitous; I just want you to know how I see it. Respectfully, Dick."[24]

When Nixon took up his offer to visit the Langley headquarters, Helms was effusive. Nixon told an auditorium full of Agency personnel that their work was difficult and sometimes in conflict with the country's values. Nonetheless, he declared, he would always support them. Afterward, Helms took his pen in hand.

"My dear Mr. President," he wrote. "Again, I want to thank you for visiting the Agency Friday. From the standpoint of our people, it was everything that one could have desired. I know you could sense the lift in morale even while you were on the premises. Your warm friendliness has brought nothing but glowing remarks, even from those 'cynics' who believe they have seen it all. . . . Your words about me were humbling. I need not assure you that I will do everything I can to justify them. . . . Respectfully, Dick."[25]

After the event, Helms also thanked his security staff by name, including Office of Security veteran James McCord, for their work during Nixon's visit. "The arrangements were flawless; the security first-class without being intrusive," Helms wrote. A copy went into McCord's personnel file.[26]

Helms didn't mind serving as the butler of intelligence. He thought it part of the job.

"It's easy for intelligence people to forget that they're really a service organization," Helms told one of his biographers. "That they're really there to assist in the policymaking process through other people. [I tried] to give the President, Vice President, and the cabinet the impression that the agency was there to be useful, to be of service, to be helpful. I did my damnedest, as a result of demands placed on the agency . . . to see to it they were carried out and the agency put its best foot forward and the papers were produced in a timely fashion."[27]

In the White House, Kissinger felt well served. Helms, he said, "never volunteered policy advice beyond the questions that were asked him, though he never hesitated to warn the White House of dangers, even when his views ran counter to the preconceptions of the president or his security advisor."[28]

Early in his first term Nixon asked the Agency to prepare an assessment of the Soviet Union's mammoth new nuclear missile, known as the SS-9, which the United States had identified by satellite surveillance photos. Bigger and more destructive than any missile in the U.S. arsenal, the SS-9 worried the Nixon administration. The strategic question was whether the Soviet Union was seeking a so-called first-strike capability in which their military superiority would enable them to dictate political outcomes. The practical question was whether the multiple warheads packed into the SS-9 had individual guidance systems that would enable them to disperse and hit multiple U.S. missile silos. The answer was crucial to the administration's case for an antiballistic missile (ABM) system to deter a Soviet attack with the ability to shoot down its missiles. If a score of SS-9 missiles could distribute nuclear warheads to sixty different U.S. targets, the case for the multibillion-dollar ABM system was stronger. If twenty missiles could only hit twenty targets, the missile defense system might be optional, if not unnecessary.

Analysts from the Directorate of Intelligence said no, the multiple SS-9 warheads did not have individual guidance systems, and no, the Soviets did not seek so-called first-strike capabilities to launch a surprise attack on the United States.

Both positions contradicted Defense Secretary Laird. In the White House, aides griped, *Where did the CIA get off making policy?*

Helms told his staff that Pentagon officials had accused CIA officers of undercutting Laird's position on the Georgetown cocktail circuit. He directed his subordinates to take no public position, pro or con, on the ABM issue. He said "responsible quarters"—meaning the Pentagon and the White House—charged that the CIA's estimates were biased. At the same time, he made clear he did not share that view.[29]

The differences of opinion were bitter, Helms recalled, "as difficult a policy problem as I have ever faced." The safety of the American people, as well as government contracts worth billions of dollars, turned on the CIA's analysis.

The question of whether the Soviet Union sought a first-strike capability came up again in a National Intelligence Estimate intended to serve as the U.S. government's best information on the SS-9. The NIE reiterated the Agency's view that the Soviets did not have first-strike plans. Laird and Kissinger demanded that Helms remove the offending passage. He relented. When he felt it absolutely necessary, Helms would accommodate himself to Nixon's demands.[30]

"To many observers, inside and outside the agency, it seems that Helms had buckled under pressure," said an official biography. Never before had a cabinet secretary forced a change in the Agency's finished product. Helms felt the revision was tainted by the administration's desire to build a missile defense system, but acquiesced, he said, because no intelligence service should "assume it has achieved absolute wisdom." Helms didn't want to stake the Agency's reputation on one issue.[31] In Nixon's administration, where dissent was often equated with betrayal, Helms had to proceed carefully if he was ever going to gain the president's confidence.[32]

He made progress by making allies. Kissinger admitted that he originally "leaned towards the more ominous interpretation" of the SS-9's capabilities. Then he had his staff review the CIA's work. Helms, he realized, was right.[33] Kissinger was impressed. "He stood his ground where lesser men might have resorted to ambiguity."

12

MADMAN THEORY

Helms was not exactly welcome in Nixon's deliberations. Nor was he entirely excluded. In July, Nixon invited Helms and Cushman for a cruise on the presidential yacht, the *Sequoia*. It was an exclusive gathering of the inner circle of presidential advisers. The only other passengers (besides the crew and the waiters) were Kissinger, Secretary of State William Rogers, Defense Secretary Laird, Attorney General John Mitchell, and Joint Chiefs chairman General Earle Wheeler. Nixon may have distrusted Helms's East Coast pedigree, but he still wanted his counsel.

As the boat floated down the Potomac on a warm summer night, Nixon expounded on his plans for strategic arms limitations talks with the Soviet Union and what he called the "go for broke" approach to Vietnam.

"I call it the Madman Theory," he confided to Haldeman on another occasion. "I want the North Vietnamese to believe that I might do anything to stop the war. We'll just slip the word to them that 'For God's sake, you know Nixon is obsessed by Communism. We can't restrain him when he's angry—and he had his hand on the nuclear button'—and Ho Chi Minh himself will be in Paris in two days begging for peace."[1]

"Nixon's position was, threaten the Russians," recalled Mort Halperin. "You tell the Russians we're going to drop nuclear weapons on Vietnam if they don't get the North Vietnamese to end the war. And if they [the Russians] do get the North Vietnamese to end the war, then we'll do arms talks. We'll do trade talks.

We'll do all kinds of stuff. Kissinger conveyed this to [Soviet Ambassador Anatoly] Dobrynin, who said, 'You talk to the North Vietnamese in Paris. Just tell them whatever you want to tell them. We're not going to carry your messages."[2]

Helms thought it unlikely that U.S. escalation would break the communists' will or ability to fight. It had not done so for the past six years, and it seemed unlikely in the next twelve months. But he was steadfast in support of Nixon's refusal to negotiate an end to the war and U.S. withdrawal, which is what the former architects and overseers of the war, including Robert McNamara and McGeorge Bundy, now advocated.

In October, Nixon told Kissinger he was ready to make an unspecified "tough move" on North Vietnam before antiwar groups staged a national "moratorium" in protest later in the month. Nixon said he didn't want to be seen responding to the peace movement, which he regarded as misguided at best. The protesters beat him to the punch. On October 15, the Moratorium drew an unprecedented crowd of half a million people to midtown Manhattan. Opposition to the war now extended from hardcore communists to business executives, from liberal Republicans to religious leaders to the editors of the *New York Times*. Undaunted, Nixon instructed Kissinger to tell Dobrynin that "the president was 'out of control' on Vietnam."[3] Whatever his private doubts, Helms communicated unstinting support to the president. Nixon delivered a nationwide TV address on November 3 responding to the Moratorium and defending his refusal to meet North Vietnam's demands for withdrawal. Nixon claimed the support of a "Silent Majority" of Americans, making the case that his "Vietnamization" policy—withdrawing U.S. troops and replacing them with South Vietnamese troops—was working to extricate the United States without defeat.

The next day Helms wrote another little note:

"My dear Mr. President: May I say how impressed I was with your speech last evening. It constituted national leadership at its best. From my vantage point, I would opine that a sigh of relief went through free Asia and that its leaders quietly offered thanks for your courage and statesmanship. . . . Respectfully, Dick."[4]

That month, six hundred fifty-eight Americans died in Vietnam, the youngest was eighteen, the oldest forty-nine. Thirty-nine were named John, thirty-eight James, and thirty-five Robert. Eight died from homicides. Twelve committed suicide.[5]

Kissinger thought Nixon's madman posture was a bluff, and he was right. The country's divisions had, in effect, called Nixon's bluff. On November 15, the national coalition of antiwar groups followed up on the Moratorium to pause the war with a Mobilization to end it. Another massive crowd converged on Washington. "Official estimate was 250,000," Haldeman wrote in his diary. "By our photo count it was 325,000. Anyway, it was really huge." The demonstrators were overwhelmingly young, white, and middle class, "casualties of affluence," in Kissinger's words. They were a cross-section of educated America, a glimpse of the country's future. Their very presence proved that escalation would only inflame and embolden Nixon's opposition. His ability to mobilize national power behind dire threats of escalation was crippled. His bluff was stillborn.

The rage of the antiwar movement only steeled his determination. At night, after the politicians and the preachers had spoken, the more radical elements of the crowd staged an unsanctioned march on the Justice Department building at 7th and Pennsylvania. The protesters took down the department's American flag and hoisted a Viet Cong banner to rousing cheers. Five stories above the street, Attorney General Mitchell came out on the balcony and peered down at the rabble below. Ignoring the shouted insults floating up at him, the old Wall Street bond lawyer puffed his pipe and gave the demonstrators below the benefit of his middle finger. Fuck you. It was a popular sentiment. At year's end, polls showed two-thirds of Americans approved of Nixon's handling of the war.[6]

Helms's response to the confounding phenomenon of a failing war and a rising antiwar movement was more detached. He had his private doubts, bolstered by the Agency's assessments. But Helms was not one to criticize U.S. policy behind closed doors or to defend it in public. In Washington, Vietnam was "a bloodless war of men in well-tailored suits around waxed conference tables, a briefcase full of paper propped against every chair," wrote Thomas Powers. Helms "was the coolest of advocates, presenting his Agency's view on paper, defending them on paper, a paper general in a paper war."[7]

Cynthia Helms's son Roderick, a recent Harvard graduate, got to know his mother's new husband at family gatherings. "He was very courteous," he recalled in an interview. "He more wanted to hear what young people were thinking as opposed to selling anything or confronting us." McKelvie couldn't tell if he was a Republican or a Democrat. "He just wanted to chat and find out what we were thinking. . . . He never got after me for the long hair."[8]

OPERATION CHAOS

President Nixon saw the CIA not just as a source of information but also as an organization that could achieve his aims by secret methods. Helms was ready to oblige him, within limits. Early on, Nixon tried to get the Agency to monitor the activities of his brother Donald Nixon, a feckless businessman whose antics were a source of embarrassment. Helms refused on the grounds that the Agency's charter prohibited domestic operations.[9]

Helms, however, was glad to share the abundant take from the CIA's ongoing infiltration of the antiwar movement. He had no higher priority. In a memo he stated, "Operational priority of CHAOS activities in the field is in the highest category, ranking with Soviet and ChiComm [Chinese Communist]."[10] In May 1969, Helms met with Attorney General Mitchell to discuss "where within the government could the entire question of domestic dissidence be handled." Helms then asked Dick Ober, chief of CHAOS, to serve as a liaison with the Justice Department.[11]

Helms shared Nixon's desire to expand the wiretapping and surveillance of radicals. On a tour of Europe, Helms met with the intelligence chiefs of the United Kingdom, West Germany, Switzerland, France, and Holland. He said they all told him it was "absolutely necessary" to employ wiretaps and mail coverage to deal with security threats. "This is no problem in Europe because most countries' application of such techniques is considered an elementary tool for the internal security service involved," Helms said.[12] Such measures were problematic in the United States where ideals of privacy, civil liberties, and constitutional rights ran deep.

Like Nixon, Helms believed in the value of domestic surveillance and the CIA's right to conduct it. As Operation CHAOS grew, it attracted criticism from the ranks of the Agency. Was it really their job to spy on American college students, some wondered? Helms acknowledged the discontent and dismissed it. He sent a memo to all of his deputy directors, defending the operation and calling on all personnel to support the effort, "both in exploiting existing sources and developing new ones."[13] Domestic spying was the order of the day.

"REMIND HELMS WHO'S PRESIDENT"

Nixon came to the presidency with the hunch that the CIA had something to hide about Cuba operations in the Kennedy years —something that culminated in the assassination of President Kennedy. He deployed John Ehrlichman to find it. He veiled his specific interest in a general request. Bob Haldeman recalled that early in his first term, Nixon had summoned Ehrlichman and told him he wanted "all the facts and documents the CIA had on the Bay of Pigs, a complete report on the whole project." Haldeman and Ehrlichman were puzzled.[14] By 1969, the Bay of Pigs was a footnote to the failed struggle against Castro's now-entrenched communist government. Other than a "Cubans for Nixon" committee formed by

Manuel Artime, the CIA-supported exile leader, Cuba barely figured in Nixon's 1968 presidential campaign.

One man who thought the true story of the Bay of Pigs could help Nixon was Howard Hunt. He was still shopping "Give Us This Day" with the help of his faithful friend Bill Buckley. ("Give my love to Dorothy and to my sweet and attentive godchildren who write such terribly nice notes in impeccable Spanish," Buckley wrote to Hunt in May 1969.)[15] He was also lunching regularly with Chuck Colson as part of his efforts to get out of the CIA and into a job in the White House. "To Colson I described my role in the Bay of Pigs and Nixon's special interest in the project," Hunt recalled. The way Hunt framed the bygone issue made Nixon look good compared to the Kennedys. JFK made a commitment to Castro's foes and then "abandoned the brigade at the beachhead," Hunt later explained on Bill Buckley's *Firing Line* TV show. "Now, this commitment was made by the Eisenhower Administration in which President Nixon served as vice-president, and I believe he chaired the National Security Council in that capacity. So, in effect, the commitment that was made to the Cubans who went forward and risked their lives was nullified by a subsequent political decision of the Kennedy White House."[16]

Nixon was already thinking about the 1972 election. The Bay of Pigs was most relevant to the presumed presidential aspirations of Senator Ted Kennedy, heir apparent to his slain brothers. Nixon wanted to remind the country of JFK's biggest failure as a way of impugning Teddy before the 1972 campaign. But he couldn't obtain what he wanted.

Haldeman wrote that Ehrlichman stopped by his office six months later. "Those bastards in Langley are holding back something," he exclaimed. "They just dig in their heels and say the President can't have it. Period. Imagine that! The Commander-in-Chief wants to see a document relating to a military operation, and the spooks say he can't have it."

"Well, you remind Helms who's president," Haldeman snapped. "He's not. In fact, Helms can damn well find himself out of a job."

Helms would have the last word. He visited the White House that same day and had a long private meeting with Nixon in the Oval Office. Then Ehrlichman met with Nixon and returned disconsolate about "the Mad Monk," his nickname for the president. "The Mad Monk just told me I am now to forget about that CIA document," Ehrlichman griped to Haldeman. "In fact, I am to cease and desist from trying to obtain it."[17]

To placate the president, Helms handed over some harmless but classified material. Attorney General Mitchell was among the few permitted to the review the heavily sanitized documents. He grumbled that they revealed little more than that JFK had puffed pot in the White House.[18] At a time when antiwar demonstrators routinely smoked dope on the streets of Washington, this was not exactly usable dirt.

Helms was an obliging man, a man of routine, elegantly dressed but unpretentious. He commuted to Virginia in the same Pontiac that he had been driving for years. He wanted Nixon to know he had a friend in Langley.

"My dear Mr. President," Helms wrote on the occasion of Nixon's fifty-seventh birthday in January 1970. "This brings warm birthday greetings from all of us in the Agency. Long may you prosper! Respectfully, Dick."[19]

Nixon saved the note. He still didn't trust the son of bitch.

13

PUBLIC RELATIONS JOB

The names of Richard Nixon and Richard Helms were not often linked in public. Helms was admired inside Washington, largely unknown outside of the capital. He was not a target of the antiwar movement. He rarely met the president alone. Their relationship was discreet. Nixon wanted Mitchell to have better intelligence on the antiwar movement, which was growing more militant as Nixon's "Vietnamization" policy reduced American casualties without ending the war. Helms supplied timely intelligence from the CHAOS operation, but that did not satisfy the White House.

Mitchell summoned Helms to his office in January and February 1970 to discuss what the White House delicately referred to as "inadequacies in domestic collection."[1] Helms, the spymaster from the Main Line, and Mitchell, the bond lawyer from Queens, did not have much rapport. "Mitchell was less than expansive at the best of times," Helms said. Mitchell sometimes sat in on meetings of the interagency committee that approved CIA covert operations. Helms found him "shadowy," sometimes asking questions, sometimes remaining ominously silent. Mitchell sized up Helms as "capable but devious." Chuck Colson, it was said, would "run over his grandmother" to serve Nixon. "Helms," Mitchell gibed, "would knock off his grandmother."[2]

Eager to please, Helms offered help on the question of foreign support. The Agency had found no significant foreign funding or influence in the antiwar movement since Helms launched CHAOS in the summer of 1967. There were foreign contacts, however, that caused concern, if not heartburn. Eight Weathermen leaders had traveled to Cuba in the summer of 1969, where they met with representatives of the Viet Cong and North Korea.[3]

The threat was declared. In December 1969, the Weathermen convened a "national war council" in Flint, Michigan, with the purpose of avenging the murder of Fred Hampton, the twenty-one-year-old chairman of the Black Panther Party in Chicago, who was killed in a predawn police raid. Initially depicted as a gun battle, the raid was actually an assassination. It fulfilled the letter and spirit of the August 1967 memo from FBI director J. Edgar Hoover that launched the Bureau's Counterintelligence Program, known as COINTELPRO, in which Hoover called for the "neutralization" of black leaders. On December 4, 1969, the Cook County and Chicago police delivered, killing Hampton in his bed.[4]

What more could the Agency do on domestic threats? Helms was hamstrung by the obdurate Hoover. In a fit of pique, the FBI director, now seventy-five years old, had suspended all face-to-face meetings with CIA employees because of a perceived slight by Helms.[5] Without the FBI, the CIA did not have a partner for surveillance operations in the United States. Helms could offer the take from Operation CHAOS but not much more.

For Nixon, it was just one goddamn excuse after another. The president would never fire Hoover, still a personal hero, so he had to appease him. Nixon told Haldeman he wanted to meet with the FBI director once every three months. He assigned young Tom Huston, one of his sharpest and most conservative aides, to come up with a plan to centralize the collection of domestic intelligence in the White House. Huston, all of twenty-eight years old, summoned Helms to a meeting in his office to explain exactly what Nixon wanted. The courteous director, sharing the president's concern, was glad to oblige.

WAR CABINET

Still, there was no pleasing the president. The Agency remained a favorite target of Nixon's barbs. In mid-March 1970, Cambodian prime minister Lon Nol, backed by the country's small army, ousted long-reigning monarch Prince Norodom Sihanouk, who went into exile. The coup came as a complete surprise to Nixon. The CIA had given him no indication there might be a change of government in South Vietnam's neighbor. "What the hell do those clowns do out there in Langley?" he asked Secretary of State Bill Rogers.[6]

Helms knew the geopolitical complexities. Prince Sihanouk had kept his rural kingdom out of the war in neighboring Vietnam with ever-shifting alliances and tactics. Like Nixon, Sihanouk was perhaps too crafty for his own good. For money, he allowed the North Vietnamese communists to use Cambodian territory to ship war material into South Vietnam. To keep communists out of his government, he relied on Lon Nol, the pro-American commander in chief of the Cambodian military. When Nixon secretly authorized "Menu," a series of B-52 bombing raids on North Vietnam's depots in Cambodia in May 1969, Sihanouk did not protest. The communists, in turn, stepped up their infiltration and pressured the prince to break with the United States. Fearing Sihanouk would capitulate, Lon Nol staged a coup. Now the deposed prince was in Beijing, denouncing the Americans as imperialists, and the White House had an unexpected crisis on its hands.

Kissinger was irked. It was not until the day of Sihanouk's ouster that the Agency circulated a report that riots encouraged by Lon Nol were precursor to a coup if Sihanouk did not go along with a more pro-American policy.[7] For Helms, the failure to predict the coup was not exactly surprising given that the Agency did not have a station in Phnom Penh, the Cambodian capital. But he was not one for excuses. He would support the president.

Nixon decided denying the North Vietnamese a free hand in Cambodia would relieve pressure on South Vietnam. He supported Lon Nol's effort to add ten thousand men to the Cambodian armed forces,[8] "a poorly led wisp of an army," in the words of Neil Sheehan, the *New York Times* correspondent in Saigon. Sheehan thought it was a "lunatic exercise" to throw the Cambodians into battle against the experienced communist forces. But Nixon was desperate to buy time for his "Vietnamization" strategy, and he turned to his CIA director for help.[9]

"I want Helms to develop and implement a plan for maximum assistance to pro-US elements in Cambodia," the president told Kissinger. And he wanted to keep the plan secret, just as he had sought to conceal the bombing of Cambodia. "Don't put this out to 303 [the interagency committee that approved covert operations] or the bureau bureaucracy [of the State Department]. Handle like our [Menu] airstrikes."[10]

The president not only wanted to bolster Lon Nol, who didn't seem capable of holding off the communists, he also wanted to invade Cambodia and eliminate North Vietnam's Central Office for South Vietnam (COSVN), which managed the communist war effort in the south. Taking inspiration from George Patton, the brash general of World War II, Nixon dreamed of striking a heroic decisive blow.

The Agency's analysts were skeptical. Nixon and Kissinger assumed COSVN was an organization that was housed in a building or a base that could be bombed to good effect. The CIA believed COSVN was more like a team of officials who moved around in trucks and whose ability to function might not be curtailed by bombing. The effect of a U.S. invasion, concluded the Agency's Office of National Estimates, would be neither permanent nor crippling to the North Vietnamese. Helms didn't pass the study to the White House, prompting an unusual protest. A group of analysts circulated a petition inside the Agency criticizing Helms's decision as a betrayal of the agency's ideal of speaking truth to power.

Helms briefed Nixon and Kissinger on the escalating North Vietnamese attacks in Cambodia. The government in Phnom Penh could not long survive, he said.[11] The National Security Council considered three options: doing nothing, the preferred course of Secretary of State Rogers and Defense Secretary Laird. Kissinger's recommendation was to attack the sanctuaries with South Vietnamese forces only. The third option—using whatever forces were necessary to neutralize the two biggest bases—was favored by the Joint Chiefs and by Helms.[12]

"He felt that we would pay the same domestic price for two operations as for one," Kissinger recalled, "and the strategic payoff would be incomparably greater in the two-pronged attack."[13] At a time when most of Nixon's cabinet openly or privately opposed expanding the war, Helms urged him on.

When Nixon announced the invasion of Cambodia in a nationwide TV address on April 30, 1970, his tone was apocalyptic.

"My fellow Americans," Nixon declared, "we live in an age of anarchy, both abroad and at home. We see mindless attacks on all the great institutions which have been created by free civilizations in the last five hundred years. Even here in the United States, great universities are being systematically destroyed. Small nations all over the world find themselves under attack from within and from without.

"If, when the chips are down," he went on, "the world's most powerful nation, the United States of America, acts like a pitiful, helpless giant, the forces of totalitarianism and anarchy will threaten free nations and free institutions throughout the world."

The antiwar movement that Nixon and Mitchell thought they had contained back in the fall surged again. College campuses erupted in protests. Panicky National Guardsmen shot four students dead at Kent State University in Ohio. Police killed two more at Jackson State in Mississippi. Another huge crowd descended on Washington. The image of a "pitiful helpless giant" was all too apt for a nuclear superpower wasting blood and treasure on a brutally ineffectual war against a resilient peasant army while tormented internally by the bitter division of its people.

Helms knew the Vietnam venture was misbegotten, on the grounds that intervening in a country as alien to the United States as Vietnam (or Cambodia) required at least a ten-year commitment. "In a decade, the operatives might achieve command of the necessary languages and the desired in-country familiarity with the cultures and terrain," he wrote in his memoir. Failing such a commitment, his credo was as cautious as it had been since before the Bay of Pigs. "Do not intervene on the ground unless prepared to make an all-out effort. And do not count on a secret intelligence agency being able to pull political folly away from the blaze."[14]

The United States had never made that commitment in Vietnam, much less Cambodia. Washington's "all-out effort"—resisted by JFK, embraced by LBJ, and extended by Nixon—never broke the communists' will to keep fighting to liberate their country from foreigners. Yet when Nixon and Kissinger expanded the war into Cambodia, repeating all the mistakes Helms warned about, the director endorsed the policy.

"Many found the casting of another nation into the furnace morally abhorrent," wrote Neil Sheehan.[15] Not Helms. He agreed with his friend Stewart Alsop, who wrote in his weekly column for *Newsweek* that the president was guilty of a half measure. Nixon wasn't tough enough, it seems.[16] Sometimes Helms spoke truth to power, but when it came to Cambodia, power was his truth. Nixon appreciated that.

"PUBLIC RELATIONS JOB"

Howard Hunt knew this day was coming. He had imagined it in the opening scene of his 1967 thriller *One of Our Agents Is Missing*, which took place outside the Langley headquarters.[17]

"Peter Ward pushed through the heavy glass double doors, tugged his tweed cap lower on his forehead and turned up the beaver collar of his off-white raincoat. He went down the broad stone steps and followed the walk around to the visitors parking area, gusty wind wetting his face with mist.

"Behind the wheel of his leased Spyder he started the engine and gazed rebelliously at the impersonal façade of the CIA's headquarters building, eyes lifting to an expanse of lighted curtained windows on the seventh floor that marked the domain of Deputy Director Avery Thorne. Peter had come from an hour's conference with Thorne, with results that far from pleased him."

In February 1970, Hunt had just come from an hour's conference with Deputy Director Tom Karamessines, with results that ended his twenty-year career at the Agency.

The problem was Hunt's passion about the Bay of Pigs. Paul Gaynor, chief of the CIA office known as the Security Research Service (SRS), learned from a source in the publishing industry about the circulation of a pseudonymous un-published memoir about the Bay of Pigs operation titled "Give Us This Day," written by one "Edward J. Hamilton," purportedly a longtime Agency employee.[18] "A review of the first few pages of the manuscript clearly show this to be the work of E. Howard Hunt," an aide reported to Gaynor.

As a component of the Office of Security, SRS was responsible for counter-intelligence as it applied to CIA staff employees. It was, in the words of journalist Jim Hougan, "a tabernacle within the inner sanctum." Gaynor was a former brig-adier general in the army with long experience in counterintelligence and inter-rogation. He had managed the BLUEBIRD and ARTICHOKE programs in the early 1950s, which evolved into the notorious MKULTRA mind-control program. He was reputed to maintain a "fag file" of known or suspected homosexuals whom he could bar from government employment. He also coordinated many of the domestic spying activities associated with Operation CHAOS.[19]

Gaynor gave the manuscript to Walter Pforzheimer, curator of the Agency's Historical Intelligence Collection, the man who had uncovered the true name of "David St. John" five years before. Pforzheimer confirmed Hunt's authorship, telling Gaynor that the manuscript was "the most comprehensive story of a CIA operation that has ever been written for publication to my knowledge. . . . It far exceeds in detail anything written on the Bay of Pigs."

Hunt's manuscript was favorable to the Agency. "The villains of the piece," said Pforzheimer, "are certain liberal figures in the Kennedy Administration (Schlesinger, Goodwin and Stevenson) and to some extent the President himself. In his concluding chapter, the author's bitterness is undisguised against those in the Administration and the press who took the opportunity of the Bay of Pigs incident to attack and denigrate CIA."

Hunt recounted returning from Havana in March 1960 with the recommen-dation that "Castro be assassinated before or coincident to the invasion." Such comments, Pforzheimer warned, "would be unfortunate if published, in view of current charges in the press of various CIA 'assassinations.'"[20]

Gaynor was irate. He went straight to Tom Karamessines, who called Hunt in for an explanation. Facing two stern men, Hunt weaseled. He said he knew nothing about such a manuscript, then he admitted he had written it for his own personal interest. Gaynor interrupted. They had information that the manuscript had been reviewed and rejected by two publishers, Gaynor said. A third publisher, Walker & Company, was known to have seen the manuscript in the last two weeks. Hunt finally fell silent. The well of his prevarication had run dry.

Karamessines cited the dangers of publishing such an outspoken manuscript. He didn't need to spell out the details. If a CIA officer published a book saying the Agency had tried to kill Castro, the liberals on Capitol Hill would raise holy hell. The press would sensationalize it. The communists would love it. What was he thinking? Karamessines ordered Hunt to retrieve all copies of the manuscript.[21]

Gaynor wasn't satisfied. He asked his Office of Security colleague, Jim McCord, to investigate how Walker & Company had obtained the manuscript. McCord was a natural choice. He had served as Gaynor's deputy at SRS from 1959 to 1963. They were not social friends, but in the office they had a "close working relationship," Gaynor said. He described McCord as "a quiet religious man, deeply devoted to his family, totally patriotic."[22] McCord did not know Hunt at the time. They would not meet for two years. In the meantime, McCord investigated his future partner in crime for flouting agency rules.[23] And so one Howard Hunt fiasco would beget another.

Hunt counted on Helms. Back in January, the director had given Hunt his blessing to retire as soon as he found another job.[24] Hunt assured Helms that everything was under control. "Paul Gaynor tells me he is retrieving the pirated Ms. copy from Walker & Co,"[25] he wrote in a note on government stationery. Hunt had alienated more than a few colleagues at the Agency. Helms was his trump card, and he played it to good effect.

"Dick Helms came to the rescue in the spring of 1970," the relieved Hunt recalled, "agreeing to allow me to retire early and recommending me to the public relations department of several large companies." In his autobiography, Hunt made no mention of his unauthorized shopping of "Give Us This Day," or Karamessines's dressing down, only the happy ending. "Eventually I was hired by Robert Mullen, former press aide to President Eisenhower," he wrote.[26] The Robert Mullen Company was a global public relations firm that collaborated with the CIA.

Why Helms, a stickler for correct behavior, indulged the wayward Hunt again and again is a mystery of male bonding. Perhaps the attraction of opposites was felt: the buttoned-up Helms taking vicarious pleasure in the antics of his brash buddy. Maybe, like Castro and Cubela at the onset of the Cuban revolution, they shared "the bond of the beginning." They had gone to war as young men, and that would also count for something between them. In any case, for Helms, a man of tidy arrangements, the Mullen Company position was practical. Hunt might still be useful, albeit in a new capacity.

To a biographer, Helms murmured he had only seen Hunt "infrequently" in the 1960s, which hardly did justice to Helms's indulgence of Dorothy's spying or his promotion of the Peter Ward books or the wedding gifts from Howard. When an incredulous congressman asked in 1973 if Helms had really written a job recommendation for Hunt, by then a convicted burglar, Helms claimed he could not recall doing so. He knew the man mostly from his file, he implied. "There was nothing about his record which would stop me from saying 'Here is a man who writes very well,' because he does write very well," Helms explained. "This was a public relations job."[27]

That was sort of true, but not very. The position that Helms arranged for Hunt was, in fact, a cover for secret activities. The Mullen Company had served the Agency since 1963 when it helped set up the Committee for a Free Cuba, the CIA's response to the Fair Play for Cuba Committee. When Robert Bennett, son of Utah senator Wallace Bennett, bought the company in 1971, he was introduced to the firm's case officer, Martin Lukoskie. The Mullen Company was especially useful to the Agency because it handled Washington business for the Hughes Tool Company, a CIA contractor controlled by Howard Hughes, one of the wealthiest men in the world.

Helms needed to keep current on the troublesome Bob Maheu, the spook with solid gold cuff links, who now held a senior position in the Hughes organization. The Agency "was considering utilizing the Mullen Hughes relationship for a matter related to a cover arrangement in South America and to gather information on Robert Maheu" said one Agency memo.[28] So the Mullen Company where Hunt now worked served Helms in two sensitive matters: Bob Maheu and the Hughes organization.

Hunt's perch at the Mullen Company was arranged by Francis O'Malley of the Central Cover Staff, which maintained the false identities of Agency operatives. To congressional investigators O'Malley explained that he maintained contact with Hunt because he became "instrumental in discussing several aspects of the cover operations" at the firm. Hunt, in turn, relied on O'Malley for assistance as needed: finding a retired CIA secretary, locating an experienced lockpick, and selecting a security firm that could do electronic countermeasures to detect wiretapping.

Hunt still had a collaborative relationship with the Agency after he retired, not that he was entirely trusted. "Mr. Hunt was in the habit of making glib comments which were not necessarily accurate," O'Malley said. He added, he "was sure Mr. Hunt had lied to him on a number of occasions."[29]

All in all, the hapless spy novelist had moved on in life rather smartly. On the day Nixon announced the Cambodia "incursion," Hunt sat for his exit interview at the Agency. He disclosed that his new job might involve travel to the Mullen Company offices in London and Tokyo. He checked in with Tom Karamessines, who told him to "stay in touch."[30] He did just that.

To formalize the Agency's new relationship with Hunt, the Central Cover Staff needed to grant him a security clearance. The staff's chief wrote a memo to Karamessines saying that the Office of Security "believes you have an interest in Mr. Hunt and is unwilling to grant a clearance to CCS without being assured you do not have an overriding interest or objection."

Karamessines, of course, had an interest in Hunt. He was his agent, and more to the point, a friend of the director's, a trusted and daring operative whose action orientation more than compensated for his sometimes questionable judgment. Hunt received the clearance.[31]

A public relations job indeed. Hunt was retired from the CIA yet "aware of two cover placements" at the Mullen Company."[32] He had no formal connection with the Agency but remained in contact with Karamessines, who had been his case officer since 1963. Hunt didn't have formal operational duties for the DDP, but he was available for sensitive, deniable undercover missions. Like his alter ego Peter Ward, Howard Hunt had become an odd job man for the boss he admired, the director who was gaining favor in Richard Nixon's White House.[33]

WINK

The collaboration of Richard Nixon and Richard Helms deepened in the summer of 1970 as the agile director accommodated himself to the president's vision of a stepped-up campaign against domestic radicals.

Nixon was enraged, baffled, confounded, and mystified by what his country had become. The young men with long hair, the Negroes with their Afros, the girls without bras, the casual use of drugs, the noisy rock music. *Laugh-In* was one thing. He had nothing against young people, but this so-called counterculture was a menace. The American people had chosen him because he was like them. Responsible. Hard-working. God-fearing (not that Nixon often saw the inside of a church). He depicted himself working for the "Silent Majority" against the noisy minority, the insolent longhairs, the pusillanimous liberals, the ungrateful blacks, and, by God, he would prevail.

The threat was real. "Terrorists caused no fewer than 174 major bombing and bombing attempts on campus in the school year 1969–70," Nixon wrote in his memoir. ". . . With as many as a thousand estimated members, the Weather Underground [the new non-sexist name of the Weathermen] separated into secret floating commando type units. As with the Black Panthers, there was no way of knowing where or how they were going to strike."[34]

"Now that this season of mindless terror has fortunately passed," Nixon went on, "it is difficult—perhaps impossible—to convey a sense of the pressures that were influencing my actions and reactions during this period. I turned for assistance in my effort to the various intelligence agencies. Working together, they developed a program to counter revolutionary violence."[35]

The program, drawn up by Tom Huston, authorized the intelligence agencies to expand domestic surveillance with increased powers of wiretapping, burglary, and use of informants. The Huston Plan, as it became known, was a Nixonian vision that went momentarily into effect in the summer of 1970 and then vanished, though not for lack of support from Helms.

Huston's plan created a new interagency Intelligence Evaluation Committee, based in the White House. Representatives of the FBI and the national security agencies would be granted a host of new powers to investigate, surveil, and harass the antiwar and black nationalist movements, reporting to the president's staff every week or two. Nixon would finally have the apparatus he wanted in order to put down the leftist threat. Helms had no objection, as long as certain CIA equities were respected.

In June, Nixon seized the moment. He summoned Helms, Hoover, Admiral Noel Gayler, director of the National Security Agency, and General Donald Bennett, director of the Defense Intelligence Agency, to a meeting in the White House. It was no routine get-together. Shocked by the convulsion that followed the invasion of Cambodia, the president felt he had to fight back against the enemies of the state. In his diary, Haldeman called it a "historic meeting," one "generated by [the president's] complete dissatisfaction with the results of intelligence gathering."[36]

In the Oval Office, Nixon and Hoover sat side by side in front of the fireplace under Gilbert Stuart's portrait of George Washington, with the FBI director glaring at the president. Helms sat attentively to the president's left, opposite Admiral Gayler. Nixon, with typical awkward indirection, barely spoke of the protests and bombings that animated his action. He did mention meeting the president of Venezuela and complained of black militants who exported revolution to the Caribbean. He suddenly turned to Hoover and asked if he had any problems with Huston's plan.

Hoover said no, but his body language spoke otherwise. As always, the FBI director was tightly packed into a blue three-piece suit. Helms had cultivated him over the years, requesting meetings, sending memos, flattering relentlessly, all with indifferent success. Hoover did not defy Nixon, even though he had no intention of going along with this scheme. Nixon asked Helms the same question. Any problems? Helms said no.

Nixon told the security chiefs that Hoover would head the new Intelligence Evaluation Committee with deputy FBI director William C. Sullivan, chief of the Internal Security Division, in charge of day-to-day operations. Because Sullivan was close to counterintelligence chief Angleton, he was acceptable to Helms.[37] Angleton served as the CIA's representative to the working group. Dick Ober, chief of the CHAOS operation, sat in as an observer at the first meeting. The Agency's interests were protected, and the president's purposes served. "The heart of the matter," said Helms, was to "get the FBI to do what it was not doing."[38]

Key to the plan was Nixon's intention to formally ease existing controls on the government's right to engage in wiretapping, burglary, and surveillance in national security matters. In late June, men gathered at Hoover's office for a final review of Huston's recommendations. The CIA's contribution was a paper titled "Definition of Internal Security Threat-Foreign," which addressed only the slight foreign connections of the antiwar movement.[39]

Hoover then used the meeting to teach his bureaucratic rivals a lesson. The FBI director read the text of Huston's plan aloud, adding a dissenting footnote to each major point, stating the FBI's reservations about the proposed change. Did the other directors have any objections? Helms, Gayler, and Bennett could not object. This was what the president wanted. They endorsed the plan with Hoover's footnotes. It was now on paper. The CIA, NSA, and DIA favored the expansion of surveillance of Americans. The FBI did not. Helms recognized a bureaucratic master at work. He leaned back in his chair and winked at Huston, as if to say, *If you think you are going to outmaneuver J. Edgar, think again.*[40]

On paper, the Huston Plan had unanimous approval. Huston gave Haldeman the intelligence chiefs' recommendation that the president remove all restraints on methods of intelligence collection. Huston prepared a directive for Nixon's signature that formally ordered the termination of restrictions on mail opening and break-ins (termed "black-bag jobs") to address perceived national security threats. The order also loosened constraints on electronic surveillance and sanctioned increased intelligence gathering on college campuses.[41]

Helms went along to get along. It was Mitchell and Hoover who objected.

Mitchell hadn't even been told about the centralization of intelligence in the White House until Huston's draft directive arrived on the president's desk in late July. Mitchell was disturbed at the scope of the plans. Looking ahead to 1972, Mitchell planned to run Nixon's reelection campaign. Leaks from inside the bureaucracy had bedeviled the White House from the first days of his administration. What if this domestic spying operation leaked before the election? Mitchell advised the president not to sign. Without Nixon's signature, Hoover refused to participate.

The Huston Plan, in existence for five days, expired on the spot. There was no agreement and no Intelligence Evaluation Committee.[42]

"The president was strongly in favor of it," Helms told journalist James Rosen. "He was constantly stating that the FBI was not giving sufficient support to these matters, and that this was something that ought to be done. But once Mitchell got to him, that was pretty much the end of it," he said. Helms's tone implied *Easy come, easy go*.[43]

Huston Plan or no, the Nixon administration carried out a robust spy program aimed at American dissidents, complete with coordinating committees to fine-tune the surveillance. How ongoing Agency practice differed from the abandoned Huston Plan is not easy to discern in hindsight. Helms and the other Agency chiefs who signed on to Huston's plan didn't think they needed new powers. What they required was a formal justification for what they already wanted to do.

None of the FBI or CIA surveillance programs were curtailed when the Huston Plan fell apart. Indeed, the FBI, even with Hoover's apparent opposition, loosened restrictions on recruiting informants, widened the scope of watch lists to catch radical fugitives, and reinstituted a mail-opening program. At the CIA, the demise of the Huston Plan did not affect Operation CHAOS, which continued full bore. As Huston put it, "All these things that were in the plan were all on every intelligence agencies' [sic] desirable list, you know, and had been for a very long time."[44]

As evidenced by his wink, Helms was just as amused as he was disappointed by Hoover's objections. He shared Nixon's desire to act aggressively, but, like Hoover, he didn't care to put such a policy in writing.[45] When it came to the legality and constitutionality of the Huston Plan, Helms did not exhibit the civil liberty sensitivities of Hoover and Mitchell, reactionaries not known for their constitutional nuance.

Nixon noticed. When the president had a nasty assignment that fall, he summoned the director to the Oval Office.

14

SLEDGEHAMMER

At seven thirty in the morning of October 22, 1970, the chauffeur for General René Schneider, commander in chief of the armed forces of Chile, pulled up outside the general's home in Santiago. Schneider was a career military officer, schooled in the Prussian tradition that émigrés from Germany had brought to the coastal South American country in the nineteenth century. Schneider slipped into the back seat of the four-door Mercedes-Benz, briefcase at his side, and the car headed to his office at the Ministry of National Defense.

Schneider was an apolitical officer, faithful to Chile's tradition of civilian control of the armed forces, which had blessed the country with more than a century of democratic rule and peaceful transfers of power. A cultured man, he listened to Beethoven and appreciated Picasso. His library held volumes by Shakespeare and Gabriel García Márquez.[1] He had a wife, two sons, a daughter, and little reason to suspect the CIA had marked him for death.

Schneider was a target precisely because he wasn't political. Salvador Allende, running as a socialist parliamentarian, had narrowly defeated conservative Jorge Alessandri and Christian Democrat Radomiro Tomic in the presidential election held six weeks earlier. Allende's leftist agenda of nationalizing industries, wealth distribution, and support for socialism internationally alarmed the military, businessmen, and conservative society. But he had won the election legitimately and enjoyed support among the middle class and the poor, as well as in labor unions and universities. In the summer of 1970, Schneider gave an interview in which he said the Chilean armed forces had no role to play other than to allow a peaceful transfer of power.[2] Because Allende had not won a majority of the vote, the election had to be decided by the Congress on October 24. The Congress traditionally voted to confirm the candidate with the most votes, in this case Allende.

That Schneider refused to intervene was an intolerable affront to Nixon's and Kissinger's pride. In a brief meeting on the afternoon of September 15, they ordered Helms to come up with a solution to their problem in Chile.[3] Thirty-seven days later, Helms delivered.

As Schneider's chauffeur made his way down the Boulevard Martín de Zamora in the morning traffic, a blue Dodge Dart, a white Ford Falcon, and a Willys Jeep pulled up alongside the car. The jeep rammed Schneider's car, forcing it to stop. A young man named Jaime Melgoza Garay jumped out of one of the cars with a Colt pistol in his hand. Another man ran up to the Mercedes-Benz wielding a sledgehammer and smashed the rear left window.

Schneider was pulling his 6.35-caliber Star pistol but hadn't managed to fire when he was wounded. As the family's lawyer later told a Santiago courtroom with clinical precision, "Melgoza's shot, fired from the left side with his Colt 45 pistol, . . . fractures the metacarpal and the far anterior end of the right forearm, damaging the general's right shoulder." Two more men then ran up behind the Mercedes-Benz, firing into the back window.

The chauffeur swerved around the attackers and raced to the military hospital, occasionally looking back at his wounded passenger. He saw Schneider, stretched out "with blood on his forehead and his hand . . . the General tried to get himself upright against the back of the front seat, but since he was struggling, I saw him lie back down across the top of the briefcase."[4]

Schneider died three days later.

MAINTAINING GOODWILL

No one in the Nixon White House was under any illusion that Chile was strategically important to the United States, least of all Helms. All CIA estimates on Chile agreed it had little significance, economically or militarily. The country was "a dagger pointed at the heart of Antarctica," joked the cynical Kissinger.

Chile mattered as Cold War theater. While Allende embraced Cuba as an ally, he never modeled his Popular Unity movement on the Cuban revolution and did not seek to transform Chile into a Cuba-style one-party state. No matter. Allende's success, the White House feared, would embolden leftists in Chile's neighbors, Peru, Uruguay, and Argentina.

Nixon and Kissinger hadn't been paying attention, Helms said. He had told the 303 Committee back in April 1969 that if they wanted to head off a leftist victory in 1970, they had better act. "They didn't want to accept responsibility themselves for not having gotten on the thing properly," he carped.[5]

Helms had been hearing a lot about Chile. In May, his former boss John McCone, now a member of the board of directors of ITT, a multinational conglomerate with extensive holdings in Chile, approached Helms privately. He wanted to discuss a program to support candidate Jorge Alessandri, whose conservative policies would benefit the company's bottom line.[6] In June, Kissinger called for more funding of Allende's opponents, saying, "I don't see why we need to stand by and watch a country go Communist due to the irresponsibility of its own people."[7] The CIA dispensed money, political commentary, favorable news stories, even anti-Allende graffiti.[8] There were direct payments to Agustín Edwards, publisher of the *El Mecrurio* newspaper, who met with Helms on September 15. One "key to a coup," he told Helms, "would involve neutralizing Schneider so other Army officers could take action."[9]

Nixon called Helms to his office that day with Kissinger and Mitchell sitting in. Helms later said Nixon acted at the behest of a friend. In an oral history, Helms recalled Nixon saying, "Don Kendall has been in touch with me, referring to his long-time friend, the chief executive of PepsiCo. Nixon told Mitchell, 'Kendall was my first client when I set up to practice law in New York. He is an awful nice fellow, and I think we ought to do anything for him we can. He is very interested in this Chile matter and business down there. . . . We ought to really try to help.'"[10]

Since Chile's political parties were reconciled to Allende's victory, the CIA sought to create a "coup climate" with a package of economic, political, and psychological warfare, dubbed Track II.[11] This secret war would be waged without knowledge of the State Department. Helms brought in Dave Phillips, his top operations officer in the Western Hemisphere Division, to come up with a plan to thwart Allende's victory. Nixon and Kissinger said ten million dollars was no object.

"I installed myself in [a] cubicle from which I would direct the small task force,"[12] Phillips recalled. He said he spent twenty hours a day advancing a scheme to do something, anything, to keep Allende from taking office. At night, Phillips slept on the couch in the office. By day Karamessines shuttled to the White House with updates.[13] The plan was to remove General Schneider to prevent Allende from taking office.

But how? Phillips summoned Tony Sforza, the undercover operative from the Miami station who had assisted in the recruitment of Rolando Cubela. As documented in personal papers he gave to his family before his death in 1985, Sforza was an "outside" agent, meaning he didn't operate under official cover like a CIA officer working out of an embassy.[14] Posing as a gambler named Frank Stevens, he held a key position in the Agency's Western Hemisphere Division. He ran a network of 150 Cuban informants known as the AMOTS from 1961 to 1967. Originally, the AMOTS were set up to comprise a new intelligence agency in a pro-American government after Castro was overthrown.[15] As that possibility faded, Sforza said, the AMOTS "monitored exile activities by penetrating groups or collecting information from friends of group members."[16]

Sforza had played a leading role in the 1964 defection of Juana Castro, Fidel's sister, a propaganda coup that boosted his standing in the Agency. In a memo about his CIA career, Sforza wrote that Helms had given him a medal and a pay raise for his work in Cuba. He felt "deeply honored" by Helms's generosity.[17]

Sforza had been entrusted with lethal missions. In May 1967, he was sent to Bolivia, where he oversaw the CIA's manhunt for Che Guevara. He translated Guevara's diaries for the Agency and collated photographs of him and his guerrilla band. When Guevara was executed, Sforza sent the photos to Langley, another intelligence coup. Three years later, he was summoned by Helms's men.

"I went to Washington and spoke with Mr. Thomas Karamessines and Mr. Phillips," Sforza later told Senate investigators in a secret testimony. "I was given a file to read on the Chilean situation. . . . My only instructions were concerning contact with Agency personnel in Chile," a claim that his interrogators frankly disbelieved.[18] Surely, Tony Sforza had a lethal mission.

From his Washington hotel room, Sforza wrote to his wife in October 1970, stressing he could not say anything about his new assignment except that it "sounds like it might be 'very interesting.'"[19] He then traveled to Santiago, where he met with station chief Henry Heckscher, the man who ran the last phase of the AM-LASH operation for Helms. Sforza spent a week meeting his Chilean contacts.[20] The CIA men approached Brigadier General Roberto Viaux, an ultra-rightist military man who had been cashiered for trying to overthrow pro-American president Eduardo Frei in 1969. Heckscher told Langley Viaux was "the only military leader of national stature [who] appears committed to denying Allende the presidency by force."[21]

In his Senate testimony, Sforza denied meeting Viaux, but he said his Chilean contact asked "about weapons, tear gas and insurance policies" for his men, which is exactly what Viaux asked other CIA officers for. Sforza's controllers in Langley countered with an offer of unlimited funds to "bribe arsenal commanders to provide arms."[22]

Nixon didn't know all the details of Track II but his appreciation of Helms was growing. Before leaving on an overseas trip, the president invited the CIA director to take advantage of his presidential perks. Helms replied a week later with a little note.

"My dear Mr. President: It was most thoughtful of you to offer me the use of Camp David and the [presidential yacht] SEQUOIA during your absence. Circumstances did not work out so that this could be done, but perhaps it will be possible to have an opportunity some other time. . . . Respectfully, Dick."[23]

Covert action could not wait. The next day Helms ordered the Santiago station to "sponsor a military move" using "all available assets and stratagems to create a coup climate." He stressed "Every hour counts, all other considerations secondary." Bill Broe, chief of the Western Hemisphere Division, recalled Helms took a greater interest in Track II than any other operation at the time.[24]

Kissinger later said that as he and Nixon learned more of the details, the effort was abandoned. "Nixon was briefed at various times on Track II by Tom Karamessines, head of CIA covert operations, always pessimistically," Kissinger wrote in his memoirs. "All CIA reports to [Alexander] Haig and me were similarly negative. The effort was terminated by me on October 15."[25]

Kissinger did nothing of a sort, as the declassified records makes clear. Karamessines testified that when he told Kissinger the chances of success were less than one in twenty, Kissinger told him to discourage Viaux from premature action, not to stand down.

Helms certainly didn't stand down. "It is firm and continuing policy that Allende be overthrown by a coup," he told the Santiago station. "We are to continue to generate maximum pressure toward this end, utilizing every appropriate resource. . . . There is great and continuing interest in the activities of [the Chilean conspirators] and we wish them optimum good fortune."[26]

Sforza admitted to the investigators that he met his Chilean contact "five or six times" to discuss plans for a coup and the kidnapping of General Schneider. General Camilo Valenzuela, chief of the Santiago military district, proposed kidnapping Schneider, flying him out of the country, blaming the left, and using the pretext of searching for Schneider to raid communist-controlled neighborhoods as the first stage of the coup. Sforza reported that Viaux "expects some 10,000 casualties in Santiago area before leftist mobs are put down."[27]

Sforza said that his superiors at the CIA station instructed him to say that they recommended against the kidnapping. When told his Chilean contacts were going ahead anyway, Sforza said he was told by the Agency to leave the country.[28]

Karamessines briefed Kissinger on the plan.[29] Valenzuela asked for tear gas grenades, machine guns, and ammunition, along with $50,000 for a team of un-identified abductors. The CIA supplied the money and arranged for the U.S. military attaché to deliver the weapons to a Chilean officer in Santiago at two a.m., October 22.[30]

"But before this group could act," Helms explained in his memoir, "a fragment of General Viaux's original band of golpistas attempted to kidnap General Schneider."[31] Helms wanted to tell an exculpatory story to history, but no kidnapping was attempted, as he surely knew. He laid the blame on Valenzuela, not Viaux. However, the difference between General Viaux's henchmen and General Valenzuela's was, in the words of Helms's official biographers, "narrowly framed." The Viaux men who assaulted Schneider had participated in two earlier "kidnap" attempts in previous days that were organized by General Valenzuela. There may have been two groups, but it was all one effort, funded and encouraged by the CIA.

In a post-action memo to the Santiago station, division chief Dave Phillips portrayed Schneider's assassination as a positive development. He spoke for his boss Helms, telling subordinates that "a maximum effort has been achieved and now only Chileans themselves can manage a successful coup. The Chileans have been guided to a point where a military solution is at least an option to them."[32]

That was wishful thinking. Allende's victory was ratified by the Chilean Congress, and Allende took office. Schneider's funeral was attended by tens of thousands of people. In a graveside ceremony, Defense Minister Sergio Ossa said, "He gave his life as a martyr to democracy and to his devotion to the institutions of his country."[33]

The CIA hastened to generate postmortem reports to obfuscate Track II. One memo claimed implausibly that Schneider's death was "totally unplanned and un-foreseen," which was totally uninformed. In fact bloodshed was not unexpected nor unrewarded. A member of Viaux's gang who avoided capture after the ambush of General Schneider contacted the Agency a few weeks later. "In an effort to keep previous contact secret, maintain the good will of the group, and for humanitarian reasons," a CIA memo reported, "$35,000 was passed."[34]

Such was the Dick Helms that friends and admirers did not care to think about too closely, the gentlemanly planner of assassinations who expressed his goodwill to the men who shot Schneider in the back because the general respected civilian rule. Nixon and Helms cast themselves as tough-minded defenders of the Free World, and they killed a defender of democracy to prove it.

And it still wasn't enough. In the increasingly paranoid White House, Haig, Kissinger's deputy, thought "left-wing" officials at CIA had undermined the president's policy of blocking Allende.[35] At year's end, former director John McCone paid a visit to the Langley headquarters. He told one of Helms's aides that he had spoken to Kissinger, who said, "Everybody's down on Helms for failing to take drastic action to stop Allende."[36]

15

BLACKMAIL

Flattery worked. Helms was diligent, attentive to Nixon's perennially wounded pride. When the president did a nationally televised interview in January 1971 with four network correspondents, Helms tuned in. Nixon discussed the war, the economy, and student unrest. The group discussion format played to his strengths: his analytical rigor, his mastery of detail, and his command of policy. Helms responded with a note in his neat cursive.

"My dear Mr. President, Without I hope being thought presumptuous, may I say how effective I found your appearance on television last evening. You were persuasive and constructive, all in a 'real world' context, and it came over as a most impressive performance in the best Presidential tradition. It gave even me a big lift. . . ."[1]

Nixon was grateful but daunted. The problems his administration confronted in early 1971, he later recalled, "were so overwhelming and so apparently impervious to anything we could do that might change them that it seemed possible I might not even be nominated for re-election in 1972." Unemployment hit 6 percent, the highest in a decade. The dollar hit a record low.[2] Expanding the war into Cambodia had not relieved pressure on the South Vietnamese government. It had merely opened another battlefront for the communists. In the Senate, leading Republicans, men whom he had helped over the years—Chuck Percy in Illinois and Hugh Scott in Pennsylvania—were rebelling against the war that everyone hated. Nixon's claim that he was "winding down" the conflict was losing credibility, even if the death toll was less appalling. Two hundred fifty-nine men died in Vietnam that month. They came from every state in the union except for Maine and Vermont. Two hundred twenty-three were white, twenty-six were black. There were four homicides and three suicides.[3]

While Nixon brooded, Helms waltzed. He relished his job, ran laps in the basement of the CIA headquarters, played a moderately competent set of tennis on the weekends, and got to bed early. Helms loved ballroom dancing. He and Cynthia attended the parties of the Waltz Group, a network of like-minded couples in government, law, and the press. Once a month they put aside the business of power in favor of Brahms.[4]

Tom Hughes, the director of Intelligence and Research at the State Department, and his wife, Jane, were also regulars at the events held at the Sulgrave Club in Dupont Circle. The mood was gay, the banter flowed, and Helms enjoyed himself, Hughes recalled in an interview. "He was an excellent dancer and an avid gossip, always in control. I'd look over and there would be Helms rolling his eyes because Cord Meyer was drunk again."[5]

Other evenings, Dick and Cynthia read spy novels aloud to each other. Helms didn't care for the fictions of John le Carré, the nom de plume of David Cornwell, a former MI6 man whose dour tales of the Circus, a fictional version of the British service, did not glamorize the Cold War. Le Carré's bestseller *The Spy Who Came in from the Cold* had been made into a movie with Richard Burton, and never had Helms's profession looked less heroic. "He found Le Carré too dark and cynical," Cynthia said.[6]

Helms got his fill of the dark and cynical on page B7 of the *Washington Post* on January 18, 1971, where syndicated columnist Jack Anderson, successor to the retired Drew Pearson, published a nasty and all-too-accurate column headlined "6 Attempts to Kill Castro Laid to CIA."[7]

The shadow of JFK's assassination fell on Dick Helms once again.

MAHEU'S RETURN

"Locked in the darkest recesses of the Central Intelligence Agency is the story of six assassination attempts against Cuba's Fidel Castro," Anderson's column began. The story was true, as Helms knew better than anyone. Anderson was referring to Inspector General John Earman's top-secret report of May 1967, which recounted the Mafia and AMLASH plots in dispassionate detail. Helms's predecessor John

McCone, now retired and serving on corporate boards, was quoted as saying he had objected to the plots.

Then came the nasty but true part.

"To set up the Castro assassination, the CIA enlisted Robert Maheu, a former FBI agent with shadowy contracts who had handled other underworld assignments for the CIA out of his Washington public relations office," Anderson wrote. "He later moved to Las Vegas to head up billionaire Howard Hughes' Nevada operations."

Anderson was describing the same events Drew Pearson reported in March 1967 but with more detail. Helms knew the story could have only come from Maheu himself.

"Maheu recruited John Rosselli, a ruggedly handsome gambler with contacts in both the American and Cuban underworlds to arrange the assassination," Anderson went on. "The CIA assigned two of its most trusted operatives William Harvey and James (Big Jim) O'Connell to the hush-hush murder mission."

Helms was not a man prone to self-deception. With its naming of names, Maheu was sending a blunt message to both the White House and the CIA. He was reminding the president of their collaboration in throttling Aristotle Onassis's monopoly on Middle East oil shipments back in 1954. He was warning Helms that he could spill secrets on the Castro plots that would raise JFK questions.

Déjà vu blackmail. Maheu had squeezed RFK and the CIA men in 1962, forcing the Justice Department to drop the charges of snooping on mobster Sam Giancana's girlfriend. In 1967, he and Rosselli had floated the story of the Mafia plots to Drew Pearson, via his attorney Edward Morgan, to fend off the Long Committee. Now Rosselli was under grand jury investigation for running a rigged high-stakes gambling casino at the swank Friars Club in Los Angeles. If convicted he faced deportation to Italy, where he was born but had never lived. Maheu's lawyer called his CIA contacts to say that Rosselli's lawyer was putting out the word that unless someone interceded on his behalf Rosselli was going to make a "complete expose" of his activities with the CIA.[8]

That did the trick. Maheu came to Washington for a meeting at the Justice Department, which he later recounted to researcher Michael Ewing.[9] Maheu explained to Attorney General Mitchell, whom he called his "close friend," that he had a problem with a subpoena. If compelled to testify, he would talk about the Castro plots, Maheu emphasized. "There [is] a CIA report that can verify this," he said, which was true. Maheu was referring to the 1967 inspector general's report.

By insinuating that the Mafia plots might have led to JFK's assassination, Maheu increased the pressure on all concerned. The JFK story was back in the news. The *New York Times* reported that retired Dallas police chief Jesse Curry had just published a book saying he did not believe the Warren Commission report and called for a new investigation.

And what was the JFK story? Maheu told Mitchell the same story he told Anderson: the Mafia bosses had sent a team to Cuba to kill Castro. The team had been captured, and Castro retaliated with Oswald. There was a core of fact—the CIA had enlisted the mob bosses to kill the revolutionary they detested. The rest was window dressing. There was no evidence—no documents or testimony—that Castro "turned around" a CIA assassination plot. But the core of the story was enough. By the end, Mitchell was shaking in amazement. He offered Maheu a deal. Instead of going before the grand jury, he would be interviewed by Justice Department officials. Maheu did not need to talk about his assistance to the Agency. "I assured them, I intended to keep my word and maintain the secrecy of the mission," Maheu said.[10]

Helms apparently blessed the deal. A month later, an unnamed Agency official met with the commissioner of the Immigration and Naturalization Service. "The purpose of this effort was to intercede . . . on behalf of Mr. Rosselli in the action being initiated for deportation," read one memo. "It was determined that this Agency would be kept informed of the progress of the action against Mr. Rosselli in an effort to forestall public disclosure of his association with the United States government." In short, Maheu and Rosselli had blackmailed the CIA once again.

It was a fallen world in which Dick Helms lived. Later that month, he spoke at a private family memorial for Frank Wisner at CIA headquarters on the fifth anniversary of his death. Cynthia was best friends with Frank's widow, Polly. Only friends and family were invited. The director recalled Wisner's foundational role in building the American clandestine service. Wisner's conception of the Free World—the empire of American influence in righteous struggle against communism—had defined the Agency's mission. Helms reflected too on the crushing pressures of a life in secret intelligence. He spoke of Wisner's "night of dark intent" when he killed himself. This disparity between Wisner's Free World fervor and the despair that drove him to pick up his shotgun chastened Helms.

"He sought perfection," Helms lamented, "which we all must acknowledge, is yet to be attained by any wise man in the world of ambiguity and imperfection."[11]

"WITH YOU ALL THE WAY"

The world of ambiguity and imperfection often made Dick Nixon uncomfortable. He yearned for clarity, control, knowledge. His file card memory wanted data, dates, transcripts. He wanted to know what had happened, who said what, and why. In February 1971, he ordered recording devices placed in the White House, just as John Kennedy had.[12]

The first conversation captured between Nixon and Helms was a fight. It came halfway through a dismal meeting on February 27, 1971, about Laos, where South Vietnamese forces faced a powerful communist offensive. Admiral Tom Moorer, chairman of the Joint Chiefs, gave the battlefield statistics in a soft Virginia drawl. "They reported ten tanks destroyed, one by artillery, nine by tank fighting arms."

Nixon broke in with a blunt challenge to Helms.

"One point, Dick, that concerns me is our intelligence people are saying our intelligence is inefficient, inadequate, bad," Nixon spat, "and that's the reason we're running into more resistance that was expected."

"Mr. President," Helms perked up. "This is precisely what we expected."

Nixon interrupted him by reading from a *New York Daily News* story about the fighting.

"Quote. 'A high official said.'"

Helms was still talking and Nixon repeated himself louder.

". . . a high official said . . ."

"What that high official doesn't know," Helms barked back, ". . . before the operation kicked off, we identified all those units."

The president and the director were shouting at each other.

"What are you talking about?" Helms said.

They talked over each other until Helms finally gave up. The room fell quiet.

"Find the high official who said . . ." Nixon said, almost to himself.

Was Nixon implying Helms was the high official quoted in the article? He almost certainly wasn't. Helms didn't talk to the tabloids. Nixon was just in a bad mood because his invasion of Laos was sputtering. Easier to blame the CIA than acknowledge the enemy's strength.

"All right, go ahead," the president said morosely. "That's about it."

Admiral Moorer resumed the dismal briefing.

A week later, Helms was back in the Oval Office for another meeting of the war cabinet. Entering the room, he wasted no time quoting one of Nixon's most vociferous defenders on the editorial pages of the *Washington Post*. "I was talking to our friend Joe Alsop," he blurted, "and he understands this . . ."

Helms wanted to show his support. Nixon needed an audience.

"The mood of the country at the moment is negative and it will continue to be for the next couple of weeks because of television," Nixon said. "Television has created doubts. The network news coverage of the offensive had been negative. They show this horrible killing, they show the helicopter people. . . . They show the South Vietnamese getting killed. And the people get the idea that the United States is taking a hell of a licking. And that's why we're gonna win."

The logic was loose, but the conviction was not. As always, Nixon believed sheer willpower could turn things around.

"This country doesn't lahk to lose," drawled Moorer. "This country doesn't lahk to lose. We have got to win this."

"And I just feel so strongly now that's why we popped them here," Nixon yelped. "We popped them here and the same thing was true in Cambodia last year . . ."

Helms came to the aid of his beleaguered commander in chief.

"I have no personal reservations about any of these decisions, Mr. President," he declared. "I'm with you all the way. These are my profound convictions. I think that the U.S., if we stick our tails between our legs and come slinking out of Vietnam would effectively, as you say, finish us as a world power."

Nixon, heartened, wanted more wisdom from his counselor.

"What about Cuba?" he asked. "My conviction is very strong. . . . We cannot relent in our policy toward Cuba. . . . They're still of course bent on revolution. . . . If we threw in the towel with Cubans, the effect in Latin America could be massive, in encouraging Communists."

"Do you, from the intelligence and everything else, think we should hold the course on Cuba?" Nixon pressed. "Or should we start being nice to Castro?"

"Sir, I testified about a year ago on this question," Helms replied, "and I gave you the answer then. I was opposed to the idea of relenting on Cuba. I'm just as opposed today and in fact even more so. I think what's happened in Chile makes it even more advisable to keep a tough line on Cuba."

What's happened in Chile. The failure to prevent a leftist victory weighed on both of them. The assassination of General Schneider had accomplished nothing. For Helms that meant it was no time to let up on Cuba.

"What I'm afraid is a wave in Latin America anyway is going to crash on the beach a lot faster," he explained. He anticipated a wave of popular support for the left in Latin America, driven by global opposition to the war in Vietnam. "It's a lot easier for this country to handle Cuba the way we handle her now, than to start these little pacifying moves which are really cosmetic and just make it difficult to face the problem."

"'Do this, or that, or the other thing with the damn Cubans?'" Nixon snarled. "To hell with them."[13]

Just like that, Helms was back in Nixon's good graces.

EDUARDO

Howard Hunt, in linen suit and wraparound sunglasses, puffed his usual pipe at the monument to the fallen solders of the Bay of Pigs on Southwest 8th Street in Miami's Little Havana. He and Dorothy loitered as a crowd gathered. It was the tenth anniversary of the failed invasion, an emotionally potent occasion for Hunt to reunite with some old friends.

Hunt had stuck a note in the mailbox of Macho Barker, his deputy on Operation Zapata, whom he hadn't seen in years. He said he wanted to meet him and Musculito too. Musculito was the nickname of muscular Rolando Martínez, the veteran boat captain who had run many a mission for the Agency.

"Eduardo was a name that all of us who had participated in the Bay of Pigs knew well," said Martínez in an oral history. "Eduardo had been the maximum representative of the Kennedy administration to our people in Miami. He occupied a special place in our hearts. . . . He blamed the Kennedy administration for not supporting us on the beaches of the Bay of Pigs. So, when Barker told me that Eduardo was coming to town and that he wanted to meet me, that was like a hope for me."[14]

After abrazos all around, the three men and Dorothy went out to eat. Hunt told his Cuban friends how bad he still felt about the Bay of Pigs, avowing "the whole thing is not over yet."[15]

"He made us believe if we would help, the influence that he might have, later on, will be of benefit for our fight against Castro," Martínez said. He was certain Hunt was talking about Agency-approved business.

"We were going to work in national security because they had formed an organization that was between the CIA and the FBI," he said. "He convinced us. He selected our names for clearance, and, later on, he came and said, 'You have the clearance.' . . . Where am I going to suppose he is finding out about us? With the CIA."[16]

Hunt insisted his misadventures in political burglary began when he went to work for the Nixon White House in July 1971. He was responding, he said, to the publication of the Pentagon Papers and the revelation that former Defense Department analyst Daniel Ellsberg was the source.

Rolando Martínez and Bernard Barker said otherwise. They said Hunt was looking for "national security" operatives ten weeks before he went to work at the White House, which was ten weeks before Daniel Ellsberg became a household name. Hunt wasn't working for the White House at that time. He was working for the Mullen Company with a security clearance from Tom Karamessines for an undisclosed project.[17]

"I CAN ASSURE YOU"

As Hunt recruited help in Miami for national security work, Helms pressed for authority in Washington to conduct more aggressive operations against the radical antiwar movement and other targets. Policy measures would echo in political crime.

Helms was not averse to conducting covert operations in the United States, even if that was forbidden by the Agency's charter. In February 1971, an Agency break-in team entered the second floor of a photography shop in Fairfax City, Virginia. Helms authorized the entry as part of an investigation of an Agency employee who ran the studio with Orlando Nuñez, a former Cuban government official. While working in the CIA records division, the employee tried to find out what Agency files existed on Nuñez.[18] The surreptitious entry was justified, Helms said, because the Agency sought evidence of a Cuban penetration operation. It found none.

Helms favored such measures as a matter of policy. He convened a meeting with Hoover, Admiral Gayler, and John Mitchell. He wanted to discuss "a broadening of operations, particular of the confidential type in covering intelligence both domestic and foreign."

The grumpy Hoover said he was "not at all enthusiastic . . . in view of the hazards involved."[19] Helms talked up "further coverage of mail." He offered some choice classified details about the LINGUAL program, which opened and copied international correspondence of several thousand Americans every year. He followed up by sending a letter to Mitchell formally requesting the end of Hoover's freeze on domestic wiretaps. Mitchell approved.[20] Nixon couldn't count on Hoover to implement his domestic surveillance agenda, but he could count on Helms.

Not the least of Helms's contributions was to plausibly deny that such an agenda existed. As the butler of intelligence, he was especially convincing. In April 1971 he made a rare public appearance to send a reassuring message. The Agency did not have or seek the power to spy on Americans, he told the annual conference of the American Society of Newspaper Editors.

"I can assure you," he explained to several hundred editors and publishers assembled in a Washington hotel ballroom, "that except for the normal responsibilities for protecting the physical security of our own personnel, our facilities and our classified information, we do not have any such powers and functions [in the area of domestic intelligence]. We have never sought any; we do not exercise any. In short, we do not target on American citizens."[21]

Well intentioned or not, that was a falsehood. Two CIA operations, authorized by Helms, LINGUAL and CHAOS, targeted thousands of American citizens on a daily basis. Between 1970 and mid-1972, the CHAOS operatives distributed 1,064 reports and 75 special studies in the Langley headquarters while receiving more than 5,800 cables and 2,400 dispatches.[22] Targeting American citizens, in other words, was not forbidden. It was routine. Helms believed that function could be plausibly denied in service of national security.

He wasn't wrong. The desire to believe in a law-abiding CIA director was strong in the Washington press corps. The editors of the *New York Times* placed their story of Helms's speech at the top of the front page under the headline "Helms Defends the CIA As Vital to a Free Society."[23] An accompanying sidebar declared, "Richard McGarrah Helms: His Mission Is Facts."[24]

"WE'LL GET THEM"

Nixon was starting to feel better. Chinese leader Chou En-lai responded positively to his feelers about discussing the future of the two nations' relationship. The vision that Nixon had nurtured since his 1967 *Foreign Affairs* article—to reconcile the world's most powerful nation with the world's most populous nation—might finally be achieved. "I told the President the tide was turning," said the unctuous Kissinger. "We were beginning to see the outlines of a new international order."[25]

Helms was clued in. To conduct the secret negotiations, Kissinger replaced the U.S. Navy facility he had been using with a secure communications channel set up by the CIA.[26] "Helms knew how to limit the flow of cables," Kissinger said. "He handled backchannels discreetly and competently."[27]

Nixon was cheered on May 1 when Attorney General Mitchell delivered a crushing blow to the antiwar movement. With expectations of up to 250,000 protesters coming to Washington, Defense Secretary Laird called up 10,000 troops. "If the government won't stop the war," went the movement's new slogan, "the people will stop the government." The crowd was smaller than expected, and the demonstrators failed to shut down the capital. The offices of Congress, the courts, and the Executive Branch functioned normally. The protesters smashed windows, slashed tires, blocked fire trucks, abandoned cars on the bridges over the Potomac, and dumped trash in the street. In a massive sweep that a federal judge later ruled unconstitutional, Washington police arrested more than seven thousand people. They were held in Robert F. Kennedy Stadium and then released. "For his bloody victories over the movement—the Days of Rage, the New Mobilization, Kent State and May Day, John Mitchell was never forgiven," wrote the attorney general's admiring biographer.[28]

A grim satisfaction emanated from the president in the summer of 1971 that was shared by Chuck Colson, White House strategist. Nixon invited Colson along with Kissinger, Haldeman, and Ehrlichman for an evening cruise on the *Sequoia*.

"After the craft passed by Washington's Tomb at Mount Vernon," Colson recalled, "Nixon and his men gathered in the wood paneled dining room, drank wine and scotch, dined on New York strip steak and corn on the cob, and plotted their political futures. While the yacht drifted along the darkening waters of the Potomac, Nixon looked ahead to 1972 and the battles that were to come against Congress and others over Vietnam and his domestic agenda."

Colson observed the president stroking the rim of his wineglass with a pointed finger.

"One day we will get them," Nixon growled. "We'll get them on the ground where we want them. And we'll stick our heels in, step on them hard and twist—right, Chuck, right?"

The glowering president looked around for approval. Kissinger smiled and nodded. Haldeman said nothing. Ehrlichman jerked his head back to stare at the ceiling, a silent dissent. "You're right, sir," vowed Colson, the true believer. "We'll get them."

With the benefit of hindsight from a prison cell, Colson saw the cruise on the *Sequoia* as a voyage to self-destruction. "They who differed with us, whatever their motives, must be vanquished," he recalled. "The seeds of destruction were by now already sown—not in them but in us."[29]

Helms wasn't there that night, but he was not one to discourage his boss. *No personal reservations. . . . Keep a tough line. . . . I'm with you all the way.* In his season of retribution Dick Nixon could count on Dick Helms.

"GET THIS SON OF A BITCH"

On Sunday, June 13, 1971, the *New York Times* published a front-page story headlined "Vietnam Archive: Pentagon Study Traces 3 Decades of Growing U.S. Involvement." The bylined author, veteran correspondent Neil Sheehan, quoted extensively from a secret Defense Department study of U.S. policy in Vietnam as it evolved from President Truman to President Johnson. Nixon's first reaction was mild, recalled John Dean, former White House counsel. "He said, this is good for us. This will really be a problem for the Democrats because they are the ones who've been deceiving. It's not reached Republicans. And so, he felt very comfortable about it."[30]

Henry Kissinger returned to Washington the next day and, in Dean's view, pressed "the president's manhood button." Dean quoted Alex Butterfield, the deputy chief of staff who was perhaps the most frequent daily observer of the president's moods, as saying, "Everything changed with Nixon after the leak of the Pentagon Papers and . . . after his meeting with Henry."

Soon Nixon was raging against the man who had supplied the *Times* with the secret history, Daniel Ellsberg, a former Pentagon analyst turned war critic. Nixon loathed him. "We've got to get this son of bitch," he told John Mitchell, Nixon's hatred was visceral, bubbling up from the depths of his insecurities and resentments. Ellsberg was everything Nixon loathed, a creature of Harvard, who was both Jewish and countercultural. Nixon called him, derisively, "Ellstein" or, simply, "the Jew," the embodiment of the hated outsider.

"Don't worry about his trial," Nixon hissed to Mitchell. "Just get everything out. Try him in the press. Everything, John . . . that there is in the investigation . . . leak it out. We want to destroy him in the press. . . . There's where we won the Hiss case. I didn't try it in the goddam courtroom. But I won it before it ever got to court."[31]

Many years later, Nixon calmed himself.

"What Ellsberg had done was despicable and contemptible," he wrote in his memoirs. "I felt there were serious concerns about what he might do next. There were rumors and reports of a conspiracy," most of which proved phantoms of Nixon's imagination.

Nixon asked Haldeman to get him a copy of the Pentagon file on Anna Chennault and the events leading up to Johnson's bombing halt in 1968. The file was supposedly held by former Pentagon official Leslie Gelb, now a fellow at the Brookings Institution, a liberal think tank. "I wanted the documents back," Nixon recalled in his memoirs. "When I was told the documents were still at Brookings, I was furious and frustrated. Top secret reports were in the hands of a private think tank in the hands of antiwar Democrats. I said I wanted it back, even if it meant getting it surreptitiously."[32]

"Yes, but you need somebody to do it," Haldeman said.

"That's what I'm talking about," Nixon said. "Don't discuss it here. You talk to Hunt."

"Helms says he's ruthless, quiet, careful," Haldeman said.

It was a revealing aside. Helms sometimes protested that he didn't even know Hunt was working at the White House in July 1971. In fact, Helms had recommended him to Haldeman.

"He's kind of a tiger," Colson said. ". . . He spent 20 years in the CIA overthrowing governments."

"I want the break-in," Nixon stormed. "Hell, they do that. You're to break into that place, rifle the files, and bring them in. Just go in and take it, period. . . . Bob, now you remember Huston's plan?" Nixon barked. "Implement it!"[33]

The Huston Plan, which supposedly died the year before, was still an operative concept in the Nixon White House a year later. The president wanted his policy implemented and Hunt was the man to do it.

16

THE "WHO SHOT JOHN?" ANGLE

In this season of fury, Chuck Colson called Hunt once again. "With the right resources," he asked his fellow Brown alumnus, could he make "a major public case against Ellsberg and his co-conspirators?" Colson was intent on "nailing any son of a bitch who would steal a secret document of the government and publish it." The Ellsberg case, he said, channeling Nixon, "won't be tried in court. It will be tried in the newspapers."

Hunt welcomed the job. He believed the country was endangered by a "counterculture government" that was supported by journalists, clergymen, scientists, and lawyers and aided by "moles such as Ellsberg who were deeply entrenched in the government." In some ways, Hunt said, "this was a mirror image of the events . . . that the CIA had perpetuated in other countries such as Guatemala to effect regime change. Perhaps that's why it seemed so frightening . . ."[1]

Hunt was hired as a White House security consultant[2] and installed in an office with David Young, a former Kissinger aide on the NSC staff, and Gordon Liddy, a former FBI agent detailed from the Treasury Department. They worked out of Room 16 in the Executive Office Building. As their job was plugging leaks in the press, they put a sign on the door calling themselves "The Plumbers."

Hunt and Liddy bonded at first sight. "Liddy was a wired, wisecracking extrovert who seemed as if he might be a candidate for decaffeinated coffee," Hunt said.[3] Liddy effused that Hunt "was knowledgeable in the area of intelligence operations and had a command of the English language one associates with brains and a first-class education."[4] They were buddies, at least for a while.

Hunt went to work. Introduced to Ehrlichman, he said he needed help with identification and disguises. Ehrlichman called deputy director Bob Cushman and told him to expect a call from Hunt. "You should consider he has pretty much carte blanche," he said. Cushman promised "full cooperation." He then notified Howard Osborn, chief of the Office of Security, who knew of Hunt's penchant for trouble. Osborn said his reaction was "one of wonderment, since, to my knowledge, [Hunt] knew nothing about security."[5] Osborn kept his opinion to himself.

Nixon himself wanted Hunt. "I wanted someone to light a fire under the FBI in its investigation of Ellsberg," Nixon wrote in his memoirs. "If the FBI was not going to pursue the case, then we were going to ourselves. . . . I urged that we find out everything we could about his background, his motives, and his co-conspirators, if they existed. I was also determined not to sit back while the Democratic architects of our involvement tried to make me pay for the war politically. I wanted a good political operative who could sift through State and Defense files and get us all the facts on the Bay of Pigs, the Diem assassination, and Johnson's 1968 bombing halt." Nixon had found his "good political operative."[6]

Hunt, alas, bungled his first assignment. He knew Nixon wanted to blame JFK for Diem's murder in 1963, the better to wrongfoot Ted Kennedy, who he expected would be his opponent in the 1972 presidential campaign. Hunt arranged an interview with Lou Conein, a veteran of the CIA station in Saigon who was deeply involved in the 1963 coup that deposed Diem. Conein also knew Ellsberg from Saigon. Seeking dirt on Ellsberg and the details of how Kennedy abandoned a U.S. ally, Hunt invited Conein to talk in Ehrlichman's office. He arranged to have the room "wired" to capture the story on tape. Conein arrived, plopped down on the couch, and proceeded to tell stories as he and Hunt drank whiskey until late in the evening. When Hunt asked for the tape, the technician said he had concealed it under the cushions of the couch. He extracted the machine, which had been crushed when Conein sat on it. Hunt, Langley's answer to Inspector Clouseau, had no recording of the conversation and no memory of what Conein had said.[7]

Hunt visited Cushman a few days later, feeling full of himself.

"I've been charged with quite a highly sensitive mission by the White House," he whispered, "to visit and elicit information from an individual whose ideology we aren't entirely sure of. . . . [F]or that purpose they asked me to come over here and see if you could give me two things: flash alias documentation . . . and some degree of physical disguise, for a one-time op a. In and out." He was talking about black-bag jobs, an unauthorized entry.[8]

"I don't see why we can't," Cushman shrugged.[9] He asked his executive assistant, Karl Wagner, to contact the Technical Services Division and "tell them they were to furnish Mr. Hunt with the necessary papers to indicate an alias."[10] Wagner instructed the acting chief of TSD to "furnish a physical disguise and alias documentation to an individual who didn't want his identity known to TSD officers . . . the matter was extremely sensitive and being done for the White House." Wagner cleared the request with Sam Halpern, assistant to Tom Karamessines.[11]

This ready servicing of Hunt's demands would later require some explaining. Helms's defense, offered later in multiple Capitol Hill appearances, was subtle and multilayered. Helms swore he knew and approved of Cushman's provision of credentials and wig—but did not ask for any details about what use they would be put to. As for Hunt's request for a CIA profile of Ellsberg: David Young had called Howard Osborn and told him Kissinger and Ehrlichman had been very impressed with a paper prepared by the Office of Medical Services on Fidel Castro. Young asked for a similar profile on Ellsberg. Osborn told him only the director could make the decision.

"We didn't know Mr. Ellsberg," Helms told Young. "We didn't have any information on him, why were we being asked to make a study of this kind?" Young pleaded with Helms, stressing the study had been given "highest priority" by Ehrlichman and Kissinger and that the CIA was the only agency with such a capability."[12]

"All right," sighed Helms, "let's go ahead and give it a try."[13]

With May Day mobs rampaging and the nation's secrets at risk, Nixon wanted action and Hunt supplied it. Helms was just doing his job by facilitating. If Helms didn't know that Hunt had proposed a blackmail operation to Colson, it was because he didn't micromanage. With his leftist politics and prolific love life, Ellsberg embodied the counterculture the CIA men feared. Hunt proposed that he and Liddy would break into the offices of Ellsberg's psychiatrist, Dr. Lewis Fielding, in Beverly Hills, California, in search of information to discredit the new hero of the left. Hunt secured White House approval and solicited still more support from the CIA, asking for false credentials for Liddy and a camera suitable for indoor photography. Cushman approved and informed Helms, who didn't ask any questions.[14] He had deniability, even if it wasn't entirely plausible.

Hunt and Liddy flew to Los Angeles. They surveyed Fielding's office in preparation for a burglary. They took a series of photos showing the building, inside and out. They snapped a photo of Dr. Fielding's white Volvo with its visible California license plates. When Hunt returned to Washington, he gave the film to a CIA technician who developed the photos. The technician gave the originals to Hunt and made copies for the files of the Technical Services Division.[15] He was working for the White House and sharing the take with his former employer. That was the spymaster's modus operandi.

The same day the photographs of Dr. Fielding's office were reviewed at CIA headquarters, Helms decided Hunt's mounting demands for help had become intolerable. While the CIA official history would claim the two events were not connected, Senator Howard Baker concluded, "it was only after these photographs were developed and examined that the CIA technician dealing with Hunt was ordered to cut off all support."

Helms had an explanation, of course. He told Ehrlichman that Hunt was "bad news," confiding that the Agency "had kept Mr. Hunt on a little longer than they should have." Several years before, Hunt had been separated "from more operational tasks because he was overly romantic," Helms explained, ". . . [but] we had continued him because he had some serious financial problems relating to a sick child and we did not want to have a disgruntled ex-employee."[16]

In fact, Hunt was not disgruntled. He was reporting to Helms all the while. Rob Roy Ratliff was a career CIA officer who served as the Agency's representative on the National Security Agency in 1971. Peter Jessup, former station chief in Tel Aviv and aide to counterintelligence chief Angleton, had held the job before Ratliff. Both were career officials in good standing. Both said they received packages from Hunt for delivery to the director's office in 1971 and 1972.

"I was aware that Hunt had frequently transmitted sealed envelopes via our office to the Agency," Ratliff said in a statement given to Senate investigators. "We had receipts for those envelopes but were unaware of their contents." Ratliff said Jessup "told me that he had opened one of the packages," which appeared to contain "gossip" information about an unknown person. Jessup, he said, "assumed it had something to do with a psychological profile of that person." Ratliff said he had no knowledge of "whether Hunt had arranged with Mr. Helms or whether Hunt had prevailed on another Agency official because of some past connection." Ratliff "found ∴ hard to believe an individual of the Agency would become involved in something like that without some approval from higher authority within the Agency."

Ratliff added that his secretary reported that Hunt had once visited his predecessor for a visit behind closed doors. When they emerged, his predecessor said he was "amazed, shocked and bewildered by the things Hunt had told him that he was doing."[17]

Helms said he "didn't recall any such thing." Hunt admitted to sending "occasional things over to the CIA" in sealed envelopes but said they only concerned a problem he had with his retirement annuity.[18]

Hunt had carte blanche. Helms had plausible deniability. It still wasn't enough. Nixon was demanding more. It was Bay of Pigs time again.

"DIRTY LINEN"

With South Vietnamese president Thieu running for reelection unopposed in October 1971, Nixon was on the defensive. Some senators were talking about cutting off aid unless Thieu allowed his opponents to run. Nixon seized the moment to highlight JFK's perfidy. "I would remind all concerned that the way we got into Vietnam was through overthrowing Diem and the complicity in the murder of Diem," Nixon said at a press conference.[19] With Republican opposition to his war policy mounting, Nixon wanted to make the issue partisan, to contrast his Vietnam policy to Kennedy's. This would lay the groundwork for his 1972 campaign and give the press something to chew on besides coups and casualties.

The next day he and his advisers discussed how to impugn the Democrats with historical documents. Ehrlichman recommended the Plumbers in Room 16. "We have a couple of fellows under Krogh—Liddy and Hunt—who know what they're doing."[20]

In their next meeting Nixon articulated his new 1972 campaign strategy: keep the origins of the Vietnam War "front and center" so that the Democrats would squabble about it. Haldeman and Ehrlichman agreed that the murder of Diem was the best line of attack. Like Hunt, Nixon had heard Lou Conein's account of the November 1963 coup and thought it was damning to the memory of JFK. Nixon suggested selected Republican senators might demand that Conein be released from the silence required by his Agency oath. "Let the CIA take a whipping on this one," Nixon said.[21]

Hunt took charge. With a phone call from the White House, he was cleared for access to the State Department archives. He read all the cables between the Department and the Saigon Embassy in late 1963. "What kind of material have you dug up in the files that would indicate Kennedy complicity in Diem's death?" Colson asked. Hunt said no single cable would prove it. "You'd have to take a sequence of three or four cables, be aware of their contents and speculate on what was missing from the sequence," he explained.

"Do you think you can improve on them?" Colson asked.

Hunt went to work forging two cables that would damn JFK by making it look like he refused to give asylum to Diem and Nhu. (In fact, Henry Cabot Lodge, acting on JFK's orders, had told Diem "if I can do anything for your physical safety, please telephone me.")[22] It was, for all intents and purposes, a CIA-sponsored psychological warfare operation aimed at Ted Kennedy and the Democratic party. Colson then passed photocopies of the forged cables to a reporter from *Life* magazine who expressed interest but wanted to see the originals.[23]

Nixon ordered Ehrlichman to go to Langley. Over breakfast with the ever disdainful Helms, Ehrlichman asked for Agency files on a host of controversial events: the 1958 landing of U.S. Marines in Lebanon, the 1961 assassination of Dominican dictator Rafael Trujillo, the Bay of Pigs, the 1962 Cuban missile crisis, and the death of Diem in 1963.[24] Helms said he would look into it.[25] When Ehrlichman followed up with a phone call, the silky director lamented that even he did not have access to one of the Bay of Pigs reports. He expressed concern about who might see the files that the president wanted. He mentioned Hunt by name, suggesting he could not be trusted with the Agency's "soiled linen."[26] Helms knew his friend's animus against JFK and his penchant for putting his politics ahead of the Agency's interests. Ehrlichman returned to the White House with little to show for his errand, save more excuses.

The impatient Nixon summoned Helms for a late morning meeting. Ehrlichman briefed him shortly before the director was scheduled to arrive.

"He would not give me any of the Diem stuff until he had an opportunity to talk with you," Ehrlichman complained. ". . . I said 'Well, nobody's going to see this stuff except the president, me and . . .' He said, 'Well, this is incredibly dirty linen.' He said, 'I just wouldn't feel comfortable about it without talking to the president first.'"

"Now on the other stuff," Ehrlichman went on, referring to the Bay of Pigs files, "I asked for a lot of background material, a lot of nuts and bolts, cables, cable traffic and internal memos. He didn't give me any of that. He gave me only summaries and post-mortems. What he gave me is useful stuff but we've really got to have the internal stuff."

"What the hell, do you mean?" Nixon griped. "Kennedy didn't know these things? Johnson didn't know these things?"

"The thing he wants to say to you," Ehrlichman replied, "is that, in all fairness to Kennedy, this stuff shouldn't be spread all over the newspapers."

"Maybe we should just get rid of Helms," Nixon groused. "It will have to come to that pretty soon."

"I was kind of mysterious with him about why you were doing all this," Ehrlichman said.

"Why do we want the Kennedy stuff?" Nixon interjected. "He murdered Diem."

That was the message Nixon was honing. He knew all about Hunt's handiwork with the forged cables, and he was pleased. "*Life* magazine has their tongue out a mile," he bragged. "To do a special issue on the cover about the assassination of Diem."

"Helms is scared to death of this guy Hunt we got working for us," Ehrlichman added, "because he knows where a lot of the bodies are buried."

Ehrlichman offered a plan.

"Supposing we get all the Diem stuff and supposing there's something we can really hang Teddy and the Kennedy clan with. I'm going to want to put that in Colson's hands and we're going to want to run with it," he said. "I think what you will say to him [Helms] is that you have to make the decision [to declassify]. And you have a perfect right."

"That's right," Nixon harrumphed. "I'm the president. The CIA is not."

At that moment, Dick Helms was ushered into the Oval Office.

"Let me come to this delicate point that you've been talking to John about," Nixon started, as Helms took a seat. "John's been talking to me about it, and I know he talked to you about it. Maybe I can perhaps put it in a different perspective than John. You probably wondered what the hell this was all about."

Helms probably had some idea.

It was a matter of diplomacy, Nixon said. "I just want to be sure that I am fully aware of everything that we've ever dealt with Russians in the past. What they did, and what we did. What was politics, what was not politics. . . . For the purposes of my information I need to know all that."

With the niceties out of the way, Nixon was ready to level.

"Now to get to the dirty tricks part of it," he growled. "I know what happened in Iran. I also know what happened in Guatemala, and I totally approve both. I also know what happened with the planning of the Bay of Pigs under Eisenhower and totally approved of it.

"The problem was not the CIA," Nixon went on. "The problem was that your plan was not carried out. It was a goddamn good plan. If it had been backed up at the proper time. If he'd just flown a couple of planes over that damn place . . ."

He was talking about John F. Kennedy and the Bay of Pigs.

"My interest there is not the internal situation, the fight in the CIA," Nixon confided. "My interest there is solely to know the facts, and, in the event, things heat up . . . this becomes an issue."

What issue? He was talking about the politics of the presidency.

"The problem with the whole Pentagon Papers issue . . . it impaired the whole security system of the United States . . . , it whetted the appetite on every goddam scandal monger in town," he ranted. ". . . Did he lie or want to know the truth, about everything else that happened? . . . What Johnson's thoughts were and why he bombed. Did he lie?"

He was referrring to the business of assassination.

"We should have never lost the Chilean elections . . ." he said, cold and clear and furious. "Once we got to the point we did, we should have done something more *effective* than what we did do."

It was a blood oath between two men of power. Nixon would take responsibility for Schneider, but Helms had to do his part: give up the intelligence on Diem and the Bay of Pigs.

"What I want, what I want, Dick," Nixon rasped, "regarding any understanding, regarding any information, I do not want *any* information, that comes in from you on these delicate and sensitive subjects, to go to *anybody* outside . . ."

Helms said nothing.

"This is my information, me and you," Nixon said. "Ehrlichman will be my ears."

Helms, the butler of espionage, spoke for the first time. He limited himself to one word.

"Exactly."

"I need it for a defensive reason," Nixon explained. "For a negotiation."

"I quite understand," Helms said, not understanding a bit.

"The 'Who shot John?' angle," Nixon began, launching into a stream of consciousness monologue about the secrets he sought and the pressures he faced. This was Nixon's id running rampant in the annals of history.

"Is Eisenhower to blame? Is Johnson to blame? Is Kennedy to blame? Is Nixon to blame?" he ranted. "Etcetera, etcetera, etcetera. It may become, not by me, but it may become a very, very vigorous issue. If it does . . ."

Nixon raved but with reason. In the context of a demand for secret records of the Kennedy presidency, his invocation of the "'Who shot John' angle?" can only refer to one thing, the JFK assassination. The angle was the press coverage of the continuing controversy about Dallas. Nixon wanted to assure Helms he would not raise the "Who shot John" question, but if the JFK story again became a "vigorous issue" in the press—as it did after Drew Pearson's column in March 1967, after Clay Shaw's trial in February 1969, and after Jack Anderson's column in January 1971—Nixon would protect the Agency.

"I need to know what is necessary to protect, frankly, the intelligence gathering and the Dirty Tricks Department, and I will protect it," Nixon avowed. "Hey, listen, I have done more than my share of lying to protect you, and I believe it's totally right to do it."

The tape of Nixon and Helms's tête-à-tête confirms Haldeman's belief that when Nixon spoke of "the whole Bay of Pigs thing," he was making a coded allusion to the assassination of JFK. When he asked for files on the Bay of Pigs Nixon had the "Who shot John?" angle in mind. It was, Haldeman wrote, "the president's way of reminding Helms, not so gently, of the cover-up of the CIA assassination attempts on the hero of the Bay of Pigs, Fidel Castro, a CIA operation that may have triggered the Kennedy tragedy and which Helms desperately wanted to hide."[27]

Nixon had read Anderson's column about Bob Maheu and Johnny Rosselli and the Castro plots. Nixon knew Maheu from the 1950s, knew how he operated. He almost certainly knew Mitchell had cut a deal with Maheu, though he might not have known the Agency was protecting Johnny Rosselli from deportation. Nixon didn't have a problem with the Agency's dirty tricks around Kennedy. *I have done more than my share of lying to protect you, and I believe it's totally right to do it.*

Nixon just wanted to know how the Mafia plots related to Kennedy's assassination. "If I *don't* know then, then what do you have?"

The CIA had shared the Mafia plots with President Johnson. Maheu told his version to Mitchell. Nixon wanted the whole story, including the "Who shot John?" angle.

"I don't believe that you can say, well, . . . the director of the CIA . . . is the only one who is to know what happened in certain circumstances. The president is to know, and that the president's successor is not to know?"

Nixon rapped the desk with his knuckles.

"I am not [*thump*] going to embarrass [*thump*] the CIA because it served . . . I believe in Dirty Tricks," he yelled.

Ready to deal, Helms said nothing.

"I think the way we ought to do it," the president said, "is to set up a method of communication. Whereby you and I and John, you can trust him. I have him in

the domestic council but as my lawyer. He handles all the . . . sensitive [stuff]. . . .
You can rely on the fact that John is the contact. But also, you can rely on the fact
that you and I will talk if something hits the fan."

"You've got to tell us what we did," Nixon suddenly implored.

"We did the Chilean thing," replied Helms, the chilly spymaster. "And we did
a few other things." He might have been thinking of secret operations he ran for
the White House. *LINGUAL (mail opening). AMLASH (assassination). CHAOS
(undermining the antiwar movement.* "By God we can do some more." He was
ready do Nixon's bidding. "Sir," he explained, "we only have one president at a
time."

Helms showed his fealty by offering up files on Diem's assassination.

"As a matter of fact, sir, the reason I want to speak to you," he began, ex-
tracting a sheaf of papers. "Various documents I didn't even know existed. I was
not told about it at the time. It was a review that John McCone asked to have
made about the Diem period. He was the director. I was down the line . . ."

Suddenly, the director was earnest, helpful, ingenuous.

"So, when I saw this document," Helms went on. "I thought this was the kind
of document that it would be irresponsible if I didn't go to the president and tell
him what this document was, before I handed it over, why it's so sensitive . . . I've
got a copy right here."

He handed over a 1963 memo about Diem, written by McCone, along with
reports on his meetings with the president and secretary of state. It was the sort of
raw intelligence that Nixon demanded.

"Sir, I'm working entirely for you," Helms said. "Anything I've got is yours."

Helms had appeased Nixon with the Diem material and surrendered nothing
on JFK.

"That's really the case," Nixon beamed, gift in hand. "That's really the case."[28]

The president was starting to trust the son of a bitch.

17

OUR SIDE

AIRTEL TO DIRECTOR FBI (62–115691)

Based on information developed through investigation to date under captioned matter, it appears that one or more unknown individuals executed seven break-ins against official Chilean establishments and residences of Chilean officials in the New York City area. They were as follows.

The FBI's file on Frank Sturgis, soldier of fortune from Miami, specified both the dates and places of the seven reported break-ins. ("Sometime during the weekend April 9–11, 1971, in Apartment 11-A at 35 East 38th Street, which at the time was the residence of Javier Urrutia, President of the Chilean Development Corporation.")

The men who became famous as the Watergate burglars were suspected in a string of similar "black-bag jobs" in 1971. The targets were all associated with the Allende government, which Nixon and the CIA still sought to overthrow. The goal: to obtain blackmail information. At least that's what Sturgis told journalist Andrew St. George, prompting the FBI to open an investigation on Sturgis. Sturgis later denied breaking into the Chilean Embassy in Washington and broke with St. George and called him a "fucking liar."[1]

Sturgis and St. George had first crossed paths in Cuba in 1958. St. George was a photographer and journalist who traveled to the Sierra Maestra for *Life* magazine to cover Castro's guerrilla war against the Batista regime, while Sturgis was delivering guns to the 26th of July movement from Florida. A decade later, after the Watergate burglary, St. George renewed the acquaintance.

Sturgis told him he had been investigating a rumor that Allende had made a deal with the Democratic Party through Sol Linowitz, a Washington attorney and Democratic Party activist. Allende's government would funnel money to the presidential campaign of South Dakota senator George McGovern in return for concessions, if and when McGovern won the presidency in 1972. Linowitz was an important McGovern advisor, Sturgis said, and would be influential in formulating the Democratic Party's platform on Cuba and Latin America. Sturgis and his good friend Rolando Martínez entered and searched Linowitz's office. The intent, he said, was to publish any embarrassing information developed in the course of this breach, but no compromising documents were found. Linowitz later confirmed there had been a break-in at his office.

Some of the surreptitious entries, Sturgis said, required considerable planning with clerks, maids, maintenance men, and switchboard girls cultivated for information and assistance in these entries. Plenty of money was available for these endeavors, he added.

No information about these activities reached Helms, according to a statement later given to Senator Baker's investigators. "The Agency had no information or reports prior to 17 June 1972, which might have suggested or referred to domestic clandestine operations by those individuals associated with or who took part in the Watergate break or the break-in of Dr. Fielding's office."

That wasn't quite true. Hunt had lunch with Tom Karamessines on October 14, 1971, after he and Liddy broke into Dr. Fielding's office. And Helms's office had received packages from Hunt, transmitted through Rob Roy Ratliff and Peter Jessup via the CIA office in the National Security Council.[2]

Truth be told, Helms was doing his damnedest to serve the president. When the Office of Medical Services had finished the psychological profile of Ellsberg, Helms delivered it to David Young, who was working with Hunt and Liddy in Room 16.

"We are, of course, glad to be of assistance," Helms wrote in his cover memo. "I do wish to underline the point that our involvement in the matter should not be revealed in any context, formal or informal. I am sure you appreciate our concern."

Did this injunction indicate awareness of an illegal action, a possible violation of the Agency's charter banning operations on U.S. soil, a Senate investigator later wondered? The memo was "most unfortunately worded," Helms admitted.

He knew he was walking close to the line of improper behavior, not that he was deterred from crossing it occasionally.

"DEEP APPRECIATION"

He was a soft-spoken man, said the widow Miriam Furbershaw to the inquiring FBI agents. He wanted to rent the room in the basement of her home in suburban Silver Spring, Maryland. He had good credentials, said he was an air force colonel, recently retired, and he made a good impression. His name was James McCord.

McCord had retired from the Office of Security in August 1970. His final job evaluation praised his "imagination, ingenuity, and drive," as well as his "innate stubbornness" as "a very principled individual who once convinced he has hit upon the proper course of action will usually yield only by direction."[3]

Helms appreciated his service. When McCord went into business as a security consultant, he hung an autographed photo of the director bestowing an award on him. It was signed and personally underlined, "With deep appreciation, DICK HELMS."[4] On recommendation of a friend in the Secret Service, McCord was hired by the Committee to Re-elect the President as chief of security in October 1971.[5]

McCord told Mrs. Furbershaw that his family lived in Baltimore and he needed a place to receive mail and stay overnight for occasional work at the Pentagon. She told him she had two rules: no smoking in the bedroom, and no women overnight. McCord agreed. He paid the rent with a single one-hundred-dollar bill and moved in. During installation of a phone line in the basement, she said that a telephone company technician informed her there was considerable "bugging equipment inside her tenant's apartment."

One winter night, when McCord wasn't there, she went down to the apartment. Much to her surprise, she found a young girl—she couldn't have been more than seventeen years old—curled up in a chair. Mrs. Furbershaw quickly retreated upstairs. The following morning she saw McCord and the girl drive away early. She went downstairs. The state of the bedsheets was shameful. McCord was a "rotten womanizer," she thought, and with helpless young girls, which made it worse.

Later in the day McCord came back, alone. Furious, Furbershaw insisted he leave immediately. Pack up and get out, she said. McCord offered her more money. She wouldn't have him there for any amount of money, she said. Pack up your belongings and get out. Now! And take these sheets with you, the only thing they're good for is burning. McCord left. After that Mrs. Furbershaw said she received postcards at the house from women who obviously had been in the apartment, filled with lewd references to their experiences there. That's the last she knew of James McCord until she saw his picture in the *Washington Post* in late June 1972 alongside a story about a burglary.[6]

What McCord was doing at Mrs. Furbershaw's apartment with young women and bugging equipment is anybody's guess. McCord, by all appearances, was a family man, religious and conservative. He might have had a secret life. His secret might have been professional only, namely mounting operations to compromise others. As an officer in the Security Research Staff, McCord had worked for Paul Gaynor, who was known to maintain files on suspected subversives, homosexuals, and other security threats. "Historically," noted Jim Hougan, "the Office of Security was the launching point for domestic operations involving prostitutes, as well as the repository for all data, tape recordings and photographs collected in the course of such operations."[7]

MUDHEN

Nixon's latest problem—and Helms's too—was Jack Anderson, successor to Drew Pearson as a sensationalist syndicated columnist. Anderson was not one of those liberals who sniped at Nixon from a privileged perch. He was born less than thirty miles from Nixon's birthplace in dusty southern California. Like Nixon, Anderson had grown up in a struggling working-class family with dour parents and strict religious instruction. During World War II he became a reporter for the military newspaper *Stars and Stripes*.[8] He joined Drew Pearson's staff as an assistant and learned the muckraking trade from a master. Pearson and Anderson schmoozed with lawyers, lobbyists, and lowlifes over breakfast, lunch, and dinner, as well as drinks late into the night—and then wrote up the most provocative tidbits in the morning.

Anderson loved to lob bombshells at the Nixon White House, and on December 14, 1971, a big one exploded. In a column about Pakistan and India on the brink of war, Anderson published verbatim transcripts of minutes of a recent top-secret meeting of State, Defense, CIA, and NSC officials, chaired by Henry Kissinger. Officially, the United States was neutral. In the meeting, Kissinger complained, "I'm getting hell every half hour from the president that we are not being tough enough on India." Nixon, he said, wanted "to tilt in favor of Pakistan."

The specificity of the quote was powerful. The committee's deliberations were classified at the very highest level. This wasn't the usual fare of a Washington pundit, an anonymous quote from someone in the room. This was the official transcript. Diplomatically, "the leak was embarrassing," said Nixon. "From the point of national security it was intolerable."[9] Helms and his colleagues were jolted by the revelation. Anderson "obviously got a hold of the documents themselves," he said, "and we were all somewhat awed."[10]

Nixon's plumbers investigated the leak, along with the Defense Department security officials. They learned that a twenty-one-year-old navy yeoman, Charles Radford, who worked in the Joint Chiefs of Staff liaison office in the National Security Council, had been rifling "burn bags" in Kissinger's office after hours. Radford passed scores of documents to the generals of the Joint Chiefs, who felt left out of Nixon and Kissinger's back-channel negotiations with longtime enemies China and Russia. Radford was also friends with Anderson, a fellow Mormon.

Radford was arrested and grilled. He confessed he'd been stealing documents from the White House. Ehrlichman reported to Nixon that Radford, with the implicit approval of his superiors, "has systematically stolen documents out of Henry's briefcase, Haig's briefcase, people's desks, any place . . . and every place in the NSC apparatus that he could get his hands on—and has duplicated them and turned them over to the Joint Chiefs, through his boss. This has been going on for thirteen months."[11]

Nixon took the news calmly. As a connoisseur of dirty tricks, the president was barely offended when one was pulled on him. "I was disturbed—although perhaps not surprised—that the JCS was spying on the White House," he wrote in his memoir.[12] And then Nixon lashed out. Anderson was becoming a media star thanks to his revelations. The so-called Anderson Papers were compared to the Pentagon Papers in terms of impact. When Nixon demanded the CIA put Anderson under surveillance and identify his sources, Helms complied.

Howard Osborn, chief of security, assigned a team of sixteen undercover officers to mount round-the-clock surveillance of Anderson's home in Northwest Washington. Eight different vehicles—equipped with two-way radios, binoculars, and cameras with telephoto lenses—were deployed in what was dubbed Project Mudhen. It was, in the words of Anderson's biographer, "a massive and illegal covert operation."[13]

True to its avian namesake, Mudhen was a comical bird. Anderson's teenage kids noticed the CIA spy team right away and turned the tables on them. "We drove around to where they were," said Anderson's son Kevin, then fifteen years old, "We pulled up behind them and blocked them in. We started taking pictures and they put on their sunglasses and pulled up newspapers to block their faces." Finally, the embarrassed spooks screeched away in their government-issued cars.[14]

Helms was unabashed. He insisted that he had an obligation *not* to abide by the Agency's charter, which bans operations in the United States. "The Director is responsible for the protection of agents and sources . . . ," he told James Rosen. "And so I thought I had a perfect right to find out, if I possibly could, who was providing him with this information."[15]

The information, however, was hardly relevant to the CIA's mission. The Security Research Staff, headed by Paul Gaynor, studied Anderson's personal behavior and found nothing more scandalous than a few speeding tickets. A twenty-five-page assessment of Anderson's "sensationalistic" reporting concluded that he "exhibits a flamboyant attitude," maintained "a network of informants whom he did not pay," and was "a liar" whose politics were hard to discern. In other words, he was a fairly typical Washington columnist.

Helms's dedicated service paid dividends. That same month a CIA officer in New York obtained a copy of a book proposal by Victor Marchetti, a former assistant to Tom Karamessines, who intended to tell all about the Agency. That was no small threat to Helms. Marchetti had handled classified material and heard sensitive conversations in the director's suite.

Helms decided to approach Nixon directly, not something he did lightly. The president promised his support. The Justice Department argued the Agency's case in court and secured an injunction permanently restraining Marchetti from publishing the book. The action saved the CIA a world of trouble.[16] When Marchetti's manuscript was finally published with redactions in 1975, it "changed national attitude," said *New York Times* columnist Anthony Lewis, instigating new skepticism toward the CIA and its "total exemption from the scrutiny to which the Constitution generally makes a government subject."[17] In 1971 the public remained ignorant of how the CIA actually worked, and Helms was grateful. It was, he felt, the only favor Nixon had ever done him. He wrote a note to John Ehrlichman thanking the White House for this "historic litigation on behalf of the Central Intelligence Agency."[18]

Nixon and Helms had become partners.

"EXPLOITABLE FOR THE MOVIES"

Gordon Liddy and Howard Hunt were "living high, wide, and handsome."[19] So said Earl Silbert, the first prosecutor to investigate the Watergate burglary. They were "James Bond–type characters" who lived the life of cinematic spies, Silbert wrote in his diary, later donated to the National Archives. The redactions for reasons of privacy hint at the antics of these macho adventurers.

"They're chasing around the country, staying in first class hotels of theirs, pursuing women," Silbert wrote, "all kinds [LINE REDACTED] switching off, Hunt wanting to do a scene . . . [HALF A LINE REDACTED]."[20] When it came to hotels, Silbert observed, "They had very good taste. The Playboy Plaza Hotel on Miami Beach, the Fontainebleau Hotel in Miami Beach are truly very luxurious . . ."[21]

In Miami, Hunt and Liddy planned for defending the July Republican presidential convention, where Nixon expected to be nominated for a second term. With the help of Bernard Barker, Hunt and Liddy interviewed candidates for a "riot squad" of counterdemonstrators to take on the expected hordes of antiwar protesters. One of them was Frank Sturgis, whose reputation for violence preceded him. "The men were exactly what I was looking for," Liddy rumbled in *Will*, his best-selling memoir. "Tough, experienced and loyal. Hunt and I interviewed about a dozen men. Afterward Howard told me that between them they had killed twenty-two men, including two hanged from a beam in the garage."

Hunt and Liddy were also shopping for women, with blackmail on their minds. They interviewed prostitutes for the prospective mission of bedding down with Democratic politicos in view of hidden hotel room cameras in the Fontainebleau.

"Hunt and Barker kept recruiting dark-haired and -complexioned Cuban women," Liddy complained. "They were very good-looking, but their English left something to be desired." Sturgis came to his rescue, said Liddy, by offering "two stunning Anglo Saxons." Living a life of fantasy, these men were prone to delusion, and it would catch up with them.[22]

Hunt continued to count on the CIA for help. He called on the graphics desk at the Agency to generate three-by-four-foot charts illustrating the plan the Plumbers called Gemstone. At a meeting with John Mitchell, Liddy digressed about how he would confound the Democrats with prostitutes, secret cameras, and thugs-for-hire. Mitchell filled and refilled his pipe. "Gordon," he finally breathed. "That is *not* what I had in mind."[23] The attorney general told them to come up with a plan that was less expensive and more realistic.[24] Crushed, Liddy and Hunt scaled back, but did not altogether abandon, their ambitions to surveil and blackmail Democrats on behalf of Nixon's campaign committee.

Hunt did not limit himself to White House business. He also seemed to be working for the agency, said Douglas Caddy, a lawyer who worked at Mullen Company and shared an office with Hunt. In an interview, Caddy said Hunt introduced him to CIA counsel Larry Houston in April 1972. "They asked me if I would take up residence in Nicaragua to set up a tourist hotel where they would lure members of the Sandinista movement," the leftist guerrillas then seeking to overthrow the country's pro-American dictatorship. They wanted a three- or four-year commitment. Caddy declined.[25]

Hunt's ambiguous profile—a former CIA man riding high in a White House job—led more than one Agency hand to start asking questions. In Miami, Rolando Martínez, still employed as AMSNAP-3, wrote up what he'd learned about Hunt and Artime's schemes in Nicaragua.[26] Jake Esterline, the former Bay of Pigs organizer, now chief of the Miami station, cabled Langley to say that Hunt was giving the impression his White House position "could be of importance to his Cuban friends." He asked Lawrence Sternfield, chief of Cuban operations, if Hunt really did have such a job.[27] Sternfield talked to Cord Meyer, now serving as assistant deputy director for plans. Meyer, in turn, consulted with DDP Tom Karamessines, who was effectively Hunt's case officer. Karamessines told Esterline to "cool it."[28] Hunt was protected from on high.

Helms had not forgotten his buddy, not at all. In May 1972, he and Cynthia attended a screening of the new hit movie *The Godfather* at the invitation of Paramount Pictures. It was a small intimate gathering at the headquarters of the Motion Picture Association of America. Helms mingled with MPAA chief Jack Valenti and White House staffers, including John Ehrlichman. Picking up on the popularity of a new TV spy series, *Mission Impossible*, Paramount executives had proposed a series about the CIA. Agency officials decided such a show would be "unwise" but gave Paramount the right of first refusal if they changed their mind.

Helms still liked the idea of a movie series. He brought along several of Hunt's Peter Ward novels and passed them to Charles Bludhorn, chairman of Gulf & Western, a corporate conglomerate that owned Paramount and assisted the CIA under a program code-named LPCHRIS. Bludhorn, in turn, passed the books to Martin Davis, his senior vice president.

Davis said the books were "a bunch of crap" that "couldn't possibly do the Agency any good." In response, Helms let Cord Meyer do the talking. Meyer told Davis the studio should exercise its own judgment, "and there is no pressure from the Agency on the matter."[29]

Helms wasn't one to push a string. He had done what he could for Hunt, even getting him a meeting with Valenti, one of the most powerful men in Hollywood. His dream of Hunt as the next Ian Fleming wasn't dead. Not yet.

SEX TALK

Hunt and McCord both said they met for the first time in April 1972. Whether that was true or not, they were introduced on that occasion by Liddy, who had learned of McCord's expertise in electronic surveillance. McCord was, in Hunt's estimation, "a thick-necked, wide-jawed man with a prominent brow, who look as if he was straight out of central casting—as a thug. It was hard to draw him out, and I would find him to be aloof and withdrawn during most of our acquaintance."

McCord Associates was doing well, thanks to referrals from Agency's personnel office. Recently retired officers looking to supplement their pensions came calling and McCord interviewed a dozen of them. He wanted Earl Harter, considered a genius of surreptitious entry, for his security team at the upcoming Republican convention. He spoke with Dr. Edward Gunn, the wizard of poison pills and pens, about joining his nonprofit Center for Protection and Safety Studies.[30] He knew too that Hunt had circulated his Bay of Pigs manuscript without authorization and gotten his wrist slapped. McCord wasn't averse to working with Hunt but he wasn't impressed either.

Liddy told Hunt and McCord that "the principals"—meaning the men in the White House—now wanted the Plumbers to break into the Democratic National Committee, which had offices in the Watergate office complex. According to Liddy, his superiors had information that the DNC was receiving illegal contributions from the North Vietnamese. "In retrospect, these were probably Nixon's paranoid delusions," Hunt said. "But at the time we were told that the information was fairly concrete. Additionally, Miami contacts relayed a companion rumor that Fidel Castro was clandestinely funding the Democrats, as well."[31] These baseless claims were mostly an excuse to burglarize the Democrats.

Hunt said Bernard Barker, his deputy from the Bay of Pigs operation, would serve as team chief and undertake a survey of the DNC offices. Liddy said his White House superiors also wanted to wiretap and burglarize the apartment of DNC chairman Larry O'Brien, who also lived in the Watergate. O'Brien's ties to the Howard Hughes organization were one of Nixon's obsessions. He had long endured criticism for taking money from Hughes and wanted to give the same treatment to the Democrats.

McCord provided the electronics. He approached Michael Stevens, owner of

Stevens Research Laboratory in Chicago, seeking eavesdropping devices. Stevens, a CIA contractor, asked for confirmation that this was official business. McCord showed Agency identification, and Stevens received a letter from the CIA authorizing the purchase.[32] The transaction punctured the Agency's later statement that it had no knowledge of McCord's activities after his retirement. Like Hunt, McCord could still count on the institutional support from Langley.

McCord put down $4,000 on a $15,000 purchase. He came away with four telephone bugs, eight high-fidelity tape recorders concealed in suitcases, and three bugs capable of feeding into the nation's highly classified satellite communications network."[33] He was clearly planning for more than one job. The Plumbers had ambitions.

Hunt brought in the Cubans. When Macho Barker came to Washington, Hunt drove him by the Watergate. "That's our next job," Hunt said. "There's reports that Castro's sending money to the Democrats."[34] Rolando Martínez, who had notified the Miami station of his contacts with Hunt, came with his friend Sturgis. Barker brought along Virgilio González, a skilled lockpick. Hunt introduced the Cubans to McCord, saying "they were working for a super-secret White House organization which had some of the functions of both the FBI and CIA."[35]

They set up a listening post in a room in the Howard Johnson's motel on Virginia Avenue across the street from the Watergate complex. McCord and the Cubans attempted their first entry into the DNC offices on Friday night, May 26. They failed, fostering recriminations. McCord did not procure all of the necessary equipment, leading Liddy to conclude that he was a coward.[36] The lockpick, González, didn't have the right tool to gain entry, and the mission was aborted. Hunt sent González to Miami in the morning to get the tools and come back the same day, which he did. At eleven o'clock on Saturday night, May 27, they successfully broke in.[37] As Hunt and Liddy monitored the operation by walkie-talkie from the listening post, McCord set about planting the bugs—meaning miniature transmitters—while Martínez photographed documents selected by Barker.

According to McCord, Liddy set two priorities for the bugs: Larry O'Brien and other senior Democrats. The Senate Watergate Committee concluded that McCord placed electronic bugging devices in the telephones of O'Brien and a newly appointed official of the DNC named Spencer Oliver, who was not a senior Democrat. In his book, McCord said he had been asked to install only one device, but he brought a second. "I found an office with a direct view across the street at the Howard Johnson's Motel, pulled the curtain and made the installation in the phone."[38]

That was not O'Brien's office, which was on the other side of the building.[39] It was the office of Oliver, whose father was a Washington labor lobbyist who had worked with Robert Mullen in the 1950s. Hunt, it turns out, had met Oliver. When Robert Bennett contemplated selling the Mullen Company, he thought of Oliver as a potential buyer. When Mullen, Bennett, Oliver, and Hunt had dinner, Hunt was "less than enthusiastic" about having the liberal Oliver as his boss. Hunt later claimed he didn't even know Oliver worked at the DNC at the time of break-in. "It came as a total surprise to me . . ." he wrote in his memoir. "I couldn't conceive why his phone was bugged. I thought it must have been an error and Mr. Liddy indicated to me he thought too, that McCord had made a mistake."[40]

McCord didn't think it was a mistake. He brought in a former FBI agent named Alfred Baldwin to monitor the wiretapped conversations. Baldwin listened to the conversations and gave handwritten notes to McCord, who passed them to Liddy's secretary. She typed them up and gave them to Magruder and Mitchell. McCord shared the transcripts with Hunt. An intelligence collector, he kept carbon copies for the Agency's files.[41]

McCord instructed Baldwin to record all calls relating to political strategy or sexual affairs. Because Oliver traveled for his job, the phone line the burglars bugged was often used by his secretary, Ida "Maxie" Wells, and her friends in the office. Wells later said she was "kind of appalled by the culture of casual sex and adultery in the office and gossiped about it with friends." She said other secretaries in the office used Oliver's phone line to talk "to their sweeties."

"The conversations were of a sexual nature," Baldwin recalled in a deposition years later, "but they weren't asking for money, they weren't the type I would classify as prostitution, or call or escort service. . . . They were people who knew each other, conversations to arrange dates or rendezvous or dinner, whatever, and sexual relationships to follow . . ."

Oliver later told journalist Robert Parry that he thought he had been targeted because of his opposition to George McGovern, the liberal South Dakota senator who was emerging as the frontrunner for the Democratic nomination. He connected the tap to his efforts to block McGovern's nomination. Baldwin had said much the same to the FBI. "All political conversations were related to the policy of getting rid of McGovern."[42]

But sex talk was a priority, as McCord made clear. "When you hear anything involving McGovern, let's hear that," he told Baldwin. ". . . [If] two people are talking about sex they had, if there is any names, I want to know it."

Two weeks later, Liddy came into Hunt's office at the Mullen Company. "We have to go into the DNC headquarters again," he said. "McCord screwed up somehow. Evidently, he bugged the wrong telephone line. He was supposed to bug O'Brien's."

"I'm against it, Gordon," Hunt said. "My men got McCord in and out of the target premises, and if he fouled up his part of the operation, I don't think we should have to go again." But Hunt relented to Liddy's arguments. "I've been arguing against it for days," he told McCord. "But Liddy's boss is adamant."

Hunt went home to have dinner with Lisa and St. John at Witches Island. Dorothy was vacationing in England with Kevan and David.

"If anybody should have developed a second sense by now, it should have been me," Hunt lamented in his memoir, "after all I'd been through in life. . . . But if I felt uneasy, I suppressed it, kissing my children good night and telling them that I was seeing Mr. Liddy that evening."[43]

"OUR SIDE"

Nixon and Helms knew nothing of what their underlings were up to that day and night. They were men of power who delegated authority and trusted subordinates to carry out their orders. They conferred by phone during lunch hour. Nixon wanted to share a confidence. President Luis Echeverría of Mexico had arrived for a state visit.[44]

"I just left President Echeverría," Nixon said. "He took me aside. He doesn't speak any English, but he says, 'I'm seeing Director Helms this afternoon.' And I said, 'Good.' I said, '. . . he has authorization to speak directly to you for me.'"

"Right," Helms murmured.

"So you should tell him that I talked to you, and so forth," Nixon went on. "I don't know what game they're playing there [in Mexico], but he's strong. He wants to play the right games."

"Well, thank you very much, sir," Helms said. "Dick Walters is going with me and we're going to have about an hour's chat with him." (General Vernon "Dick" Walters, who had served as Nixon's translator on his overseas, had succeeded Cushman as Nixon's man at the CIA.)

"I went into why we had to finish Vietnam in the right way," Nixon interjected, forever needing to justify himself. "Why it was important for us to hold the line against aggression all over the world, particularly in the Western Hemisphere. Because nobody else was there to do it. And he said he's on our side all right." They were a team, Nixon emphasized. *He's on our side.*

"Oh that's great Mr. President," Helms said. "Right. Thank you."[45]

That night, with Pat away on the West Coast, and Rose Mary Woods staying in her apartment in the Watergate, Nixon boarded Air Force One for a flight to Florida and a weekend getaway. Helms went home for dinner with Cynthia and then early to bed. It was June 16, 1972.

18

THE SOREST SPOT

It took twenty hours for anyone on Dick Helms's staff to notify him about the arrest of his friend Jim McCord and four Cuban associates in the offices of the Democratic National Committee in the Watergate complex. Or so Helms said. It was plausible, as most of Helms's stories were. But was it actually true? That was harder to ascertain.

McCord, Martínez, Sturgis, Barker, and González were intercepted at two thirty in the morning by three undercover officers of the Washington, D.C., police department.[1] Tipped off by a security guard, the cops entered the offices, guns drawn. Hunt and Liddy, watching through binoculars from their command post in Room 712 of the Howard Johnson's hotel, saw cops detaining Martínez and Barker in Maxie Wells's office. They were setting up a camera to photograph documents in her desk. Martínez had a key to the desk, which he tried to hide. The cops seized the key and took a picture of it. Forty years later, Martínez, while sitting for an oral history for the Nixon presidential library, deflected all questions about that key. Half of his oral history remains classified a half century after the break-in, proof positive that the burglars' target and intentions that night remains a sensitive matter for the CIA.

The five men were taken to the precinct house on M Street to be photographed and fingerprinted. Contemplating their disastrous predicament, they gave aliases and said little. Barker identified himself as "Frank Carter." Martínez called himself "Gene Valdez." González called himself "Raoul Godoy." Sturgis gave his birth name, "Frank Fiorini." McCord identified himself "Edward Martin," the name on Hunt's CIA-forged driver's license. Hunt had given the fake card to McCord right before the break-in.

Hunt and Liddy fled the crime scene. After seeing the cops collar McCord and the Cubans, they cleaned out their hotel room and fled in near panic. Hunt gave Liddy a ride to Virginia and then returned to the Howard Johnson's to evacuate a second room used by Alfred Baldwin to monitor the intercepted conversations. Baldwin hauled away McCord's eavesdropping equipment. Hunt hurried to his office in the Executive Office Building to retrieve his incriminating notebooks. Then he went across the street to his office at the Mullen Company to call his lawyer and Barker's wife in Miami. He drove home to Potomac and roused his son St. John. He wanted to get rid of his typewriter. It was a poignant moment, the aspiring spy novelist needed to toss the tool of his trade.

"He woke me up in the wee hours," recalled St. John Hunt. There was "a pond across the street on General Griffith's property. He was the owner of this huge mansion up on the hill. I used to go there fishing with my brother. We dumped the typewriter in there."[2]

The next morning McCord's wife, Ruth, called Penny Gleason, a security officer who worked at McCord Associates. She asked Gleason for help finding a lawyer, evidently relaying a request from her husband. She also asked Gleason to take down the autographed photo of Helms hanging in McCord's office. After June 17 McCord sought to erase his connection to Helms.

In Miami, station chief Jake Esterline heard about the arrests from a friend in the Secret Service at three in the afternoon. The burglars, arraigned in court around that same time, were asked their names and professions. McCord, still posing as Edward Martin, said he was a security consultant who had worked for the CIA. "Holy shit," murmured Bob Woodward, a twenty-eight-year-old Metro reporter for the *Washington Post*, who was in the room. Woodward hustled back to the *Post* newsroom.[3] Around five o'clock, someone at the *Post* called the CIA's Public Affairs Office for comment on an "Edward Martin" arrested at the Watergate.[4]

Yet it wasn't until five hours later, ten o'clock that night, that Helms received a call from Howard Osborn, chief of the Office of Security, notifying him of the arrest of McCord and company. Or so the Agency's story went. Cynthia Helms recalled her husband receiving a call late at night.[5] But fourteen months later, under oath before the Senate Watergate Committee, Helms had a good forgettery about when exactly he learned of the Watergate arrests.

"It is my impression that I heard about it, read about it in the newspapers and heard it on the radio," he frowned as he groped for the details of a momentous event in his life, "but this is not any lapse of memory. This is just one of those things that this far back it is hard to know just exactly who might have told me or how I might have heard it."

Helms later agreed that he received a call from Osborn in the evening of June 17 but that didn't mean that the director hadn't already heard the news from someone else, perhaps his old friend Hunt. On the witness stand Helms would not be pinned down. "Certainly it was big news from the moment it happened," he said.[6]

Nixon was more forthright. The president read about the break-in in the Sunday morning edition of the *Miami Herald*. The headline read "Miamians Held in D.C. Try to Bug Demo Headquarters." His professed unconcern sounded a little forced. "I scanned the opening paragraphs . . ." Nixon recalled. "It sounded preposterous. Cubans in surgical gloves bugging the DNC!"[7]

Nixon called Haldeman, who was in California. Haldeman checked with Jeb Magruder at the Committee to Re-elect the President. "It was Liddy and McCord," Magruder squeaked, which Haldeman found evasive. Hunt was working for Liddy, Magruder added, which worried Haldeman, who knew of Liddy's eccentricities. "It has to be some crazies over at CRP, Bob," Nixon said. "That's what it was. And what does it matter? The American people will see it for what it was: a political prank. Hell, they can't take a break-in at the DNC *seriously*. I've got some real business to go over with you."[8]

Early the next day, Liddy showed up at McCord's office, which he had visited before. Stephen Anderson, a newly hired security officer at the firm, recalled a colleague telling him that Liddy asked for the keys to all the cabinets and desks. "He apparently spent hours going through the desks and pulling stuff out and taking it over to a shredding machine," Anderson said in an interview. "That was the first indication to me that something was not kosher."[9]

The arrests were certainly real business for Helms. Naturally, Watergate was the primary topic at the director's Monday morning staff meeting. The response to any inquiries about the burglars, Helms said, should be "limited to a statement that they are former employees who retired."[10] Bill Colby, the former Far East division chief serving as one of Helms's top deputies, recalled his boss's injunction: "Stay cool, volunteer nothing, because it will only be used to involve us."

Unconcern was Helms's mantra. "Mr. Osborn's call to me was a perfectly routine matter," he said. He was to be notified if any Agency employee got in trouble, which in a large organization, happened regularly. It was all perfectly routine.

Except it wasn't. That day Helms received a visit from Colby and Karl Wagner, executive assistant to General Cushman. They felt obliged to tell the director about the camera and disguises they had provided to Hunt the summer before in connection with the burglary of Dr. Fielding's office. Helms said the Ellsberg business had nothing to do with the break-in, so it wasn't an issue. And from that moment on, Helms sought to obfuscate the fact that the CIA had been helping Hunt on orders from the White House.[11]

As always, Helms controlled the intelligence. Wagner gave Helms his memos on the Technical Service Division's assistance to Hunt. The deputy TSD chief handed over his notes and copies of the photographs of Ellsberg's psychiatrist's office. Sidney Gottlieb, a senior official in TSD, gave copies of the photos to Colby. If Helms did not know of Hunt's role in the burglary at Dr. Fielding's in the summer of 1971, he certainly knew by the evening of June 19, 1972, although he would indignantly insist otherwise.[12]

Helms had an elegant explanation, of course. He didn't know what the casing photographs showed, he explained to Watergate investigators. "Even though Dr. Fielding's name was discernible on a wall that was photographed," he said with utmost sincerity, "no one in the Agency who had seen the picture had identified Dr. Fielding or was aware that his office had been broken into."

The explanation was hard to credit. Helms was shown the photos by his staff because Hunt was involved in the Watergate burglary. Hunt and Liddy took the photographs in preparation for a burglary. Helms was mystified but not curious enough to ask a single question about the photos.[13] Cynthia Helms spoke of her husband's "amazing powers of observation which his years in intelligence had honed to an extraordinary degree."[14] Helms's story—and he stuck to it—was that those powers simply failed him.

Helms's biggest problem was Hunt, whose name was found in Barker's and Martínez's address books, seized by the police, and leaked to reporters. On Tuesday, June 20, a front-page *Washington Post* headline exposed Hunt's connection to the burglars: "White House Consultant Tied to Suspect in Bugging Case." Helms's pal was now a fugitive. The situation was far from routine even for a CIA director.

Hunt, pacing the floor at Witches Island, ducked phone calls from the irritating Bob Woodward. He phoned Dorothy, still on vacation in England, to tell her his name and picture were in the *Post*. "The important thing is for you not to cut short your vacation," he said. "I'm sure this whole thing will blow away just as soon as the right people do what they're supposed to do."

The right people. That meant Howard's friends on the seventh floor, Dick Helms and Tom Karamessines. Hunt hoped to be rescued, yet again, by the boss. Dorothy decided to stay on vacation. Howard flew to Los Angeles that night.

UNDER CONTROL

The next morning, Nixon spoke with Haldeman for more than an hour in the Oval Office. Haldeman, taking notes, said Nixon was sounding paranoid in the wake of the burglars' arrests. He asked that the Executive Office Building be checked "to make sure I was not being bugged."[15] That conversation, recorded by the White House taping system, would become notorious when it was revealed that eighteen minutes of talk had been erased.

Haldeman told Nixon that McCord was going to say that he was working for the Cubans, who had been planting the bugs for their own reasons. Hunt had either disappeared or was about to, he said, adding that one of the burglars, Barker, had been Hunt's deputy during the Bay of Pigs. Haldeman also mentioned that Hunt had been involved in the "Diem thing."

"I recalled that Colson had alluded to Hunt's intelligence background," Nixon said later. "I asked Haldeman how Hunt was involved in the Watergate incident. He said on the night of the break-in Hunt had been waiting across the street in the motel room from which the bugs would be monitored."

Nixon conceived of a cover story. "Whatever the case, the involvement of Cubans, McCord and Hunt made it appear to be a Cuban operation," he reasoned. "It would protect us from the political impact of the disclosure of the CRP's involvement and it would undercut the Democrats by calling attention to the fact that the Cuban community in the United States feared McGovern's naive policy toward Castro."[16]

Nixon called Haldeman that evening. He was feeling better. "This thing may be under control because of the Cubans who went in there," he said. "A lot of people think the break-in was done by anti-Castro Cubans."

"Well, I've never understood, myself, what the Cubans were doing there," Haldeman said.

"Tell Ehrlichman this whole group of Cubans is tied to the Bay of Pigs," Nixon said.

"The Bay of Pigs?" wondered Haldeman. "What does that have to do with this?"

"Ehrlichman will know what I mean," he said.[17] Ehrlichman was in the room when Nixon brought up the "who shot John angle" with Helms.

When Haldeman asked Ehrlichman, he said, "I'm staying out of this one." Between Nixon and Helms was suddenly a dangerous place to be.

Helms went up to Capitol Hill for a closed-door meeting with the Senate Foreign Relations Committee meeting about the proposed Anti-Ballistic Missile Treaty. In passing, Helms was asked if he wanted to volunteer any information on the former CIA employee, James McCord, who had been arrested at the Watergate.

"I will volunteer anything you would like," Helms said agreeably, a reliable indicator that he would do anything but. "I just want to distance myself from my alumnus," adding, "I don't have—I can't conceive of what this caper was all about. I really can't conceive it."[18] Because the senators knew nothing of Helms's "deep appreciation" for McCord, or the CIA all-star team that was working out of McCord Associates, the former director felt no need to disabuse them of their innocence.

The next night a suspicious fire broke out at McCord's house in Rockville, Maryland. Another connection between the burglars and the Agency was cauterized.

AMATEUR ARSONISTS

In his odd Watergate memoir, *A Piece of Tape*, James McCord said the real story of the Watergate affair was the "illegal misuse" of the CIA by the Nixon administration. The fire at his house had nothing to do with it. That's not what Senator Baker and staff found. They concluded that McCord's wife and friends destroyed evidence that linked McCord to the Agency.

McCord's version of the story was frightening. The fire came in the aftermath of a bomb threat on June 19, McCord wrote. A male caller, he said, had told his wife Ruth that a bomb would go off in their house within twenty-four hours. Ruth took the children and went to stay with a friend. McCord, still in jail, instructed her to go back to the house and clear out "newspapers, magazines and other fire hazards which a spark might set off." He also told her to burn a folder of his CIA retirement papers. "It contained nothing related to Watergate," McCord claimed. "I simply wanted none of our personal papers to be spread over the front yard in case a bomb did go off."[19]

McCord speculated that the bomb threat came from the Nixon White House, which he said wanted to get into his house and remove evidence of his work for Mitchell, Dean, and Magruder. In his account, McCord did not mention the name of his friend Lee Pennington, who joined Ruth McCord in destroying his papers.[20]

McCord's boss, Paul Gaynor, told a more verifiable version of the same story. Gaynor liked McCord and was not one to impugn a colleague. He told Edward Sayle, a subordinate in the Security Research Staff, that Lee Pennington, a former FBI agent and close friend of McCord's, had gone to the McCord home on June 22. Gaynor knew Pennington because he was a longtime confidential SRS informant, paid $250 a month by sterile check untraceable to the U.S. government.[21]

Pennington knew a thing or two about sensitive material. He was the executive secretary of the American Security Council, a right-wing group that maintained an extensive archive on communists, socialists, liberals, civil rights activists, homosexuals, and others they suspected of subverting the U.S. government. McCord had been tapping Pennington for information since he joined the Agency in the early 1950s. Pennington's relationship to McCord, said one CIA employee, was "like father and son."[22]

Since McCord's retirement Pennington supplied information to the CIA via his new case officer, a man named Lou Vasaly. Pennington also mentioned the incident at McCord's house to Vasaly, explaining he searched for documents "that might link the Agency with Mr. McCord." He said he joined Ruth McCord in tossing such material into the blazing living room fireplace.

As the amateur arsonists fed the blaze, they forgot to open the flue in the fireplace. The house soon filled with smoke, driving Pennington and Ruth McCord outside coughing and gagging. So while McCord acknowledged there was a fire at his house, his account left out a detail that his former colleagues found relevant: that his wife and Pennington had destroyed evidence linking him to the Agency.

McCord didn't say anything about Liddy's shredding paper at his office the day after the burglary but he admitted that he kept a wealth of incriminating evidence on his property at the time. His car, returned by Alfred Baldwin on the night of the arrest, contained two tape recorders, two electric typewriters belonging to Hunt, and other electronic equipment removed from the Howard Johnson's motel. All of the gear, McCord said, was "rapidly traceable to their original source of purchase," the CIA contractor in Chicago.

McCord said he also had $18,000 in cash, a copy of a letter signed by John Mitchell authorizing McCord to obtain information from the Internal Security Division of the Department of Justice about possible violent protests at the Republican National Convention, and some notes from early 1972 mentioning not only Mitchell's name but also the names of John Dean and Jeb Magruder. McCord said he destroyed all of this evidence on his own, including "carbon copies of recent wiretap logs."[23] That was a telling detail. McCord wasn't just a technician. He was a collector. He kept the take from the wiretaps at the Watergate and elsewhere for the Agency's use.

Helms was truthful when he said the CIA was not involved in organizing the Watergate break-in. No CIA official told the burglars where to enter surreptitiously—those orders emanated from the White House and the Committee to Re-elect the President and the intelligence collected by the burglars went back to their sponsors. But the Agency harvested the fruit of Hunt and McCord's work. McCord kept copies of the wiretap logs at his home; Hunt passed material to Helms through the Agency's office at the NSC. The burglars worked for the White House and the Agency shared in the take. It wasn't a CIA conspiracy. It was opportunistic intelligence collection, which was Helms's métier.

What was in the wiretap logs that the burglars obtained McCord never said, but Jeb Magruder did. Two days after the break-in, Mitchell ordered him to get rid of the transcripts the burglars had delivered. The file was about "four or five inches thick," Magruder recalled in his memoir. The stack of papers consisted of photographs and transcripts of telephone conversations. In his Connecticut summer house, he skimmed the file as he sat by his fireplace tossing the paper into the flames, all the while "chuckling at the graphic details of the social lives of [DNC staff]."[24]

The CIA "had information as early as June 1972 that one of their paid operatives, Lee R. Pennington, Jr. had entered the James McCord residence shortly after the Watergate break-in and destroyed documents which might show a link between McCord and the CIA," Senator Baker later concluded.[25]

Howard Osborn, chief of the Office of Security, didn't share the information with the FBI, which likely saved Helms's job.[26] If Osborn didn't know about the bonfire at the McCords', Helms could plausibly deny that he knew. The story stayed within the Office of Security. Investigators would not learn about the blaze at the McCords' home until twenty months later, by which time Dick Helms was thousands of miles from the scene of the crime.

"A LOT OF HANKY-PANKY"

It was a routinely hectic day in the life of the president. He had an 8:30 breakfast in the Family Dining Room of the White House with leaders of the House of Representatives who were going to travel to China as part of the opening up of relations he had orchestrated with Kissinger. From there Nixon went to the Oval Office.

"Now, on the investigation," Haldeman said almost before they sat down. The chief of staff was a man of disciplined routine, now taxed by the undisciplined antics of Liddy and Hunt. "You know, the Democratic break-in thing, we're back in the problem area because the FBI is not under control."

J. Edgar Hoover had died in May and Acting Director L. Patrick Gray could not control his own agency. "Their investigation is now leading into some productive areas, because they've been able to trace the money [found in the burglars' possession]," he said. "And it goes in some directions we don't want it to go."

Nixon brooded as Haldeman rambled on about the new facts and new names filtering in. He had spoken with White House counsel John Dean and heard from John Mitchell, and he had come up with a plan. "The way to handle this now," Haldeman said, "is for us to have Walters call Pat Gray and just say, 'Stay the hell out of this . . . this is ah, business here we don't want you to go any further on it.'"

That was plausible. The FBI agents working the Watergate case assumed that Cuban burglars in suits with sophisticated gear and stacks of hundred-dollar bills had to be CIA operatives. "They'll stop, if we take this other step . . ." Haldeman promised. "It's got to be Helms and, ah, what's his name . . . Walters," the new deputy director.

Haldeman said he would call them in.

"All right, fine . . . ," Nixon said, warming to the idea. "We protected Helms from one hell of a lot of things."[27]

That was true. The Justice Department suppressed the book of renegade agent Victor Marchetti and cut a deal to ensure the silence of Bob Maheu and Johnny Rosselli. Nixon had rejected Haldeman's suggestion that they reopen the investigation of JFK's assassination.[28]

"You open that scab there's a hell of a lot of things," Nixon said, rehearsing the threat once more, "and that we just feel that it would be very detrimental to have this thing go any further. This involves these Cubans, Hunt, and a lot of hanky-panky that we have nothing to do with ourselves."

Hanky-panky like the Bay of Pigs and the question of Who shot John?

"You call them in," Nixon growled. "Play it tough. That's the way they play it and that's the way we are going to play it."

The meeting was breaking up when the president added more detail to his message for Helms and Walters, who were due any minute.

"When you . . . get these people in," Nixon started, "Say, 'Look, the problem is that this will open the whole, the whole Bay of Pigs thing, and the President just feels that, ah, without going into the details . . . don't, don't lie to them to the extent to say there is no involvement, but just say this is sort of a comedy of errors, bizarre, without getting into it, the President believes that it is going to open the whole Bay of Pigs thing up again. And, ah because these people are playing for keeps . . . they should call the FBI in and say that we wish, for the country, don't go any further into this case. Period!"

Nixon excused himself for a meeting with his economic team, from Treasury Secretary George Shultz on down. He took a break for a photo session. Mr. and Mrs. Carlos Dixon, dairy farmers from Arkansas, smiled proudly for the cameras with their two children, unaware they had interrupted the president's efforts to obstruct justice. The Dixons departed, and Haldeman returned to receive a set of refined instructions for the CIA director.

"This fellow Hunt," he resumed, "you know, he knows too damn much and he was involved, we happen to know that. And [if] it gets out that . . . this is all involved in the Cuban thing, it's a fiasco, and it's going to make the FBI and the CIA look bad. It's going to make Hunt look bad, and it's likely to blow the whole, uh, Bay of Pigs thing which we think would be very unfortunate for CIA and for the country at this time, and for American foreign policy, and he just better tough it and lay it on them . . ."

Haldeman had his orders. He headed for Ehrlichman's conference room on the second floor of the West Wing where Dick Helms and Dick Walters waited expectantly.

"A DEVIOUS HARD-NOSED SMELL"

"I am tall," Helms recalled. "Even in those day Dick Walters had a certain bulk and Ehrlichman's mere presence took up some space," which is to say Helms still detested the man. They had scarcely wedged themselves into straight-backed chairs around the conference table in the small room when Haldeman marched in.

Four tense men sat face-to-face. Haldeman asked Helms what connection the CIA might have with the Watergate break-in. "The CIA had no connection with Watergate," Helms said. From the start he spoke broadly, not just of the burglary at the DNC but all of "Watergate." There was no connection, he insisted. "Elegantly put," Haldeman sniffed in his memoir, "with just the right tone of injured innocence."[29]

Haldeman explained the president's plan. "It has been decided that General Walters go see Pat Gray and tell him that further investigations . . . could lead to the exposure of certain Agency assets and channels for handling money," he said.[30] "The president asked me to tell you this entire affair may be connected to the Bay of Pigs, and if it opens up, the Bay of Pigs may be blown."

Those few words threw the tiny room into turmoil.

"The Bay of Pigs hasn't got a damned thing to do with this!" Helms shouted.

Silence. The four men stared at each other. Helms's sudden rage subsided. Ehrlichman's dark, intense eyes roamed under his thick brows. He never trusted Helms, thought he was a blackmailer. The upright Haldeman, shocked by Helms's violent reaction, wondered what was so explosive about the Bay of Pigs story. Helms regained his composure. "I have no concern about the Bay of Pigs," he said. He always denied he shouted. He recalled saying, "There's nothing about the Bay of Pigs that's not in the public domain."

In later years, Helms acknowledged that "the whole Bay of Pigs thing" was a Nixonian threat with a "devious, hard-nosed smell." It conveyed, said one CIA historian, "a desire to touch a sore spot, to apply pressure."[31] Helms called the threat "incoherent," which didn't explain why the phrase had caused him, a master of self-control, to lose his temper.[32]

"The whole Bay of Pigs thing," as Haldeman correctly intuited, was Nixon's way of referring to a sinister nexus that could end Helms's career if disclosed. Drew Pearson and Jack Anderson had published the broad outlines of the story in 1967 and 1971. *The Mafia plots to assassinate Fidel Castro had somehow backfired leaving too many people, including Nixon, to wonder who shot John.* While the Mafia men blamed Castro, others—like Howard Hunt in retirement—said CIA personnel might have been involved in the Dallas ambush. Helms himself had said *Make sure we had no one in Dallas on that day.* The director lost his temper in the June 23 meeting because Nixon had found the sorest of spots and squeezed hard.

Helms went along as a convincing messenger. He had served as an interpreter for Eisenhower and Nixon. He spoke at least five languages fluently and had served as military attaché in three European capitals. He told Walters to go see the FBI director. "You must remind Mr. Gray of the agreement between the CIA and the FBI that if they run into or expose one another's assets they will not interfere with the other," he said.

Walters took the message straight to Gray at FBI headquarters on Pennsylvania Avenue. In the director's office suite, he passed a young military officer, Colin Powell, who was waiting for an appointment. Per Helms's instructions, Walters reminded Gray of the working agreement between the CIA and the FBI on such matters.[33] After investigating the five suspects, Walters said, "It would be better to taper off the matter."[34]

Haldeman went back to the Oval Office and told Nixon the threat had worked. After telling Helms the Watergate investigation "tracks back to the Bay of Pigs, . . . he said we'll be very happy to be helpful."[35]

And, in the moment, Helms was helpful. He would later insist that he resisted Nixon's cover-up plans from the start. Not in that first week, he didn't. In the June 23 meeting, the director acquiesced to the White House order to tell the FBI to limit the Watergate investigation. Walters delivered his message: *Better to taper off the matter.*

19

THE RUSE

Helms, the civil servant, wanted to be helpful.

"I was being asked about an operational matter," he later explained of the explosive June 23 conversation. "That was what was concerning me. What did they have in mind? What were they up to? It did not occur to me that the President of the United States would be asking me to perform an illegal act right there in the White House." But he admitted he did not want to cross Nixon, adding the credo of a Washington survivor: "Anybody who thinks you can say the president's wrong . . . lives in a very dangerous life in the executive branch."[1]

John Dean, an ambitious lawyer just hired by Haldeman as White House counsel, wanted to prove his toughness. Just thirty years old, he summoned Walters to the White House the following Monday. He wanted to make sure the burglars didn't talk about their connection to the White House. Walters told Dean that further checking showed the FBI investigation did not threaten any CIA activities. "I could not say that further investigation would jeopardize Agency sources," Walters explained.[2]

Dean was frantic. He asked Walters to come again the next day. Could the CIA have participated in the burglary without him knowing it?" he wanted to know. "Impossible," Walters replied. Dean suggested Barker had been involved in a break-in at the Chilean Embassy.[3] Walters said the Agency didn't know anything about it.

Dean kept probing. He said some of the suspects were "wobbling." Walters said no matter how scared they were, they couldn't implicate the CIA because the Agency wasn't involved in the break-in. Dean didn't believe it. He wondered if the CIA would provide bail money for the defendants. "Would it be possible for the CIA to pay the salaries of these individuals while they served their jail sentences?" he asked. Walters raised the possibility with Helms, who said he would have to clear it with the chairmen of the House and Senate Armed Services Committees. In other words, forget it. Following Dean's proposed course, Walters added, "would only enlarge the problem."[4]

Helms wanted to be helpful without compromising the Agency. In advance of a scheduled meeting with Gray on June 28, he briefed two colleagues who wanted to accompany him: Ted Shackley, the new chief of the Western Hemisphere Division, and Lawrence Sternfield, chief of Cuban operations. He wrote a memo for the record to Walters. "I informed them that the Agency is attempting to 'distance itself from the investigation' and that I wanted them along as 'reference files' to participate in the discussion when requested," he wrote. By "reference files," Helms meant that Shackley and Sternfield would answer any questions about the Cubans.

"I told them I wanted no free-wheeling . . . hypothesis or conjecture about responsibility or likely objectives of the Watergate intrusion," Helms went on. He didn't need speculation because he knew enough already. "At such a meeting it is up to the FBI to lay some cards on the table," Helms wrote. "Otherwise we are unable to help." The director staked out a hard line. He would not share anything until he knew who the FBI wanted to question.

"In addition," he closed, "we still adhere to the request that they confine themselves to the personalities already arrested or directly under suspicion and that they desist from expanding this investigation into other areas which may well, eventually, run aground of our operations."[5]

Walters's message to the FBI on Friday was *better to taper off the matter*. It echoed in Helms's memo five days later: *desist from expanding this investigation*.

The meeting never happened. Ehrlichman called Gray and told him to cancel. Gray then called Helms. The acting FBI director was surprised Helms didn't ask why the meeting was called off. "Instead, he gave me two more names [of CIA officers] not to interview," Gray recalled. They were Karl Wagner, Cushman's assistant, and John Caswell, an officer in Technical Services Division. Both provided help to Hunt while he was scheming to discredit Ellsberg. "They're active CIA agents," Helms told Gray, no doubt apologetically. "Their names have to be kept secret."[6]

Helms closed by offering a tip. He said he'd heard that Howard Hunt worked

for Ehrlichman. That was a Helmsian masterstroke, the first of several that summer. In one conversation, Helms had blocked the FBI's Watergate agents from
investigating CIA support for Hunt while nudging the Bureau to investigate Ehrlichman, whom he loathed. It worked, with lasting impact. The burglary at Dr.
Fielding's office and the Chilean break-ins would not become public knowledge
for ten months. In that crucial formative year, Watergate was a story about White
House burglars, not CIA burglars.

Only later did Gray realize that Helms shielded the two officers because they
knew all about Hunt and the campaign to smear Ellsberg. It never occurred to
Gray that the CIA director might be lying to him. Gray was one of the many
people in Washington who believed in the story of the law-abiding CIA director.

"Nowhere in my entire upbringing, from childhood through the Navy and
into the highest levels of government service, had I ever been given any reason to
suspect that in private conversation the Director of Central Intelligence would be
anything less than brutally honest with the acting director of the FBI," Gray wrote
in his memoir. "In the Defense Department's dealings with Congress and the
executive branch, we had always relied on the 'presumption of regularity' working
in both directions. . . . We may have disagreed, and we might even have disliked
one another, but we didn't lie to one another. The high public trust we all held
simply didn't allow for it."[7]

Helms had a different conception of the public trust, one that enabled him to
retain his reputation and high position while Pat Gray, believer in the "presumption of regularity," was swept into disgrace.

UNFLAPPABLE

Henry Kissinger admired Dick Helms's quality of unflappability. It was on display on June 30 when he delivered the director's annual State of the Agency
address to an auditorium full of CIA employees. If beset by a uniquely complex set of problems, the director showed no signs of worry. He wanted to tell a
humorous story.

"I was reminded coming down here," he said, "of a story which may be old to
some and new to others but I'll take a chance and tell it anyway because I think
that in its peculiar way it sets a sort of a focus on the kind of life we lead in the
Agency and some of the uneven problems we have."

There were a couple hundred people in the room—analysts, operatives, clerks,
researchers, division chiefs—more than a few of whom were wondering about the
arrests at the Watergate.

"This is the story of a traveling salesman," Helms began. The crowd tittered in expectation of a bawdy joke. "Don't start laughing because it doesn't come out the way you think it does.

"About midnight one night [the salesman] got a flat tire on a bridge across a roaring stream," Helms said. "As the rain pounded down, he got out and got his jack out and got himself organized to change the tire. In the process of this he took the hubcap off the offending wheel and he put it up on the edge of the bridge on a little stone parapet and then he took the lugs off the wheel and put them very carefully inside the hubcap. Then he got himself down to get the tire off. But as he gave it that extra lurch, . . . off went the hubcap and the lugs into the roaring stream.

"The rain was still pelting down," Helms continued. "He got up, tried to remember exactly how far it was to the next town, or how far he'd come from the town he'd been in before. As he was focusing on this problem, he saw a strange little figure standing behind a fence just on the other side of the stream looking at him intently. He wondered how long that man had been there and he was uncomfortable because of the lateness of the hour. But anyway he turned to him and said, 'I've had a flat tire here and maybe you saw what happened. . . .'"

The director had the room's attention.

"So the little man said, 'What's your problem?' And the driver explained in great detail just what had happened to him. The little man said, 'Look, instead of walking to one town or the other, why don't you just go around the automobile and take one lug off the other three tires and put those lugs on the fourth tire and that will enable you to drive to the next town where then you can get yourself properly taken care of in a garage.'

"The traveling salesman thought about this. His eyes visibly brightened. But he began to get very pensive and had a very strange feeling. And suddenly he said, 'Isn't that building over there the insane asylum?'

"The little man said, 'Yes, 'tis.'

"And he said, 'Well, are you an inmate?' And the little man said, 'Yes, I am.'

"He said, 'Well, how were you able to figure out this thing?'

"And the little fellow said, 'Well, I may be crazy but I don't have to be stupid.'"

As knowing chuckles filled the auditorium, Helms coughed slyly. "Maybe you see what I mean."[8]

What he meant was clear enough for his audience. The men and women of the CIA might be a little crazy, but they knew how to solve problems that confounded most mortals.

The director's dance with the president was a little crazy, at least in its latest incarnation. There was nothing like the Nixon-Helms relationship in the Agency's twenty-five-year history. Harry Truman shuffled directors until he found one he trusted, General Walter Bedell Smith. Allen Dulles's relationship with Eisenhower was one of arm's-length respect. The friendship of Dulles and Kennedy, poisoned by the Bay of Pigs, congealed to mutual patrician disdain. Kennedy tolerated the overbearing John McCone while Johnson tired of him and welcomed Helms as an adviser. Nixon and Helms, by contrast, were enemies, allies, confidantes, and now, potentially, partners in crime.

In the wake of the arrests at the Watergate, they both sought to impede the FBI's investigation of the burglars in fear of what disclosure might bring. For Helms, it was his friendship with Hunt, his relationship with McCord, the national security operations that they had carried out, and the reporting that came back to the Agency. For Nixon, it was his knowledge of the use of Hunt and Liddy as campaign spies and White House plumbers. For both, the Watergate arrests threatened to expose the subterranean politics of assassination—the Castro plots, Diem's demise, Dallas, and the elimination of General Schneider that they had to hide.

In this perilous situation, Helms had one advantage that Nixon did not. For the president, it was illegal to conceal or destroy material evidence, suborn witnesses, or dissemble to law enforcement. For Helms, not so much. He had authority, derived from the language of the 1947 National Security Act, to protect the Agency's sources and methods. Helms's successful effort to prevent the FBI from interviewing witnesses knowledgeable about Hunt's role in the targeting of Ellsberg, for example, may have been unethical, but it was not illegal. As CIA director, Helms had discretion to hide certain activities from law enforcement. As the duly sworn president, Nixon did not. And that would make all the difference in determining who would fall first.

As for the Watergate break-in, Helms said at the end of his State of the Agency address, "I don't know what's behind it. I don't know who put up the money. I don't really know anything about it. But I want to put your mind at rest; the Agency had nothing whatever to do with it."[9]

Nothing whatever was his story, and he was sticking to it. It just wasn't completely true. Helms knew that the White House was behind the burglars. He had recommended Hunt to Haldeman. Helms knew a lot, and he put his colleagues' minds at rest by disclosing none of it.

Helms followed up with a second ingenious move: he left town. The calm audacity! The effortless mastery! The sangfroid! As Dave Phillips noted, Helms's style in running covert operations ran to "controlled boldness." In the Watergate fiasco, he played the subtlest of variations: passive boldness.

On July 1, exactly two weeks after the Watergate arrests, Helms departed for a tour of Agency facilities in Australia and New Zealand—previously scheduled, he insisted. No director had ever felt the need to visit the region, but now, it seems, was the time.[10] Helms spent the next three weeks out of the country. Before leaving, he duly signed the papers formally designating Dick Walters as acting director.

The working vacation had the benefit of removing him from Washington. Helms was still in charge but at an immense distance. He could always be reached on a secure line in an emergency, but that would be complicated for all concerned. He had massaged the president's demands. He had laid down the law for his subordinates. If something disastrous happened, it wouldn't technically be on his watch. He expected the White House demands to continue, but that was Walters's problem for the duration. Helms just *had* to inspect the station in Sydney.

The FBI soon came calling. Acting Director Gray spoke to Acting Director Walters on July 6. "I can't hold up on this anymore," Gray said. He needed formal notification that the FBI's investigation should taper off, with respect to certain CIA activities. Walters expressed surprise. "But Pat," he said, "I told Dean to go ahead," adding that the Agency had no objection to expanding the investigation.

Gray was confused. Dean hadn't told him anything. Walters's message was suddenly very different from what he had said on June 23 (*better to taper off the matter*) and what Helms said in their call on June 28 (*desist from expanding the investigation,* and *you can't talk to Wagner or Caswell*). When Gray asked for a memo saying the investigation might compromise CIA operations, Walters had reached the limit of the Agency's passive cooperation. The CIA men might agree to something like that orally, but they would not put it in writing. Walters said—"with some emotion," he recalled—that he would not say that the FBI investigation threatened Agency operations.[11]

Gray called Nixon. What the president knew about the burglars' activities and when he knew it would forever be unclear. At that point, Nixon wanted Helms to head off the FBI, and, as far as he knew, the CIA director had done just that. Gray warned the president that certain people on his staff "are trying to mortally wound you by using the FBI and CIA."

Nixon was all smooth confidence. This Watergate fuss would pass. It was too transparently a Democratic ploy, and he had ways to make it go away. What did it matter what Walters said to Gray?

"Pat, you just continue your aggressive and thorough investigation," the president purred. Nixon, like Helms, would make no overt demands. That was the end of CIA interference in the FBI's investigation, Gray said in his memoir. "No more attempts were made by anyone in the CIA or the White House."[12]

For three weeks, Helms had cooperated with Nixon. Now the interests of the president and the director were diverging. The loser in the process was the hapless fugitive Howard Hunt.

DOROTHY

In his hour of need, Hunt's marriage improved. Dorothy and Howard reunited in Chicago. He flew in from Los Angeles. She had returned from England to Washington, trying to reassure the family that everything was going to be okay. Her cousin in Chicago called her and suggested she pay a visit. Dorothy caught a flight to Chicago.

"The reunion was if not joyous—given the circumstances—warm, loving and without recrimination on her part," Hunt wrote in his memoir. Dorothy was kind in that way. At that time, Dorothy wanted a divorce, said St. John Hunt. "Around nineteen sixty-eight or sixty-nine, I think was when she first started talking about divorcing my father, and then by seventy-two she was all set."

Howard recounted the miserable sequence of events, finishing with his faith that he and his accomplices "would be taken care of company style," implying the Company, the CIA, would come to his rescue. By the time she flew back to Washington, Hunt stopped skulking. "Her positive reinforcement gave me the morale boost that I needed and renewed energy to confront the situation."

Hunt hired William Bittman, a former Justice Department prosecutor now with Hogan & Hartson, a prestigious D.C. law firm. He told Bittman he "resented being cast in the role of a fugitive" and "was ready to speak to whatever government agencies were looking for him." He paid his retainer in hundred-dollar bills.

Hunt expected help from "the right people" in Langley and didn't get it. Somehow, he learned that John Dean had pressed Dick Walters for legal and living expenses. "Walters opted out of doing things Company style," Hunt noted bitterly. Fortunately, he added, "Haldeman rode to the rescue," ordering a subordinate to disburse $75,000 to the defendants.[13]

Dorothy went to work as Howard's courier, negotiator, and all-around secret agent. Through Bittman she met a man identified only as "Mr. Rivers" who asked her to estimate the expenses for the five men under arrest, plus her husband and Liddy. She called McCord, Liddy, and Barker, who gave their estimates. Mr. Rivers told her to go to a particular pay phone in Dulles Airport where she would find a key to a locker. She found the money in the locker, just not as much as promised. Instead of five months of expenses for her husband and the others, she found three.[14]

Dorothy delivered a share to Jim McCord, now out on bail. When they met at the Lakewood Country Club in Rockville, she mentioned that Paul O'Brien, a lawyer for the Committee to Re-elect the President, had expressed the view that the burglary was a CIA operation. Dorothy assumed it was, but McCord denied it.[15] He emphasized the point with fundamentalist conviction: *Watergate was not a CIA operation!*

When Dorothy got home she sliced open a letter from family friend Bill Buckley.

Dear Dorothy,

I don't know where Howard is obviously but get word to him that if I can help I stand ready to do so. How are you?

Lots of love

Wm. F. Buckley Jr.[16]

BACK CHANNEL

When Dick Helms returned from his working vacation, the handwritten report of Bob Bennett's case officer was waiting on his desk. Bennett, owner of the Mullen Company and employer of Howard Hunt, was a CIA informant. The case officer, Martin Lukoskie, transmitted Bennett's reporting to the Agency on a regular basis. He wrote out his first post-Watergate memo by hand "because of the sensitivity of the information."[17]

He reported that Bennett was protecting the Agency from reporters who came calling about Hunt's job at the firm. Some suspected the Mullen Company might be a front for CIA operations, an accurate conclusion that Bennett sought to discourage. Bennett bragged that he had dissuaded reporters from the *Post* and *Star* from pursuing a "*Seven Days in May* scenario," implicating the CIA in a Watergate conspiracy. He was referring to the best-selling book and Hollywood movie about an incipient military coup against a liberal president deemed soft on the Soviet Union.[18] Bennett didn't want reporters thinking the CIA was plotting against Nixon. Bennett later bragged of feeding information, not for attribution, to Bob Woodward of the *Washington Post*, who was said to be "suitably grateful." The Mullen Company's association with the CIA would not be reported by the *Post* for almost two years.[19]

Bennett reported that he had contacted Edward B. Williams, lead attorney for the Democratic National Committee, which was suing the Committee to Re-elect the President for violating its rights in the burglary. Bennett wanted to "kill off" any reference to the Agency's relationship with the Mullen Company in the course of the litigation. Williams agreed, which was no surprise.[20] Williams and Helms were social friends and Mullen's ties to the Agency could only complicate the DNC's litigation against the Republicans.

Helms believed he had put the matter behind him. At least that's what his official biographers said. Their conclusion was cheerful. "By mid-July 1972 the Watergate incident no longer involved him or CIA," they wrote of Helms. "He had made it clear that any assistance the CIA had given Howard Hunt was merely to help staunch the unauthorized flow of national security information. He had repeatedly denied the CIA had any direct connection to the break-in."[21] Then Helms received a clandestine letter from his friend Jim McCord, the connection which Helms preferred to conceal.

"From time to time, I'll send along things you may be interested in from an info standpoint," McCord wrote in an unsigned letter to the director's office in early August. Someone, perhaps Elizabeth Dunlevy, Helms's longtime secretary, passed the letter to Office of Security "as a routine piece of junk mail."[22] Chief Howard Osborn recognized McCord's handwriting because McCord had worked for him for most of his career.

"This is a copy of a letter that went to my lawyer," McCord wrote. The accused burglar, now out on bail, had retained Gerald Alch, an associate of F. Lee Bailey, the famous criminal defense attorney. The White House was seeking to blame the Agency for the burglary, McCord said, noting that "leaks this week by the prosecutor and/or the FBI to the NYT are trying to infer this was a CIA operation. . . . Rest assured I will not be a patsy to this latest ploy. . . ."[23]

Osborn took the letter to a meeting with Helms and Larry Houston, general counsel for the Agency.[24] Helms asked for their advice. Houston said they did not have to turn it over to Watergate prosecutor Earl Silbert. Osborn said they did. Helms did not hesitate. He told Osborn to file the letter away and say nothing.[25]

Helms's controlled boldness bought him precious time. McCord was facing serious criminal charges. The Agency was publicly denying any relationship with him. Yet the defendant was sharing his legal strategy with the director. If there was no relationship, Helms would have had no reason to withhold the letter from the prosecutors. There was a relationship, which Helms had to hide. McCord's missive made clear he wanted to protect the Agency and his former boss without implicating them. He wanted a back channel to the Agency while navigating his legal ordeal. The CIA did not turn the letter over to the Justice Department for nine months, by which time McCord was no longer Dick Helms's problem.[26]

THE PENNINGTON RUSE

Two weeks later came Helms's true masterstroke—the deft operational response that confounded law enforcement and protected the Agency's equities. In a summer of supple spy work, the Pennington ruse was sheer genius.

It began ominously for Helms. On August 18, a special agent in the FBI's Alexandria office asked the Agency for a name trace on a "Mr. Pennington," said to have been McCord's supervisor. Frederick Evans, in the Agency's Personnel Security division, recalled a conversation with Edward Sayle of his staff. Sayle had said that Pennington told him he had "entered Mr. McCord's office and home" and destroyed "any indication of connections between the Agency and Mr. McCord."

The Watergate investigators were also interested. Earl Silbert wrote in his diary that he and senior FBI agent Angelo Lano were working on "the problem of trying to locate this fellow Pennington. We are still trying to locate him as possible source of information for the equipment that McCord had."[27]

The question of how to handle the FBI's query went to Howard Osborn, chief of the Office of Security, who did not make major decisions without consulting with Helms.

"Pennington's file was very closely held," Osborn explained when grilled by Senate investigators two years later. So somebody at the Agency—it was never clear who—provided the inquiring minds at the FBI with the name of Cecil Harold Pennington, no relation, a former Office of Security employee who was retired and had never been McCord's supervisor. Cecil Pennington was duly interviewed. He sincerely denied knowing McCord or burning anything, which of course was true.[28] The CIA had sent the FBI on a fool's errand with beneficial results.[29] Prosecutors did not learn about the fire at McCord's house while preparing their indictments of the burglars. "Pennington had been interviewed," the unsuspecting Earl Silbert wrote in his diary, "and he had nothing to do with the removal or destruction of property that Baldwin had brought out to the McCord residence."[30]

The Pennington ruse threw the FBI off McCord's trail, which bought Helms all the time he needed. The Watergate investigators only learned about the flame-fest at McCord's home after he had pled guilty to the burglary charges. They only caught up with the real Lee Pennington eighteen months later, and he denied all. They never learned why McCord kept carbon copies of the conversations he wiretapped or what he did with them.

Helms, now in his seventh year as director, showed few outward signs of stress. On the weekends he played tennis, still sporting his long linen trousers last stylish before World War II. Once a month he and Cynthia went to the Sulgrave Club for the Waltz Group, where Helms favored friends with his slightly twisted grin. Cynthia had formed a women's environmentalist group, which advocated for the banning of lead paint and phosphates in detergents. Helms was a convert. He started buying recyclable toiletries and talking up the ecological crisis. "It gave him something to chat about at social events," his wife observed, "and an excuse not to discuss his work, particularly Vietnam."[31]

Cynthia's son, Rod McKelvie, asked Helms how he slept at night with so many hot topics on his mind. Helms confided that he focused on "recreating tennis games in his mind. Back and forth. Back and forth," McKelvie recalled him saying. "He fell asleep to the distraction."[32]

Helms was a self-satisfied and self-aware man, not so stodgy as he looked. Above all, he would survive. *I may be crazy, but I don't have to be stupid.*

20

PRECIPICE

Nixon was cruising to reelection in the fall of 1972 as his well-laid plans paid off. The antiwar movement never did disrupt the Republican convention in Miami, where he was nominated virtually by acclaim for a second term. He played statesman over the summer, hosting Soviet premier Leonid Brezhnev for a state visit of a Russian leader to Washington. The disorganized Democrats, hobbled by the divisions generated by the war, nominated Senator George McGovern, the most liberal candidate in the field. While Hunt and Liddy never got the chance to mount schemes of surveillance and blackmail against the Democrats, they were hardly needed. By Labor Day, Nixon was ahead thirty points in the polls.

In the White House, Watergate was a concern, not a worry. On September 15, the five burglars were indicted, along with Hunt and Liddy, on charges of conspiracy, burglary, and violation of wiretapping laws. The indictment noted that the telephone bugged was "used primarily . . . by Spencer Oliver and Ida M. Wells." Curiously, the burglars had not focused on Larry O'Brien, the Democratic party chief who was supposedly the prime target. They were more interested in the Democrats' private lives.

The president, following developments closely, asked John Dean to come to the Oval Office. Besides the seven defendants, the president crowed, there was no evidence that anyone else was involved. Dean agreed the damage had been controlled, although he privately thought otherwise. On Capitol Hill Congressman Wright Patman, a Texas populist, sought to open a an investigation and was rebuffed thanks to Democratic defections. The press was losing interest in the story. Nixon wanted to turn the table on his critics by revealing how President Johnson had spied on him during the 1968 campaign. He wanted the world to know he was the victim, not the perpetrator, of illicit wiretapping.[1]

Nixon wanted "peace with honor" in Vietnam and thought it within reach. He believed his first term had demonstrated to Moscow and Beijing that the United States would not cut and run on its ally in Vietnam. Now dealing from a position of strength, he believed he would get the terms he wanted from Hanoi. (The North Vietnamese felt they had the upper hand because the Americans finally seemed serious about signing a withdrawal agreement.[2]) Nixon had to sell the agreement, which included allowing North Vietnam to keep its forces in South Vietnam, to President Nguyen Van Thieu, who balked at a provision calling for the creation of a coalition government, including the National Liberation Front. Hanoi charged the Americans had reneged and refused to sign. On the brink of a peace agreement, Nixon decided to escalate bombing of the North to force the communists to sign an agreement that the South Vietnamese could accept.

Helms was not a party to Nixon and Kissinger's decisions. His skepticism about the effectiveness of bombing was known. He did contribute finished papers from the Intelligence Directorate, which didn't please Nixon at all. "We're having some trouble in finding out even now how effective [bombing] is," Helms told CIA staffers in June.[3]

The director was looking forward to retirement. Helms had served Nixon for four years, for the most part loyally. He backed him on the toughest calls: Cambodia and Chile. He used CHAOS and LINGUAL to support his internal security policy. He handed over the Diem file and kept the Ellsberg matter under wraps. His men, Hunt and McCord, came well recommended to the Committee to Reelect the President. It wasn't Helms's fault they screwed up on June 17. As Helms liked to say, the Agency's "skirts were clean." He wanted to stay in his position for perhaps one more year and then retire.

Helms had become an admirer of the president, however strange and mercurial he could be. Nixon was the best prepared president, Helms insisted, better than Eisenhower, Kennedy, or Johnson. Each of those men had their strengths, he said, but Nixon had the best overall grasp of foreign affairs and domestic politics.[4] And for all of his class resentment, Nixon still wanted Helms to like him. It was almost poignant. In October 1972 Nixon invited the director to an exclusive dinner at the White House for four high-ranking visitors from London. These were the top men at the British Home Office and the Exchequer, men of power and money who epitomized the enduring Anglo-American alliance. Nixon wanted to impress Helms, and he did. Afterward, Helms penned another little note.

"My dear Mr. President: May I thank you most warmly for including me in one of the most pleasant dinners I have ever attended at the White House. You were in such good form Friday evening that, even if we had not had the delicious dinner in the Blue Room, it still would have been a memorable occasion. . . . Respectfully, Richard Helms."[5]

"POTENTIALLY EMBARRASSING"

In the Watergate affair, Helms played consigliere to Nixon's godfather. When law enforcement pressed for explanations, the director supplied answers crafted with care. In late October, Earl Silbert submitted a series of questions to the Agency. He wanted to clarify three factual issues: Hunt's knowledge of the cover operations at the Mullen Company; the forged identification and disguises supplied to Hunt in the summer of 1971; and the Agency's contacts with Rolando Martínez.[6]

The answers were as modulated as Helms himself. Yes, Hunt was knowledgeable about the assets acting under Agency control at Mullen—but he wasn't one of them. Yes, the credentials and wigs were provided—but Helms didn't know why. Yes, Martínez was on the payroll—but not for surreptitious entries. Helms asked his staff to write up the details on blank memoranda with no identification of the CIA as the source. Helms took the package of answers to a meeting at the attorney general's office in the Justice Department. He was accompanied by Larry Houston, his general counsel.

In handing over the package to Nixon's new attorney general, Richard Kleindienst, Helms stressed that the enclosed information was "irrelevant" to the Watergate investigation, because all contact with Hunt terminated in August 1971. He put the point delicately but firmly. The package need not be conveyed to the prosecutors unless, in the unlikely event, it was needed for rebuttal at trial.

Silbert wanted to see the package and Kleindienst was in no position to object. The prosecutor came away with more questions.[7] The CIA said that Hunt was retired and they'd had no dealings with him for two years, which wasn't true. Silbert had trouble understanding why Hunt would supervise a break-in if he wasn't working for the CIA. Who else did that sort of thing? And why did the burglars target the unimportant Spencer Oliver, not his well-connected boss Larry O'Brien?

"We were never able to determine the precise motivation for the burglary and wiretapping," Silbert told the Senate Judiciary Committee, "particularly on the phone of a relative unknown Spencer Oliver."

Silbert believed McCord was responsible.

"Baldwin had told us that McCord wanted *all* telephone calls recorded, including personal calls. . . ." Silbert wrote. "Many of them [were] extremely personal, intimate and potentially embarrassing. We also learned that Hunt had at some time previously met Spencer Oliver at Robert R. Mullen and Company and opposed his joining the firm because he was a liberal Democrat. Therefore, one motive we thought possible was an attempt to compromise Oliver and others . . . for political reasons . . . [but] we never had any direct proof of this since neither Hunt or Liddy . . . would talk to us."

Hunt would later scoff at Silbert's speculation but there was no doubt that McCord's wiretaps had captured "personal, intimate and potentially embarrassing" material on Democratic politicians and party workers. Hunt could not deny that. Al Baldwin and Jeb Magruder both received and read such material.

In the fall of 1972 Hunt did not want to explain his actions to anyone. He wanted money for his legal fees, his family, and his Cuban friends, and he wanted it yesterday.

"A NEW ERA"

On November 5, 1972, Nixon won reelection in a landslide, prevailing with voters in every state except for Massachusetts and the District of Columbia. More than forty-seven million Americans had voted for him. "The support was wide and deep," Nixon exulted. He won a majority of votes from manual workers, Catholics, union families, and people with only a grade-school education. No Republican president had ever done that.

Nixon had wound down the war in Vietnam, at least for Americans. Only twenty-one American men died in combat that month, the lowest number of monthly fatalities since 1964.[8] Nixon could credibly claim his Vietnamization policy had succeeded.

Yet a melancholy settled over Nixon in the White House on the evening of his triumph. He had a toothache. He was still brooding about Watergate, a political toothache. The Republicans had failed to win Congress. Kissinger had yet to pin down the Vietnamese on the exact language of a peace treaty. "Whatever the reasons, I allowed myself only a few minutes to reflect on the past," the restless Nixon said. "I was confident that a new era was about to begin, and I was eager to begin it."[9]

The next morning, the senior staff of the White House were called for a meeting in the Roosevelt Room. Expecting a celebration of the president's victory, they were told to hand in their resignations. Nixon left and Haldeman spelled it out. The president wanted to make some changes. The same message went out to the Cabinet: hand in your resignations.

Helms was lunching at CIA headquarters that day with Alexander Haig, Kissinger's deputy. He told Haig of his desire to serve one more year as director and then retire.[10] When Helms got back to his office, Walters informed him of Nixon's order. He was writing his letter of resignation. Helms advised him not to.

"Unlike other presidential appointees, it had become customary for the DCI and the director of the FBI to remain in place during a change of administration," Helms explained in his reasonable way. He was not a political appointee, so he didn't have to resign. Nor did Walters. "In keeping with this practice I did not submit my resignation to Nixon," Helms recalled.[11]

A lesser man might have resorted to ambiguity, or the path of least resistance. Helms wanted to keep his job, as long as possible. He wanted control over when and why he left the government service. He wanted to see the president face-to-face.

THE APPEARANCE OF POWER

The burglars, released on bail until trial, had ample time to contemplate their predicament.

Hunt was angry and so was Dorothy. She complained about the unreliable "Mr. Rivers" who delivered money on behalf of the White House. When Rivers didn't provide the sums promised, she was the one who had to call the families of the Cubans and tell them. She thought Rivers was ignoring her because she was a woman. When he arranged for her to meet another intermediary, Dorothy sensed that the president's men, having won the election, were going to abandon them.[12]

McCord paced. "Jimmy came to me during the Watergate trials and asked me to turn state's evidence," Macho Barker recalled. "He said he was not going to be a scapegoat . . . I told him that not only would I not do this, but that he shouldn't either. I said, 'Look, Jimmy, you're going to have to shave every morning and look in the mirror. This is too big for someone like me. When something like this is big, leave it alone; it will take care of itself.'"

Barker and the Cubans were more fatalistic than their American associates. Exiled from their own country, they had lost to Castro and learned to live with defeat. Not McCord and Hunt. McCord mentioned "one or two or three things he was involved in that he was going to expose if they didn't give him immunity," Barker recalled.[13]

"I said, 'No, Jimmy. There is nothing behind this, except we are caught, and we have got to take our punishment," Barker said. "Mentally, Jimmy was not prepared for things to go wrong. The appearance of power caused these people to think they had connections and would not have problems, so they broke down."

That was McCord and Hunt. Their friendship with Helms gave them the appearance of power. When the director didn't do what Hunt called "the Company thing"—rescue them—the two former CIA men felt stranded. While McCord and Hunt were tormented by their dangling fate, the Cubans didn't complain. Sturgis, Barker, Martínez, and González said little beyond that they believed the break-in was government-approved business.

The Cubans were taken care of by Manuel Artime. He launched a Watergate defense fund to raise money to support the burglars and their families with an enticing twist for donors. All they had to do was write a check. Artime gave them cash for the amount of the check.

In other words, the burglars' defense fund was a money-laundering operation. Whose money was laundered was never disclosed. To reporters covering the Watergate events, Artime was merely a Bay of Pigs veteran and friend of Hunt's.[14] None knew of his long service to the Agency as AMBIDDY-1, much less his role in passing a gun to Rolando Cubela in the AMLASH conspiracy. Artime was another connection between the burglars and the Agency hidden in plain sight.

While Hunt stewed in his feelings of abandonment, McCord actually thought like a spy.[15] In a bid to get the charges against him dropped, he called the Israeli Embassy. He knew their phone lines were tapped by the FBI. He asked to speak to a consular official, explaining that he was involved in the Watergate scandal. Without giving his name, he inquired about obtaining a visa to travel to Israel. McCord was counting on U.S. intelligence intercepting the call and passing the information to the Justice Department. When the prosecutors used his apparent intention to flee the country against him, he would threaten to reveal that his conversation had been overheard. The prosecutors would then face the embarrassing prospect of admitting in open court that the United States wiretapped a friendly nation. McCord calculated that the government would drop the case against him rather than jeopardize U.S. foreign relations.[16] The gambit overestimated the efficiency of U.S. intelligence. Earl Silbert and his prosecutors were never told that McCord was preparing to flee. McCord called the Chilean Embassy and tried the same trick. It didn't work.

Hunt felt abandoned. He called Colson at the White House.

"Commitments that were made to all of us at the outset have not been kept," Hunt barked, "and there is a great deal of unease and concern on the party of the seven defendants. . . . What we've been getting has been coming in very minor dribs and drabs. . . . This is a long haul and the stakes are very, very high. . . . This thing must not break apart for foolish reasons."

Hunt was ready to talk about numerous high-level conspiracies he had undertaken for the U.S. government if his demands were not met. That could have been a reference to the plots to kill Castro (which he wrote about in the unpublished "Give Us This Day"), or the possible involvement of CIA personnel in the JFK assassination (which he would write about in his autobiography), or the burglary at Dr. Fielding's office or any number of dirty tricks he had played in his career.

"We think now is the time when a move should be made," Hunt warned, "and surely the cheapest commodity available is money."[17]

CAMP DAVID

Helms received notice he was to meet with President Nixon at Camp David. Taking off from the White House, he endured the noisy thirty-minute helicopter ride to the presidential retreat in Maryland's Catoctin mountains. He was thinking, optimistically, that he would stay on as director, and they could talk about next year's budget.

At the Aspen Lounge, the main building of the compound, the ever-unfriendly Haldeman ushered Helms in to meet the president. Nixon and Haldeman perched on the couch. Helms took a chair. After Nixon made small talk—"several rambling disjointed observations," said Helms—the president came to the point. Nixon said how much he appreciated the fine job Helms had done as director. Helms heard Nixon say he wanted some changes at the top of his administration. *People get tired, find themselves trapped in old positions, falter, give in.* Nixon wanted a new DCI. Ever gracious, Helms said he understood perfectly, he served at the president's pleasure, and he deftly inserted his demand into the conversation. Perhaps a good time for a changeover, he suggested, would be the following March when he turned sixty years old, the Agency's mandatory retirement age.

Nixon was taken aback. He expressed surprise that the CIA had such a policy. Helms sensed Nixon shifting gears mentally, as if he wanted to make a deal. The president suddenly asked if he would like to be an ambassador. Since the thought had never occurred to Helms (or so he said), he asked the president for time to think about it. They measured each other anew, circled some more, all of their mutual history filling the time between awkward bursts of conversation, memories going back to that briefing on Hungary in the vice president's office around the time Frank Wisner went mad. They didn't have to speak words that had already been spoken, only weigh memories for intentions.

Dear Mr. President . . . I like the dirty tricks. . . . a goddamn good plan. . . . the black world. . . . . . lacked the will. . . . martyrs of tomorrow . . . warm birthday greetings. . . . our involvement should not be revealed . . . We never should have gone . . . the Chile thing. . . . the who shot John angle. . . . . . knows too damn much. . . . . You open that scab, there's a hell of a lot of things. . . .

"What about Moscow?" Nixon blurted.

Helms said the Russians might not appreciate the presence of a spymaster in their capital. Nixon asked if there was any place he might like to be an ambassador. Helms proposed Iran, which made a certain amount of sense. He knew the country's supreme leader, the shah, who was an alumnus of La Rosey. He and Cynthia shared an interest in Persian culture, and he would leave government on a high note. Nixon said he was amenable. Helms said he would think about it.[18]

Haldeman was glad to see him let go. "It was basically a friendly meeting," the chief of staff wrote in his diary, "although Helms was a little surprised and obviously disappointed to be moving out after 25 years."[19] Haldeman called back a few days later to ask if Helms had accepted the ambassador position. Helms temporized for a few more days—it was hard to leave the director's chair—and realized his time was up. He finally said yes.[20]

It was Watergate, Helms concluded. Nixon and Haldeman were firing him because he didn't quash the Watergate investigation.[21] He had done what he could but, as always, they wanted more. At the Langley headquarters, Dave Phillips said most people thought Helms had been kicked downstairs by a vindictive Nixon.[22] Elsewhere, the suspicion arose, unbidden, that Helms had secured his soft landing in the court of the Peacock Throne by implicitly threatening to reveal what he knew of Watergate and other events. John Ehrlichman wrote as much in a thinly disguised roman à clef about Nixon's presidency that culminates with newly married CIA director Bill Martin blackmailing President Richard Monckton at Camp David.[23]

Helms would be forever sensitive on the subject. Twenty-two years later in retirement, he somehow obtained a pre-production script of Oliver Stone's forthcoming biopic about Nixon. One tense scene depicted Helms (played by a chilly

Sam Waterston) alluding to the Bay of Pigs and, implicitly, the assassination of JFK, when talking to Nixon (played by the gloomy Anthony Hopkins). Helms was indignant at the prospect of seeing such dialogue on the big screen. His attorney sent a letter to Stone threatening to sue over a "false and defamatory" scene depicting "an invented exchange between Ambassador Helms and President Nixon in which Ambassador Helms is depicted as threatening the President with incriminating documents."[24]

Stone cut the offending scene from the theatrical release, for reasons of length, he said. He included it in the director's cut for commercial release on disc and cable. Helms took no action.

"I never blackmailed Nixon in any form, manner or kind," Helms said with affable steel, "and nobody can prove anything to the contrary because nothing to the contrary ever happened. I worked for the President of the United States. I would have been disloyal, treasonable, anything you want to call it if I had tried such a trick . . ."[25]

As cagey responses go, it was revealing. Helms seem to recognize that, under the circumstances, such a "trick" was conceivable. What he knew could harm Nixon. That he did not need to say.

"BLOW THE WHITE HOUSE OUT OF THE WATER"

Dorothy and Howard escalated their demands.

"We are protecting the guys who are really responsible," Howard bitched to Colson. "And of course that is a continuing requirement, but at the same time, it is a two way street."[26] He dashed off a letter to Kenneth Parkinson, a senior official at the Committee to Re-elect the President, threatening to "blow the White House out of the water."[27] Hunt's warnings were heeded. On December 1, John Mitchell authorized use of $350,000 from the Committee to Re-elect the President to pay off Hunt and the Cubans.[28]

The anxious McCord felt cornered. He was convinced Silbert and the prosecutors were out to blame the CIA for a White House operation. When the *Washington Star* carried a story reporting that "reliable prosecution sources" were saying McCord recruited the four Cubans and that they believed they were working for the president on an extremely sensitive mission, McCord suspected a plot, as he often did.

"This was laying the groundwork for the false claim that I was the 'ringleader of the Watergate plot,'" he later wrote, "which would draw attention away from Hunt and Liddy." McCord suspected the story came from Hunt. He sent telegrams to Hunt and Barker asserting the story was untrue. He said if Hunt didn't correct it, he would.[29] Hunt, who had nothing to do with the *Star* story, thought McCord was "unstable." Dorothy felt uneasy around McCord. There was just "something wrong" about him, she said.[30]

And so the burglars awaited their trial, scheduled for early January. To ease his financial worries, Hunt was trying to finish another spy novel. Dorothy told him she didn't like the ending. "The way you have it," she said, "the good guys win. But Howard, you know it isn't always that way in real life. More often than not, the good guys lose—so why not end it that way?"

Like how? Hunt wanted to know.

"Well, the girl for one thing," Dorothy said. "The hero doesn't get the girl and the villain, well, he gets away. That's how I'd end it if I were you. Besides," she added, "if you don't do it that way I won't type it for you."[31]

On the morning of December 8, Dorothy caught a flight to see her cousin in Chicago. Hunt returned to his typewriter to rewrite his ending.

"A PINATA IN THE SHAPE OF A MAN"

"The aircraft was in a nearly wings level, nose-high attitude when it first penetrated the uppermost branches of a 20-foot tree," said the accident report of the National Transportation Safety Board. "After this contact, the aircraft impacted trees, houses, utility pole cables, and garages before it came to rest across the foundation of one of the destroyed houses." The trail of destruction left by the crash of United Flight 553 in the neighborhood west of Chicago's Midway Airport ran for more than six hundred feet. "Portions of both wings and the fuselage from just aft of the cockpit to the rear galley door were consumed by the post-crash fire," said the report.[32]

Dorothy Hunt, sitting in seat 1A in the first-class section of the cabin, was killed instantly. Of the fifty-five passengers on board, forty died in the crash. The pathologist who examined the bodies of the victims said those in first class suffered violent trauma, described as "disruption of head, torso, upper and lower extremities by burns and apparently some explosive force." The pathologist corrected his "bad choice of adjectives." Explosive force was not a reference to the presence or the effects of a bomb, he said. He was describing "injuries caused by high-energy impact."[33] While St. John Hunt and others would later argue United 553 was sabotaged, the NTSB found no evidence that anything other than pilot error was responsible.

Hunt's children heard news of the plane crash in Chicago on the radio and rushed to tell him. They wondered, hope against hope, if their mother was among the survivors. Howard sought to comfort his nine-year-old son David and broke down crying himself. "Unquenchable tears fell from my eyes," he later wrote, and the boy comforted the man, patting his arm. That night Hunt flew to Chicago, not knowing if Dorothy was still alive. The next day he was called to the Cook County morgue. A clerk emerged to dump some jewelry from a plastic bag onto a table.

"I stared at the blackened pieces with bile surging in my throat and tears clawing my eyes," Hunt recalled. There was Dorothy's wedding ring. He picked it up. "Ashes dropped from it leaving black smudges on my hand. . . . Her chapter bracelet had been half melted."

"Can you identify these Mr. Hunt?"[34]

Pity the poor spy. Hunt was a scoundrel, a would-be assassin, a burglar, a liar, a racist, and a cheat. He was also a loving father of four, facing jail time, and he had just lost his best friend and companion of twenty-two years. He was, in his own description, "a pinata in the shape of a man, someone who had been battered until his insides spilled out leaving only a sorrowful and empty shell."[35]

He scrawled a note to Bill Buckley.

"Dear Bill, If you hadn't heard Dorothy was killed in yesterday's Chicago plane crash. I am absolutely desolate. Howard."[36]

Rescue workers sifting the wreckage found $10,000 in cash in Dorothy's Hunt's purse. Hunt said the money was for an investment in a Holiday Inn, which sounded contrived. The FBI interviewed Michael Stevens, the man who had supplied electronic equipment to McCord back in May. He said that the money was intended for him, as final payment for the eavesdropping gear.[37] Hunt's version was perhaps easier on his conscience. If Dorothy was paying off McCord's debt, she had died as a direct consequence of his work, just as he had imagined in the David St. John novels, where Peter Ward felt guilty that his wife Su-Li had been killed because of his profession. If he told the world that the stack of hundred-dollar bills in Dorothy's purse was for an investment, then she was taking care of her family, not his business. He couldn't bear to think otherwise.

A broken man, Hunt could fight no more. He passed $21,000 in cash from the White House to Manolo Artime for distribution to Barker and his men.[38] He told his lawyer he was going to plead guilty, say nothing, and take his chances on getting a presidential pardon within a year.

"EVERY TREE IN THE FOREST WILL BURN"

Jim McCord did not like the way the lawyers were talking. Just before Christmas he met with his attorney, Gerald Alch, at the Monocle restaurant on Capitol Hill. Alch said he had just come from meeting with Bill Bittman, Hunt's lawyer.

"Alch suggested that I use as my defense that the Watergate operation was a CIA operation," McCord recalled. "I heard him out on the suggestion, which included questions as to whether I could ostensibly have been recalled from retirement to participate in the operation." Alch mentioned the possibility of calling former CIA officer Victor Marchetti as a witness "to describe CIA training in which its employees were trained to deny CIA sponsorship of an operation if anything went wrong.[39] Alch even raised the possibility of calling Helms as a witness.

McCord had heard enough. To even consider calling the outgoing director to the witness stand was intolerable to McCord. He wanted a new lawyer, and he made his views clear to the Agency by sending another letter to Paul Gaynor, his former boss in the Security Research Staff.

"Dear Paul," he wrote, "there is tremendous pressure to put the operation off on the company [i.e., the CIA]. Don't worry about me no matter what you hear."

McCord didn't just want to defend himself. He had a media strategy to defend the Agency. "The way to head this off is to flood the newspapers with leaks or anonymous letters that the plan is to place the blame on the company for the operation," he told Gaynor. "This is of <u>immediate </u>[and he underlined the word] importance because the plans are in the formative stage and, can be pre-empted now, the story is leaked so the press is alerted."[40]

McCord sent three more letters to Gaynor in the coming weeks, each complaining about his legal defense team and constructing his own defense.

Asked why he received the letters, Gaynor said, "I imagine McCord was assuming I was still in the same position I had when he left, and that he knew I would have direct channels of communications directly with the director of security, I would report to him, I would see these letters would get somebody's attention."[41] Gaynor did just that. He passed the letters to his boss, Howard Osborn, chief of the Office of Security and confidante of Helms.

Alch rejected McCord's charge that he wanted to concoct a CIA defense using falsified evidence. He said he raised the possibility of Agency involvement because all the Cuban defendants believed, on Hunt's assurances, that they were on an officially approved mission. It was a logical avenue to pursue in McCord's defense.

Alch knew nothing about McCord's back-channel communications with the Agency. About his intentions, Alch could only speculate.

"Let's just suppose that Mr. McCord was in contact during the trial and before the trial with some representative of the CIA, a former colleague," he told congressional investigators. "And let's just suppose he was accepting discreetly, unbeknownst to me, counsel from whoever this CIA contact was, and acting at the advice of this contact to protect the CIA but still keeping me above the surface as far as these activities are going and just wanting me to give him the best trial and the best record for appeal purposes."

Thus McCord's own lawyer did not dismiss the possibility that McCord coordinated his legal strategy with the Agency—and perhaps with Helms himself. "He was obviously doing a lot of things I didn't know about," Alch said, "and that could have been one of them."[42]

In his memoir, McCord denounced Earl Silbert and his fellow prosecutors for pursuing the question of blackmail, as if they had any choice. Their only cooperating witness, the former FBI agent Alfred Baldwin, testified the calls he monitored for McCord involved sex as much as politics. That indicated the burglars might have been seeking blackmail material. McCord indignantly denied the suggestion, but Silbert believed Baldwin. The witness, he said, was a frustrated single man who recalled the conversations in all their salacious detail. And Silbert knew nothing of Lee Pennington's work for the Security Research Staff, which indicated McCord's long-standing interest in collecting intelligence on the personal lives of "disloyal" people—an elastic category that often included liberals and Democrats—another possible motive for seeking blackmail material.[43]

McCord regarded any talk of calling current or former CIA employees as a plot against the Agency. It certainly constituted a threat to Helms. Any cross-examination of Agency personnel in court might reveal facts the Agency had taken pains to conceal: that Hunt was a friend of Helms and had been reporting to Tom Karamessines for years; that Hunt and Barker plotted to kill Castro in 1961; that Hunt and Liddy had burglarized the office of Ellsberg's psychiatrist; that the Mullen Company was a front for CIA operations; that the "retirement" of Hunt and McCord was a façade for continuing reporting relationships; and that McCord ordered his wife and friends to burn evidence of his connections to the CIA after his arrest. Helms had a great deal to lose if CIA witnesses were called to testify.

With the burglars' trial scheduled to open in early January 1973, McCord's self-appointed mission was to protect Helms. McCord believed that Nixon had fired Helms at the Camp David meeting as preparation for laying the blame for the burglary on the CIA. He was sure the Nixon White House, the Justice Department, and the press were about to go after Helms.

He wanted to get his message to the White House too.

"I am sorry I have to write this letter," McCord wrote to his friend Jack Caulfield, a former New York cop working at the White House.[44] "If Helms goes and the Watergate operation is laid at the feet of the CIA where it does not belong," he said, "every tree in the forest will fall. It will be a scorched desert. The whole matter is at the precipice now. Pass the message if they want it to blow they are on exactly the right course."[45]

21

ESCAPE

In his season of triumph, Nixon returned to replaying Richard Rodgers's stirring anthem, "Victory at Sea." The man from Whittier was now master of the globe. Entering his second term, he had a mandate from the voters and the will to prevail. Interest in Watergate abated and Vietnam negotiations were proceeding. When North Vietnam stalled on the final terms of a peace treaty, he ordered another wave of war. He authorized B-52 bombing strikes on sixteen major transportation, power, and radio targets in Hanoi. Within twenty-four hours, 129 B-52s took part in bombing raids.

The explosions were awesome, the destruction vast, the civilian death toll uncounted. Whether such violence actually forced changes in North Vietnam's strategy remained unproven. The United States had already dropped more than three million tons of bombs on North Vietnam by the time Nixon took office in 1969, compared to two million in all of World War II.

"Only Nixon and Kissinger, coming in fresh and thinking, we know how to launch a threat campaign, could convince themselves that this was going to do the job," said whistleblower Ellsberg, who originally favored the war. "By the end of the first term, they had dropped 4.5 million tons of bombs—but to no effect."[1] The North Vietnamese and the Viet Cong were still fighting and still demanding complete U.S. withdrawal.

The editorial reaction to the Christmas bombing raids was broad and harsh. Senator William Saxbe, Republican of Ohio, said the president "appears to have lost his senses." The *Washington Post* editorialized that the bombing caused millions of Americans to begin "crying in shame and to wonder at the President's very sanity."

The critics were "disgraceful," Nixon scoffed in his diary. They "cannot bear the thought of this administration under my leadership bringing off the peace on an honorable basis which they have long predicted would be impossible. The election was a terrible blow to them," he said, "and this is their first opportunity . . . to strike back."[2] Nixon felt vindicated when the North Vietnamese returned to the negotiations a few weeks later. He was inaugurated for a second time on January 20, 1973, and the Paris Peace Accords were signed six days later.

Dick Helms had moved on. He wouldn't be director much longer, and he felt no need to flatter the president. He and Cynthia attended an elegant and exclusive dinner party where Kissinger got up to speak about the peace he and Nixon had negotiated in Vietnam. As they left the dining room, Helms leaned over to Cynthia. "Nonsense," he whispered, "they don't have any peace."[3]

"RETENTION OF THE LETTER"

"It would appear we have headed them off at the pass," McCord wrote to Paul Gaynor on the eve of the burglars' trial. "The crisis appears to be over."

The crisis was the looming possibility that McCord's lawyer or Hunt's might call CIA witnesses, including Helms. McCord berated Gerald Alch and said he was firing him. "I repeated I would not stand for it, nor would I sit still for any other defense attorney trying to do it," McCord said. ". . . Alch met with me again and assured me the issue was dead, that he would not try it again, nor would anyone else."[4]

Two days later, McCord reported again to Gaynor. The prosecutors had tried to get all the defendants to plead guilty, "thus protecting those higher up from involvement," McCord wrote. He and Liddy refused. "Now the prosecution is planning to state the motive of at least some of the defendants was blackmail."[5] At trial, the prosecutors asked to introduce transcripts of the conversations the burglars had intercepted in the DNC offices. A lawyer for the American Civil Liberties Union objected on privacy grounds, and Judge John Sirica upheld his argument. The question of blackmail as a motive for the Watergate burglary was never addressed in court.

Jack Caulfield passed McCord's message about his defense strategy to John Dean, who consulted with John Ehrlichman in the White House. They knew Hunt planned to plead guilty and say nothing in hopes of executive clemency. Dean had heard that the burglars' attorneys planned to blame Watergate on the CIA by convincing "those dumb D.C. jurors that they were watching the *Mission Impossible* show." Now McCord was balking.

"No one knew why," Dean said. "I wondered whether the Agency had reached him."[6]

McCord had certainly reached the Agency via the back channel to Helms through Gaynor, a matter that required discretion. Knowing that Helms would soon be leaving the Agency, Howard Osborn took the folder of letters to Helms and asked for guidance as to what he should do with them. Helms reviewed the file and—deft touch—directed Osborn to check with General Counsel Houston. If the latter had no objection, Osborn was to—delicate phrase—"secure retention of the letter."

Houston had no objection. Osborn kept McCord's letters in his safe.[7] Helms had evidence of his former employee's intentions, state of mind, and legal strategy. And he had counsel's permission not to share it with the court—a tidy package that lent credence to Gerald Alch's speculation that McCord was coordinating his legal strategy with "some representative of the CIA, perhaps a former colleague," perhaps his appreciative friend, the outgoing director.

The trial of the burglars was anticlimactic. While all of Washington still wondered what the burglary was all about, the proceedings in Judge Sirica's courtroom clarified nothing.

The Cuban defendants pled guilty to all counts. Under questioning from Sirica, they said they acted on behalf of liberating Cuba and uncovering Castro's supposed connections to McGovern.

Hunt pled guilty on all counts, saying, falsely, that he had no knowledge of "higher-ups" in the conspiracy. He deprecated his former colleague. "McCord was a low-level security man," he said.[8]

McCord contested the charges oddly. He told Gaynor that he had "evidence of the involvement of Mitchell and other sufficient evidence to convince a jury, the Congress and the Press," but he did not present it during the trial. Instead, Alch offered a "defense of duress," arguing that McCord thought it necessary to get intelligence from the Democrats to protect Republican officials from bodily harm. "Ridiculous," snorted Judge Sirica.[9] McCord was convicted. Investigators would not learn of McCord's back channel to Helms for four more months.

SHREDDED

The FBI agents working on the background check for ambassadorial nominee Richard McGarragh Helms heard many words of effusive praise.

"General Robert E. Cushman, U.S. Marines Corps, highly recommends Helms for the position of Ambassador," reported the Alexandria, Virginia, field office.

Former director John McCone told the Los Angeles field office that the "appointee is totally responsible concerning security matters. Highest respect for the appointee's intelligence and integrity."

Dr. Louis Tordella, deputy director of the National Security Agency, said he "would highly recommend him for any position of trust in the U.S. government."

Senate majority leader Mike Mansfield of Montana "considers him forthright and practical in his approach to foreign-policy. . . . And has no question concerning his patriotism, morals, reputation or choice of associates."

Another twenty-two people vouched that Helms was "a dependable, trustworthy, dedicated and conscientious person."

"If there is any question regarding Helms' loyalty," quipped Secretary of State William Rogers, "we're all in a lot of trouble."

When this package of praise reached Acting Director Gray, he passed it to the White House with a summary memorandum on Helms's "character, loyalty, ability, and general standing."[10]

Just when Helms was certified the most trustworthy of men, he then betrayed the trust bestowed on him. With his well-earned reputation for integrity, Helms was well positioned to pull a fast one, and he did. Such was his skill that his admirers could not hold it against him. They too wanted to believe in the law-abiding spymaster, and he gave them sufficient grounds.

It happened when Senator Mansfield announced the establishment of a select committee, headed by Senators Sam Ervin and Howard Baker, to investigate the Watergate affair. Mansfield sent identical letters to Helms and eight other people involved in the Watergate events, including John Dean and Richard Kleindienst.

"I am writing to request that you not destroy, remove from your possession or control or otherwise dispose of or permit the disposal of any records or documents which might have bearing on the subjects under investigation," he wrote, referring to "the break-in at the Democratic National Committee headquarters, [and] the reports of political sabotage and espionage."

When John Dean received Mansfield's "request," he assumed that any violation of its terms might expose him to contempt of court charges.[11] A spy not a lawyer, Helms took the opposite course. He ordered his secretary, Elizabeth Dunlevy, to start disposing of records that he knew full well "might have some bearing" on the Watergate investigation.

Like Nixon, Helms had installed a taping system in his office that enabled him to record telephone calls and room conversations. The tapes were routinely transcribed. Helms and Dunlevy made a cursory review of three file drawers of the transcripts and decided none were related to Watergate. Helms ordered the material shredded and the taping system removed.[12] Dunlevy later said she destroyed transcripts of either telephone or room conversations with Nixon, Haldeman, Ehrlichman, and other White House officials.[13]

Helms said he could not recall any conversations with the White House burglar but he didn't exclude the possibility.

"Did you have telephone conversations with Mr. Hunt?" he was asked in a court deposition in 1984.

"I don't recall any, but I may have," Helms said. "If he was in the Agency, I would normally have talked to him there, but I don't recall any conversations with him. I did not have any telephone conversations with him after he went to work for the White House."[14]

Helms shrugged off criticism. The destruction of his personal material was "a routine part of vacating his office," he explained to the Rockefeller Commission. ". . . He assumed that anything of affirmative value had been transferred from the tapes and he felt obligated [that] the records of confidential conversations between him and others should not become part of Agency files."[15]

Helms's definition of "related to Watergate" was exquisitely narrow. The fire at McCord's place? Not related to Watergate. Hunt's job at the Mullen Company? Not related to Watergate. The packages Hunt sent to his office? Not related to Watergate. The destruction of Helms's personal archive of files, tapes, and transcripts was completed before the end of the month. If you could believe the former director, none of it was related to Watergate.

THE QUESTION

On the morning of February 5, 1973, Helms showed up at Room 4221 of the Dirksen Senate Office Building for a scheduled meeting of the Senate Foreign Relations Committee, with his old friend and sometime nemesis Senator J. William Fulbright of Arkansas presiding. It was a friendly session devoted to Helms's nomination as ambassador to Iran.

"I believe Director Helms has established a reputation that may well have saved the Central Intelligence Agency from a good deal of additional criticism because of the respect that all of us have for him as a person and the way he has operated," said Senator Stuart Symington, Democrat of Missouri. Senator Chuck Percy, Republican of Illinois, added Helms "was a superb public servant."

Fulbright inquired about the Agency's ties to the Watergate burglars.

"They had all retired," Helms said. "They had left. I have no control over anybody who has left."

Fulbright said he just wanted to confirm that Hunt and McCord were former CIA men.

"Yes sir," said Helms. "Hunt was and McCord was."

The questioning moved on to CIA funding for the National Student Association and Radio Free Europe, and the session was soon over.

"C.I.A. Discloses It Trained Police From 12 Agencies," announced the front-page headline in the *New York Times* the next day. In response to a question from New York congressman Ed Koch, John Maury, CIA liaison to Congress, had disclosed an Agency training program that assisted local police in the handling of explosives, wiretaps, and organization of intelligence files. Koch charged the Agency was flouting the 1947 National Security Act, which stated that "the Agency shall have no police, subpoena, law-enforcement powers, or internal-security functions."[16]

Fulbright called Helms back for questioning, this time in executive session. The seven senators and the outgoing director met in a conference room in the Capitol. Helms was exasperated.

"What is involved here is nothing but what we regard as a public-spirited act," Helms began. Four or five years before, he said he had dinner with a group of police chiefs and was appalled to learn many departments did not have intelligence files.

"So I said, 'Well, if there's one thing we know how to do in the Central Intelligence Agency and that is how to set up intelligence records and files . . . and as an individual American citizen who's interested in law and order and decency in his community, if there is any way that we could help instruct you as to how these files are set up I would be glad indeed to have a man available."

The program taught techniques developed for the war in Vietnam, Helms said. "We developed a system where treating a cloth with chemical and wiping off a man's hands you can tell whether he had dealt with explosives or not," he boasted.

Fulbright interjected that the issue was "not your very sophisticated methods.

It is whether or not it is proper for you to directly become the mentor of our po-lice." "Oh no," said Helms, sounding surprised that Fulbright didn't care about his support for "law and order and decency."[17]

Fulbright wanted to know more about the burglars, starting with Rolando Martínez. This was the first time Helms testified under oath about Watergate. With the scandal exploding, the stakes were rising. He skied around the facts, like they were poles on a slalom run.

"Mr. Martinez was never an employee of the Central Intelligence Agency," Helms said. He was merely a part-time employee as of June 1972. "He was on a re-tainer of $100 a month at that time."[18] What Helms did not say was that Martínez was a full-time contract employee from 1963 to 1969.

As for McCord, "he actually was an employee of the Agency . . . up until 2 years," Helms allowed, as if searching his memory, "2 or 3 years ago."

"But since then he has had no relationship?" Fulbright inquired.

Since then McCord had displayed the autographed photo from Helms in the office of McCord Associates. He had interviewed or hired a dozen former Agency employees, some of whom Helms knew quite well. He had used Agency references to buy eavesdropping equipment. His longtime confidential informant Lee Pennington had helped Ruth McCord burn CIA documents in the wake of the break-in. And McCord had sent Helms four private back-channel communi-cations about his defense strategy.

"None whatever," Helms replied.[19]

As for Howard Hunt, Helms could barely remember him.

"My recollection is that he resigned rather than retired." He squinted. "I am not sure exactly."

"About when?"

"About two, two and a half years ago," Helms said.

The dating of Hunt's retirement, at least, was accurate. In the three years since then Helms had shielded Hunt from the repercussions of shopping his Bay of Pigs manuscript and written a letter of recommendation that helped him land the job at the Mullen Company. Hunt had been given a security clearance by Tom Karamessines, received assistance from the Office of Medical Services on the Ells-berg personality profile and obtained equipment from General Cushman's deputy for the break-in at Dr. Fielding's office. And Hunt had honored Tom Karamess-ines's parting words at his exit interview: stay in touch.

"He had no relationship to the CIA since then?" Fulbright asked.

"No, sir," Helms lied sincerely.[20]

The questions moved on to other subjects in the news: heroin production in Southeast Asia, the assistance to local police, and the purpose of the Agency's Domestic Contacts Division. The senators were not unfriendly, but they were no longer deferential. And then the shadow of JFK's assassination returned, if only for a moment.

Senator Symington of Missouri mentioned President Harry Truman, who had just died six weeks earlier. Symington proceeded to read aloud the column that Truman had written in December 1963, one month after JFK was killed in Dallas.

"I never thought when I set up the CIA that it would be injected into peacetime cloak and dagger operations," Truman had written. Much to Helms's discomfort, Symington read to the former president's conclusion. "There is something about the way the CIA has been functioning that is casting a shadow over our historic position and I feel we need to correct it."

Symington's aside was a sign of the new mood, the new morality, among even these mostly sympathetic senators. The events of Watergate had revived Truman's post–November 22 warning about "peacetime cloak and dagger operations." Once willing to look the other way, the senators now asked questions, if only because the Watergate affair begged them. *Who are these people? What is going on here?*

At the time virtually nothing was known publicly about the CIA's activities in Chile, where Allende's leftist government still held power.[21] Symington, who had been briefed on some secret Chile operations, was curious.

"Did you try in the Central Intelligence Agency to overthrow the government of Chile?"

"No, sir," said Helms, which might be parsed as truthful. The CIA had given money to the pro-American Christian Democratic candidate but that was for the 1970 election, not a coup. Helms himself had authorized payment to the men who ambushed General Schneider, but the payment was intended to foster a "coup climate," not a specific plan of overthrow.

"Did you have any money passed to the opponents of Allende?"

"No, sir," Helms said. That was in no way true. The Agency funded Agustín Edwards, the anti-Allende publisher, and paid off General Viaux, the ultra-rightist coup plotter.

"So the stories you were involved in that war are wrong?"

"Yes, sir," Helms affirmed falsely. "I said to Senator Fulbright many months ago that if the Agency had really gotten in behind the other candidates and spent a lot of money and so forth the election might have come out differently."[22]

That fateful exchange—three simple questions and three routine denials—was over in minutes, but the words would last for years as a defining moment for Congress, the Justice Department, the CIA, and Helms. It was the moment when the Agency's impunity, born in 1947, began to come to an end.

A PRIVATE WORD

Helms had one last Oval Office meeting with Nixon before he and Cynthia left for Tehran. The president, it seemed, still wanted his counsel. With his new national security adviser Brigadier General Brent Scowcroft at his side, Nixon cross-examined Helms on U.S. policy in the Persian Gulf. Helms said U.S. and British interests were similar but not identical. In Mexico, Nixon complained that President Echeverría had "ostentatiously rolled out the red carpet" for a state visit by Allende. Helms said Echeverría had sent word that his statements were for "domestic consumption" only.

After twenty-five minutes of conversation, Nixon asked Scowcroft for "a private word" with the ambassador. Scowcroft left the room so the two men could talk alone.[23] It is the last time Helms and Nixon are known to have spoken during Nixon's presidency. The burglars were coming to trial, and Helms was going overseas. Their conversation was not recorded.

After four years in power, Helms's and Nixon's bond was more fraught than friendly, intricate but not emotional, collaborative but not close. They were two men of power threatened by an ongoing criminal trial, an imminent Senate investigation, and the ongoing transformation of Washington political culture. Two men who needed and feared and admired and mistrusted each other. Two scorpions, backing away from a long and wary dance.

22

THE WITNESS

James McCord had a new lawyer and a new strategy. As the March 23 sentencing hearing for the burglars approached, his attorney, Bernard Fensterwald, urged him to talk.

Bud Fensterwald, as he was known, was an improbable choice of counsel for McCord. A native of Nashville, he came from a wealthy Jewish family, went to Harvard and Harvard Law School, and made a career on Capitol Hill. He was a liberal and a Democrat, and McCord was neither. While McCord was a proud CIA man, Fensterwald had built a career challenging governmental secrecy and abuses of power.[1] His reputation lent credibility to McCord's new strategy of blaming the White House.

According to Fensterwald's son, McCord hired his father on the recommendation of McCord's friend Lou Russell, a down-on-his-luck private investigator who hung around the Howard Johnson's hotel across from the Watergate complex and supplied information to cops, lawyers, and his friend McCord. (Russell told the FBI that he had dinner with McCord two nights before the break-in.[2]) Fensterwald later boasted to a Democratic politico that he had convinced McCord to talk.[3] His son said the same: "My understanding was that Bud wrote the letter that went to John Sirica and offered to help raise one hundred thousand dollars for bail, of which he was forty thousand short," said Bernard Fensterwald Jr. "And so he put the forty thousand in himself there."[4]

On March 20, 1973, Fensterwald accompanied McCord to Judge Sirica's chambers where he delivered a letter setting forth what he called "the facts of perjury, suppression of evidence and political pressure" coming from the White House. In his memoir, McCord said he wrote the letter himself and did not show it to his attorney.[5]

Three days later, at the sentencing hearing, a poker-faced Judge Sirica read McCord's letter aloud in court. "The air was electrified. It was almost as though no one was breathing for fear of missing a comma or phrase," McCord recalled. The judge deferred sentencing McCord, pending his cooperation with the newly established Senate Watergate Committee.[6]

When Hunt's turn came, he chose not to talk about who was behind the burglary. Instead he begged for mercy.

"Your honor, I stand before you, a man convicted first by the press and then by my own admission, freely made even before the beginning of the trial," Hunt said. "Since the seventeenth of June I lost my employment, then my beloved wife in consequence of my involvement in the Watergate. Today I stand before the bar of justice, alone, nearly friendless, ridiculed, disgraced, destroyed as a man." What he did, Hunt said, "was unquestionably wrong," but they were first offenses in "a life of blameless and honorable conduct. . . . My fate—and that of my family—my children—it is in your hands."

Sirica responded without pity. He sentenced Hunt to forty years in jail. He sentenced Sturgis, Barker, Martínez, and González to thirty-five years. "I sat in stunned, nauseated silence," Hunt recalled.[7]

McCord's letter and the harsh sentences were a sensation. After nine months, one of the burglars was finally ready to talk, and the rest would pay for their silence. McCord issued a statement reiterating what he said in his letter to Sirica. "There was political pressure applied to the defendants to plead guilty and remain silent." And: "Watergate was not a CIA operation. . . . The Cubans may have been misled by others into believing it was a CIA operation. I know for a fact it was not."[8]

McCord got a lenient sentence while the others faced the possibility of decades behind bars. McCord would be sentenced to one to five years in prison and would serve only four months.[9]

The Watergate case was breaking open. Suddenly, news reporters following the lead of the *Washington Post* were everywhere, "swarming over officials' lawns and back porches, sticking microphones in faces which had barely swallowed their morning eggs," wrote *New York Times* reporter J. Anthony Lukas. "And the more resourceful reporters managed to dig out secret testimony, naming big names, high places, and titillating machinations."[10]

Dick Helms could not escape the furor. He returned from Iran for a closed-door hearing of the Senate Foreign Relations Committee. Knowing his testimony would immediately leak in the media feeding frenzy, Helms asked for a public hearing. He got it.

The first question concerned the burglary of Ellsberg's psychiatrist's office, which had just been revealed.

"I would like to say right now that the first time I ever heard that Daniel Ellsberg had a psychiatrist was when I was in Shiraz, Iran, a week ago," Helms said facing twelve senators in front of a standing-room-only crowd in the Dirksen Senate Office Building.

Helms's recollection about that moment in Shiraz was probably untrue—he had seen the casing photographs of Dr. Fielding's eleven months before. Yet as one cover story unraveled, Helms had seamlessly stitched a new one into place. Ever since the arrest of the burglars the Agency insisted it had no dealings with Hunt and McCord after their retirement in 1970. That was Helms's first cover story, which he had retailed to the committee back in February. "About this Watergate business, you have asked the relevant questions," he shrugged at that time. "I have no more information to convey and I know nothing about it. Honestly, I don't."

It turns out he did have more information. He just didn't convey it. Too many people knew too much and were starting to talk. John Dean, fearing his own legal culpability in meeting Hunt's demands for hush money, had turned state's witness. He told prosecutors about the White House campaign against Ellsberg, including the burglary at his psychiatrist's office. Hunt, testifying before a federal grand jury, disclosed the Agency's help with the preparations for the entry at Dr. Fielding's office.

On April 25, the Justice Department shared the information with Judge Matthew Byrne, who was presiding over Ellsberg's trial in Los Angeles. Having failed to block publication of the Pentagon Papers, Nixon's Justice Department had charged Ellsberg with conspiracy and violation of the Espionage Act. The next day Judge Byrne declared a mistrial and cited the Fielding break-in as the reason. Around the same time, investigators learned of McCord's undisclosed back-channel communications with Helms for the first time.

The former director had some explaining to do. The now-defunct cover story of "no dealings" metamorphosed into a more plaintive tale: Helms said he had reluctantly surrendered to pressure to do a personality profile of Ellsberg in 1971 but knew nothing about the burglary of his psychiatrist's office.

"The Agency was not aware that Hunt and Liddy were preparing to commit a crime?" asked an incredulous Senator Fulbright.

"They were not, to the best of my knowledge," Helms avowed. "I never heard anybody in the Agency mention any such thing. As a matter of fact, in the context of that time, no crimes have been committed. . . . no crimes were contemplated, nobody had given us the slightest indication that anything underhanded was afoot." Helms admitted he had seen "photographs of an unidentified building and I did not know what it was."

In the face of Fulbright's skepticism, Helms essentially pleaded his innocence of the profession he had mastered. The most accomplished spy in America just couldn't discern the meaning of those ten photos in the file of his friend Hunt, a career undercover officer seeking to discredit Ellsberg. *Nobody had given us the slightest indication.*

Helms's sinuous actions had shaped the larger Watergate narrative to his advantage. The Agency adopted a familiar trope. When it came to Hunt, "the Agency's right hand didn't know what [its] left hand was doing and vice versa."[11] For the most part, it worked. For the press corps and the Democratic Congress, the Watergate story was the abuse of power by the Nixon White House. The nature of the CIA involvement remained off the public record. The reason for the break-in and scope of the Watergate burglars' other activities—the intrusions at the Chilean Embassy and the offices of Chilean officials—were not investigated by the Senate Watergate Committee.

As Helms massaged his story, his successors at the Agency had to deal with the consequences, setting in motion the events that would lead Helms to be condemned in a court of law. His mastery set the stage for his undoing.

THE FAMILY JEWELS

Nixon's choice to succeed Helms as director of Central Intelligence was James R. Schlesinger, a brusque economist. "Schlesinger's forte was management, his only knowledge of intelligence was that gleaned from work in defense analysis," wrote historian John Prados. "He was really an economist with a Harvard PhD."[12] He came to the Agency with a reputation as a troubleshooter and a mandate from Nixon to shake things up.

Schlesinger had barely started in his new job when he himself was shaken up. The Agency, he was told, had previously helped Hunt and Liddy as they prepared to break into Dr. Fielding's office to search for information that could be used to discredit Ellsberg. "What else have you people been hiding from me?" Schlesinger snarled.

The answer came within a few days. The Agency had received and not disclosed four letters from McCord, one of them personally addressed to Helms. With this revelation, Schlesinger erupted.

"His anger over this had to be experienced to be believed," recalled Bill Colby, the target of his wrath, "and I experienced it both barrels."[13]

On the spot, Schlesinger made a fateful decision. He directed, in writing, that all Agency employees were to report immediately on any current or past practices that might fall outside CIA authority.

Rob Roy Ratliff, a career officer, formerly the Agency's representative on the National Security Council, paid a visit to Schlesinger's office. Hunt, he said, had "frequently transmitted sealed envelopes via our office to the Agency." He thought that "Mr. Helms was probably aware of some of Hunt's activities" but did not know for sure. Schlesinger was "surprised and unaware of such a link," he said.[14] Ratliff provided the names of Peter Jessup and another officer who saw transmission of Hunt's packages.

Ratliff was not the only employee to come forward. By late May the CIA inspector general had a summary of the dubious activities running to more than twenty pages. The full collection of reported complaints would run to close to seven hundred pages.[15] A wag dubbed the collection "the Family Jewels," slang for testicles. In other words, valuable and vulnerable. (Helms, rarely vulgar, insisted "family jewels" was an OSS term for closely held intelligence.[16]) Helms thought that Schlesinger's intent was clear: "to make sure nothing like this"—namely, CIA support for Hunt and the back channel to McCord—"ever happens again."

"Less clear," Helms complained, "was the standard to be used in judging the activities which might fall legally beyond the agency's legislative charter. The National Security Act of 1947 was deliberately cast in terms vague enough not to offend the elements of Congress and the public who might be shocked at the thought of the United States admitting that it was arming itself with a national intelligence service."[17]

Contrary to Helms's implication, the Family Jewels were not composed of complaints from the naive or uninitiated. They came from the Agency's managers and rank-and-file employees. Most of the incidents they deemed problematic had been approved by Helms, including Angleton's mail-opening program (LINGUAL); infiltration of the antiwar movement (CHAOS); mind-control experiments (MKULTRA); the use of Mafia bosses in the Castro assassination plots; the surveillance of dissidents and the proposed centralization of domestic intelligence collection in the White House (the Huston Plan).

The CIA was flailing. Mark Felt, deputy director of the FBI, told the *Post's* Bob Woodward on background that Hunt was blackmailing the White House, that McCord's life had been threatened, and the CIA might be spying on the *Post*. His message: "The cover-up had little to do with Watergate but was mainly to protect the covert operations."[18]

Helms was relieved when the manic Nixon suddenly moved Schlesinger to head the Defense Department. In his four months as director, Schlesinger had orchestrated the dismissal of some one thousand employees, a significant number of whom came from the Directorate of Operations, the new, more candid name for the old Directorate of Plans. "The bond between management and personnel," Helms lamented, "was seriously damaged."

Helms's longtime friend Bill Colby took over as director. Like most CIA people, Helms was glad to see a career officer in the director's chair. Keen to shore up the Agency's diminished credibility on Capitol Hill, Colby briefed congressional leaders on the tenor of complaints from Agency personnel. The chairmen of the Senate and House Armed Services Committee agreed that if the Agency was addressing the issues, Congress need not investigate.[19]

Helms was unhappy that Colby had shared the internal complaints outside the Agency, but the gambit worked, at least initially. The stories in the Family Jewels stayed secret. Helms's defenses were holding, thanks to the gentlemanly agreements that prevailed between the Agency's leadership and the barons of Capitol Hill. In retrospect, Helms found it "astonishing" that the existence of the Family Jewels did not leak for another fifteen months.[20]

NASTY SURPRISE

One sensitive matter that leaked right away was the short-lived Huston Plan. John Dean still had a copy, which he turned over to Judge Sirica, saying it contained national security material not related to Watergate. With the sentencing of the burglars and the revelation about Ellsberg, the short-lived plan was politically radioactive. Senator Ervin obtained a copy and told reporters it was "an operation to spy on the American people," an indicator of the administration's "Gestapo mentality." The fear of the CIA as a secret police organization, first voiced when the Agency came into being in 1947, had returned. Nixon issued a statement defending the plan as necessary and legitimate in the face of an increasingly violent antiwar movement. The CIA, he noted, supported the Huston Plan.

The cascading revelations of wrongdoing forced Attorney General Elliot Richardson to appoint a Special Prosecutor to take over the Watergate investigation. Earl Silbert handed off his investigation to Archibald Cox, a former Solicitor General under President Kennedy, with a memo summarizing the case and what he had learned, especially about Helms.

Silbert showed no deference to the once untouchable director.

"The CIA record of disclosure in this case is a sorry one," Silbert wrote. "Mr. Helms never disclosed to anyone the June 23rd meeting at the White House with Haldeman and Ehrlichman. He knew of General Walters' meetings with Dean and did not disclose them. When this office pressed for CIA information re Hunt and Liddy, he approached Mr. Kleindienst to give him the file. CIA did not want this office to see it, unless needed on rebuttal at trial.

"Eventually, upon our insistence, we did see it," Silbert went on. "CIA maintained a continuous objection to using any CIA information in the Government case-in-chief, probably because of obvious potential embarrassment to CIA over the technical assistance to Hunt and Liddy in July/August of 1971." Helms's failure to disclose the letters from McCord, he added, was "inexcusable."[21]

Richard Ben-Veniste, one of Cox's prosecutors, explained how Helms had deflected the law and compromised its reputation in service of Nixon's White House.

"Disclosure of the White House approaches [to the CIA] could have had a radical impact on the direction of the original Watergate investigation," Ben-Veniste wrote in his Watergate book *Stonewall*. "Disclosure of McCord's letter would at the least have aroused prosecutors' suspicion. There was no question the CIA was impudently protective of the Nixon administration in its handling of the Watergate matter and that it unnecessarily weakened its position in the eyes of the public."[22]

Later that summer Helms returned to Washington to answer questions. "A charming and informal man, Helms put on an impressive display of apparent candor and sympathy," Ben-Veniste recalled. "He explained frankly the tradition of protecting the agency from political entanglement and cited that motive as the reason he had been reluctant to cough up information about Watergate."

As for the pressure from the White House, "Helms admitted that he knew perfectly well that the agency was being importuned but said that he felt well out of it to extract the agency from these pressures and retire gracefully to the sidelines, where the agency could get on about its own business." Helms assured the prosecutors that "it was obvious to him at the time that this was a political gambit by the Nixon palace guard."

The prosecutors were satisfied, and Helms returned to Tehran. Not long after, said Ben-Veniste, "a new batch of documents from old CIA files brought with it a nasty surprise. For the first time, the prosecutors saw Helms's memorandum of June 28, 1972, about his phone conversation with Pat Gray. This was the memo in which Helms stated that he had asked Gray "to desist from expanding this investigation into other areas which may well, eventually, run afoul of our operations. . . ."

"The memo," Ben-Veniste noted, "expressed an opinion that was one hundred and eighty degrees around from the opinion Helms had told us he actually held at the time. What made the memo even more peculiar," said the prosecutor, "was that General Walters claimed *he never received it*. [Emphasis in original]"

Helms was recalled from Iran for another interview. Ben-Veniste quizzed him about the memo, pointing out to him that it seemed to say just the opposite of what he said about the June 23 meeting at the White House.

"Helms was sorry, but he just couldn't explain it," Ben-Veniste recalled. "The memo was unfortunately phrased. True it was hard to reconcile what he wrote with his state of mind: What could he say? Helms was sure that the memo was delivered to Walters."

Ben-Veniste wondered if Helms had recently created the document and back-dated it a year "for the specific purpose of corroboration of the White House line" that the Watergate investigation threatened to uncover confidential CIA operations.

"It seemed far-fetched to suppose that Helms might be blackmailed by the White House," Ben-Veniste wrote. But when he later heard the White House conversation in which Nixon said, "We protected Helms from a hell of a lot of things," he realized it was possible. "Not till later disclosures about the intelligence community's abuses in other fields did the full import of the President's statement fit into place," Ben Veniste said.[23] Behind Helms's cover story lay a host of CIA practices he didn't care to defend publicly.

Ben-Veniste never resolved in his own mind whether Helms obstructed justice or not. "Richard Helms," he said in an interview, "was very good at making you see things the way he wanted you to see them."[24]

23

MAGNIFICENT

In early August, Helms returned yet again to Washington to testify before the Senate Watergate Committee. On the long flights from Tehran to London to Washington, he had time to contemplate his appearance. Whether Helms knew it or not, Jim McCord was ready to show his support. On the day Helms was scheduled to testify, McCord published an article titled "What the FBI Almost Found" in the *Armed Forces Journal*, a publication of the Defense Department. In the piece McCord explained that he could have told the FBI all about the White House officials behind the burglary but insisted he didn't because the FBI, under Nixon's control, could not be trusted. Along the way, McCord admitted destroying evidence at his house in the aftermath of the break-in.

The article was, in the phrase coined by Ehrlichman, "a modified limited hangout," an admission of wrongdoing on a lesser point to hide a greater offense, in this case the involvement of CIA informant Lee Pennington in destroying evidence at McCord's house right after the burglary. McCord shared his less incriminating story exclusively with Connie Chung, a young CBS News correspondent. McCord invited her to his Rockville home to watch Helms's appearance on TV.

In the Senate Caucus Room, Helms did not wait long to deliver his message to the senators, the cameras, and the standing-room-only crowd.

"*The agency [thump] had nothing [thump] to do [thump] with the Watergate* *break-in [*thump*]!"* he shouted. *"I hope all the newsmen in the room hear me clearly now."*[1]

Under the bright lights, Helms described the Watergate burglars as "amateur-ish in the extreme," explaining that "breaking and entering and not getting caught is a very difficult activity, and for it to be done properly, one has to have trained individuals who do nothing else and who are used to doing this frequently and are trained right up to the minute."

"And was McCord in that category?" Senator Baker inquired.

"Obviously not," said Helms as laughter rippled through the room.

When Baker and Thompson's cross-examination grew hostile, Senator Ervin defended the former director, saying his performance at the CIA was "magnificent." He downplayed Helms's occasional bouts of amnesia with a series of quotations from scripture, each phrased slightly differently. In his windy way, Ervin declaimed that Helms's story about his conversations with Pat Gray was no more inconsistent than the words of Matthew, Mark, Luke, and John. While the Christian Bible was not a frequent point of reference in Helms's personal life, much less his professional duties, he was pleased by Ervin's soliloquy. "Thank you, Mr. Chairman," he smiled.[2]

McCord didn't mind absorbing the derision of his former boss in service of his larger purpose. In his interview with Chung, broadcast on national TV that night, McCord defended his role in the burglary, saying Hunt and Liddy were in charge and that he, McCord, did not set up the operation or determine how to carry it out. McCord had airtime to absolve the Agency and throw the blame on senior White House officials. The ex-CIA man reinforced the former CIA director's claim that the CIA wasn't involved.

"I believe there is a very massive cover-up attempt that's going on," he said, "covering up the cover-up, so to speak, of last summer and in turn trying to cover up the events preceding that. My personal opinion is that Mr. Haldeman, Mr. Ehrlichman, and Mr. Mitchell have perjured themself in testimony."

Helms left the Senate hearing room satisfied. Outside in the high-ceilinged hallway, a reporter from the *Post* asked if he resented having to appear before the committee. Helms reserved his best bon mots for Kay Graham, but he didn't mind schooling her minions in the ways of Washington.

"It's part of the job," he shrugged. "If you do it, you get the whole ball of wax. Obviously, I'd rather not be here. I'm not cheerful about being here but one takes life as it comes."[3]

Hunt watched the Watergate hearings from his new residence: the federal

prison in Danbury, Connecticut. In the prison TV room, he wasn't offended by
Helms's disavowals of their friendship. He heard it as a tacit promise of support.
"Yesterday Helms confirmed Intelligence practice to care for families of captured
agents," he wrote to Buckley. He still believed his friend would come to his aid.[4]

THE ROSE MARY STRETCH

A mile and a half away at the White House, President Richard Nixon hosted the
president of Gabon for a state visit.[5] Nixon felt a new confidence. The avalanche of
headlines in the spring—the conviction of the burglars, the charges of cover-up,
and the forced resignations of Haldeman and Ehrlichman—was giving way to a
more normal political season. In May, the president brought home the American
prisoners of war from Vietnam to a rapturous reception that Nixon relished as a
rebuke to the antiwar movement.

His biggest problem was the discovery of the recording system he had installed in the White House. The revelation, made by his former deputy chief of
staff Alexander Butterfield in an interview with Senate investigators, inflamed the
Democrats and the press. Special Prosecutor Cox demanded the president turn
over the tapes of nine key conversations—the very most sensitive of which was
with Helms. That Nixon would not do, not voluntarily. When Judge Sirica ruled
he had to turn the tapes over, Nixon appealed.[6]

"If I were to make public these tapes, containing as they do blunt and candid
remarks on many subjects that have nothing to do with Watergate, the confidentiality of the office of the President would always be suspect," Nixon said. "Persons
talking with a President would never again be sure that recordings or notes of
what they said would not at some future time be made public, and they would
guard their words against that possibility. . . . I shall therefore vigorously oppose
any actions which would set a precedent that would cripple all future Presidents."[7]

In September, Nixon asked Rose Woods to transcribe the tapes that the special prosecutor was seeking via subpoena. "I thought it would only take her a few
days to finish the whole lot," Nixon said, "but she found the quality of the tapes
was so bad and the voices so hard to distinguish, she had to go phrase by phrase."
It took Wood twenty-nine hours to complete one conversation between Nixon,
Ehrlichman, and Haldeman that occurred on June 20, 1972, three days after the
burglary. Amid this typing marathon, Woods came into the president's office in
the Executive Office Building "visibly agitated," in Nixon's words. He recalled
that she said "she might have caused a small gap in the Haldeman part of the June
20 tape."

She explained that the Secret Service had given her a new tape recorder that morning. Unlike the manually operated Sony she had used previously, the Uher 5000 machine had a foot pedal control that would help speed up the work considerably by allowing Woods to type without having to continually shift position back and forth from typewriter to tape recorder. She told Nixon she had been using the machine only about half an hour when she finally came to what seemed to be the end of the Ehrlichman conversation. She heard Haldeman talking when she received a phone call. When she finished the call and listened to that portion of the conversation, all she could hear was "a shrill buzzing sound." She had accidentally erased the tape. The eighteen-and-a-half-minute gap was born.[8]

Nixon assured Woods that the conversation was not covered by the subpoena, although in fact, it was. In October, as Special Prosecutor Cox demanded the tapes, Nixon fired him, leading to the resignation of Attorney General Elliot Richardson and his top deputy. Nixon was forced to name a new special prosecutor, Leon Jaworski, to whom the White House disclosed that a portion of the June 20 tape had been erased. Suspicion immediately fell on the president. In the ultimate act of loyalty to Nixon, Woods went before the U.S. District Court in Washington in November with the Uher machine to explain how she, not the president, had erased the tape.

"What did you do after the phone rang?" asked prosecutor Jill Wine-Volner, one of the youngest Watergate prosecutors and one of the few women. She recalled in her memoir that Woods, at "fifty-five . . . was nearly twice my age, petite but fierce, dressed that day in a color-blocked turquoise, chartreuse, and orange sheath topped with a strand of pearls."

"'I had to take those off first,' she said in a hostile tone, delicately pointing to the headphones resting on the ledge. With that slight movement of her fingers, her foot lifted from the pedal.

"The tape stopped cold," Wine-Volner recalled. Even if Woods had mistakenly pushed Record instead of Stop, releasing the foot pedal would have halted the tape. "Rose had lied and I had caught her." Woods insisted that she had accidentally erased the tape, though she could not explain how.

Woods repeated her performance at the White House later that day. As the photographers' shutters clicked, Woods contorted herself to reach the phone while holding down the pedal of the tape recorder. It was tortuous position, impossible to sustain for eighteen minutes. It was dubbed the Rose Mary Stretch.[9] Her sacrifice for Nixon defined her place in history. When Woods died three decades later, photographs of the Rose Mary Stretch would top her obituary.[10]

Woods became the butt of jokes, and Wine-Volner felt sorry for her.

"I saw something of myself in the president's trim, copper-haired secretary," she wrote, "in the way we both had to survive in a world of men who'd often bullied and belittled us."[11]

With both Nixon and Helms, the most loyal subordinates sometimes suffered the most.

"NOT BY THAT NAME"

As Nixon flailed, Helms sailed. From Tehran, Helms monitored Watergate events. In November, *Harper's* magazine published "The Cold War Comes Home," an account of the Watergate affair written by Andrew St. George, the journalist who had known of Frank Sturgis from his days covering Fidel Castro in the Sierra Maestra.

Most sensationally, St. George reported that Helms was informed about the break-in at seven o'clock in the morning by a call from a watch officer.

"Ah well," he quoted Helms telling the watch officer "They finally did it. . . . A pity . . . They really blew it. . . . If the White House tries to ring . . . just tell them you reported McCord's arrest already, and I was *very* surprised."

Based on conversations with Sturgis, St. George wrote that all the Cubans involved believed they were on a CIA-sanctioned mission because of assurances from Hunt and Barker. Sturgis claimed that his work in the anti-Castro cause was well known to Agency officials, saying that "my own situation involved the Agency's knowledge and approval of my operations and their indirect financing of them."

These revelations triggered a barrage of questions from Capitol Hill. Senator Baker sent seven questions to the Agency on behalf of the Watergate Committee. Senator Fulbright sent a letter for the Foreign Relations Committee. Congressman Lucien Nedzi called St. George to testify before the House Armed Services Committee, followed by CIA director Colby.

St. George appeared accompanied by counsel, who was none other than the ubiquitous Bud Fensterwald. The story about Helms, St. George testified, came from a source he had known a long time who had heard it from the watch officer. When pressed on whether he was absolutely sure of the accuracy of the quote, St. George replied by quoting Helms as saying he had "no recollection" of when he was notified. When told that Helms insisted he was called at night and that he had uttered no such words, St. George stuck with his story, which was hearsay at best.[12]

Senator Symington came to Helms's defense.

"What protection does a man have who is willing to undertake this position for his country?" he asked. "[W]hat protection does he have from slander and yellow journalism? . . . What is his protection?"

Helms had protection from his many friends in the journalism business. Tom Braden, a retired CIA officer turned syndicated columnist, denounced Baker. In a column headlined "Can He Blame It On CIA?" Braden charged the skepticism of the ranking Republican on the Watergate committee about the Agency's role was "the last turn in the defense of Richard Nixon."

Helms kept up appearances. He met with the new special prosecutor, Leon Jaworski, in late November, the last event recorded in Inspector General John Richard's draft history of the affair. "The agency's pattern of cooperation and responsiveness has been set and will undoubtedly continue," he wrote.[13]

Back in Tehran, Ambassador Helms met with the shah and extolled his regime to visitors. He benefited as the focus of the Watergate investigation was passing from the special prosecutor to Congress. Since Cox's firing, Democrats had called for Nixon's impeachment. In February 1974, House Speaker Carl Albert granted the Judiciary Committee authority to investigate whether sufficient grounds existed to impeach Nixon of high crimes and misdemeanors under Article II, Section 4, of the Constitution. As the dimensions of Nixon's crime grew, the details of the burglary faded in importance.

And then the post-burglary fire at McCord's house flared anew. Helms was drawn back into the Watergate vortex by his former colleagues. As the House prepared for impeachment hearings, Walter Pforzheimer prepared a letter for Colby's signature certifying that all CIA records had been shared with investigators, only to learn that the two security officers who heard about the blaze insisted their memos be given to Congress. They told the story of how McCord's wife and friend had burned evidence of his connections to the Agency. They told the story of the Pennington ruse. Colby had no choice to comply.[14]

In March 1974, Helms was called back from Iran to testify before the House Armed Services Committee. He had some explaining to do. Chairman Lucien Nedzi had been surprised to learn that the former director was friends with one of the burglars. Helms conceded he knew Hunt rather better than he had previously disclosed.

"What is wrong with knowing someone better than I have admitted," he shrugged. "I have admitted I know him. Now, how well is 'well.' He is like hundreds of others in twenty-five years that I knew."[15]

It was true that Helms had many friends at the Agency, but how many had he sent on a yearlong paid sabbatical to write spy novels? How many did he confide in about his marriage? How many did he introduce to Jack Valenti? How many did he recommend to Bob Haldeman? His pal Hunt was the only CIA employee so favored.

Helms's intact reputation suffered when Congress had learned he had shredded of his tapes, something even Nixon had not done.

Helms insisted he had honored Senator Mansfield's request to preserve all records related to Watergate. "Senator Mansfield has always treated me very well since I have been in public life," he explained, "and I would do nothing to offend Senator Mansfield."[16]

Nedzi asked if he knew Lee Pennington. As with Ben-Veniste, Helms knew how to parry when cornered by a knowledgeable interrogator.

"No, I don't know a Pennington," he said. "Maybe I did know one at some time in my life."

"You were never aware of his being an informant or a source for the Office of Security?" Nedzi asked.

"Not by that name," Helms snapped. "You know, somebody might have used some other way to describe him, but I don't know any Pennington."

"You were never made aware of Lee Pennington having anything to do with McCord or anybody in the Agency?"

Helms knew better than to answer a precise question.

"Look, Mr. Chairman," he replied, "if you want to tell me what this thing is all about. I am delighted . . . since I didn't know the man, I didn't think it made any difference, but if I can be helpful, if you want to identify with me what the problem is, then I can be more specific."

Nedzi folded. "I think the fact that you don't know anything about it is sufficient," he said. What McCord destroyed and why was never established. The perpetrator of the Pennington ruse was never identified. The interrogation was over.

Howard Baker was not so generous. He and his staff had continued to investigate the CIA's role, as the Watergate Committee prepared its final report. Marc Lackritz, one the attorneys for the majority staff, said that Baker and his counsels "remained determined to hang the whole break-in, wiretapping, and cover-up on the agency," which he called an "illusion/fantasy."[17]

Baker called in Helms once again. Because of the importance of the witness, Senator Ervin and chief counsel Sam Dash sat in on the meeting. Helms brought along Senator Symington for moral support. Baker wasted no time asking the question the Democrats sidestepped, Fred Thompson recalled in his memoir.

"Did any of the destroyed tapes contain conversations with the president?"

Helms's eyes flashed. "No," he said.

"Did they contain any conversations with Haldeman?"

"No," Helms said in an even louder voice.

Thompson was reminded of Helms's outburst during his public testimony to the committee but sensed "he seemed more tense, not quite so confident."

"What about conversations with Ehrlichman?" Baker inquired.

"No!" Helms shouted. He did not know that Elizabeth Dunlevy had told Baker that some of the destroyed tapes did contain conversations with Nixon's closest aides. When Symington tried to make peace, Thompson insisted on answers. He rehearsed all that Baker's staff had learned: the Mullen Company as a CIA proprietary, Hunt's support from the White House; Martínez's reporting on Hunt, and the Pennington ruse.

"Helms stared straight ahead and did not speak," Thompson recalled. There were some things he simply would not talk about. Eventually, the conversation moved on, as Helms repeated what he said in his public testimony.[18]

Despite the rough treatment behind closed doors from Baker, Helms was still shielded by the traditional gentlemanly agreements of Capitol Hill that had protected the Agency for his whole career.[19] With the Senate investigation coming to a close, and the House impeachment hearings getting underway, Helms was free and clear of the Watergate's taint, or so it seemed.

24

GHASTLY

The ways of Washington had changed in just a few years. The war and Watergate taught Congress that the president and the CIA could no longer be trusted. The civil rights movement elected black representatives to Congress and legitimized the idea that human rights should be part of U.S. foreign policy. Feminism swept a wave of women into politics and the professions. Congress modified the seniority system that stifled legislative initiative. Junior members investigated matters once ignored: multinational corporations in Chile, drug trafficking in Panama, prisons in South Vietnam. The antiwar movement faded and the militant left self-destructed while Nixon's "silent majority" absorbed the countercultural changes that emboldened reformers and distressed conservatives. A new moralism took hold in Washington, liberal in spirit and intolerant of hypocrisy. Nixon's presidency was under siege from without and eroding from within.

The self-made Nixon, so astute in his rise to power, could not comprehend the new realities. He imagined that the White House tapes, now sought by Special Prosecutor Jaworski, might exculpate him. Daughter Tricia, by contrast, felt hopeless. Her father, she wrote in her diary, "has repeatedly stated that the tapes can be taken either way. He has cautioned us that there is nothing damaging on the tapes." But, she added, "he has cautioned us that he might be impeached because of their content." Knowing her father, "the latter is the way he really feels." Nixon cited Tricia's observation in his memoirs, noting that "sometimes people around you understand things better than you understand them yourself."[1]

On April 30, Nixon sought to preempt impeachment by releasing a compilation of the transcripts of fifty White House conversations.

"I am confident the American people will see these transcripts for what they are," Nixon said in a televised address, "fragmentary records from a time more than a year ago that now seems very distant, the records of a president and a man suddenly being confronted and having to cope with information which, if true, would have the most far-reaching consequences not only for his personal reputation but, more important, for his hopes, his plans, his goals for the people who had elected him as their leader. In giving these records—blemishes and all—I am placing my trust in the basic fairness of the American people."[2]

The American people were mostly impressed with the prolific profanity of White House chatter, excised from the transcripts with the instantly immortal phrase "expletive deleted." The White House had censored its obscenities, but many still found the dialogue offensive. The editors of the *Wall Street Journal* saw nothing in the transcripts to justify impeachment. "Still there is such a thing as moral leadership . . . the 'bully pulpit,'" they wrote. "This is what Mr. Nixon has sacrificed once and for all." The *Chicago Tribune*, long supportive of Nixon's presidency, called for his resignation, as did other traditionally Republican newspapers like the *Omaha World-Herald*, *Kansas City Times*, *Miami Herald*, and *Providence Journal*.[3]

Jaworski filed suit for sixty-four White House tapes that he said were relevant to his investigation. Nixon sat down to listen to the tapes, including the June 23 conversation where he and Haldeman schemed to head off the Watergate investigation by ordering Helms to restrain the FBI. "I didn't recognize the tape then as the 'smoking gun' it turned out to be," Nixon rued in his memoir.

The currents of Watergate were converging. In May, the House Judiciary Committee opened its impeachment hearings. The following month the Senate Watergate Committee issued its final report, a devastating summary of a wide range of illicit activities, from the cover-up of the Watergate burglary to the Republican (and Democratic) violation of campaign contribution laws to Nixon's personal finances, including the allegation, never proven, that Nixon's friend Bebe Rebozo gave $50,000 to Rose Mary Woods.

In introducing the twelve-hundred-page report, the committee called attention to the larger pattern and identified what it said were the root causes of the scandal.

"The Watergate break-in cannot be understood unless viewed in the context of similar White House activities," the report declared. "[F]rom the early days of the present administration the power of the President was viewed by some in the White House as almost without limit, especially when national or internal security was invoked, even criminal laws were considered subordinate to Presidential decision or strategy."[4]

The adoption of the Huston Plan in July 1970, the committee declared, was a key step on the road to the Watergate. "The President approved the use of illegal wiretapping, illegal break-ins and illegal mail covers for domestic intelligence purposes," the report stated, adding that the CIA, NSA, and the military services supported the Huston recommendations.[5] The justification for the policy became justification for the Watergate crimes.

Baker could not convince the majority to include his findings about the CIA in the report, so he filed a forty-three-page appendix with his views. Baker did not take issue with the committee's report. He just said there was more to investigate. He described the role of the Mullen Company in covert activities. He detailed the support given to Hunt by the Agency's Technical Services Division, which, he said, raised the question of "whether the CIA had advance knowledge of the Fielding break-in." He recounted the Pennington ruse, and noted Helms's destruction of his office tapes.[6]

Perhaps most importantly, Baker concluded that "congressional committee oversight did not function effectively as a deterrent to those who may have sought to utilize governmental intelligence and investigative agencies for unlawful or unauthorized purposes." The traditional arrangement, in effect since 1947, in which the CIA director reported to exactly one senator had failed to protect the democratic process from those who might abuse it in the name of national security. Baker called for "closer supervision of Central Intelligence Agency activities by the appropriate congressional oversight committees," an increasingly popular idea that Helms had always resisted.[7]

"I CALLED ROSE"

The end for Nixon came suddenly and unmercifully and it implicitly involved Helms. On July 24, the Supreme Court ruled unanimously that the tapes must be turned over, and the House Judiciary Committee approved three articles of impeachment. Nixon reluctantly made the tapes public on August 5, including the June 23, 1972, conversation in which his enigmatic threats about the "whole Bay of Pigs thing" indicated his intention to enlist the CIA in his obstruction of justice.

"President Nixon personally ordered a cover-up of the facts of Watergate within six days after the illegal entry into the Democrats' national headquarters on June 17, according to three new transcripts," wrote Bob Woodward and Carl Bernstein on the front page of the *Washington Post*, under the headline "The Plan: Use CIA to Block Probe."[8]

Nixon's supporters on the House Judiciary Committee called for him to resign.[9] The next day, a trio of Republican leaders visited the White House. They were Barry Goldwater, the former standard-bearer and now a patriarch of the party, Hugh Scott, the Senate Republican leader, and John Rhodes, the House Republican leader.

Nixon asked how many senators would vote against the three articles of impeachment. Goldwater said sixteen, perhaps eighteen. He said he was prepared to vote for Article 1, the obstruction of justice count. Nixon knew his presidency was over. In the agonizing moment where he contemplated his ruin, he could not bring himself to face his family. He turned to his most loyal friend, Rose Woods. She had been there at the start, for the Checkers speech and the ordeal in Caracas, the defeats and the triumphs. Now she was the only person in the world he could face.

"After the meeting," Nixon said, "I called Rose and asked her to tell the family that a final check of my dwindling support in Congress had confirmed that I had to resign. . . . My decision was irrevocable and I asked her to suggest that we not talk about it anymore when I went over for dinner."[10]

That night Nixon asked Kissinger to join him in the Lincoln Sitting Room, one of his favorite places in the White House, where he relaxed in an overstuffed brown leather armchair with a stereo system and his record collection. Nixon was drinking when Kissinger arrived.

"Will history treat me more kindly than my contemporaries?" he asked, tears in his eyes. Certainly, Kissinger told him. Nixon asked him to get down on his knees with him to pray. "The President prayed out loud, asking for help, rest, peace and love," Woodward and Bernstein reported.

"How could a President and a country be torn apart by such small things?" Nixon wept. Later he asked Kissinger, "Henry, please don't tell anyone that I cried and that I was not strong."[11]

"GLAD HE WAS GONE"

In Tehran, Dick and Cynthia Helms got a call from their friend Hugh Sidey, *Time* magazine correspondent, who alerted them to the fact that Nixon was going to speak on television that night.

"Dick, as usual, was unperturbed and went to bed at his normal time," Cynthia recalled. "I arranged for the young marine who stood guard through-out the night to wake me at 4:15 a.m. The president was scheduled to speak at 9 p.m. in Washington, which would be 4:30 a.m. our time. Wearing my dressing gown, I grabbed a large shortwave radio, took it into the garden to find a spot where the radio reception was best, and found a station in Sweden that was carrying the broadcast live. Sitting in that fragrant garden beneath a starry sky more than six thousand miles from Washington I listened to Nixon announce his resignation. The suspense finally got to Dick, who threw open the upstairs bedroom window with a clatter during the speech to lean out and ask me what had happened."

She relayed the news.

"Nixon had no love for my husband," she recalled, "so we were glad he was gone."[12]

The next morning, Nixon boarded a helicopter to leave the White House for the last time.

"The memory of that scene for me is like a film frame forever frozen at that moment," Nixon wrote in his memoir. "The red carpet, the green lawn, the White House, the leaden sky. The starched uniforms and palace shoes of the honor guard. The new President and his First Lady. Julie. David. Rose. So many friends. The crowd, covering the lawn, spilling out into the balconies, leaning out of the win-dows silent, waving, crying. . . . The flag on top of the house, hanging limp in the windless, cheerless morning. I raised my arms in a final salute. I smiled. I waved good-bye. I turned into the helicopter, the door was closed, the red carpet was rolled up. The engines started. The blades began to turn. The noise grew until it almost drowned out all thought."[13]

Nixon retreated to his home in San Clemente, California. Gerald Ford, former congressman from Michigan, took over as president. At the Pentagon, the generals of the Joint Chiefs of Staff made a decision about their own tapes. The meetings of the Joint Chiefs had been recorded and transcribed ever since the cre-ation of the JCS in 1947. The day after Nixon was driven from office by the rev-elations on the White House tapes, the generals ordered the destruction of all the transcripts. The records, the chiefs decided, did not constitute official minutes but rather the reporter's version of events and thus did not have to be preserved under federal records laws. All transcripts of the generals' conversations about every major issue of the Cold War from the Korean conflict, the nuclear arms race, the Bay of Pigs, Operation Northwoods, JFK's assassination, the Six-Day

War, the Tet Offensive, the arms control talks, and the opening to China were all shredded. Like Helms, the generals made sure they would not suffer the same fate as Nixon.[14]

"DEAD CATS"

Helms emerged from the Watergate scandal as an éminence grise of Washington, a wise man above the fray of politics and polemics. In the fall of 1974, actor and director Robert Redford invited Helms to serve as a consultant on the set of his CIA thriller, *Three Days of the Condor*, which he was filming in New York City. Helms had never lost his interest in books and movies about his profession.

Helms was seen as a compelling, slightly mysterious man of power who commanded respect even from afar. Redford was the brainy star with a social conscience. "I was desperate to get a shot of the two of them together," said photographer Terry O'Neill, "but everyone was very tight-lipped about his visits to the set" in New York's Central Park. "I first saw them sitting together from a distance. It was perfect, both having coffee in Styrofoam cups, an eerie and foggy city in the background and two very powerful men sitting in their coats on director's chairs. I couldn't believe what I was seeing. I knew I couldn't move a muscle because I didn't want to draw any attention to myself. I quietly put on a long lens and snapped."[15]

The black-and-white photo captured Helms at his most untouchable, and that aura vanished just as quickly as it was captured on film.

On September 8, 1974, President Ford pardoned Nixon, ensuring that the former president would not face criminal trial and provoking charges that the Watergate cover-up continued. Congress was asking more questions about the CIA in Chile. President Allende had been overthrown in September 1973 by a military coup that established a brutal pro-American dictatorship. The question of CIA involvement led back to Nixon and Kissinger's Track II policy that culminated in the ambush of General Schneider. Details of the payments to General Viaux leaked from Capitol Hill and were reported in the *New York Times* and *Washington Post*.

Amid this bad publicity, the CIA's general counsel set up a panel of officers to review whether Helms had testified truthfully about Chile—he had not, they said. Director Bill Colby was prepared to sit on the finding, but his lawyers said he had no choice but to refer the matter to the Justice Department. Attempting to hide Helms's misleading testimony would only explode later. On December 21, 1974, Colby disclosed the Agency's qualms about Helms's testimony to the Justice

Department, which took the issue under advisement. That single decision would end the two men's friendship and land Helms in a court of law.[16]

The same day that Colby met with the Justice Department, Seymour Hersh, investigative reporter for the *New York Times*, was putting the finishing touches on his latest scoop. He had learned from CIA sources about the problematic operations cited in the Family Jewels, especially the surveillance of the antiwar movement (CHAOS) and Angleton's mail intercept program (LINGUAL). When Hersh called Colby for comment, the director invited him to his office in the Langley headquarters. Hersh said his sources told him that the Agency had engaged in "massive" operations against the antiwar movement involving wiretaps, break-ins, mail intercepts, and surveillance. The *Times* was going to publish the story soon, he said.

"Colby sought to set him straight," said historian John Prados. "CHAOS was limited to figuring out if the antiwar movement was under foreign control," Colby said. He insisted Hersh had nothing more than "a few incidents of the Agency straying from the straight and narrow." Whatever had happened under his predecessors was over. Colby had discontinued CHAOS, fired Howard Osborn, disbanded the Security Research Staff, and was hoping to force Angleton's retirement. Colby wanted credit for cleaning up after Helms. "There is certainly nothing like that going on now," he insisted.[17]

Hersh sent word to Helms in Tehran seeking comment. Helms refused. With neither Colby nor Helms denying the details in the story, Hersh's editors played it up with a triple-decker headline in the Sunday edition of December 22, 1974.

HUGE CIA OPERATION REPORTED
IN U.S. AGAINST ANTIWAR FORCES,
OTHER DISSIDENTS IN NIXON YEARS

"Helms Reportedly Got Surveillance Data in Charter Violation" declared the subhead. The ambassador thought he had escaped Watergate. In fact, his nightmare was just beginning.

Helms was furious about the *Times* story. Colby was defensive. He demanded Angleton's resignation and sent a report to President Ford. In a six-page single-spaced letter with nine classified appendices, Colby summarized the most troublesome stories in the Family Jewels: the CIA held files on fourteen past and present members of Congress, had surveilled thousands of Americans, and had been involved in operations involving organized crime and mind-control experiments.[18]

Colby believed the Agency could only regain credibility by repudiating the abuses of the past. Helms's friend Cord Meyer blamed Colby for "atrociously bad judgment and appalling naivete."[19] But was Helms's judgment that was called into question. The former director bore "direct and substantial responsibility for the CIA abuse in Project Lingual," wrote historian Prados. "Helms not only approved James Angleton's proposals for the mail-opening, he rode shotgun thereafter—backing expansions, turning aside complaints, keeping an eye for outside challenges, intervening with Cabinet officers when the project came under fire, and ordering measures to reduce visibility—and flap potential—all the while pushing for action. And all of this in service of something CIA acknowledged as illegal from the start."[20]

And contrary to Helms's claims that the CIA only acted at the behest of the president, Nixon had never been told about CHAOS or LINGUAL. "In more than four thousand hours of unguarded conversation recorded on the White House tapes, the president never once referred to CIA surveillance or mail-opening," Prados noted.[21]

Coming four months after Nixon's resignation and three months after Ford's pardon, the *Times* story stoked the fears of an out-of-control CIA voiced by Senator Baker and others. Ford named Vice President Nelson Rockefeller to head a commission charged with evaluating CIA activities within the United States that "give rise to questions of compliance" with the National Security Act of 1947.

For the first time, the Agency was going to be investigated by outsiders. Skeptical of the independence of the Rockefeller Commission, Democratic leaders in the House and Senate announced the creation of separate investigative committees to also probe the CIA's alleged abuses.

"These stories are the tip of the iceberg," Helms warned Kissinger, who passed the story to Ford. "If they come out, blood will flow. For example," he said. "Bobby Kennedy personally managed the operation on the assassination of Castro."[22]

The claim was not implausible—RFK was hawkish on Cuba up until the day his brother was murdered—but there is also reason to doubt Kennedy knew about the AMLASH operation. If the attorney general managed the Castro plot, why did Helms tell Desmond Fitzgerald not to inform RFK about his meeting with Rolando Cubela in October 1963? Helms was in a tight spot, facing questions he had always managed to avoid. He had never been a partisan, but if Democrats wanted to score points off his Agency, he could play that game.

Helms went to the White House.

"Frankly, we are in a mess," Ford told him. "I want you to tell me whatever you want. I believe the CIA is essential to the country. It has existed to perform a function. . . . The CIA needs to remain a strong and viable agency. It would be a shame if the public uproar forced us to go beyond and question the integrity of the CIA. I automatically assume what you did was right, unless proved otherwise."

"I've been in service 32 years," replied Helms. "At the end, all one has is a small pension and a reputation—if any. I testified in Watergate. I didn't dump on President Nixon, and I stuck to the truth. I intend to fight this matter. . . . The CIA is the President's creature. . . . If allegations have been made to Justice, a lot of dead cats will come out." (He was referring to a pastime of nineteenth-century American politics: hurling feline corpses at the opposition candidate.) "I intend to defend myself," Helms raged. "I don't know everything which went on in the Agency; maybe no one really does. But I know enough to say if the dead cats come out, I will participate."

"I have no doubt about your total integrity," Ford replied. "I plan no witch hunt, but in this environment I don't know if I can control it."[23]

He couldn't. After Helms returned to Tehran, Ford had a meeting with the editors of the *New York Times* where he expressed concern that the impending investigations might delve into matters the U.S. government simply could not discuss. Like what, a *Times* editor asked? "Like assassination," blurted out Ford, before hastily taking his answer "off the record."[24]

CBS News correspondent Daniel Schorr picked up word of the conversation and confirmed it with his sources. On February 28 he broadcast a two-minute story on the evening news, leading with a sensational revelation: "President Ford had reportedly warned associates that if current investigations go too far they could uncover several assassinations of foreign officials involving the CIA."[25]

The story was soon confirmed. The Agency had sought unsuccessfully to assassinate three foreign leaders, Fidel Castro in Cuba, Patrice Lumumba in Congo, and Rafael Trujillo in the Dominican Republic. (Other parties killed Lumumba and Trujillo, according to the Agency.) "While I have been mistaken in suggesting actual murders," Schorr later wrote, "my report opened up one of the darkest secrets in the CIA's history." As Ray Cline, the former deputy director for intelligence, put it, "the fig leaf had fallen off and we were out of the Garden of Eden."

The Rockefeller Commission, originally charged with investigating the domestic spying allegations, added the assassination of foreign leaders to its portfolio after Schorr's report. "This was the post-Watergate Congress," Colby observed. "The old power structure of the Congress could no longer control their junior colleagues and hold off their curiosity about the secret world of intelligence. In this new era, CIA was going to have to fend for itself without that longtime special Congressional protection."[26]

The state of the country was "ghastly," in Helms's view, and it only got ghastlier. A week later, Geraldo Rivera, host of ABC's *Good Night America* program, broadcast Abraham Zapruder's home movie of President Kennedy's assassination on national TV. Millions of Americans witnessed JFK's violent death for the first time.

25

INTERROGATION

If Dick Helms ever saw Abraham Zapruder's film, he did not see fit to mention it in his memoirs or to his biographers. The CIA had obtained a copy of the film from the Secret Service within twenty-four hours of the assassination, and some of Helms's colleagues are known to have viewed it.

The Agency's National Photographic Interpretation Center, led by Helms's friend Dino Brugioni, magnified individual frames of the film into three-by-four-foot storyboards seeking to identify the sequence of gunfire that struck Kennedy and Governor Connally. John McCone, Helms's boss, saw the storyboards and the film. He told Robert Kennedy that he thought JFK had been hit by gunfire from two different directions.[1] Jane Roman, senior liaison officer for the Counterintelligence Staff, requested a copy of Zapruder's film from the FBI in October 1964, saying it was needed "for training purposes." If McCone, Brugioni, and Roman had access to the film, it is plausible, if not likely, that Helms saw it too.

Zapruder's film was "the most famous underground movie in America," wrote Lee Winfrey, TV critic for the *Philadelphia Inquirer*.[2] After Kennedy's assassination, Zapruder gave a copy of the film to the Secret Service and sold the rights to *Life* magazine for $150,000. *Life* published individual frames in its assassination coverage but did not release the film for broadcast in deference to the Kennedy family. Jim Garrison played the film for the jury in the trial of Clay Shaw, and bootleg copies had circulated on college campuses. But until Geraldo Rivera broadcast the film on March 6, 1975, it had never been seen by a national audience.

In twenty-six seconds of grainy color film, the nightmare unfolded, with narration by Robert Groden, a photographic analyst who obtained a copy of the film. Kennedy's motorcade was seen turning onto Elm Street.

"Before the sign the president is waving to the crowd," Groden said. "When he comes out from behind the sign, he is shot, and the Governor Connally is shot . . . and now at the bottom of the screen the head shot."

The studio audience gasped as Kennedy's head was blasted backward.

"That's the shot that blew off his head," Rivera announced unnecessarily.

Rivera showed the film again in slow motion, and it just got ghastlier the second time: the happy procession snaking through sunlit America . . . the president jolted by a shot from behind . . . his hands raised . . . the First Lady looking at him quizzically . . . the backward snap of the head . . . the corona of blood.

"The Warren Commission said that all of the shots were fired from behind by a lone assassin," Groden explained. "The head is thrown violently backward, completely consistent with a shot from the front."[3]

In the pixilated colors, Americans saw an event that had been etched indelibly into memory. Just about every American older than the age of five in 1963 remembered where they were when they heard the news from Dallas. Now, twelve years later, they had an image of what had actually happened.

Rivera's show generated "an enormous reaction—more letters, more phone calls, more comment from important people and word of mouth in the industry than from any other Rivera show," wrote Stan Isaacs, columnist for *Newsday*, the tabloid of suburban Long Island, New York. "TV people were impressed by considerable reaction that came from middle America," he wrote, prompting Rivera to host another show three weeks later. This ninety-minute special featured another agonizing replay of the film, followed by a debate between critics and defenders of the Warren Commission.[4]

The official story that Kennedy had been killed by a lone gunman, never terribly credible according to public opinion polls, was called into question. "In the aftermath of Watergate and its stunning revelations," wrote John J. O'Connor of the *New York Times*, "the whole of recent American history has been opened to re-examination. The darkly improbable can no longer be casually considered impossible."[5]

While O'Connor tut-tutted about "easy sensationalism," viewers asked hard questions about the veracity of their government. Kay Gardella, TV critic for the

New York Daily News, called the show "ghoulish,"[6] but many more called it reve-
latory. For a decade, the government—and the CIA—had assured the people that
Kennedy was killed by a gunshot from behind. Zapruder's film indicated otherwise
to millions of Americans. The implication: the government was lying about the
murder of a president. After Rivera's two shows, the Rockefeller Commission had
no choice but to investigate new allegations about JFK's assassination, including
claims, never substantiated, that Howard Hunt and Frank Sturgis were in Dallas
on that day. The commission's staff viewed the Zapruder film.[7]

The revelation of the plots to kill Castro raised more questions for Ambas-
sador Helms. When the CIA shared the 1967 inspector general's report with the
Rockefeller Commission, staffers realized the Agency had never disclosed to the
Warren Commission that Nestor Sanchez was delivering a lethal weapon to Rolando
Cubela, a.k.a. AMLASH, on the same day JFK was shot dead. Among those who
were duped was former assistant counsel to the Warren Commission David Belin.
He had just been selected as executive director of the Rockefeller Commission. He
was embarrassed and angry.[8]

"Did anyone with the CIA tell any member of the Warren Commission or
any lawyer serving on the Warren Commission staff that such plans had been underway?" Belin wrote to the Agency. "If the Commission was not told about his,
why was it not told and who made the decision not to deliver such information to
the Warren Commission?"[9]

Helms hastened back from Tehran once again, now the target of the government he served. He made sixteen trips to Washington during his tenure as ambassador. "A single trip was grueling," said Cynthia. "It took as many as eighteen
hours, with a brief stop to change planes in London . . . went to bed soon after
he arrived, and then testified before one of the committees the following day for
hours on end. . . . He sometimes completed the 12,680-mile round trip in four
days. It took a terrific toll on him both physically and mentally."[10]

Compounding Helms's predicament, his interrogators acted like they didn't
trust him, even men he thought were friends. The Rockefeller Commission insisted he testify, on the record, about sensitive CIA missions—"the Dirty Tricks
Department" in Nixonian parlance—that he had undertaken for the president. As
if he had done something wrong by serving the White House. Helms was baffled
and infuriated by this turn of events.

The news from Vietnam only made matters worse. A North Vietnamese offensive that began in January had captured provincial capitals of Pleiku and Da-
nang by March. President Ford could not convince Congress to make good on

the promises of the disgraced Nixon to protect the South Vietnamese at all costs. Helms knew that Nixon and Kissinger had not made peace in 1973, and now the worst had come to pass. The United States was done with Vietnam. President Thieu had abdicated, and Saigon was about to fall. The war that Helms had helped prosecute for a decade was lost. He was in a foul mood.

Helms testified in one of the most secure rooms in the capital—the windowless penthouse built for the Joint Committee on Atomic Energy in an office annex across the street from the White House. He started by filibustering.

"The business about the assassination of Castro, I have read about this in the papers," he started, "I have heard about it from associates. It has been kicked around whether this was a viable proposition or not. I have no doubt it was written into various plans as one of many options, but I don't recall any successful effort that was made in this direction, and since Castro is alive and apparently well in Havana, the extent to which this was serious I have never ascertained."[11]

Amid the verbiage, Belin pressed a point.

"Well, there is evidence in the record, Ambassador Helms, that there were plans made to try and assassinate Premier Castro of Cuba, that there were several series of plans, and that the plans, at least one or two of the stages, included the delivery of poison pills developed in the Agency to be placed in food or drink—"

"Who authorized this particular operation?" Helms asked. He knew the answer. It was Dick Bissell who ran the poison pill project. Let him take the heat.

"This is one of the areas that we are trying to ascertain," Belin said, "and I suppose my first question along this line was whether or not you had any knowledge of the existence of such a plan?"

"Not that I recall," he dodged.

"And you indicate that you never knew of such a plan?"

Of course, Helms knew of the poison pill plan. He thought it was foolish. But he wasn't going to be pinned down.

"I don't recall any plan," he lied.[12]

Belin was supposedly a friend, yet the unfriendly interrogation did not stop.

"Do you have any recollection of a project known as Project Amlash?" Belin inquired.

Helms played dumb and pushed back.

"Amlash?" he said. "By that name? Not anymore."

"Did you ever—"

Helms interrupted him, "Don't forget, Mr. Belin, that there were hundreds of these things."

"Do you have any recollection of any man by the name of Rolando Cubela?"

Helms had to be careful. Since the Commission obviously had the 1967 inspector general's report, ignorance was not an option.

"Let's see," he said, as if plumbing the depths of memory. "Was he the fellow who eventually ended up in Paris or Madrid or something of this kind?"

Helms had an excellent memory. His agent Nestor Sanchez had met Rolando Cubela in December 1964 to arrange delivery of the FAL rifle. The meeting was in Madrid.

"Do you remember that eventually arms were delivered to Mr. Cubela in Cuba?"

Helms was not going to be the fall guy for an inquisition.

"I don't have any doubt about it," he snapped. "I think we delivered arms all over the place in connection with Cuba. I mean let us not for a moment think that the Kennedy administration wasn't dead serious about getting rid of the Castro government . . . this was a government operation."

Belin wanted to know about General Schneider, and Helms had to worry again.

"President Nixon called you or contacted you to ascertain if anything could be done to prevent his investigature, that is, Allende's investiture by the Chilean legislature," Belin asked. "Do you remember that call?"

Of course Helms remembered it. He would describe the meeting to journalists Thomas Powers and James Rosen, among others. He wrote about it in his memoir. Belin was asking about the September 15, 1970, meeting where Nixon and Kissinger ordered Helms to do something about Allende's victory.

"No," lied Helms. ". . . I knew this subject had come up, but I thought it came up in the context of the 40 Committee deliberations [the 40 Committee being the interagency panel that approved covert operations]. I don't recall a conversation with President Nixon. I don't say I didn't have one. I just don't recall it in that form."

Belin wanted to know about the false flaggers and the provision of arms to General Viaux's gang. He laced his question with a hard fact.

"Do you recall any request made by the president or anyone else in the White House that the Agency funnel funds, also even perhaps submachine guns, to see if something could be done to prevent the legislature from electing him?"

Helms recovered smoothly.

"My recollection . . . was that having investigated this, we came to the conclusion there was no way to prevent his investiture," he fibbed. "And I do not recall anything about machine guns."

The aggressive questioning went on for two days, followed by a four-hour session with the commission members. Helms emerged shell-shocked and jetlagged, incredulous that his secret operations were being thrown to the wind of public opinion. He was an intelligence chief turned ambassador, and he was now being treated like a perpetrator, and when he left the room, who should appear in his face but the obnoxious Daniel Schorr of CBS News. He had been the first to report the assassination plots.

"I extended my hand in greeting with a jocular welcome back!" Schorr recalled. "I was forgetting that I was the proximate reason for his being back."

Helms knows Zapruder's film. . . *JFK's hands raised . . . the First Lady looking at him quizzically . . . the backward snap of the head . . . the corona of blood.*

"You son of a bitch," he raved. "You killer, you cocksucker! Killer Schorr, that's what they are to call you!"

Helms turned away. Schorr pursued him.

"I must say Mr. Schorr, I don't like what you had to say in some of your broadcasts on the subject," Helms barked. "As far as I know, the CIA was never responsible for assassinating any foreign leader." Helms did not care to think of General Schneider as a foreign leader.

"Were there discussions of possible assassinations?" Schorr asked.

Helms's temper rose again.

"I don't know when I stopped beating my wife, or when you stopped beating your wife," he shouted. "Talk about discussions in government! There are always discussions about practically everything under the sun!"[13]

For a poised man, it was an unusual loss of control. Three years before, Helms had erupted when Haldeman told him the Watergate investigation threatened to open up "the whole Bay of Pigs thing." Now, amid a barrage of questions about Castro, poison pills, AMLASH, and "Who shot John?" he exploded again.

Nothing threatened Dick Helms more than the shadow of JFK's assassination.

26

THE PURITAN ETHIC

The next two years of Dick Helms's life were often miserable. To his continuing consternation, the government he served rebuked him. The Rockefeller Commission released its report in June 1975 covering a host of questionable CIA activities during Helms's tenure: the Castro assassination plots, the mail-opening program, and the surveillance of domestic dissident groups. It also conducted a narrow study of issues relating to the JFK assassination. The commission endorsed the scientifically dubious claim that the backward snap of Kennedy's head seen in the Zapruder film was caused by a neuromuscular reaction to a shot from behind. More plausibly, the commission refuted claims that Howard Hunt and Frank Sturgis had been in Dallas on November 22. Given the commission's conservative cast and mild conclusions about long-secret illicit activities, the Rockefeller report was dismissed by many as a whitewash.

Still, one of its recommendations stung Helms. "The best assurance against misuse of the Agency," the commission concluded, "lies in the appointment to that position of a person with judgment, courage and independence to resist improper pressure and importuning, whether from the White House, within the Agency or elsewhere."

Helms took that personally, objecting to the notion "that a fellow who had made a career of intelligence, as I had, didn't have the strength to stand up to a president who wanted certain things done, that I would be afraid for my job or not able to stand up to the pressure. I resented that."[1]

He resented Frank Church, the ambitious Idaho Democrat who chaired the Senate Select Committee on Intelligence Activities. The Church Committee opened its hearings in September 1975 on the sensational topic of biowarfare. Nixon had ordered destruction of all lethal toxins to bring the United States into compliance with a new international treaty. Someone at the CIA had saved a small amount of one toxin. It was not a major issue for the committee, not compared to assassination, domestic spying, and mind control experiments. In a show of cooperation, Colby gave Church a small battery-powered dart gun that could kill in seconds and leave no trace. The gun had never been used, he said. But, like Zapruder's film, the dart gun was a potent image capable of shaping public opinion. The spectacle of Church holding up the pistol on national TV, said John Prados, "blew the roof off" the CIA scandal.

"For many in Congress and the public, what mattered was that all these revelations of past misbehavior did not square with America's image of itself as an innocent," observed one CIA staff historian. "It was psychologically uncongenial to learn that CIA had intervened in other countries, contributed to the deaths of certain foreign leaders, tried to assassinate others, done business with gangsters, developed deadly toxins, and interfered with the rights of Americans. Other countries' secret agencies might do these things, but never ours."[2]

Helms blamed Colby for cooperating with Church, and he blamed Church, who he thought was running for president at the expense of the Agency.

"He felt this was a great launching platform to bring his name before the public and get a lot of media attention, which it certainly did," Helms groused. "And there was no reason not to hold such an investigation if they felt it desirable . . . But it struck me that Senator Church's political ambitions ran far ahead of his interest in really doing a thoughtful and serious job."

Helms had allies in President Ford and Henry Kissinger. In late October 1975, the president summoned Colby to the White House for an early morning meeting. Ford told him he wanted to restructure the national security system. In other words, he was fired. Ford replaced Colby with former Texas congressman George H. W. Bush, whose oil drilling company, Zapata Petroleum, had long lent support to the CIA. He also fired Defense Secretary (and former CIA director) James Schlesinger. That same day, Colby stopped by Schlesinger's house to commiserate.[3] "You know," Schlesinger said ruefully, "Dick Helms outlasted us both."[4] The suggestion was that the old secretive CIA had outlasted the new transparent CIA.

Helms hardly felt victorious. He thought he had served the American government well. And what did he get for his trouble? The Church Committee released an interim report on "Alleged Assassination Plots Involving Foreign Leaders" that exposed a host of sensitive lethal operations in which Helms had a hand.[5] The report, endorsed by both Democratic and Republican senators, took care to put its findings in historical context, especially about the challenge that revolutionary Cuba posed to the American empire.

"Following the end of World War II, many nations in Eastern Europe and elsewhere fell under Communist influence or control," the report began. "The defeat of the Axis powers was accompanied by rapid disintegration of the Western colonial empires. The Second World War had no sooner ended than a new struggle began. The Communist threat, emanating from what came to be called the 'Sino-Soviet bloc,' led to a policy of containment intended to prevent further encroachment into the 'Free World.'"

The tone was not hostile to the CIA.

"[I]t was considered necessary to wage a relentless cold war against Communist expansion wherever it appeared in the 'back alleys of the world,'" the interim report went on. "This called for a full range of covert activities in response to the operations of Communist clandestine services. The fear of Communist expansion was particularly acute in the United States when Fidel Castro emerged as Cuba's leader in the late 1950s. His takeover was seen as the first significant penetration by the Communists into the Western Hemisphere. United States leaders, including most Members of Congress, called for vigorous action to stem the Communist infection in this hemisphere. These policies rested on widespread popular support and encouragement."[6]

But the consensus in Washington was no longer so indulgent of the Agency's impunity. The interim report went on to offer four major findings, all of which implicitly or explicitly rebuked Helms. The committee could not confirm that the Castro plots were authorized by Presidents Eisenhower, Kennedy, or Johnson, which Helms thought was normal, not noteworthy. "You've got to protect the president from the dirty stuff," he told reporters coming out of one hearing.[7]

The second finding didn't name Helms, but it was clearly aimed at him and his colleagues from Bissell to Karamessines. "Certain officials may have perceived that, according to their judgment and experience, assassination was an acceptable course of action." That was true.

The interim report also criticized "agency officials" for "failing on several occasions to disclose their plans to superior authorities, or for failing to do so with sufficient detail and clarity." Helms scoffed. As he testified to the committee, "I can't imagine anybody wanting something in writing, saying, I have just charged Mr. Jones to go out and shoot Mr. Smith."[8]

Finally, the report chided U.S. officials for "not ruling out assassination," which Helms found presumptuous. If a president wanted an assassination capability to achieve U.S. goals, who was the CIA to deny it?

When his irritation with Colby and Church subsided, a more philosophical Helms blamed larger historical forces.

"Americans are peculiar in this particular respect," he explained. "As one very wise American said to me one day, 'Look, this is simple. The American people want you to go out and do these things, they just don't want to be told about them, and they don't want to have them on their conscience.' Period. I think that's true. That's part of our Puritan ethic."[9]

Helms's predicament going into 1976, the bicentennial of the American nation, was not just personal. It was cultural. Helms was no Puritan but he embodied the white Anglo-Saxon Protestant culture that had dominated the U.S. government for two hundred years, and the CIA for twenty-five. In the culture where Dick Helms was born, bred, and elevated, there was also a strain that would judge him with a Puritan ethic.

"HIRED TO LIE"

"Did Richard Helms Commit Perjury?" asked Mort Halperin, Kissinger's former aide, in an article for the influential *New Republic* in March 1976. "The Justice Department has been investigating Helms with perjury in mind for more than a year," Halperin reported. "The current explanation for the delay is that [the Justice Department] has asked the Senate Intelligence Committee for the information not yet made available."[10]

Halperin exemplified the generation of Washington policymakers who defected from the Cold War consensus as the war in Vietnam consumed a generation of young men and divided American society. Like many others in the government, he thought the CIA had to be held accountable lest another corrupt president enlist the Agency in his schemes.

With the Family Jewels under review by the Justice Department, Helms had to worry about his testimony on Chile and his bland denials that he had anything to do with the ambush of General Schneider. That brief exchange with Senator Symington in February 1973 haunted him.

"Did you try in the Central Intelligence Agency to overthrow the government of Chile?"

"No, sir."

"Did you have any money passed to the opponents of Allende?

"No, sir."

"So the stories you were involved in that war are wrong?"

"Yes, sir."

With the CIA memoranda that the Justice Department made public during the House impeachment hearings, Helms also had to worry about his on-the-record denials of domestic surveillance, and his evasive testimony about his friendship with Hunt and the back channel to McCord.

"For 20 years there was an agreement between Justice and the CIA never to prosecute CIA people," wrote Halperin. "To break it retroactively may seem unfair. Helms was hired to lie for his country, and no one told him that that did not include lying to Congress."

Helms could no longer count on the discretion of senior U.S. officials. Too many people had been burned by the Nixon-Helms partnership. Edward Korry, former U.S. ambassador in Chile, wrote a letter to Attorney General Edward Levi about the Track II operation that culminated in Schneider's death. On Nixon's orders, Helms had not told Korry about Track II. To exculpate himself, Korry talked about what Helms had done. Levi was a respected University of Chicago law professor appointed by President Ford to restore the credibility of the Justice Department that had been shredded by the Watergate scandal. "The letter piqued interest," Cynthia Helms recalled, "and the government began to present testimony to a grand jury in the summer of 1976."[11]

Helms called his friend Edward Bennett Williams and asked if he would represent him while the Justice Department deliberated. Williams's clients over the years had included the *Washington Post*, the Democratic National Committee, Teamster boss Jimmy Hoffa, and even Senator Joe McCarthy. "Of course, Dick," Williams said. "I'll handle it myself from here on." Helms's spirits improved, albeit only slightly. "I knew the road ahead would be bumpy," he said.[12]

In February 1976, the Justice Department agreed to drop a possible criminal case against Helms related to the 1971 Fairfax City break-in that was done in response to a possible Cuban penetration operation. "It was impossible to prove he [Helms] had intent to violate anyone's civil rights," an anonymous Justice Department source told *Washington Post* reporter Bob Woodward. "It is regrettable that this puts him out of reach of the law and [may] seem to be an endorsement of breaking and entering."[13]

All the while, Helms carried on as ambassador in Tehran.

"The Agency had some history in Iran," wrote Cynthia Helms, with no small understatement. The United States and the United Kingdom, she said, had "cooperated in orchestrating a military coup against the democratically elected government of Prime Minister Mohammad Mossadegh." Two decades later, Ambassador Helms often spoke to the shah, his fellow alumnus of La Rosey boarding school, alone without any aides.

"My husband spoke candidly to the shah, as he had spoken to presidents of the United States," said Cynthia. "He never thought it made any sense to shade the truth in speaking to those with true power. He warned the shah about the insidious cancer of corruption in Iran and advised him to loosen his autocratic style."[14]

Frances FitzGerald, the journalist, saw a different Helms. Her father died in 1967, so she no longer saw Helms socially. But when she came to Tehran on assignment for the *New Yorker* magazine, Helms was generous in sharing contacts and arranging interviews with the Iranian officials. What she learned startled her.

"Virtually all the Americans there who were working in Iran, not just in government, but in business, all said how wonderful the Shah was and everybody loved him," FitzGerald said in an interview. "So it came as a huge shock to me, to find out that wasn't the case." Iranian officials told her the Shah was corrupt and out of touch. "I mean, even his prime minister told me that." FitzGerald was sure that Helms knew the embassy's assessment of the shah was flawed. "He was not stupid," she said. "Plus, he didn't say anything that I could quote . . . He was too smart."[15]

"THE OLD IMPLICIT RESPECT"

At his home in San Clemente, Nixon brooded on his unfair fate. Like Helms, he conceded no ground to his critics. When President Ford required him to issue a statement of contrition at the time of his pardon, Nixon offered only "regret and pain" at the anguish caused by his "mistakes and misjudgments."

After serving a short prison sentence, the born-again Chuck Colson stopped in to see Nixon in 1976 and found the ex-president suspicious about the CIA and the Watergate burglary. "He believes he was set up," Colson told an interviewer.

"He'd love to know why. And he's very depressed by what's continuing to happen to the country."[16]

Helms wasn't feeling much better. He was ready to retire. In October, he submitted his resignation to Ford in advance of the November 2 election, in which Ford narrowly lost the presidency to Governor Jimmy Carter of Georgia.

"Washington looked the same, as beautiful as ever," wrote Cynthia Helms about their return in early 1977, "but something fundamental had shifted in the political atmosphere during our absence. The old rules that had governed relations between the Central Intelligence Agency and Congress had gone out the window. The old champions of the agency on Capitol Hill had literally died or been cowed into silence by the lust for exposés. The old, implicit respect for an experienced Washington insider, the gentleman's agreement that one could take the word of a man of integrity, had utterly disappeared."[17] The possibility that Helms himself might have contributed to the loss of respect with his slippery public words and furtive private deeds in the Watergate affair did not occur to his loyal wife.

Too much of what Helms called the CIA's "dirty linen" had come to light. The Watergate Committee interviewed Johnny Rosselli about the Mafia plots in February 1974. Rosselli had been convicted in the Friar's Club case but never deported, thanks to the CIA's intervention.[18] On advice of counsel, he refused to answer questions about his dealings with Bob Maheu before 1967.[19] In June 1975, the Church Committee called Sam Giancana to testify. Five days before his appearance, Sam Giancana was shot in the face six times by an unknown visitor to his Chicago apartment.[20] When retired CIA official John Whitten heard the news, he wondered "if they looked into Bill Harvey" as a possible killer.[21] Giancana's assailant was never found.

The Church Committee recalled Rosselli to testify in April 1976.[22] Still not satisfied with his answers, the committee wanted to question him again in three months. Rosselli, who had successfully blackmailed the CIA in 1962 and 1971, was in a position to do so again. When he couldn't be found, Senator Baker, a member of the committee, knowing that Rosselli feared for his life, called on the FBI to investigate. Three days later Rosselli's body was found stuffed in an oil drum floating in a Miami bay. He had been strangled.[23] His killer was never found. Bill Harvey could not have been involved because he died of a heart attack in June 1976. After the second gangland killing of the CIA's assassination partners, Helms no longer received the benefit of Washington's doubt.

The question of whether to prosecute the former director for his Chile testimony landed on the desk of President Carter's attorney general, Griffin Bell, a former federal appellate judge.[24] Bell recalled "considerable pressure" to drop the case against Helms. The man had friends. Bell heard from, among others, Averell Harriman, former diplomat and Democratic party statesman, Eric Sevareid, CBS News correspondent, and Zbigniew Brzezinski, Carter's national security adviser. The president summoned Bell to say he had been told that prosecuting Helms would give away the nation's greatest secrets. The attorney general replied that the administration could avoid that danger if the president would authorize him to negotiate a plea bargain. Carter agreed.

"It was indisputable to me that Helms had not told the Senate Committee the truth," Bell wrote later, "but it was equally clear to me that he had lied to prevent divulging an agency secret" as required by his CIA oath. Bell called Ed Williams to say he didn't think disclosure of secrets at trial was a problem. "A man would hardly lie to the Senate to keep from divulging his agency secrets and then divulge other secrets to avoid being prosecuted," he explained.

"You've touched on a problem," Williams allowed.

"Having touched on it," Bell replied, "let's solve it."[25]

Bell spoke to Benjamin Civiletti, assistant attorney general in charge of the Criminal Division, who authorized one of his prosecutors to present the Justice Department's case against Helms to Williams.[26]

"GROVEL ON THE FLOOR, NO."

In search of vindication, Nixon accepted an invitation from David Frost, a British talk show host, to discuss Watergate and his presidency. In an internationally broadcast interview in May 1977, Nixon was unrepentant, lawyerly, defensive, and selectively self-deprecating. Because of Ford's pardon, Nixon would never stand before the bar of law, as Helms would. Because of his disgrace, he sought a hearing in the court of public opinion.

The show attracted a huge audience, both because Nixon had not spoken publicly and Frost, an affable host not known for his American political expertise, was an unexpected interviewer. Frost didn't mince words.

"Reviewing now, your conduct over the whole of the Watergate period," he said to open the interview, "with the additional perspective now of three years out of office and so on, do you feel that you ever obstructed justice, or were part of a conspiracy to obstruct justice?"

"I will express an opinion on it," replied Nixon, "but I think what we should do is to go over it—the whole matter—so that our viewers will have an opportunity to know what we are talking about."

And so Nixon and Frost returned to June 23, 1972, and his conversation with Bob Haldeman about the CIA, the "smoking gun" conversation that ended Nixon's presidency.

"So you invented the CIA thing on the 23rd, as a cover?" Frost asked.

"No," Nixon said. ". . . If a cover-up is for the purpose of covering up criminal activities, it is illegal. If, however, a cover-up as you have called it, is for a motive that is not criminal, that is something else again. And my motive was not criminal. I didn't believe that we were covering up any criminal activities."

This was not so different than what Helms believed. Black-bag jobs carried out by CIA employees with national security responsibilities were not criminal, so covering them up was not criminal either. The Justice Department did not entirely disagree, as evidenced by the decision not to charge Helms for the 1971 surreptitious entry in Fairfax, Virginia.

"But surely," Frost objected, "in all you've said, you have proved exactly that that was the case; that there was a cover-up of criminal activity because you've already said, and the record shows, that you knew . . . that Hunt and Liddy were involved. At the moment when you told the CIA to tell the FBI to 'Stop period,' as you put it, at that point, only five people had been arrested. . . . Your intent is absolutely clear. It's stated, again: 'Stall this investigation here, period.'"

"The foreseeable, inevitable consequence," Frost went on, "if you'd been successful, would have been that Hunt and Liddy would not have been brought to justice. How can that not be a conspiracy to obstruct justice?"

"How many times do I have to tell you," Nixon countered, "that as far as these seven were concerned, the concern that we had—certainly that I had—was that men who worked in this kind of a covert activity, men who, of course, realize it's dangerous activity to work in, particularly since it involves illegal entry, that once they're apprehended, they are likely to say anything."

The problem, Nixon insisted, was "that a man like Howard Hunt, who was a prolific book writer, or any one of the others under the pressures of the moment, could have started blowing, and putting out all sorts of stories to embarrass the administration, and as it later turned out, in Hunt's case, to blackmail the president to provide clemency, or to provide money, or both."

In the end, Nixon's defense amounted to another "modified limited hangout," the public admission of a minor wrongdoing designed to hide a major misdeed. Nixon, the lawyer, admitted no malfeasance. Nixon, the politician, appealed for sympathy.

"While technically I did not commit a crime, an impeachable offense," he told Frost, ". . . these are legalisms, as far as the handling of this matter is concerned; it was so botched up. I made so many bad judgments. The worst one, mistakes of the heart, rather than the head, as I pointed out. But let me say, a man in that . . . top job—he's got to have a heart, but his head must always rule his heart."[27]

27

To help with Helms's defense, Edward Bennett Williams brought in Gregory Craig, a thirty-two-year-old associate in his law firm. Craig was a leading indicator of change in Washington. He had been a leader of the antiwar movement at Yale, signed public letters against the war, and spoke at teach-ins. When he read about CIA director Richard Helms during the Watergate hearings, one word came to his mind: "nefarious." Now Williams wanted Craig to do the legwork on Helms's legal defense.

To his surprise, he and Helms hit it off immediately.

"He was a well-read, cultivated, and cultured man who seemed to me to have all the sensibilities required of civilization . . . ," Craig recalled in an interview. "He was charming and he was witty. And he was also very good at getting your attention and your loyalty, which I think probably was a career maker."

Craig liked his merry side. "He loved to gossip and trade stories and wink and nod and laugh," he recalled. "He was always well-dressed. He was totally in control all the time." Craig went on to become senior counsel at Williams & Connolly. He represented President Bill Clinton during his impeachment trial and served as White House counsel for President Barack Obama. He was a Democrat proud to say Dick Helms was a friend for life.

Helms did not talk about his relationship with Nixon, Craig said, except to admit that after Nixon was reelected in 1972, he knew he would not be reappointed.

Craig got the impression that Helms harbored a certain contempt for Nixon. "Dick was a bit of a snob and elitist," he said. "He treasured being surrounded by the Ivy League elites. He saw Nixon as a climber and a parvenue. Although [Nixon] was very, very smart, he was not someone that Dick Helms, given the choice, would have socialized with."

Helms was baffled by his legal predicament, Craig recalled. The combination of Vietnam and Watergate had transformed Washington.

"It was unthinkable that the Establishment could turn against Dick Helms," he said. "That was one of the mysteries about the whole case for him to figure out. He could not understand with all these powerful friends and with all these connections and with all these people who he had helped and become socially close to them and that still retained positions of influence and power, that this could nonetheless still be done to him. It was a nightmare to him. It took an enormous amount of fortitude and grace not to lose it."

As for his successor Bill Colby, Helms nurtured a simmering animus for his decision to turn over the Family Jewels to the Justice Department. "I don't think he called him a coward," Craig said, "but he certainly said he showed a lack of spine. . . . I think Dick felt that he represented the whole institution [of the CIA] and that Colby was his evil mirror twin who was torpedoing, sabotaging, undermining, [and] defeating an institution that had served the nation well."

Helms was disappointed with his friend Senator Stuart Symington.

It was Symington who asked the question about Chile that led to all his troubles. "And Symington knew the answer to that question before he asked it," Craig said. "Helms could not understand why he did that."

Williams pounded the table for his client, literally. Williams and Craig were meeting with the Justice Department prosecutors when Williams all but dared them to bring the case to trial. "Ed slapped the table. Whap! And he said, 'You understand that if this prosecution goes forward, there will be no more secrets.' And he slaps the table again. Whap! 'No more secrets!' That was memorable."

The Justice Department had no appetite for a trial. Griffin Bell respected Helms for his service in government. But President Carter had been elected on a pledge to restore "a government as good as the people," and that meant doing business in a new way. The outsiders from Georgia in the White House had no particular investment in the cozy Capitol Hill understandings that, for better or worse, had facilitated the work of the clandestine service. Carter wanted to make clear that no CIA director or cabinet secretary, had a license to lie to Congress.

After Williams and Craig heard the government's case, they met with Helms.

"It was a pretty difficult case to defend," Craig admitted. The story of General Schneider "was a chapter in his life in the CIA where he was not particularly proud of what they did and how they did it. And he may have wanted to reduce the role that he played in it by telling me, and through me, by telling his legal team that this was really not his idea. That he was not enthusiastic about it. He thought it had . . . no chance of success and could blow up."

Craig was making the best possible case for his friend and client. But if *U.S. v. Helms* had come to trial, a central issue would have been what exactly Helms concealed with his false statements. And the paper trail the Justice Department had in its possession was detailed. It showed a line of command that ran from Nixon and Kissinger to Helms to Tom Karamessines to Dave Phillips to Tony Sforza to General Viaux's gang to the ambush of the general's car to the sledgehammer in the window, and the gunfire that ended the life of a blameless military officer. That was not a story Helms cared to defend in court.

The only defense, Craig said, was that "he had two conflicting obligations, and he did not intend to break the law or to commit a crime. You can't successfully prosecute someone for a major felony of that nature unless you can prove that he intended to commit a crime, knowingly committing a crime here. The defense would be Dick's state of mind when he went into that hearing. He was not intending to mislead or misrepresent or commit perjury."[1]

The Justice Department offered a deal. If Helms would plead guilty to making false statements (a misdemeanor, not a felony) and pay a $2,000 fine, the two-year sentence would be suspended, and Helms's CIA pension would not be threatened by his conviction.

In post-Watergate Washington, the deal struck top TV news correspondents as lenient.

Brit Hume of *ABC News* said the case was a test of whether "the Carter administration would have the stomach to bring criminal charges against the former CIA chief."

"The prosecutor's eagerness to plea-bargain and avoid a trial," said Fred Graham, CBS News legal correspondent, "demonstrate how the secrecy and power of the CIA tends to make it difficult and distasteful for the government to enforce its law against a CIA director."

President Carter released a statement saying he thought the Justice Department's decision "upholds the authority of law in Congress and at the same time protects legitimate national security interests."[2]

Helms was ready to go to trial. "He had the mental fortitude," Craig said. "He had all his friends ready to stand up for him and hold his jacket. We had a raft of character witnesses. But again, this is going to be a D.C. jury, which was hostile to Nixon, sympathetic to Carter." Cynthia Helms said she and her husband talked about the case and doubted any D.C. jury would appreciate the nuances of his defense. Williams made the same point.

A plea bargain, advised Craig, "would be one day of agony, maybe a week of agony, which would be unpleasant. But then he could go on and live his life, rather than spending the next two and half years in combat. Dick Helms was practical if nothing else." The reality, Craig added, was that the agreement "was unbelievably favorable to Richard Helms."

Helms took the advice of counsel. Williams asked Bell for one symbolic concession. Helms would not plead guilty. He would plea "nolo contendere," no contest. Helms, ever attentive to the historic record, could say that he did not admit guilt, that he simply did not contest the charges.

IN THE BASEMENT

As part of the plea agreement, Helms had to go to the U.S. Marshall's office in the basement of the D.C. courthouse to get his fingerprints taken and stand for a mug shot, just another man in the never-ending parade of miscreants corralled by law enforcement in the nation's capital. The walls were drab, the lights fluorescent.

"It was, by any measure, a demeaning kind of exercise for someone who had been at the height of government, who had been meeting with heads of state and briefing very famous and very important people," Craig recalled. "He was totally a champ all the way through. There was no one watching. So he wasn't doing it for the history books, he was doing it for himself. And I think for his own sense of who he was. He was polite. He took it very seriously. He never made light of what he was going through. I was really impressed with his poise and his control, and his decision about how to handle this personally."[3]

It was the last place Richard McGarrah Helms ever expected to be. In the basement of the D.C. courthouse, brought low by the American system that lifted him so high, judged for his loyal service to the CIA and to the unrepentant Richard Nixon. When he finally had his day in court, on November 4, 1977, Helms experienced the full variety of America's peculiar righteousness. In the course of a few hours he was condemned and celebrated, convicted and congratulated.

Accompanied by Williams and Craig, Helms went to the federal courthouse in Judiciary Square to appear before Judge Barrington Parker, an African American Republican appointed by President Nixon. At a pretrial hearing a few days before, Parker had objected to the reports of plea bargaining between the Justice Department and Helms. Parker made it clear he did not feel bound to accept any agreement.

"Helms and Williams smiled and chatted as they waited for Parker to take the bench . . ." the *Washington Post* reported, "but became increasingly grim as the sentencing procedure wore on."[4]

Williams rose to praise Helms's career and character, saying his client "found himself impaled on the horns of a moral and legal dilemma" when he testified under oath before the Senate committee. He had taken an oath never to divulge classified information.[5]

"Is that paramount to the oath that he took before the Foreign Relations Committee?" Judge Parker interjected.

"I think it is not paramount, your honor," Williams replied, adding that he was mentioning it only to show the dilemma.

"Were there not other alternatives open to him, Mr. Williams?" the judge asked. "He could have very easily stood back and considered very carefully the other alternatives . . . and I am sure that he is experienced in meeting situations such as these."

When Williams said Helms did what he thought was in the best interest of the country, Parker interrupted with a reference to Watergate.

"There have been a number of defendants before this court within the last five years who have weighed this question as to what is in the best interests of the United States," the judge said, "and you have seen what has happened."

Williams insisted that Helms was different, because "self-interests were at work in those cases. There was no self-interest at work in this case. There was no self-gain."

Rising to speak for the Justice Department, Ben Civiletti repeated the government's position that a conviction was enough to "uphold the principle of the rule of law and the paramount duty compelled by oath-taking" and that a jail term would serve no useful purpose.

Parker asked the defendant to rise. While reluctantly accepting the plea agreement, he castigated Helms with the voice of a Puritan.

"You now stand before this court in disgrace and shame," Parker declared. "You considered yourself bound to protect the agency whose affairs you had administered and to dishonor your solemn oath to tell the truth before the committee," Parker thundered.

Helms, whose arms had been at his side, began gripping the lectern stiffly as the judge's tirade continued.

"If public officials embark deliberately on a course to disobey and ignore the laws of our land because of some misguided and ill-conceived notion and belief that there are earlier commitments and considerations which they must first observe, the future of our country is in jeopardy.

"There are those employed in the intelligence security community of this country, . . ." the judge went on, "who feel that they have a license to operate freely outside the dictates of the law and otherwise to orchestrate as they see fit. Public officials at every level, whatever their position, like any other person must respect and honor the Constitution and the laws of the United States."[6]

"Dick was stunned," Cynthia Helms recalled. "When he came over to me in the front row of the courtroom, he was literally shaking. It was a devastating experience for him."[7] Cynthia was furious. Her husband "just took it and tucked it away," said Craig. He said he never heard Helms express a negative word about Judge Parker.[8] The hearing was over.

Outside, on the steps of the courthouse, Williams held forth for a gaggle of reporters, with Helms at his side. "Dick Helms will wear this conviction like a badge of honor," Williams declared. Asked about Judge Parker's speech, Helms said, "I don't feel disgraced at all. I think if I had done anything else, I would have been disgraced." He had done nothing wrong. "There are endless secrets and confidentiality between foreign governments and this government which must remain secret and confidential, even from Congress," he told the reporters.[9]

After thanking Williams for "standing up for the team," Helms excused himself to attend a regularly scheduled luncheon of CIA retirees at the Kenwood Country Club in suburban Bethesda, a half-hour drive from Capitol Hill.

"The news of my conviction had been on the radio," Helms wrote in his memoir, "and to my complete surprise, every one of the several hundred guests rose and applauded thunderously." Someone fetched two large baskets and passed them around. These quickly filled with cash and checks that exceeded Helms's $2,000 fine. "It had been a really rotten day," said the choked-up Helms, "and I hoped that I managed to mask at least some of my emotion."[10]

It was an American denouement. Judge Parker spoke for the American tradition that defined its creed in fidelity to words, that aspired to be a "City on a Hill," the country that enacted the Fourteenth Amendment, sponsored the Nuremberg trials, and passed the Civil Rights and Voting Rights acts, a government of laws, not men.

Helms's supporters represented the American tendency founded in existential struggle against the Soviet Union and communism, a government that defined itself by actions in Berlin, Havana, and Saigon and did not apologize for Guatemala or Iran or the Bay of Pigs, a government they believed was led by good men in a just cause, the creed of the Free World.

Richard Helms and Richard Nixon rose in public life on the strength of the Free World creed, and they fell from power as the idea lost all credibility in Vietnam and Watergate. The wars that Nixon and Helms waged in Indochina were lost. The scandals they generated at home were investigated like few others in American history. Nixon escaped legal judgment. Helms did not. Justice was denied and then served, albeit gently. The president fell first. The spymaster fell farther. The events known as Watergate were over.

EPILOGUE

In January 1978, two months after his appearance in federal court, Dick Helms went to lunch at the Metropolitan Club, a few blocks north of the White House, an emporium of wood paneling and chintz upholstery where lawyers, lobbyists, and politicos do their murmuring business. The former director suddenly found himself looking at Howard Hunt, his friend who had served thirty-three months in prison before his release from federal prison at Eglin Air Force Base in Florida in March 1977. Helms had never come to his rescue or spoke up on his behalf, not even after he lost Dorothy.

With a gulp in his throat Helms recalled the moment while being cross-examined in a court deposition years later.

Q. When was the last time you saw Mr. Hunt?

A. Saw Mr. Hunt? I believe I saw Mr. Hunt way across the Metropolitan Club dining room four or five years ago, but I'm not sure that it was he."[1]

It certainly was Hunt who was also eating at the club that day. After his release, Hunt had embarked on a lucrative lecture tour, resumed his novel-a-year writing schedule, and proposed marriage to Laura Martin, a Spanish teacher from Georgia who corresponded with him while he was in prison. Hunt recognized Helms, the buddy who believed in him, the former boss he idolized as "Avery Thorne," the former friend who abandoned him while he was on hazaradous duty. Hunt could not forgive him.

"I was lunching in D.C. at the Metropolitan last month," he wrote to Bill Buckley in February 1978. "Dick Helms was nearby and we stared wordlessly at each other. Appropriate, I thought, Dick having testified so often that he didn't know me."[2]

The improbable and ultimately doomed friendship of Dick Helms and Howard Hunt was the seed of the Watergate affair, which grew into the collaboration of the gentlemanly spymaster and the paranoid president. While the savage, dishonest war in Vietnam discredited the U.S. government and emboldened the Congress, the counterculture, and the press corps, Nixon and Helms stayed the course set by the National Security Act of 1947, which prescribed an aggressive global defense of American interests overseas and management of public opinion at home.

As that strategy foundered in Southeast Asia, the arrest of McCord, the wiretapper; Sturgis, the soldier of fortune; Martínez, the boat captain; Barker, the wing man, and González, the lock pick, exposed a criminal class cultivated by the Agency to serve U.S. policy purposes. A lawless White House and an agency with impunity suddenly began to lose the respect and the deference they had once enjoyed on Capitol Hill, in newsrooms, and among the general public. The Agency's impunity, once tolerated and even admired, came to be seen as incompatible with a self-governing democratic Republic. Nixon and Helms were swept from power to disgrace as a bipartisan reform movement took power in Washington.

The results reshaped the U.S. government. Nixon and Helms were the last president and director to exercise the impunity in national security affairs that their predecessors had enjoyed since the end of World War II. In 1975, the legislative branch imposed its will on the CIA for the first time. The defunct system in which the Director of Central Intelligence reported only to the chairmen of the Senate and House Armed Services committees was replaced. In 1977 the House of Representatives established a permanent committee on intelligence to oversee the work of the Agency. The Senate did the same in 1979. In between, Congress passed the Foreign Intelligence Surveillance Act, requiring U.S. intelligence agencies to obtain permission to spy on American citizens. Impunity was supposed to be replaced with accountability. That didn't quite happen.

Watergate, ironically, wound up fortifying the CIA's power in the American scheme of government. The post-1975 intelligence oversight system has endured, albeit weakly. Oversight didn't stop top agency officials from conspiring in the 1980s with the Reagan White House in the Iran-Contra affair to nullify a congressional ban on CIA support for brutal counterrevolutionary forces in Central America. Nor did oversight influence the Agency as senior officials implemented a harsh, illegal, and ineffective torture regime after the September 11 attacks. And when the Senate Intelligence Committee investigated in 2014, the CIA prevailed on President Obama to block full public release of its findings. By nominally sharing responsibility for covert operations with Congressional leaders and staff, the oversight system diffused responsibility, which helped the Agency regain legitimacy and influence.

In Cuba, all of the CIA's efforts to overthrow the communist government ended in failure. Castro's one-party state compiled an abysmal record on human rights while preserving Cuban sovereignty and preventing capitalism from gaining a foothold on the island. As part of his efforts to engage the United States diplomatically, Castro released several thousand political prisoners in August 1979, including Rolando Cubela, a.k.a. AMLASH. His friend, Santiago Morales, freed at the same time, said, "He was done with politics."

Cubela moved to Madrid, where he remarried and worked as a cardiologist. "He had a good life," Morales went on. "He was a great guy. But he never got rid of his past." Cubela later moved to south Florida to be closer to relatives and to the parents of his martyred friend José Antonio Echeverría. As of October 2021, Cubela was living in a nursing home in Miami.

"In the end, I think he had been beaten by the events," Morales said. "It was a miracle he was alive."[3]

In Guatemala, the successors of the client regime installed by Howard Hunt and company in 1954 imposed a military dictatorship that provoked a leftist rebellion in the 1980s that was, in turn, crushed by a genocidal counterinsurgency war supported by the Reagan administration and the CIA. In 1999 President Clinton felt obliged to apologize for U.S. support of "military forces and intelligence units which engaged in violence and widespread repression."[4] By that time Guatemala had become a failed state.

In Chile, the assassination of General Schneider demonstrated to right-wing officers that Washington would support any effort to oust Allende. The neoliberal dictatorship established by General Augusto Pinochet in 1973 felt confident enough of Washington's support to assassinate Allende's former foreign minister in 1976 with a car bomb less than two miles from the White House.

As for the "whole Bay of Pigs thing," Helms kept the secrets and the Agency wrote the JFK story, or least the first draft. But Harry Truman intuited that the Directorate of Plans, as run by Dick Helms, was somehow complicit in JFK's death and events lent credence to his conviction. When the AMLASH conspiracy was exposed in 1975, the CIA lost control of the secret history of Kennedy's assassination. The Church Committee found the Agency's investigation of Kennedy's murder "deficient," calling into question the process that produced the lone gunman theory. The CIA's own historian found the Agency's response "passive, reactive, and selective."[5] The House Select Committee on Assassinations concluded that "in all probability" there had been a conspiracy but could not identify the perpetrators.[6]

In 1997 the Assassination Records Review Board uncovered Operation Northwoods, illuminating the anti-democratic and conspiratorial mindset that pervaded in the highest echelons of the Pentagon and CIA. The board also declassified the pre-assassination Oswald file, showing Helms's testimony to the Warren Commission was misleading. Senior undercover officers on his staff knew far more about the accused assassin than he ever admitted. When Bob Maheu and Johnny Rosselli used their knowledge of the story to blackmail the Agency, Nixon demanded the whole story. He never got it. Helms controlled the JFK record, albeit with a cost.

When Helms insisted, "I have not seen anything, no matter how far-fetched or grossly imagined, that in any way changes my conviction that Lee Harvey Oswald assassinated Kennedy, and that there were no co-conspirators," most Americans did not believe him and for good reason.[7]

As memories of Watergate faded and the U.S. government recovered from defeat in Southeast Asia, Nixon and Helms were rehabilitated and reunited in cordiality. The former president believed his former adversary had been wrongly condemned for dissembling about the assassination of General Schneider. When President Ronald Reagan bestowed the National Security Medal on Helms in 1983, Nixon sent his congratulations.

"You suffered a great injustice simply because you were carrying out the assignment which I felt was vitally important to the national security," Nixon wrote. "The attempt to castrate the C.I.A. in the mid-seventies was a national tragedy. Let us hope the recognition you have so justly received will assist in reversing that negative trend."[8]

With the dissolution of the Soviet Union and the end of the Cold War in 1991, Nixon and Helms could claim victory in the war against communism, and bask in their reputations as elder statesmen.[9] When Nixon died in April 1994 every living former president attended his funeral, as well as friends such as Rose Mary Woods, admirers such as Gordon Liddy, and rivals such as Howard Baker and George McGovern. Helms's name did not appear on the guest list.[10]

In 1997, on the fiftieth anniversary of the Agency's founding, Helms was honored as one of fifty CIA "trailblazers" and extolled as a leader who had a "strong impact in furthering the Agency's mission" and "cleared a path for others to follow."[11]

He may have worn his 1977 misdemeanor conviction as a badge of honor but he could not escape its shadow either. On September 10, 2001, General Schneider's sons, René and Paul, filed a civil lawsuit in U.S. District Court for the District of Columbia against Helms and Henry Kissinger for "designing, ordering, implementing, aiding and abetting, and/or directing a program of activities aimed at, and resulting in, the assassination of the Plaintiffs' father, Chilean Army Commander-in-Chief." The lawsuit was pending when Helms died in Washington, D.C., on October 22, 2002. It was thirty-two years to the day since General Schneider was ambushed in morning traffic.

ACKNOWLEDGMENTS

Thanks to Ron Goldfarb and George Witte and St. Martin's Press for supporting publishing *Scorpions' Dance*. I'm blessed to have a wise agent and independent publisher.

When I first came across Professor Luke Nichter's online collection of taped conversations between Richard Nixon and Richard Helms in 2009, I thought, "There's a story there." This book is that story, so my thanks to Luke.

Peter Voskamp helped launch the project by loaning me his library of Watergate books, including a rare signed copy of James McCord's memoir, *A Piece of Tape*.

Mark Sugg shared a cabin. Fernand Amandi shared contacts. Margot Williams provided invaluable and creative research assistance from beginning to end.

This book would not be possible without the archival documentation available at Mary Ferrell Foundation (maryferrell.org). Thanks to my friend Rex Bradford for building his indispensable site.

Thanks to John Dinges, John Hadden Jr., Noah Kulwin, and Jim Hougan, who read drafts of the manuscript and helped improve it vastly.

Many thanks to Christopher Buckley for giving me access to his father's correspondence with Howard Hunt. Thanks to Tanzi Sakib, who retrieved the correspondence from the William F. Buckley papers in the Yale Library.

Thanks to Calla Cameron, who copied material from the Richard Helms papers at Georgetown University.

Thanks to James Rosen for giving me access to his interviews with Richard Helms.

Thanks to everyone who sat for an interview.

And special thanks to the archivists who made research possible in the time of Covid. Allen Fisher, archivist at the LBJ Library, responded quickly to all my questions. So did Meghan Lee-Parker at the Nixon Library. Kris Bronstad, archivist at the University of Tennessee, scanned a wealth of material in the Howard Baker Papers. Laurie Langland scanned material from the George McGovern Collection at Dakota Wesleyan University. Hannah Soukup, oral history curator at the University of Montana, delivered material on Senator Mike Mansfield.

NOTES

INTRODUCTION

1. Testimony of Richard Helms, Ambassador to Iran, Senate Watergate Committee, Hearings Before the Senate Select Committee on Presidential Campaign Activities of the United States Senate, Ninety-Third Congress, First Session, Watergate and Related Activities, Phase One: Watergate Investigation, Washington, D.C., July 31, August 1, 2, 1973, Book 8 (Washington, D.C.: U.S. Government Printing Office, 1973), 3283 ("Helms Watergate Testimony").

2. *CBS Evening News, ABC News*, August 2, 1973, Vanderbilt Television News Archive, Vanderbilt University, https://tvnews.vanderbilt.edu/.

3. James Naughton, "Helms Says He Resisted Pressure by White House for CIA Cover-up Aid," *New York Times*, August 3, 1973, p. 1.

4. Lou Cannon, "Helms Displays His Old Skills as a Diplomat," *Washington Post*, August 3, 1973, p. A20.

5. CIA Memo, "FYI–Allegations and Answers," June 1972, found in Security File on Frank Sturgis, provided to the House Select Committee on Assassinations (HSCA) in 1978, https://www.maryferrell.org/showDoc.html?docId=104140#relPageId =1&search=Security_File%20on%20Frank%20Sturgis.

6. See chapter 3 for notes on the relationship between Hunt and Karamessines.

7. "CIA Cryptonym Database," Mary Ferrell Foundation, https://www.maryferrell.org /php/cryptdb.php?id=AMSNAP-3&search=AMSNAP.

8. Paul Meskil, "A Mission to Cuba: Tale of the Doomed Raiders," *New York Daily News*, April 24, 1975. "Flying the Nicaraguan flag, the Rex operated out of West

Palm Beach and Fort Lauderdale, Florida. It carried the latest radar and sonar equipment, five cannons, several .30 caliber machine guns and two 20-foot speed boats. Its skipper was reportedly Eugenio Rolando Martinez, a Miami real estate salesman and CIA agent who made more than 300 nocturnal runs to Cuba."

9. "Biography on Bernard Barker," August 21, 1973, CIA documents released on November 9, 2017. NARA/JFK RIF #104–10164–10186. CIA Cryptonym Database, Mary Ferrell Foundation, https://www.maryferrell.org/php/cryptdb .php?id=AMCLATTER-1&search=AMCLATTER. See also Jack Colhoun, *Gangsterismo: The United States, Cuba, and the Mafia 1933–1966* (New York: OR Books, 2013), 61.

10. Barker said, "Hunt always had the theory that the physical elimination of Fidel Castro was the proper way for the liberation of Cuba." Transcript, *NBC News,* April 3, 1974, Watergate Report, found in Howard Baker Papers, box 21, folder 30. Fabián Escalante, *The Secret War: CIA Covert Operations Against Cuba 1959–62* (Melbourne: Ocean Press, 1995), 72, 80–91.

11. In closed door testimony to the Rockefeller Commission in 1975, Sturgis testified that two FBI agents questioned him after the assassination of President Kennedy in November 1963. Sturgis asked why they wanted to talk to him. "Well, Frank," he recalled them saying, "we feel that you are one of several persons that is capable of doing this sort of thing." Leave aside the question of whether Sturgis had anything to do with the death of JFK. Sturgis volunteered the story. Testifying in secret, he wanted it on the record that FBI agents considered him a plausible suspect in a presidential assassination. Memorandum of Deposition for the Record, Commission of CIA Activities in the United States (Rockefeller Commission), April 4, 1975, p. 18, NARA/JFK RIF #178–10002–10372 (Sturgis Deposition).

12. "Assassination Plans Against Castro," Memorandum for the Record, March 21, 1975, from Mr. Cates, NPIC: May 8, 1975, and Memorandum for the Record, March 21, 1975, Mary Ferrell Foundation (https://www.maryferrell.org/showDoc.html?docId =104139#relPageId=13&search=Cates).

13. Helms Watergate Testimony, 3245.

14. Helms Watergate Testimony, 3250.

15. Stephen Kinzer, *Poisoner in Chief: Sidney Gottlieb and the CIA Search for Mind Control* (New York: Henry Holt and Company, 2019), 124.

16. Helms Watergate Testimony, 3250.

17. Helms Watergate Testimony, 3259.

18. Helms Watergate Testimony, 3272.

19. "Watergate Procedure Questioned," *San Mateo Times,* December 31, 1973, p. 26, https://www.newspapers.com/clip/31799234/the-times/.

20. H. R. Haldeman, *The Ends of Power* (New York: Times Books, 1980), 40.

21. Bob Woodward, "The Keeper of Secrets Earned His Reputation," *Washington Post,* June 27, 2007, p. A1.

CHAPTER 1: ARRIBA

1. Summary of Contact with AMWHIP/1 and AMLASH/1, September 1962, NARA/ JFK RIF 1993.07.22.14:25:33:280410, https://www.maryferrell.org/showDoc.html ?docId=101069Su.

2. Rosa Miriam Elizalde, "¿Le dice algo el nombre de Esteban Ventura?" *Dominio Cuba*, May 16, 2019, https://medium.com/dominio-cuba/le-dice-algo-el-nombre-de -esteban-ventura-bd9318d431c.

3. Colonel Rico's troops had recently seized the Directorio's arsenal of guns. *Havana Post*, October 30, 1956, p. 4.

4. Letter from Nixon to Col. Antonio Blanco Rico, February 10, 1955, Nixon Pre- Presidential Papers, Central America Trip, 1955, box 1, folder Cuba (2 of 3), Richard Nixon Presidential Library and Museum, Yorba Linda, California.

5. Hugh Thomas, *The Cuban Revolution* (New York: Harper & Row, 1977), 104.

6. Miriam Zito, *Asalto* (Habana: Casa Editora Abril, 1998), 39.

7. Santiago Morales, interview with the author, July 24, 2021. See also Samuel Cherson, "José Antonio Echevarría, guía del pueblo cubano; A los 25 años de su muerte," a monograph found in the records of the Directorio Revolucionario Estudiantil en el Exilio (DRE), Cuban Heritage Collection, University of Miami.

8. José Luis Llovio-Menéndez, *Insider: My Hidden Life as a Revolutionary in Cuba*, trans- lated by Edith Grossman (Toronto: Bantam Books, 1988), 56.

9. *Insider*, 56.

10. Jaime Suchliki, *University Students and Revolution in Cuba* (Coral Cables, FL: Uni- versity of Miami Press, 1969), 58–75.

11. Jack Colhoun, *Gangsterismo: The United States, Cuba, and the Mafia 1933–1966* (New York: OR Books, 2013), 21, citing Foreign Service Dispatch from American Embassy, Havana, to the Department of State, "Decree Creating BRAC Appears in Official Gazette," May 18, 1955, 737.001/5, and Department of State Instruction, "BRAC Activity," May 13, 1955, 737.001. "The DR's theory was that success of the revolution depended on quick and efficient action against the regime," a CIA study later noted, "and that Castro's forces alone could not achieve success."

12. *Gangsterismo*, vii.

13. Anthony Summers with Robbyn Swan, *The Arrogance of Power: The Secret Life of Richard Nixon* (New York: Viking, 2000), 179.

14. "Comó se Produjo el Atentado." *Habana El Mundo*, October 30, 1956, 1. A diagram of Blanco Rico's wounds appears on page 8.

15. George Crile III, "The Riddle of AMLASH," *Washington Post*, May 2, 1976, p. C1.

16. "I do not know who carried out the assault on Blanco Rico," Fidel Castro said, "but I do believe that, from a political and revolutionary standpoint, assassination was not justified because Blanco Rico was not a henchman." "Entrevista con Fidel Castro," *Habana El Mundo*, November 20, 1956.

17. *Asalto*, 39.

18. Henry Kissinger, *White House Years* (Boston: Little, Brown and Company, 1979), 37.

19. Scott Anderson, *The Quiet Americans: Four Spies at the Dawn of the Cold War—a Tragedy in Three Acts* (New York: Doubleday, 2020), 448.

20. Richard Helms with William Hood, *A Look Over My Shoulder: A Life in the Central Intelligence Agency* (New York, Random House, 2003), 14.

21. *A Look Over My Shoulder*, 384.

22. Vernon O. Pampell, "Richard McGarrah Helms," report, December 20, 1947, 1947 Richard Helms FBI file, available at Muck Rock, https://www.muckrock.com/foi /united-states-of-america-10/richard-m-helms-fbi-17637/#file-42377.

23. Tom Bower, *The Perfect English Spy: Sir Dick White and the Secret War 1935–90* (New York: St. Martin's Press, 1995), 322.

24. *Arrogance of Power*, 196.

25. Jim Hougan, *Spooks: The Haunting of America; The Private Use of Secret Agents* (New York: William Morrow and Company, 1978), 11.

26. Thomas Powers, *The Man Who Kept the Secrets* (New York, Simon & Schuster, 1979), 255.

27. E. Howard Hunt and Greg Aunapu. *American Spy: My Secret History in the CIA, Watergate, and Beyond* (Hoboken, NJ: John Wiley & Sons, 2007), 18–24.

28. Gore Vidal, "The Art and Arts of E. Howard Hunt," *New York Review of Books*, December 13, 1973, 6.

29. *American Spy*, 50.

30. *American Spy*, 53–64.

31. St. John Hunt, *An Amoral and Dangerous Woman*, Kindle edition, loc. 608.

32. *American Spy*, 72.

33. Richard Helms, interview by J. Kenneth McDonald. Transcript of tape recording. Washington, D.C., September 29, 1982 (hereafter Helms-McDonald interview), 26, https://www.cia.gov/readingroom/docs/9_29_oral.pdf.

34. Lincoln Cushing, interview with the author, December 11, 2020.

35. Enrique Cirules, *The Mafia in Havana: A Caribbean Mob Story* (Melbourne, Ocean Press, 2004), 9.

36. David Atlee Phillips, *The Night Watch: 25 Years of Peculiar Service* (New York, Atheneum, 1975), 66.

CHAPTER 2: DEFEATED

1. The Hall of Valor Project, "Marcos Perez Jimenez," https://valor.militarytimes.com /hero/400538.

2. British Pathé, "Tragic Incidents In Venezuela Against Vice President Nixon," YouTube, https://www.youtube.com/watch?v=EHR1dBTJrRA.

3. "A Venezuela Mob and Hero's Welcome Home," YouTube, https://www.youtube.com /watch?v=CI6P_5cgbGQ.

4. *A Look Over My Shoulder*, 163.

5. *A Look Over My Shoulder*, 164.

6. "The Riddle of AMLASH," *Washington Post*, May 2, 1976, C1.

7. Fidel Castro, *The Selected Works of Fidel Castro*, vol. 1: *Revolutionary Struggle 1947–1958*, edited and with an introduction by Rolando E. Bonachea and Nelson P. Valdes (Cambridge, MA: The MIT Press, 1972), 114.

8. Rolando Cubela Secades, "La Batalla de Santa Clara," *Bohemia*, July 1963, p. 22.

9. *Revolutionary Struggle 1947–1958*, 119.

10. "La Batalla de Santa Clara," *Bohemia*, July 26, 1963, p. 22.

11. *Gangsterismo*, 35–36.

12. "Inaugura mañana el Alcalde la primera de 15 escuelas que se estan construyendo," *Diario de e Marina*, April 21, 1959.

13. Memorandum of Deposition for the Record, Witness: Frank Sturgis, Rockefeller Commission, April 4, 1975, 20, NARA/JFK RIF #178–10002–10372.

14. To: Director, From: SAC Miami, Subject: Frank Anthony Sturgis, January 12, 1965. Sturgis FBI File, NARA/JFK RIF #124–10302–10273. A U.S. Customs agent told the Bureau that he had been allowed to read various CIA intelligence reports where Sturgis's name was frequently mentioned. "It would appear that subject is actually the source of such information."

15. Hunt said that Cushman said Nixon was the "action officer" on Cuba. *Night Watch*, 39.

16. Oral History Transcript, General Robert E. Cushman, Jr., U.S. Marine Corps (Retired), Benis M. Frank Interviewer, History and Museums Division, Headquarters U.S. Marine Corps Washington, D.C., 1984, 338 (Cushman Marine Corps Oral History).

17. *Arrogance of Power*, 182; *RN: The Memoirs of Richard Nixon* (New York: Touchstone, 2000), 202.

18. *Night Watch*, 86.

19. United States Congress, House Committee on Armed Services, Special Subcommittee on Intelligence (1975). Inquiry into the alleged involvement of the Central Intelligence Agency in the Watergate and Ellsberg matters: Hearings Before the Special Subcommittee on Intelligence of the Committee on Armed Services, House of Representatives, Ninety-Fourth Congress, First Session (Washington, D.C.: U.S. Government Printing Office, 1975), 500. E. Howard Hunt, *Give Us This Day* (Chicago, IL: Regnery Publishing, 1973), 30.

20. Memorandum for the Record, Subject: Report on Plots to Assassinate Fidel Castro, May 23, 1967, RIF #104–10213–10101 ("Report on Plots to Assassinate Fidel Castro"), 15.

21. *Gangsterismo*, 28.

22. *United States of America v. Filippo Sacco, also known as Johnny Rosselli*, United States District Court, Central District of California, NO. 1175-PH-CD, "Government opposition to Defendant's Motion to Reduce Sentence," February 17, 1971.

23. Marita Lorenz, *Marita: The Spy Who Loved Castro* (New York, Pegasus Books, 2017).

24. "Senator John F. Kennedy and Vice President Richard M. Nixon Second Joint Radio-Television Broadcast, October 7, 1960," John F. Kennedy Presidential Library

and Museum, https://www.jfklibrary.org/archives/other-resources/john-f-kennedy
-speeches/2nd-nixon-kennedy-debate-19601007.

25. Richard Nixon, *Six Crises* (New York: Touchstone, 1990), 354 n.

26. *RN*, 221.

27. Victor Li, *Nixon in New York: How Wall Street Helped Richard Nixon Win the White House* (Vancouver, BC: Fairleigh Dickinson University Press, 2018), 109.

28. *Six Crises*, 420.

29. *Six Crises*, 402.

CHAPTER 3: THE BLACK WORLD

1. *A Look Over My Shoulder,* 186.

2. Matt Reinman, "When Ian Fleming Met John F. Kennedy," May 27, 2015, Books Tell You Why, https://blog.bookstellyouwhy.com/when-ian-fleming-met-john-f.-kennedy.

3. *Give Us This Day*, 49.

4. "Mexico City Station History," pp. 342–46, NARA/JFK RIF #104–10414–10124, https://www.maryferrell.org/showDoc.html?docId=162979. See also *Night Watch*, 92.

5. *A Look Over My Shoulder,* 178.

6. *Give Us This Day*, 209.

7. Today in History: JFK on the Bay of Pigs, https://www.wnyc.org/story/86807-today -in-history-jfk-on-the-bay-of-pigs/.

8. *A Look Over My Shoulder,* 187.

9. *A Look Over My Shoulder,* 187.

10. *A Look Over My Shoulder,* 196.

11. From: Havana, To: Director, "Cable re ((deletion)) blown and Carswell, Tronsky Danbrunt under detention, September 15, 1960, NARA/JFK RIF #104–10111–10013.

12. Memorandum for the Record, Subject: John Mertz and Robert Bannerman— Relations with Charles Siragusa, October 11, 1977, NARA/JFK Doc. ID# 1993 .07.20.17:46:05:710440.

13. Memorandum for: Director of Central Intelligence. Subject: Reported Involvement of James McCord in Cuban Operations While an Agency Employee, June 28, 1974. 1993.08.11.18:17:58:620028, https://www.maryferrell.org/showDoc.html?docId =100877#relPageId=3.

14. Arthur Schlesinger, *Robert Kennedy and His Times* (New York, Ballantine Books, 1978), 647.

15. Gore Vidal, "The Best Man 1968," *Esquire*, March 1963, 5, 11. Online version.

16. *A Look Over My Shoulder,* 203.

17. *RN*, 234.

18. *RN*, 232.

19. Rose Mary Woods, "Nixon's My Boss," as told to Don Murray, *Saturday Evening Post*, December 28, 1957, p. 20.

20. Jeffrey Frank, *Ike and Dick: Portrait of a Strange Political Marriage* (New York: Simon & Schuster, 2013), 57.

21. *Ike and Dick*, 232.

22. Stewart Alsop, *The Center: People and Power in Political Washington* (New York: Harper & Row, 1968), 238.

23. Hunt HSCA testimony, Part 2, 32.

24. Hunt Church Committee Testimony, January 10, 1976, Praeger role, 67–68. Karamessines role, 63. Hunt's testimony about Praeger's collaboration with the CIA was declassified in April 2018. https://www.maryferrell.org/showDoc.html? docId=148747#relPageId=40.

25. Gus Russo, *The Outfit: The Role of Chicago's Underworld in the Shaping of Modern America* (New York: Bloomsbury, 2001), 387.

26. "An Interview with Richard Helms," *Studies in Intelligence,* Vol. 44, no. 4, September 1993, 25 (hereafter Frost-Helms interview), https://www.cia.gov/static/9845318ed4b 2db36bc185604a2c3bc40/interview-with-richard-helms.pdf.

27. Memorandum for: Deputy Director of Central Intelligence, Subject: Maheu, Robert A., June 24, 1966, CIA/JFK 104–10133–10341.

28. *Robert Kennedy and His Times*, 531.

29. Bayard Stockton, *Flawed Patriot, The Rise and Fall of CIA Legend Bill Harvey* (Washington, D.C.: Potomac Books, 2006).

30. "John Scelso," Security Classified Testimony, House Select Committee on Assassinations, May 16, 1978, 148–149, NARA/JFK RIF #180–10131–10330 ("Whitten HSCA Testimony"). "Scelso" was Whitten's pseudonym.

31. *A Look Over My Shoulder*, 152.

32. Memorandum for the Record, Subject: Report on Plots to Assassinate Fidel Castro, May 23, 1967, 64, NARA/JFK RIF #104–10213–10101. "Harvey states that on 14 May [1962] he briefed Mr. Helms on the meeting with the Attorney General, as told to him by Mr. Edwards. Harvey, too, advised against briefing Mr. McCone and General Carter and states that Helms concurred in this. On that same date, 14 May, Edwards prepared a memorandum for the record stating that on that day Harvey had told him that any plans for future use of Roselli were dropped." Helms knew that was not true. He had already approved Harvey's contact with Rosselli. See David Talbot, *Brothers: The Hidden History of the Kennedy Years* (New York: Free Press, 2007), 109.

33. *A Look Over My Shoulder*, 170.

34. Frost-Helms interview, 26.

35. Frost-Helms interview, 24.

36. *A Look Over My Shoulder*, 230.

37. Thomas Mallon, *Watergate: A Novel* (New York: Pantheon Books, 2011), 155.

CHAPTER 4: MONSTER OF SELF-POSSESSION

1. *Arrogance of Power*, 230.

2. *A Look Over My Shoulder*, 223.

3. Stewart Alsop and Charles Bartlett, "In Time of Crisis," *Saturday Evening Post*, December 18, 1962, pp. 15–21.

4. Carl Bernstein, "The CIA and the Media," *Rolling Stone*, October 20, 1977, http://www.carlbernstein.com/magazine_cia_and_media.php. "Two of the Agency's most valuable personal relationships in the 1960s, according to CIA officials, were with reporters who covered Latin America—Jerry O'Leary of the *Washington Star* and Hal Hendrix of the *Miami News*, a Pulitzer Prize winner who became a high official of the International Telephone and Telegraph Corporation. Hendrix was extremely helpful to the Agency in providing information about individuals in Miami's Cuban exile community. O'Leary was considered a valued asset in Haiti and the Dominican Republic. Agency files contain lengthy reports of both men's activities on behalf of the CIA."

5. Central Intelligence Agency MEMORANDUM FOR: Mr. Sterling Cottrell, Coordinator of Cuban Affairs, SUBJECT: Financial Payments Made by the Central Intelligence Agency to Cuban Exile Organizations, April 1963. John F. Kennedy Presidential Library and Museum.

6. Kennedy comment on November 6, 1962. *Foreign Relations of the United States, 1961–1963, Volume XI, Cuban Missile Crisis and Aftermath* (Washington, D.C.: U.S. Government Printing Office, 1996), Doc. 154, Summary Record of the 21st Meeting of the Executive Committee of the National Security Council, 394 (*FRUSA*, Vol. XI).

7. Luis Fernandez Rocha, interview with the author, November 18, 1996.

8. Note card," "Rocha, Luis Fernandes" [sic], courtesy of *Today Show*.

9. *FRUSA, Vol. XI,* Doc. 170, Summary Record of the 24th Meeting of the Executive Committee of the National Security Council, 435.

10. Luis Fernandez Rocha, interview with the author, November 18, 1996.

11. Memo for the Record, "Mr. Helms' Conversation with Luis Fernandez Rocha and Jose Maria Lasa of the DRE Regarding Their Organization's Relationship with the Agency," November 15, 1962. NARA/JFK RIF #104–10170–10022, https://www.maryferrell.org/showDoc.html?docId=156336.

12. Luis Fernandez Rocha, interview with the author, November 18, 1996.

13. "Mr. Helms' Conversation with Luis Fernandez Rocha."

14. From: JMWAVE, To: Director Cable, Re: Walter D. Newby Introduced as Rep to Handle AMSPELL Affairs, December 7, 1962, NARA/JFK RIF #104–10170–10016. "Walter D. Newby" was Joannides's pseudonym. See Memorandum to: Jeremy Gunn, Executive Director, From: Michelle Combs, Special Assistant for Research and Review. Subject: CIA-IR-21 DRE Case Officer for December 1962–April 1964. Assassination Records Review Board/ARRB Electronic Records/ARRB Electronic Files of K. Michelle Combs, Associate Director of Research and Analysis. https://www.maryferrell.org/showDoc.html?docId=207178.

15. *Six Crises*, 215.

16. Richard Reeves, *Nixon: Alone in the White House* (New York: Simon & Schuster, 2001), 29.

17. *Nixon in New York*, 24, 38–44.

18. Jack Gould, "Nixon Returning as a Guest on TV," *New York Times*, January 30, 1963, p. 6; "President Richard M. Nixon plays piano on The Jack Paar Program," https://www.youtube.com/watch?v=GGD2gprcKvQ. *Nashville Banner*, March 8, 1963, p. 8.

19. *FRUSA, Vol. XI*, Doc. 303, pp. 739–743, Summary Record of the 42nd Meeting of the Executive Committee of the National Security Council.

20. Antonio Veciana, interview with the author, September 24, 2014.

21. Max Frankel, "Nixon Proposes 'Freedom Policy' to Conquer Reds,*" New York Times*, April 21, 1963, p. 1; "Excerpts From Address by Nixon Calling for a Stronger U.S. Foreign Policy," p. 62.

22. Dan Kurzman, "Unleashing Exiles Not a Solution to Cuba Problem, Kennedy Says," *Washington Post*, April 25, 1963, p. A18.

23. *FRUSA, Vol. XI*, Doc. 321, 778, Memorandum from the Chairman of the Board of National Estimates (Kent) to Director of Central Intelligence McCone.

24. McCone to RFK, letter, May 2, 1963, RFK Papers, ser. 09, Attorney General Confidential File, box 206 (folder 2 of 3), John F. Kennedy Presidential Library and Museum.

25. Operation Northwoods: NARA/JFK RIF #202–10002–10104, https://www.maryferrell.org/showDoc.html?docId=1244#relPageId=1&tab=page.

26. David Robarge, "Angleton Unrevealed," *Washington Decoded*, https://www.washingtondecoded.com/site/2017/10/angletonbio.html.

27. Dispatch, To: Chief of Station, JMWAVE, From: Chief, Special Affairs Staff, Subject: TYPIC/Operational/CI, March 6, 1964, https://www.maryferrell.org/showDoc.html?docId=28891&relPageId=2.

28. Gaeton Fonzi, *The Last Investigation* (New York: Thunder's Mouth Press, 1993), 53.

29. Memorandum for: Deputy Director of Operations, From: David D. Gries, Director, Center for the Study of Intelligence, June 22, 1993, NARA/JFK RIF #104–10332–10013, https://www.maryferrell.org/showDoc.html?docId=189694.

30. *The Last Investigation*, 53.

31. *Night Watch*, 201.

CHAPTER 5: MARTYRS OF TOMORROW

1. Hearings Before the Select Committee on Assassinations of the House of Representatives, Ninety-Fifth Congress, Second Session, September 22, 25, and 26, 1978, Volume IV, Testimony of Richard Helms (Washington, D.C.: U.S. Government Printing Office, 1978), 173 ("Helms HSCA Testimony").

2. Jon Lee Anderson, *Che: A Revolutionary Life* (New York: Grove Press, 1997), 426.

3. "Biographical Data Sheet," Carlos Tepedino Gonzalez, June 17, 1962, NARA/JFK RIF #104–10183–10073. "Summary of Contacts with AMWHIP1 and AMLASH/1," September 1962, NARA/JFK RIF #104–10215–10210.

4. *A Look Over My Shoulder*, 229.

5. Sandy Smith, "CIA Sought Giancana for Cuba Spying," *Chicago Sun-Times*, August 16, 1963, p. 1.

6. Senate Select Committee to Study Government Operations with Respect to Intelli-
    gence Activities. Testimony of John McCone, October 9, 1975, p. 34, NARA/JKF
    RIF #157–10014–10079, https://www.maryferrell.org/showDoc.html?docId=1432
    ("McCone Church Committee Testimony").

7. McCone Church Committee Testimony, 35.

8. *The Man Who Kept the Secrets*, 381–382.

9. Report on Plots to Assassinate Fidel Castro, 87.

10. Testimony of Harold Swenson, Senate Select Committee on Intelligence Activities,
    May 10, 1976, 27. Contrary to Helms's claims, Swenson said the meetings with
    Cubela in 1963 concerned "an assassination plot against Castro," pp. 23–24.

11. Chris Whipple, *The Spymasters: How the CIA Directors Shape History and the Future*
    (New York: Scribner, 2020), 27.

12. *Nixon in New York,* 45.

13. "De Gaulle Eager for New A-talks; Seeks Views on His Idea for Nuclear Disarma-
    ment," *New York Times,* July 31, 1963, p. 2.

14. *Ike and Dick,* 257.

15. *Nixon in New York,* 67.

16. "Kennedy's 'Image' Assailed By Nixon," *New York Times,* October 27, 1963, p. 87.

17. Review of Office of Security Files on E. Howard Hunt, NARA/JFK RIF #180–
    10143–10076.

18. Henry Mitchell, "Tycoons, Trolls and Travels In a Rich and Lively Life," *Washington
    Post,* March 30, 1979, p. B1.

19. Monique Brinson Demery, *Finding the Dragon Lady: The Mystery of Vietnam's Ma-
    dame Nhu* (New York: Public Affairs, 2013), 93. "Diem and Nhu, transferred state
    lands, farms, and businesses to the Archbishop of Hue, who was Nhu's brother."

20. *Finding the Dragon Lady,* pp. 160–61.

21. *Finding the Dragon Lady,* pp. 139–40.

22. Luke A. Nichter, *Last Brahmin: Henry Cabot Lodge and the Making of the Cold War*
    (New Haven, CT: Yale University Press, 2020), 199.

23. David Halberstam, *The Best and the Brightest* (New York: Random House, 1973).
    263.

24. *Last Brahmin,* 250.

25. *Last Brahmin,* 252.

26. *Last Brahmin,* 79.

27. Richard Nixon to Henry Cabot Lodge Jr., November 12, 1963, Box 147, John Davis
    Lodge Papers, Hoover Institution.

28. *FRUSA, Vol. XI,* Doc. 376, Memorandum for the Record 885.

29. *A Look Over My Shoulder,* 226.

30. David Kaiser, *The Road to Dallas: The Assassination of John F. Kennedy* (Cambridge,
    MA: Harvard University Press, 2007), 298–99.

31. *A Look Over My Shoulder,* 227.

32. Report on Plots to Assassinate Fidel Castro, 91.

33. Contact Report, Meeting of AMLASH-1 and Matthew H. Ontrich, Paris, November 22, 1963. NARA/JFK RIF #104–10215–10227, https://www.maryferrell.org/showDoc.html?docId=108475.

CHAPTER 6: FREEDOM OF ACTION

1. Gary Mack, "The Man Who Named the Grassy Knoll." Originally published on the JFK Assassination Home page, now found at https://groups.google.com/g/alt.assassination.jfk/c/gDjDo4YA61s/m/F_HFA-oYay8J?pli=1.

2. Asked if he was certain that the head wound was caused by a shot from the front, McClelland told an interviewer, "I'm not certain of anything but I am as close to certain as I can be. . . . Many years later I saw the Zapruder film. I saw the president's limousine . . . going onto Elm Street. And as the limousine slowly proceeded down toward the Triple Underpass . . . Mrs. Kennedy . . . realized something had happened and she leaned over as if to ask him what was wrong . . . As she did that, all of sudden his head literally exploded and fell backwards and to the left, as if he had been hit by the second shot from the front" (starting at 14:00). "Robert McClelland–JFK's Last Doctor (11–12–15)," https://www.youtube.com/watch?v=ySO0pLcN5ww.

3. *RN*, 252.

4. *RN*, 252.

5. David Robarge, "DCI John McCone and the Assassination of President John F. Kennedy," *Studies in Intelligence* 51, no. 3 (September 2013): 1.

6. *Brothers*, 268. "If the American people knew the truth about Dallas," RFK told an old family friend, "there would be blood in the streets."

7. *A Look Over My Shoulder*, 229.

8. Jose Antonio Lanuza, interview with the author, March 11, 2020.

9. Luis Fernandez Rocha, interview with the author, January 24, 2007.

10. "The Pulitzer Prizes, Prize Winners by Year," The Pulitzer Prizes, http://www.pulitzer.org/prize-winners-by-year/1963. Carl Bernstein, "The CIA and the Media," *Rolling Stone*, October 20, 1977.

11. Wilkinson's husband, Robert, was a CIA officer. Robert Wilkinson Obituary, *Washington Post*, April 2, 2006, http://www.washingtonpost.com/wp-dyn/content/article/2006/04/01/AR2006040101322.html.

12. John Dille, "Daring Mission That Bared Cuba's Secrets," *Life*, November 2, 1962, p. 42.

13. From: Chief, New Orleans Office, To: Director, Domestic Contact Service, Memo Concerning Activities of Edward Scannell Butler, May 5, 1967, NARA/JFK RIF #104–10069–10052, https://www.maryferrell.org/showDoc.html?docId=32336.

14. Testimony of Thomas Karamessines, Senate Select Committee on Intelligence Activities, April 16, 1976, 17, NARA/JFK RIF #157–10014–10002.

15. Joseph B. Smith, *Portrait of a Cold Warrior: Second Thoughts of a Top CIA Spy* (New York: G. P. Putnam's Sons, 1976), 416.

16. *A Look Over My Shoulder*, 187.

17. *48 Hours*, "Part IV—JFK: Several Theories on JFK Assassination Examined," February 05, 1992, https://www.youtube.com/watch?v=e3nDUEgh05o.

18. In his 1964 job evaluation, Moore received "outstanding" ratings for "cultivation of contact to develop trust and confidence" and "exploitation of a source's complete intelligence potential." Fitness Report, J. Walton Moore, May 14, 1964, Personnel File of J. Walton Moore, NARA/JFK RIF #104–10194–10012.

19. Whitten HSCA testimony, 111. Whitten said, "I think it was the day after the assassination, Mr. Helms called a meeting of a lot of important people, including Angleton; the Chief of our Division, Mr. Karamessines, I think somebody from the Cuban show, and told them that I was in charge of the investigation and gave me broad powers."

20. *A Look Over My Shoulder*, 228.

21. George Lardner, "People Appear Puzzled, Lost as They Wander in the Rain," *Washington Post*, November 24, 1963, p. A.

22. Papers of Robert F. Kennedy, condolence mail, 1963–64, Box 131, John F. Kennedy Presidential Library and Museum. *RN*, 253.

23. Helms-McDonald interview, September 29, 1982, 26.

24. Evan Thomas, *The Very Best Men* (New York: Simon & Schuster, 2006), 308.

CHAPTER 7: THE SHADOW

1. Harry S. Truman, "Limit CIA Role to Intelligence," *Washington Post*, December 22, 1963, p. A11.

2. David Talbot, *The Devil's Chessboard: Allen Dulles, the CIA, and the Rise of America's Secret Government* (New York: HarperCollins, 2015), 571.

3. Nomination of Richard Helms to be Ambassador to Iran and CIA International and Domestic Activities, Hearing Before the Committee on Foreign Relations, United States Senate, Ninety-Third Congress, First Session, February 5, 1973 (Washington, D.C.: U.S. Government Printing Officer, 1974), 41.

4. Memorandum for Mr. Lawrence R. Houston, General Counsel, From: A.W. Dulles, Subject: Visit to the Honorable Harry S. Truman, Friday Afternoon, April 17, 2 pm. Miscellaneous Historical Documents Collection, Truman Library.

5. *The Devil's Chessboard*, 571.

6. Memorandum for Mr. Moyers, November 25, 1963, https://www.maryferrell.org/pages/Katzenbach_Memo.html.

7. David Robarge, "DCI John McCone and the Assassination of President John F. Kennedy," *Studies in Intelligence* 57, no. 3 (September 2013): 8. "Between 23 November and 5 December, the DCI briefed Johnson on assassination developments and other intelligence matters every day but two."

8. "DCI John McCone and the Assassination of President John F. Kennedy," 9.

9. From: Deputy Chief, CI/PROJECT, To: Deputy Chief CI, "Correspondence of US Defector (Lee Oswald) Who Recently left USSR Homebound," June 22, 1962, NARA/JFK RIF #104–10419–10076.

10. From: Elder, Walter, To: Director, "Note with Attachments: At the time of the Assassination there were five documents in the (Oswald) 201 file," October 20, 1975, NARA/JFK RIF #104–10322–10043.

11. "Response to HSCA Request of March 9," undated, NARA/JFK RIF #104–10051–10167.

12. Memo Re: Response to Rankin, W/C, March 5, 1964. NARA/JFK Record Number 1993.06.24.14:59:13:840170, https://www.maryferrell.org/showDoc.html?docId=98075.

13. Interview A. Egerter, March 31, 1978, by Dan Hardway and Betsy Wolf, NARA/JFK RIF #180–10142–10298, https://www.maryferrell.org/mffweb/archive/viewer/showDoc.do?docId=38449&relPageId=7.

14. Deposition of Mrs. Ann Elizabeth Goldsborough Egerter, May 17, 1978, HSCA Security Classified Testimony, 70, NARA/JFK RIF #180–10131–10333.

15. "Response to HSCA Request of March 9," 1978, NARA/JFK RIF #104–10051–10167, https://maryferrell.org/showDoc.html?docId=39186#relPageId=13&tab=page.

16. Jefferson Morley, "The Oswald File. Tales of the Routing Slips," *Washington Post*, April 2, 1995, p. C1, https://www.washingtonpost.com/archive/opinions/1995/04/02/the-oswald-file-tales-of-the-routing-slips/e4aca01d-654f-4c2e-931d-789cb6a9e76b/.

17. William Hood, interview with the author, April 11, 2007.

18. *A Look Over My Shoulder,* 145.

19. Testimony of Richard Helms, Hearing Before the Select Committee on Assassinations of the U.S. House of Representatives, Ninety-Fifth Congress, Second Session, September 22, 25, and 26, 1978. (Washington, D.C.: U.S. Government Printing Office, 1979), 10 ("Helms HSCA Testimony").

20. "DCI John McCone and the Assassination of President John F. Kennedy," 8.

21. To: Honorable Edwin E. Willis, Chairman, From: Francis J. McNamara, Director, Subject: Indefinite Postponement of hearing scheduled for December 10, December 4, 1963, Records of the House Un-American Activities Committee.

22. From: JM WAVE, TO: Dir, Re: Intention to Stay in Costa Rica, December 4, 1963, NARA/JFK RIF #104–10076–10039.

23. The Investigation of the Assassination of President John F. Kennedy: Performance of the Intelligence Agencies, Book V, Final Report of the Senate Select Committee to Study Government Operations with respect to Intelligence Activities, United States Senate (Washington, D.C.: U.S. Government Printing Office), 4. (Church Committee Report.)

24. Robert M. Hathaway and Russell Jack Smith, *Richard Helms as Director of Central Intelligence 1966–1973,* (Washington, D.C.: Center for the Study of Intelligence, 1993), 98 *(Richard Helms as DCI).*

25. *RN,* 266.

26. *RN,* 270.

27. Jim Hougan, "Nixon in the Jungle," published in *Nixon: An Oliver Stone Film,* ed. Eric Hamburg (New York: Hyperion, 1995), 24.

28. Ralph Blumenthal, "Secret Nixon Vietnam Trip Reported," *New York Times*, February 17, 1985, p. 3, https://www.nytimes.com/1985/02/17/world/secret-nixon-vietnam-trip-reported.html. A sergeant who accompanied Nixon was sworn to secrecy for twenty years, after which time he would tell the story and confirm it with a photo, signed by Nixon himself.

29. "Nixon in the Jungle," 24.

30. Testimony of John McCone and Richard M. Helms," Warren Commission Volume V, 126–27, https://www.maryferrell.org/showDoc.html?docId=40#relPageId=126.

31. "CIA Mail Watch List," September 5, 1974, Miscellaneous Church Committee Documents, NARA/JFK RIF #157–10014–10186.

32. Helms HSCA Testimony, 174–175.

33. Whitten HSCA testimony, 153.

34. Whitten HSCA testimony, 166.

35. Whitten HSCA testimony, 154.

36. Letter, Harry S. Truman to William B. Arthur, June 10, 1964, Miscellaneous Historical Documents Collection, Truman Library.

37. "Limit CIA Role to Intelligence."

CHAPTER 8: WOMEN

1. *RN*, 270.

2. Garry Wills, *Nixon Agonistes: The Crisis of the Self-Made Man* (Boston: Houghton Mifflin, 1970), 16.

3. *RN*, 270.

4. Neil Sheehan, *A Bright Shining Lie: John Paul Vann and America in Vietnam* (New York: Vintage Books, 1989), 589. Vietnam Conflict Extract Data File, Defense Casualty Analysis System (DCAS) Extract Files, created ca. 2001–4/29/2008, documenting the period 6/28/1950–5/28/2006–Record Group 330, https://aad.archives.gov/aad/ ("Vietnam Conflict Extract Data File").

5. Richard Nixon, "Asia After Viet Nam," *Foreign Affairs*, October 1967, p. 121.

6. *Ike and Dick*, 268.

7. *Richard Helms as DCI*, 6.

8. Helms-McDonald interview, September 29, 1982.

9. Richard Helms, interview by R. Jack Smith, Washington, D.C., April 21, 1982 (hereafter Helms-Smith interview), https://documents.theblackvault.com/documents/helms/4_21_oral.pdf.

10. *American Spy*, 144.

11. *American Spy*, 144.

12. "Review of the Office of Security File on E. Howard Hunt." The file includes a letter from Buckley to Hunt dated May 28, 1964, and a review of *The Invisible Government* entitled "Hate CIA Week." The letter begins, "Dear Howard: Here it is. You will note we had to cut fifteen lines because it was over. But I hope it helps. Thanks a million for all the work you did on it. . . ."

13. Letter, E. Howard Hunt (EHH) to William F. Buckley Jr. (WFB) October 3, 1964, William F. Buckley, Jr., Papers (MS 576). Part 1 Box 30. Manuscripts and Archives, Yale University Library (WFBP).

14. *American Spy*, 156.

15. Julia Cameron, "Life Without Father," *Rolling Stone*, January 31, 1974, p. 28.

16. David St. John, *On Hazardous Duty* (New York: New American Library, 1965), 13.

17. *On Hazardous Duty*, 21.

18. To: Kuhn, Steven, "The David St. John Novels," February 6, 1974, NARA/JFK RIF #104–010103–10049.

19. E. Howard Hunt, *Undercover: Memoirs of an American Secret Agent* (New York: Penguin, 1974), 134. Hunt said his assignment was developing confidential working relationships with influential Spaniards who would someday succeed the incumbent dictator Generalissimo Francisco Franco, "a delicate but hardly time-consuming political action assignment." The deputy chief of the Western European division said that if Hunt contributed any positive intelligence during his time in Spain, the division was "totally unaware of it." Memorandum for the Records, Subject: E. Howard Hunt—[Redacted] Assignment, February 27, 1974, found in Fourth Hunt Security File, NARA/JFK Record Number 1993.07.24.08:37:38:680310.

20. Memorandum for the Record, Subject: Watergate—Frank A. O'Malley, February 21, 1974, NARA/JFK RIF #104–10103–10042.

21. Hunt HSCA Testimony, Part 2, 32.

22. *An Amoral and Dangerous Woman*, Kindle edition, loc. 480.

23. St. John Hunt, interview with the author, April 2, 2021.

24. Senate Select Committee on Intelligence Activities, Testimony of E. Howard Hunt, January 10, 1976, 64 ("Hunt Church Committee Testimony").

25. WFBP, EHH to WFB, May 29, 1965, "Re: the Bermuda boat your piece will be quite useful, and if your patience holds out, perhaps you'd round out the following areas of current need. . . . Is it officially known as the Newport-Bermuda Race?"

26. *American Spy*, 156.

27. *Undercover*, 134.

28. *Undercover*, 134.

29. "The David St. John Novels," February 6, 1974.

30. For a list of all of Hunt's published works, see Mystery File, Obituary: E. Howard Hunt (1918–2007), http://mysteryfile.com/blog/?p=44.

31. David St. John, *Festival of Spies* (New York: New American Library, 1966), 90.

32. Gore Vidal, "The Art and Arts of E. Howard Hunt," *New York Review of Books*, December 13, 1973, p. 6.

33. Cynthia Helms with Chris Black, *An Intriguing Life: A Memoir of War, Washington, and Marriage to an American Spymaster* (Lanham, MD: Rowman & Littlefield Publishers, Inc., 2013), 75.

34. *A Look Over My Shoulder*, 295.

35. *Intriguing Life*, 95.

36. *Night Watch*, 155.
37. Frances FitzGerald, interview with the author, February 4, 2021.
38. Anne Karalekas, *History of the Central Intelligence Agency* (Laguna Hills, CA: Aegean Park Press, 1977), 81.
39. Vietnam Conflict Extract Data File.
40. Memorandum for: The Honorable Dean Rusk Secretary of State, Subject: CIA Involvement in Cuban Counterrevolutionary Activities—Arrest of Rolando CUBELA Secades and Ramon Tomas, GUIN Diaz March 7, 1966. NARA/JFK RIF #104–10521–10018 ("CIA Involvement in Cuban Counterrevolutionary Activities," March 7, 1966).
41. Carl Jenkins, interview with the author, April 12, 2021.
42. "La Causa 108," *CUBA* magazine, April 1, 1966, 7.
43. "Caning the Students," *Time* magazine, March 18, 1966.
44. Memorandum for the Record: Subject, The CUBELA Trial, April 15, 1966, NARA/JFK RIF #104–10103–10185.
45. "La Causa 108," 7.
46. CIA Involvement in Cuban Counterrevolutionary Activities, March 7, 1966.
47. "La Causa 108," 8; Santiago Morales interview.
48. To: Acting Director FBI, From: SAC WFO (161–8661), 1972 Helms FBI File.
49. *Nixon in New York*, 180.
50. "Nixon Is Consolidating Grip on Party," *Binghamton Press and Sun-Bulletin*, October 31, 1966, p. 11.
51. *Nixon in New York*, 191.
52. "Nixon Is Consolidating Grip on Party."
53. Vietnam Conflict Extract Data File.

CHAPTER 9: THE SILENT SERVICE

1. "The Silent Service," *Time*, February 24, 1967.
2. "The Silent Service."
3. Drew Pearson, "JFK's Death a Castro Counterplot?," *Bradenton Herald*, March 3, 1967, p. 4.
4. Ron LaBrecque, "Could Rosselli Have Linked Castro Plot to JFK Death?," *Miami Herald*, September 19, 1976, p. 1.
5. Pearson Diary, January 1967, LBJ Library.
6. *A Look Over My Shoulder*, 368. "The President was more concerned with the fundamental legality of passing official funds through various private channels than the effect the *Ramparts* fallout would have on the future of Agency projects," Helms wrote.
7. *Brothers*, 22. RFK enlisted Harvard assistant professor Daniel Patrick Moynihan and others to make discreet inquiries about organized crime bosses, renegade CIA officers, and anti-Castro Cubans.
8. Memorandum for: Director of Central Intelligence, From: J. Kenneth McDonald, Chief CIA History Staff, Subject: Survey of CIA's Records from House Select

Committee on Assassinations Investigation, February 10, 1992. NARA/JFK RIF #104–10428–10104.

9. Report on Plots to Assassinate Fidel Castro, 67; *Brothers*, 348.

10. "Dispatch Countering Criticism of the Warren Report," April 1, 1967, NARA/JFK RIF #104–10406–10110, https://www.maryferrell.org/showDoc.html?docId=9547.

11. To: Mr. Tolson, From: C.D. DeLoach, Subject: Assassination of President Kennedy, April 4, 1967, http://jfk.hood.edu/Collection/Weisberg%20Subject%20Index%20 Files/J%20Disk/Johnson%20Lyndon%20Baines%20President/Item%2038.pdf.

12. *The Man Who Kept the Secrets*, 165.

13. Report on Plots to Assassinate Fidel Castro, 94.

14. Leo Janos: "The Last Days of the President," *The Atlantic*, July 1973. "During coffee, the talk turned to President Kennedy, and Johnson expressed his belief that the assassination in Dallas had been part of a conspiracy. 'I never believed that Oswald acted alone, although I can accept that he pulled the trigger.'" https://www.theatlantic.com /magazine/archive/1973/07/the-last-days-of-the-president/376281/.

15. *The Man Who Kept the Secrets*, 224.

16. President's Daily Diary, Lyndon Baines Johnson Presidential Library, http://www .lbjlibrary.net/collections/daily-diary.html.

17. *Bright Shining Lie*, pp. 732–33.

18. *A Look Over My Shoulder*, 280.

19. Shane O'Sullivan, *Dirty Tricks: Nixon, Watergate, and the CIA* (New York: Hot Books, 2018), 142, citing "Recommendation for Honor or Merit award for James W. McCord, Jr."; "Summary of Agency Employment of James W. McCord Jr.," undated, NARA/JFK RIF #104–10123–10382; "James Walter McCord, Jr."; "Senate Select Committee on Intelligence Operations, request," Kane to Inspector General, May 20, 1975, NARA/JFK RIF #104–10123–10364; "Honor recommendation for James W McCord Jr." for August 1966, NARA/JFK RIF #104–10123–10407.

20. *Spymasters*, 38.

21. Vietnam Conflict Extract Data File.

22. Bruce P. Dohrenwend, Nick Turse, Thomas J. Yager, Melanie M. Wall, *Surviving Vietnam: Psychological Consequences for U.S. Veterans* (New York: Oxford University Press, 2019), 69.

23. Norman Mailer, *The Armies of the Night: History as a Novel, the Novel as History* (New York: Signet, 1968), 102.

24. *Armies of the Night*, 291.

25. "U.S. Marshals and the Pentagon Riot of October 21, 1967," https://www.usmarshals .gov/history/civilian/1967b.htm.

26. *Armies of the Night*, 211.

27. *Spymasters*, 39.

28. *A Look Over My Shoulder*, 322.

29. Letter, Jack Valenti to Richard Helms, October 19, 1968, Richard Helms Papers (RHP), Georgetown University Library.

30. *Undercover*, 140.

31. *Give Us This Day*, 13.

32. *Give Us This Day*, 15.

33. Letter, EHH to WFB, April 13, 1968; Letter, WFB to HH, May 24, 1968, WFBP. See also Memorandum for: Chief, Security Research Staff, From: Chief, Liaison and External Operations Branch, Subject: Manuscript: Give Us This Day, Author: Edward J. Hamilton, February 6, 1970. Fourth Hunt Security File.

34. J. Anthony Lukas, *Nightmare: The Underside of Nixon Years* (New York: Viking, 1976), 91.

35. Bill Peterson, "Hunt Claims Authorship of CIA Article," *Washington Post*, September 13, 1978, p. A9. The *Times* declined to comment on Hunt's statement.

36. Memorandum in Lieu of Fitness Report. Subject: Howard E. Hunt, GS15 Employee, 30 April 1969, CIA Op File on E. Howard Hunt, NARA/JFK RIF #104–10194–10023.

37. Letter, Jack Valenti to Richard Helms, October 19, 1968, RHP.

38. [No title], Handwritten notes, CIA Segregated Collection, Personnel file summary, Leslie Wizelman, March 7, 1978, NARA/JFK RIF #180–10142–10318.

39. *Festival for Spies*, 120.

CHAPTER 10: HONEYMOON

1. Vietnam Conflict Extract Data File.

2. *RN*, 298.

3. *Dirty Tricks*, 3.

4. *Dirty Tricks*, 1–2.

5. *Lost Crusader*, 199.

6. *A Look Over My Shoulder*, 334.

7. *The Man Who Kept the Secrets*, 254.

8. Kliph Nesteroff, "The Comedy Writer That Helped Elect Richard M. Nixon," WFMU's Beware of the Blog, September 19, 2010, https://blog.wfmu.org/freeform/2010/09/richard-nixons-laugh-in.html.

9. Greg Daugherty, "Did Nixon's 'Laugh-In' Cameo Help Him Win the 1968 Election?," History, updated October 19, 2018, https://www.history.com/news/richard-nixon-laugh-in-cameo-1968.

10. *Ike and Dick*, 309.

11. Ryan Lintelman, "In 1968, When Nixon Said 'Sock It to Me' on Laugh-In, TV Was Never Quite the Same," SmithsonianMag.com, January 19, 2018, https://www.smithsonianmag.com/smithsonian-institution/1968-when-nixon-said-sock-it-me-laugh-tv-was-never-quite-same-again-180967869.

12. "Did Nixon's Laugh-In Cameo Help Him Win the 1968 Election?"

13. *RN*, 323.

14. *The Man Who Kept the Secrets*, 251–52.

15. *Dirty Tricks*, 17–18.

16. *RN*, 322.

17. *RN*, 322.

18. *RN*, 335.

19. *RN*, 336.

20. *A Look Over My Shoulder*, 377.

21. *Intriguing Life*, 86.

22. Letter, Hunt to Helms, December 16, 1968, RHP.

23. *Intriguing Life*, 86.

24. Matthew Parker, *Goldeneye: Where Bond Was Born; Ian Fleming's Jamaica* (New York: Pegasus Books, 2015), 23.

CHAPTER 11: FLATTERY

1. Morton Halperin, interview with the author, March 17, 2021.

2. *A Look Over My Shoulder*, xi.

3. *The Man Who Kept the Secrets*, 257; *White House Years*, 36.

4. *Nixon Agonistes*, 402.

5. *A Look Over My Shoulder*, 381.

6. Judy Bachrach, "Rose Mary Woods: Facing Her Two Crises," *Washington Post*, July 7, 1974, p. H1.

7. "Miss Woods Profited on Nixon Stock Deal," *Washington Post*, December 9, 1973, p. A4.

8. "Police Team Investigates Jewel Theft," *Washington Post*, March 8, 1969, p. C2.

9. *Dirty Tricks*, 54.

10. *Nixon Agonistes*, 432.

11. *Intriguing Life*, 90–98.

12. *Richard Helms as DCI*, 11.

13. Grose, Peter, *Gentleman Spy (*Boston: Houghton Mifflin, 1994), 565.

14. *A Look Over My Shoulder*, vi.

15. *History of the Central Intelligence Agency*, 83.

16. *Richard Helms as DCI*, 11.

17. *White House Years*, 37.

18. Cushman Marine Corps Oral History, 316.

19. *The Man Who Kept the Secrets*, 288.

20. *Richard Helms as DCI*, 66.

21. *A Look Over My Shoulder*, 383.

22. *Spymasters*, 42.

23. *The Man Who Kept the Secrets*, 314.

24. Lucy Komisar, "The Art of Flattery: Letters from a CIA Director to a President, Richard Helms; Richard Nixon," *Washington Monthly*, April 1, 1996, p. 13 ("The Art of Flattery").

25. "The Art of Flattery," 13.

26. James W. McCord, "Restricted," NARA/JFK RIF #104–10224-10015.

27. *Richard Helms as DCI*, 38.

28. *White House Years*, 36.

29. *Richard Helms as DCI*, 49–50.

30. *A Look Over My Shoulder*, 387. Tom Hughes, chief of the State Department's Intelligence and Research Division, restored the CIA finding in a dissenting footnote.

31. *A Look Over My Shoulder*, 387–88.

32. *Richard Helms as DCI*, 43.

33. *White House Years*, 37.

CHAPTER 12: MADMAN THEORY

1. H. R. Haldeman, with Joseph DiMona, *The Ends of Power* (New York: Times Books, 1978), 83.

2. Morton Halperin, interview with the author, March 17, 2021.

3. *White House Years*, 305.

4. "The Art of Flattery," 13.

5. Vietnam Conflict Extract Data File.

6. James Rosen, *Strong Man: John Mitchell and the Secrets of Watergate* (New York: Doubleday, 2008), 93–95.

7. *The Man Who Kept the Secrets*, 225–26.

8. Roderick McKelvie, interview with the author, March 1, 2021.

9. *Lost Crusader*, 240.

10. Quoted in Angus Mackenzie, "Sabotaging the Dissident Press," *Columbia Journalism Review* (March/April 1981), 60.

11. Report to the President by the Commission on CIA Activities Within the United States (Washington, D.C.: U.S. Government Printing Office, 1975), 119 ("Rockefeller Commission Report").

12. To: W.C. Sullivan, From: D.J. Brennan, Jr., Subject: New Left in Europe, Comments of Richard Helms, Director of Central Intelligence, July 18, 1969, 1972 Helms FBI File.

13. Rockefeller Commission Report, 136.

14. *Ends of Power*, 26.

15. *Undercover*, 141.

16. Transcript, *Firing Line*, William F. Buckley, Jr. Subject: The CIA and Foreign Policy, January 21, 1973. Howard Baker Papers (HBP), Box 21, Folder 21.

17. *Ends of Power*, 26.

18. *Strong Man*, 148n527, citing interview with Mitchell.

19. "The Art of Flattery," 14.

CHAPTER 13: PUBLIC RELATIONS JOB

1. FBI memo, including CIA memo, Church Committee, Vol 2, Exhibit 61, SUBJECT; Interagency Committee on Intelligence (Ad Hoc) May 17, 1973, by James Angleton, https://nsarchive.gwu.edu/documents/spying-americans-new-release-infamous-huston-plan/23a.pdf.

2. *A Look Over My Shoulder*, 383; *Strong Man*, 148.

3. The Weather Underground, Report of the Subcommittee to Investigate the Administration of the Internal Security Act and other Internal Security Laws of the Committee on the Judiciary, United States Senate, Ninety-Fourth Congress, First Session, January 1975, 13 ("Weather Underground").

4. To: SAC Albany, From: Director, FBI Counterintelligence Program Black Nationalist-Hate Group Internal Security, August 25, 1967, https://vault.fbi.gov/cointel-pro/cointel-pro-black-extremists/cointelpro-black-extremists-part-01-of/view.

5. *A Look Over My Shoulder*, 270.

6. *RN*, 447.

7. *White House Years*, 465.

8. *White House Years*, 465.

9. *Bright Shining Lie*, 745.

10. *White House Years*, 465.

11. *White House Years*, 487.

12. *White House Years*, 491.

13. *White House Years*, 495, 497.

14. *A Look Over My Shoulder*, 389–90.

15. *Bright Shining Lie*, 746.

16. *The Man Who Kept the Secrets*, 277–78.

17. David St. John, *One of Our Agents Is Missing* (New York: New American Library, 1967), 7.

18. Memo, Chief, Security Research Staff, Chief, LEOB/Security Research Staff, E. Howard HUNT Jr., January 26, 1970, Hunt Fourth Security File, https://www.maryferrell.org/showDoc.html?docId=103905.

19. Jim Hougan, *Secret Agenda* (New York: Ballantine Books, 1984), 14–16.

20. Memorandum for: Director of Security, SUBJECT: Comment on Manuscript, Give Us This Day: CIA and the Bay of Pigs Invasion by Edward J. Hamilton, February 16, 1970, Hunt Fourth Security File.

21. Memorandum for: Director of Security, February 16, 1970. Hunt Fourth Security File.

22. Nedzi Hearings, Testimony of Paul Gaynor, 172.

23. Transmittal Slip, February 17, 1970, https://www.maryferrell.org/showDoc.html?docId=103905, Hunt Fourth Security File.

24. Letter, EHH to WFB, January 30, 1970. WFBP. "I've received Helms' blessing to retire as soon as I can locate a new outside job," Hunt wrote.

25. To: DDP, FROM: Howard Hunt [initialed "HH"], SUBJECT: Buckley 2 March 1970, Hunt Fourth Security File.

26. *American Spy*, 159.

27. Nedzi Hearings, 87.

28. The final report of the Select Committee on Presidential Campaign Activities, United States Senate (Washington, D.C.: U.S. Government Printing Office, 1974), 1122,

citing Executive Session Testimony of Mullen and Company Case officer, Executive Session testimony of Robert F. Bennett; Mullen and Company Case officer, memorandum for the record, April 30, 1971, Subject: Association of Robert R. Mullen and Company with the Hughes Tool Company. This document is found at Tab 16, Supplement CIA material, vol. 2 (Senate Watergate Report).

29. Memorandum for the Record, Subject: Watergate—Frank A. O'Malley, February 21, 1974, NARA/JFK RIF #104–10103–10042.

30. Confidential, Interview Report Name of Subject E. Howard Hunt, Hunt Fourth Security File, https://www.maryferrell.org/showDoc.html?docId=103905.

31. Memorandum for: Deputy Director of Plans, Subject: E. Howard Hunt—Utilization by Central Cover Staff, October 14, 1970, NARA/JFK RIF #104–10119–10322.

32. Memorandum for: The Acting Director, Federal Bureau of Investigation, Attention: Mr. Arnold Parham, Subject: Robert R. Mullen Company, 21 June 1972. Reproduced in Hearings of the Committee on the Judiciary, House of Representatives, Ninety-Third Congress, Second Session Pursuant to H. Res. 80, book 3, p. 11.

33. Memorandum for: Deputy Director of Plans, Subject: E. Howard Hunt—Utilization by Central Cover Staff.

34. *RN*, 470.

35. *RN*, 471.

36. H. R. Haldeman, *The Haldeman Diaries: Inside the Nixon White House* (New York: G. P. Putnam's Sons, 1994), 172.

37. John Prados and Luke Nichter, "Spying on Americans: New Release of the Infamous Huston Plan," https://nsarchive.gwu.edu/briefing-book/intelligence/2020–06–25/spying-americans-new-release-infamous-huston-plan#_edn8.

38. Rockefeller Commission Report, 123.

39. Rockefeller Commission Report, 123.

40. Mark Riebling, *Wedge: The Secret War Between the FBI and CIA* (New York: Alfred A. Knopf, 1994), 284–85.

41. "Spying on Americans."

42. *The Man Who Kept the Secrets*, 319.

43. *Strong Man*, 494.

44. Tom Charles Huston interview transcript, by Timothy Naftali, April 30, 2008. Nixon Presidential Library and Museum, Oral Histories. https://www.nixonlibrary.gov/sites/default/files/virtuallibrary/documents/histories/huston-2008–04–30.pdf.

45. *The Man Who Kept the Secrets*, 319.

CHAPTER 14: SLEDGEHAMMER

1. *El Caso Schneider* (Santiago, Chile: Documentos Especiales, 1972), 41–42.

2. "The CIA and Chile: Anatomy of an Assassination," National Security Archive, https://nsarchive.gwu.edu/briefing-book/chile/2020–10–22/cia-chile-anatomy-assassination.

3. *Richard Helms as DCI*, 92.

4. *El Caso Schneider*, 80.

5. *Richard Helms as DCI*, 85.

6. *The Man Who Kept the Secrets*, 290.

7. *Lost Crusader*, 325, citing United States Congress (94/1) House Select Committee on Intelligence. Hearings. U.S. Intelligence Agencies and Activities: The Performance of the Intelligence Community (Washington, D.C.: U.S. Government Printing Office), pt. 2, p. 835.

8. *Richard Helms as DCI*, 83.

9. John Dinges, "La historia incompleta de Agustín Edwards," *The Clinic*, June 13, 2014.

10. Interview with Richard Helms by Robert M. Hathaway, June 15, 1983, Washington, D.C.

11. Peter Kornbluh, *The Pinochet File: A Declassified Dossier on Atrocity and Accountability* (New York: New Press, 2003), 17.

12. *Night Watch*, 221.

13. *Night Watch*, 223.

14. This extraordinary collection documents Sforza's CIA career in Argentina, Paraguay, Cuba, Laos, and Vietnam. It includes photographic copies of Che Guevara's Bolivia diary, documentation of Sforza's multiple identities, and Sforza's Memorandum for the Record, classified "Secret," about his testimony to the Church Committee in 1975. These materials were given to and curated by Sforza's son-in-law, the late Randy Flick, who agreed to share them with me before his premature death in March 2020 ("Randy Flick Collection").

15. Memorandum for the Record, Subject Interview with [redacted] Chief of WH/4's CI Section, June 1, 1961. NARA/JFK RIF #104–10310–10020, https://www.maryferrell .org/showDoc.html?docId=16200#relPageId=42&search=AMOTS.

16. Memorandum for the Record, July 30, 1975, Randy Flick Collection.

17. Memo, "Subject: Reassignment," Randy Flick Collection.

18. Memorandum for the Record, July 30, 1975, Randy Flick Collection.

19. Letter, Tony Sforza to Gladys Sforza, October 8, 1970, Randy Flick Collection.

20. Hotel Conquistador receipt, Randy Flick Collection.

21. *Pinochet File*, 16.

22. *Pinochet File*, 21–23; *Richard Helms as DCI*, 92.

23. "The Art of Flattery," 13.

24. *Richard Helms as DCI*, 90.

25. *White House Years*, 674.

26. *Pinochet File*, 24; *Richard Helms as DCI*, 92–93.

27. *Pinochet File*, 21–23; *Richard Helms as DCI*, 92.

28. Memorandum for the Record, July 30, 1975, Randy Flick Collection.

29. *Pinochet File*, 33.

30. *Pinochet File*, 28; *The Man Who Kept the Secrets*, 302.

31. *A Look Over My Shoulder*, 406.

32. Classified Message, "Secret." Orig: David Phillips, To: Immediate Santiago, October 23, 1970; reproduced in *Pinochet File*, 73.

33. Joseph Novitski, "Chile Buries General as Martyr," *New York Times*, October 27, 1970, p. 3.

34. *Pinochet File*, 34–35.

35. Tim Weiner, *Legacy of Ashes: The History of the CIA* (New York: Doubleday, 2007), 362.

36. *The Man Who Kept the Secrets*, 304.

CHAPTER 15: BLACKMAIL

1. "The Art of Flattery," 13.

2. *RN*, 497.

3. Vietnam Conflict Extract Data File.

4. *Intriguing Life*, 96.

5. Tom Hughes, interview with the author, October 22, 2020.

6. *Intriguing Life*, 96.

7. Jack Anderson, "6 Attempts to Kill Castro Laid to CIA," *Washington Post*, January 18, 1971, p. B7.

8. Memorandum for the Record, Subject: Robert A Maheu, January 5, 1971, NARA/JFK RIF #104–10133–10033, https://www.maryferrell.org/showDoc.html?docId =13192.

9. Ewing was working for Anthony and Robbyn Summers while they wrote their book *Arrogance of Power*. Ewing-Maheu interview notes courtesy of Anthony and Robbyn Summers.

10. *Arrogance of Power*, 197; Memorandum Personal and confidential, To: Senator Ervin, From: Terry Lenzner and Marc Lackritz, Subject: Relevance to S. Res. 60 of John Rosselli's testimony about his CIA activities, undated, https://www.maryferrell.org /showDoc.html?docId=148916#relPageId=319. Found in "Miscellaneous Records of the Church Committee," NARA/JFK RIF #157–10014–10242.

11. Greg Herken, *The Georgetown Set: Friends and Rivals in Cold War Washington* (New York: Alfred A. Knopf, 2014), 348.

12. *RN*, 502.

13. "U.S.: Laos Push Doing Well," *New York Daily News*, February 23, 1971, 4. White House Tapes, OVAL 459–002a, February 27, 1971; OVAL OVAL 462–005a, March 5, 1971. Richard Nixon Presidential Library and Museum, Yorba Linda, California.

14. Eugenio Martinez, "Mission Impossible: The Watergate Bunglers," *Harper's*, October 1974, 51.

15. *Dirty Tricks*, 123.

16. Rolando Martinez Oral History, Nixon Library ("made us believe," 49:00; "organization between the CIA and the FBI," 54:00).

17. From: Deputy Director of Security, To: Central Cover Staff, Subject: Request for Utilization of Hunt in a Project, October 27, 1970, NARA/JFK RIF #104–10119–10320.

18. Bob Woodward, "Prosecution of Helms Ruled Out," *Washington Post*, February 20, 1976, p. A1.

19. "Spying on Americans," citing Church Committee, Vol. 2, Exhibit 31, "Memorandum for the File," FBI, April 12, 1971, https://nsarchive.gwu.edu/documents/spying-americans-new-release-infamous-huston-plan/18a.pdf.

20. "Spying on Americans," citing Church Committee, Vol. 2, Exhibit 31, From: William Ruckelshaus, To: Henry Petersen, "Interagency Committee on Intelligence (Ad Hoc)," May 18, 1973, https://nsarchive.gwu.edu/document/20445-national-security-archive-doc-23-fbi-memorandum.

21. *Nightmare*, 29.

22. *Lost Crusader*, 258.

23. Richard Halloran, "Helms Defends the CIA As Vital to a Free Society," *New York Times*, April 15, 1971, p. 1.

24. "His Mission Is Facts," *New York Times*, April 15, 1971, p. 30.

25. *White House Years*, 716.

26. *White House Years*, 722.

27. *White House Years*, 723.

28. *Strong Man*, 113.

29. Charles Colson, *Born Again* (New York: Bantam, 1976), 40–44.

30. Dean commented in "From the Pentagon Papers to Watergate," moderated by Julia Rose Kraut, at a conference sponsored by the University of Massachusetts Amherst, April 30, 2021, https://www.youtube.com/watch?v=whl1anjNZfo.

31. *Dirty Tricks*, 92.

32. *RN*, 512.

33. *Nixon: Alone in the White House*, p. 339.

CHAPTER 16: THE WHO SHOT JOHN ANGLE

1. *American Spy*, 177.

2. *Dirty Tricks*, 93.

3. *American Spy*, 178.

4. G. Gordon Liddy, *Will: The Autobiography of G. Gordon Liddy* (New York: St. Martin's Press, 1991), 204.

5. *Dirty Tricks*, 93; General Cushman's Call Re: Howard Hunt, Osborn to Inspector General, February 5, 1974, Hearings Before the Committee on the Judiciary, House of Representatives, Ninety-Third Congress, Second Session, pursuant to H. Res. 803, a resolution authorizing and directing the Committee on the Judiciary to investigate whether sufficient grounds exist for the House of Representatives to exercise its constitutional power to impeach Richard M. Nixon, President of the United States of America, May–June 1974, Book 7, pt. 2, p. 1040 ("HJC Hearings"). See also: Evans, MFR, August 30, 1971, NARA/JFK RIF #104–10119–10317; MEMORANDUM FOR: Mr. Alexander P. Butterfield, Deputy Assistant to the President, The White House, SUBJECT: Everett Howard Hunt Jr., July 7, 1971. Hunt Fourth Security File.

6. *RN*, 513.

7. *Ends of Power*, 161.

8. Report of the Special Subcommittee on Intelligence of the House Armed Services Committee, House of Representatives, Ninety-Third Congress, First Session, October 23, 1973, 5 (Nedzi Report); *Dirty Tricks*, 95.

9. *The Man Who Kept the Secrets*, 324.

10. Nedzi Report, 10, 20.

11. *Dirty Tricks*, 95.

12. *Dirty Tricks*, 96; "Working Draft-CIA Watergate History," 50. Obtained by Judicial Watch via Freedom of Information Act, August 2016, https://www.judicialwatch.org /documents/jw-v-cia-watergate-cia-report-00146/ ("Draft CIA Watergate History").

13. *Nightmare*, 91.

14. Helms Watergate Testimony, pp. 3233–34.

15. *American Spy*, 183–85. The acting TSD chief found the photos "intriguing," not least because the target, Dr. Fielding, was identified. *Dirty Tricks*, 107.

16. *Dirty Tricks*, 115.

17. CIA Employee Statement, January 17, 1974, HJC Hearings, Book 2, pp. 298–99. In the House Judiciary Committee report, Ratliff's statement is heavily redacted. See also: *Dirty Tricks*, 299–300. O'Sullivan found an unredacted copy of Ratliff's statement in Arden B. Schell Watergate Collection, box 2, folder 24, George Mason University. Ratliff said he felt sure "that Mr. Helms was probably aware of some of Hunt's activities and might have authorized the use of Dr. Malloy." (CIA Employee Statement).

18. *Dirty Tricks*, 302; Hunt HSCA testimony, pt. 1, p. 30. "Mr. Colson has in the past adverted to a supposed continuing intelligence liaison between then-director Helms and myself, which, in fact, did not exist," Hunt said.

19. The President's News Conference of September 16, 1971, *Public Papers of the Presidents of the United States, Richard Nixon, 1971: Containing the Public Messages, Speeches, and Statements of the President* (Washington, D.C.: U.S. Government Printing Office, 1999), 292.

20. *Strong Man*, 164.

21. *Nightmare*, 83.

22. *Nightmare*, 84.

23. *Nightmare*, 85.

24. *Nightmare*, 85.

25. *The Man Kept the Secrets*, 326.

26. *RN*, 515.

27. *Ends of Power*, 40.

28. White House Tapes, OVAL 587–007a; October 8, 1971; Richard Nixon Presidential Library and Museum, Yorba Linda, California, https://nixontapes.org/rmh.html ("Who shot John?" 17:30; "Gee, I did this for Kennedy or I did this for Johnson," 27:00; "Sir, I'm working entirely for you," 32:00).

CHAPTER 17: OUR SIDE

1. Sturgis Deposition, p. 29, https://www.maryferrell.org/showDoc.html?docId =31993#relPageId=33.

2. CIA Employee Statement.

3. *Dirty Tricks*, 146.

4. Penelope Gleason, FBI interview, June 22, 1972, https://vault.fbi.gov/watergate /watergate-part-21-22-of-1/view.

5. *Dirty Tricks*, 147–49.

6. To: Acting Director, From: Washington Field 139–166, James Walter McCord, May 25, 1973, https://vault.fbi.gov/watergate/watergate-part-62-of/view. Furbershaw told the same story to Robert Fink, researcher for James Hougan, which Fink recorded in a memo that Hougan shared with me. "Interview with Mrs. Miriam Furbershaw, 6402 Ruffin Road Chevy Chase," October 16, 1980.

7. *Secret Agenda*, 25.

8. Mark Feldstein, *Poisoning the Press: Richard Nixon, Jack Anderson, and the Rise of Washington's Scandal Culture* (New York: Farrar, Straus and Giroux, 2010), 13, 27, 35.

9. *RN*, 531.

10. *Poisoning the Press*, 162.

11. *Strong Man*, 170.

12. *RN*, 531.

13. *Poisoning the Press*, 204.

14. *Poisoning the Press*, 210.

15. Helms interview with James Rosen, February 2, 1995.

16. *The Man Who Kept the Secrets*, 313.

17. Victor Marchetti and John D. Marks, *The CIA and the Cult of Intelligence* (New York: Laurel, 1983), ix.

18. *Lost Crusader*, 243.

19. National Archives, Record Group 460. Records of the Watergate Special Prosecution Force [WSPF], Records Relating to the Watergate Break-In, Records of the Office of the U.S. Attorney for the District of Columbia, Personal Diary, Earl Silbert, 645 (Silbert Diary).

20. Silbert Diary, 167.

21. Silbert Diary, 482.

22. *Will*, 267.

23. *Strong Man*, 264.

24. *Will*, 276.

25. Douglas Caddy, interview with the author, July 9, 2021.

26. "Card Lists Re: Frank Sturgis, E. Howard Hunt, et al," NARA/JFK RIF #104–10096–10131. The report, entitled "Activities of Hunt and Artime in Miami and Nicaragua," was dated April 1972 (https://www.maryferrell.org/showDoc.html ?docId=179901#relPageId=11).

27. *Dirty Tricks*, 137.

28. *Secret Agenda*, 132, citing Baker Report in Senate Watergate Committee's Final Report, pp. 1146–49. "Hunt was White House consultant supposedly engaged in domestic activities that have nothing to do with foreign intelligence," Karamessines said: "[It] was neither necessary nor proper for CIA to check into Hunt's activities." Sternfield wrote a "strongly worded" letter to Esterline, informing him of headquarters' view that Hunt was "undoubtedly on domestic White House business, no interest to us, in essence, cool it."

29. Memorandum for: Deputy Inspector General, Subject: Movie or TV series on CIA Based on Books by Mr. David St. John, February 27, 1974, NARA/JFK RIF #104–10119–10305.

30. Testimony of Witnesses, Hearing Before the Committee on the Judiciary, House of Representatives, Ninety-Third Congress, Second Session, Pursuant to H. Res. 803, Book III (Washington, D.C.: U.S. Government Printing Office, 1973), 42–44.

31. *American Spy*, 202; *Will*, 302.

32. *Secret Agenda*, 150.

33. *Secret Agenda*, 150, citing FBI serial 139–4089–2159, May 16, 1973; *Chicago Today*, May 14–16, 1973.

34. *American Spy*, 20.

35. James McCord, *A Piece of Tape* (Rockville, MD: Washington Media Services Ltd., 1974), 23.

36. *American Spy*, 214–16.

37. *American Spy*, 214–16.

38. *A Piece of Tape*, 25.

39. *Dirty Tricks*, 194.

40. *Dirty Tricks*, 169; *Undercover*, 142.

41. *Dirty Tricks*, 173–74.

42. *Dirty Tricks*, 392.

43. *American Spy*, 226.

44. *RN*, 625. The Agency's files showed that Echeverría had been a paid CIA source for years, known by the cryptonym LITEMPO-8. Jefferson Morley, *Our Man in Mexico* (Lawrence, KS: University Press of Kansas, 2008), 94.

45. White House Tapes, WHT 025–071, June 16, 1972; Richard Nixon Presidential Library and Museum, Yorba Linda, California, https://nixontapes.org/rmh.html.

CHAPTER 18: THE SOREST SPOT

1. *American Spy*, 234.

2. St. John Hunt, interview with the author, April 2, 2021.

3. *Secret Agenda*, citing *All the President's Men*, 18.

4. Message To: Ambassador Helms, From: Cary, November 16, 1973, NARA/JFK Record Number 1993.08.10.17:55:39:000028, https://www.maryferrell.org/showDoc.html?docId=104983#relPageId=8&search=%22George_Murphy%22++FBI&tab=rif.

5. *Intriguing Life*, 14.

6. Helms Watergate Testimony, p. 3237.
7. *RN*, 626.
8. *Ends of Power*, 13, italics in original.
9. Stephen Anderson, interview with the author, December 18, 2021.
10. *Richard Helms as DCI*, 187.
11. *The Man Who Kept the Secrets*, 329.
12. *Dirty Tricks*, 210.
13. *Dirty Tricks*, 235.
14. *Intriguing Life*, 93.
15. *RN*, 631.
16. *RN*, 633.
17. *Ends of Power*, 24–25.
18. Nomination of Richard Helms to be Ambassador to Iran and CIA International and Domestic Activities, Hearing Before the Committee on Foreign Relations, United States Senate, Ninety-Third Congress, First Session, February 5, 1973 (Washington, D.C.: U.S. Government Printing Office, 1974), 95.
19. *A Piece of Tape*, 36.
20. *A Piece of Tape*, 36.
21. Nedzi Hearings, 956.
22. Nedzi Hearings, 976.
23. James McCord, "What the FBI Almost Found," *Armed Forces Journal* (July 1973).
24. Jeb Stuart Magruder, *An American Life: One Man's Road to Watergate* (New York: Atheneum, 1974), 226–28.
25. Senate Watergate Report, 1127.
26. Nedzi Hearings, 946–47.
27. President Richard Nixon's Daily Diary, June 23, 1972. White House Tapes, 741–002a, June 23, 1972, Nixon Library.
28. *Ends of Power*, 39.
29. *Ends of Power*, 34.
30. *A Look Over My Shoulder*, 9.
31. *Richard Helms as DCI*, 191.
32. Nedzi Hearings, 93.
33. Nedzi Report, 17.
34. Chronology of Discussions concerning CIA's role with reference to Mexican Operations etc., Walters Memoranda, June 1, 1973. Security File on Frank Sturgis, NARA/JFK Record Number 1993.08.05.14:42:12:750028 (Chronology of Discussions).
35. *Ends of Power*, 38.

CHAPTER 19: THE RUSE

1. Gerald S. Strober and Deborah Hart Strober, *Nixon: An Oral History of His Presidency* (New York: Harper Perennial, 1996), 352.
2. Nedzi Hearings, 46.

3. Chronology of Discussions.

4. Chronology of Discussions; *A Piece of Tape*, 117; Nedzi Hearings, 46.

5. *Dirty Tricks,* 226; HJC Hearings Book 2, 472.

6. L. Patrick Gray III with Ed Gray, *In Nixon's Web: A Year in the Crosshairs of Watergate* (New York: Times Books, 2008), 77; Nedzi Report, 19. Investigators later asked Helms, Why not let the FBI interview Karl Wagner? "Some of this goes back to the question of the covers that were in the Mullen office," he replied evenly, "that we wanted to keep from being spread all through the government, that we have people under cover there. There were some perfectly sensible reasons." Nedzi Hearings, 102.

7. *Nixon's Web*, 78–79.

8. Richard Helms, Director's State of the Agency address, June 30, 1972. CIA Records Search Tool (CREST), https://www.cia.gov/readingroom/docs/CIA-RDP82M00311R0001002.

9. State of the Agency address, June 30, 1972.

10. *The Man Who Kept the Secrets*, 337.

11. Nedzi Report, 19.

12. *Nixon's Web*, 91–92.

13. *American Spy*, 255.

14. *American Spy*, 254.

15. *A Piece of Tape*, 146.

16. WFB-Dorothy Hunt, July 18, 1972, WFBP.

17. "Meeting with Robert Foster Bennett and His Comments Concerning E. Howard Hunt, Douglas Caddy, and the 'Watergate Five' Incident," Martin Lukoskie, MFR, July 10, 1972.

18. Nedzi Hearings, 1071–73.

19. *Secret Agenda,* 320–21.

20. Senate Watergate Report, 1124.

21. *Richard Helms as DCI*, 196.

22. *Dirty Tricks*, 242; "Draft CIA Watergate History," 126.

23. *Dirty Tricks*, 241.

24. Nedzi Hearings, 164. The name of the source is deleted from the Nedzi Hearing Records.

25. *The Man Who Kept the Secrets*, 341.

26. Nedzi Report, 13.

27. Silbert Diary, 313.

28. Nedzi Hearings, 945–47.

29. *Secret Agenda*, 274–77.

30. Silbert Diary, 336.

31. *Intriguing Life*, 106.

32. Roderick McKelvie, interview with the author, March 1, 2021.

CHAPTER 20: PRECIPICE

1. *Dirty Tricks*, 254; conversation between the President, Haldeman, and Dean, September 15, 1972 (5:27–6:17), exhibit 4, *United States v. Mitchell*, Nixon Library. HJC Hearings Book 2, 594.

2. *Nixon: An Oral History*, 178. "The North Vietnamese were trying to have us not only withdraw our troops—which increasingly we indicated we were ready to do but to overthrow our friends [South Vietnamese government] as we left," said Winston Lord, an aide to Kissinger. "So the sticking point was 'Do you have a military settlement, alone, and leave the political settlement up to the two sides to battle out in the future. Or do you arrange the political future of Vietnam as the same time?'"

3. Richard Helms, State of the Agency, June 30, 1972.

4. James Rosen interview, Richard Helms, February 2, 1995. Courtesy of James Rosen.

5. "The Art of Flattery," 13.

6. *Dirty Tricks*, 260.

7. Nomination of Earl J. Silbert to be United States Attorney for the District of Columbia, April 23, 1974, Hearings Before the Committee on the Judiciary, United States Senate, Ninety-Third Congress, Second Session, Part 1, p. 65.

8. Vietnam Conflict Extract Data File.

9. *RN*, 717.

10. *The Man Who Kept the Secrets*, 310.

11. *A Look Over My Shoulder*, 410; *The Man Who Kept the Secrets*, 309.

12. *American Spy*, 261.

13. *Nixon: An Oral History*, 291.

14. *Nightmare*, 278.

15. *A Piece of Tape*, 46–47.

16. *Nightmare*, 268.

17. *Strong Man*, 336. On November 15, 1972, Haldeman, Ehrlichman, and Dean met in the president's office of the Laurel Lodge at Camp David to discuss Hunt's threats and demands for money and the Colson tape of his conversation with Hunt. Dean said he was going to New York to play the tape [made by Colson] for Mitchell. Dean said, "My instructions from them were to tell Mitchell to take care of all these problems." SWC, 2260–61.

18. *Richard Helms as DCI*, 208.

19. *Haldeman Diaries*, 540.

20. *Richard Helms as DCI*, 211.

21. *The Man Who Kept the Secrets*, 312.

22. *Night Watch*, 232.

23. John Ehrlichman, *Washington Behind Closed Doors: The Company* (New York: Pocket Books, 1977), 319.

24. Letter, John G. Kester, Williams & Connolly, to Oliver Stone, July 14, 1995. Courtesy of Oliver Stone.

25. *The Man Who Kept the Secrets*, 344.

26. *A Piece of Tape*, 83.

27. *A Piece of Tape*, 83.

28. *American Spy*, 263.

29. *A Piece of Tape*, 47.

30. *American Spy*, 259.

31. *American Spy*, 264.

32. National Transportation Safety Board, Aircraft Accident Report, United Airlines Inc. Boeing 737, N9031U, Chicago, Illinois, December 8, 1972, 9 (NTSB Report).

33. NTSB Report, 13.

34. *American Spy*, 267.

35. *American Spy*, 269.

36. Letter, EHH to WFB, December 9, 1972, WFBP.

37. *Dirty Tricks*, 418.

38. *Nightmare*, 278.

39. *A Piece of Tape*, 145.

40. Letter, James McCord to Paul Gaynor, December 22, 1972, SWC, 3840

41. Nedzi Hearings, 179–180; *Dirty Tricks*, 280.

42. Nedzi Hearings, 767.

43. *Secret Agenda*, 366.

44. *Dirty Tricks*, 149.

45. *A Piece of Tape*, 150. Letter, James McCord to John Caulfield, ud. SWC, 3839.

CHAPTER 21: ESCAPE

1. *Nixon: An Oral History*, 172.

2. *RN*, 738.

3. *Intriguing Life*, 107.

4. Letter, James McCord to Paul Gaynor, January 3, 1972, SWC, 3839.

5. Letter, James McCord to Paul Gaynor, January 5, 1972, SWC, 3834.

6. John Dean, *Blind Ambition* (New York: Simon & Schuster, 1976), 177.

7. "Draft CIA Watergate History," pp. 126–27; *Dirty Tricks*, 276.

8. *Ends of Power*, 231.

9. Stanley I. Kutler, *The Wars of Watergate: The Last Crisis of Richard Nixon* (New York: W. W. Norton & Company, 1990), 254.

10. Letter, L. Patrick Gray to Alexander Butterfield, January 19, 1973, Helms FBI File 1972.

11. "Congressional Record S. 8424-The Watergate Conspiracy" (1973); Mike Mansfield Speeches, 1105, https://scholarworks.umt.edu/mansfield_speeches/1105.

12. Rockefeller Commission Report, 203.

13. Fred D. Thompson, *At That Point in Time* (New York: Quadrangle/New York Times Book Co., 1975), 173.

14. Deposition of Richard McGarrah Helms, *Hunt v. Liberty Lobby*, NO 80–1121-Civ.-JWK, June 1, 1984, 82 (Helms Deposition, *Howard Hunt Jr. v. Liberty Lobby Inc.*).

15. Rockefeller Commission Report, 204.

16. Nomination of Richard Helms to be Ambassador to Iran and CIA International and Domestic Activities, Hearings Before the Committee on Foreign Relations, United States Senate, Ninety-Third Congress, First Session, February 5 and 7 and May 21, 1973, pp. 1–16.

17. Nomination of Richard Helms, 20–21.

18. Nomination of Richard Helms, 24.

19. Nomination of Richard Helms, 25.

20. Nomination of Richard Helms, 26.

21. Morton Halperin, "Did Richard Helms Commit Perjury?," *New Republic*, March 6, 1976, p. 15; *The Man Who Kept the Secrets*, 349.

22. Nomination of Richard Helms, 47.

23. Memorandum for: The President' Files, From: B/Gen. Brent Scowcroft, USAS, Subject: The President's Meeting with Ambassador Helms (Iran) February 14, 1973. National Security Adviser Memoranda of Conversations, 1973–1977, Gerald Ford Library, https://www.fordlibrarymuseum.gov/library/document/0314/1552557.pdf.

CHAPTER 22: THE WITNESS

1. Federal Bureau of Investigation, Subject: Bernard Fensterwald Jr., File 77–44206.

2. *Secret Agenda*, 221. Re-interview of Louis James Russell, July 5, 1972, Watergate FBI 139–4089 Section 9, Serials 734–744, pp. 26–27, https://www.maryferrell.org/showDoc.html?docId=217635#relPageId=268.

3. Karen Feld, "Unsung Watergate Figure Helped Burglar 'Sing' to Police," *Washington Examiner*, June 8, 2005.

4. Bernard Fensterwald Jr., interview with the author, January 5, 2021.

5. *A Piece of Tape*, 59.

6. *A Piece of Tape*, 61.

7. *American Spy*, 285–87.

8. *A Piece of Tape*, 61.

9. "Sentence Cut, McCord May Be Free in May," *New York Times*, April 29, 1975, p. 8.

10. *Nightmare*, 307.

11. "Draft CIA Watergate History," 47.

12. *Lost Crusader*, 259.

13. *Lost Crusader*, 259.

14. CIA Employee Statement.

15. *Lost Crusader*, 260.

16. *A Look Over My Shoulder*, 427.

17. *A Look Over My Shoulder*, 427.

18. Bob Woodward and Carl Bernstein, *All the President's Men* (New York: Simon & Schuster, 2014), 319.

19. *Lost Crusader*, 263.

20. *A Look Over My Shoulder*, 429.

21. Memorandum to: Honorable Archibald Cox, Special Prosecutor, From: Earl J. Silbert, Principal Assistant U.S. Attorney, Subject: Present Status of the Watergate Investigation Conducted by United States Attorney's Office for the District of Columbia, June 7, 1973, found in Silbert Diary.

22. Richard Ben-Veniste and George Frampton Jr., *Stonewall: The Real Story of the Watergate Prosecution* (New York: Simon & Schuster, 1977), 74.

23. *Stonewall*, 76–77.

24. Richard Ben-Veniste, interview with the author, March 20, 2021.

CHAPTER 23: MAGNIFICENT

1. Helms Watergate Testimony, 3283.

2. Helms Watergate Testimony, 3272.

3. "Officials Describe CIA Role," *Washington Post*, August 3, 1973, p. A1.

4. Letter, EHH to WFB, August 3, 1973, WFBP.

5. President Richard Nixon's Daily Diary, August 2, 1973.

6. *RN*, 909.

7. "Text of Nixon's Statement on Watergate Scandal as Issued by the White House," *New York Times*, August 16, 1973, p. 25.

8. *RN*, 918–19.

9. Jill Wine-Banks, *The Watergate Girl: My Fight for Truth and Justice Against a Criminal President* (New York: Henry Holt and Company, 2020), 1–2.

10. Patricia Sullivan, "Rose Mary Woods Dies, Loyal Nixon Secretary," *Washington Post*, January 24, 2005.

11. *Watergate Girl*, 4.

12. "I concluded that Andrew St. George didn't have any source," Fensterwald said later. "It was just a rumor that that's what Helms said. But I also think the rumor is true." Len Colodny, 1986 interview of Bud Fensterwald, Colodny Collection at Texas A&M University https://www.watergate.com/len-colodny/len-s-jfk-connection.

13. Draft CIA Watergate History, 152.

14. Nedzi Hearings, 1020.

15. Nedzi Hearings, 1047.

16. Nedzi Hearings, 1041.

17. Marc Lackritz, e-mail to the author, May 20, 2021.

18. *At That Point in Time*, 172–174.

19. Nedzi Hearings, 1048.

CHAPTER 24: GHASTLY

1. *RN*, 976.

2. *RN*, 995.

3. *RN*, 997.

4. Senate Watergate Report, 3.

5. Senate Watergate Report, 5.

6. Senate Watergate Report, 1135.

7. Senate Watergate Report, 1107.

8. Bob Woodward and Carl Bernstein, "The Plan: Use CIA to Block Probe," *Washington Post*, July 25, 1974, p. A1.

9. Jon Margolis and Jim Squires, "Impeachment Sure, Nixon Admits; Support Crumbles," *Chicago Tribune*, August 6, 1974, p. 1.

10. *RN*, 1073.

11. Bob Woodward and Carl Bernstein, *The Final Days* (New York: Simon & Schuster Paperbacks, 1976), 422–24.

12. *Intriguing Life*, 155.

13. *RN*, 1090.

14. Letter, Edmund McBride to James Hastings, January 25, 1993; Declaration of Mr. Edmund F. McBride, November 11, 1997, National Archives, Record Group 541 Records of the JFK Assassination Records Review Board, Ronald G. Haron's Files.

15. "Iconic Spotlight, Robert Redford and Richards Helms," Iconic Images, September 24, 2020, https://iconicimages.net/news/iconic-spotlight-robert-redford-richard-helms/.

16. *Lost Crusader*, 292–93.

17. Harold P. Ford, *William E. Colby as Director of Central Intelligence* (Langley, VA: Central Intelligence Agency, 1993), 100, 103.

18. *Colby as DCI*, 105.

19. Cord Meyer, *Facing Reality: From World Federalism to the CIA* (New York: Harper & Row, 1980), 207.

20. John Prados, *The Family Jewels: The CIA, Secrecy, and Presidential Power* (Austin, TX: University of Texas Press, 2013), 111.

21. *Family Jewels*, 319.

22. *Lost Crusader*, 299.

23. *Dirty Tricks*, 344, citing "Memorandum of Conversation," January 4, 1975.

24. Kathryn S. Olmsted, *Challenging the Secret Government: The Post-Watergate Investigations of the CIA and FBI* (Chapel Hill and London: University of North Carolina Press, 1996), 69.

25. *Colby as DCI*, 131.

26. William Colby and Peter Forbath, *Honorable Men: My Life in the CIA* (New York: Simon & Schuster, 1978), 402–3.

CHAPTER 25: INTERROGATION

1. Arthur Schlesinger Jr., *Journals: 1952–2000* (New York: Penguin Press, 2007), 184.

2. "The Dallas Question Isn't Quite Resolved," *Philadelphia Inquirer*, April 1, 1975, p. 36.

3. *Good Night America*, March 6, 1975, https://www.youtube.com/watch?v=wGdM7ut-Kk4.

4. Stan Isaacs, "Once Again, Who Killed John F. Kennedy?" *Newsday*, March 27, 1975, p. 143.

5. John J. O'Connor, "TV: Two Programs Exploit Subjects," *New York Times*, March 27, 1975, p. 44.

6. Kay Gardella, "Rivera Asks JFK Inquiry Conducted by Congress," *Daily News*, March 27, 1975, p. 337.

7. Memorandum to: James B. Weidner, From: David W. Belin, Subject: Matters Concerning JFK Assassination and CIA, April 21, 1975, NARA/JKF RIF #178–10002–10355, https://www.maryferrell.org/showDoc.html?docId=31985.

8. *Colby as DCI*, 125.

9. Letter, David Belin to E. Henry Noche, April 15, 1975, NARA/JFK Record Number 1993.07.08.07:57:21:560530, https://www.maryferrell.org/showDoc .html?docId=57270.

10. *Intriguing Life*, 155.

11. Testimony of Richard Helms, Rockefeller Commission, April 23, 1975, 160.

12. Testimony of Richard Helms, Rockefeller Commission, April 23, 1975, 162.

13. Daniel Schorr, *Staying Tuned: A Life in Journalism* (New York: Pocket Books, 2001), 269–71.

CHAPTER 26: THE PURITAN ETHIC

1. "Reflections of DCIs Colby and Helms on the CIA's 'Time of Troubles' (U)," *Studies in Intelligence* 51, no. 3 (2008): 51.

2. *Colby as DCI*, 100.

3. *Lost Crusader*, 325.

4. Anthony Lewis, "Farewell My Lovely," *New York Times*, November 6, 1975, p. 41.

5. "Alleged Assassination Plots Involving Foreign Leaders," An Interim Report of the Select Committee to Study Governmental Operations with Respect to Intelligence Activities, Eighty-Fourth Congress, First Session, Report No. 94–465, p. xiii ("Alleged Assassination Plots Involving Foreign Leaders").

6. "Alleged Assassination Plots Involving Foreign Leaders," xiii.

7. "Helms Says Mail Opening Was Illegal," *New York Times*, October 24, 1975.

8. "Alleged Assassination Plots Involving Foreign Leaders," 151.

9. "Reflections of DCIs Colby and Helms," 54.

10. Morton H. Halperin, "Did Richard Helms Commit Perjury?" *New Republic*, March 6, 1976, pp. 14–17.

11. *Intriguing Life*, 158.

12. *A Look Over My Shoulder*, 438.

13. Bob Woodward, "Prosecution of Helms Ruled Out," *Washington Post*, February 20, 1976, p. A1. Griffin B. Bell, with Ronald J. Ostrow, *Taking Care of the Law* (New York: William Morrow & Company, 1982), 137.

14. *Intriguing Life*, 139.

15. Frances FitzGerald interview with the author, February 4, 2021.

16. Dick Russell, "Charles Colson," *Argosy*, March 1976, p. 74.

17. *Intriguing Life*, 153.

18. Memorandum for the Record, Subject: Agency Contact with the Immigration and Naturalization Service on Behalf of Mr. Johnny Roselli. March 23, 1974, NARA/ JFK RIF #104–10133–10308.

19. To: Terry Lenzner, From: Bob Muse, Subject: Interview of Johnny Rosselli, February 2, 1974.

20. Seth King, "Giancana, Gangster, Slain; Tied to C.I.A. Castro Plot," *New York Times*, June 23, 1976, p. 1.

21. Whitten HSCA testimony, p. 149, https://www.maryferrell.org/showDoc.html?docId =251#relPageId=153.

22. Senate Select Committee to Study Government Operations with Respect to Intelligence Activities. Testimony of John Roselli, April 23, 1976, NARA/JFK RIF #157–10014–100000, https://www.maryferrell.org/showDoc.html?docId=1445.

23. Federal Bureau of Investigation, John Roselli (Excerpts), https://vault.fbi.gov /John%20%28Handsome%20Johnny%29%20Roselli/John%20%28Hand some%20Johnny%29%20Roselli%20Part%208%20of%2012.

24. *Taking Care of the Law*, 16.

25. *Taking Care of the Law*, 137–38.

26. *Intriguing Life* 160; *A Look Over My Shoulder*, 443.

27. "Transcript of Frost's Television Interview," *New York Times*, May 5, 1977, p. B10.

CHAPTER 27: JUDGMENT

1. Gregory Craig, interview with the author, October 23, 2020. *ABC News*, October 31, 1977; *CBS Evening News*, November 1, 1977; *NBC Nightly News*, October 31, 1977, Vanderbilt Television News Archive, Vanderbilt University, https://tvnews.vanderbilt .edu/.

2. *ABC News*, October 31, 1977; *CBS Evening News*, November 1, 1977; *NBC Nightly News*, October 31, 1977, Vanderbilt Television News Archive, Vanderbilt University, https://tvnews.vanderbilt.edu/.

3. Timothy Robinson, "Helms Fined $2,000, Term Suspended," *Washington Post*, November 5, 1977, p. A1, https://www.washingtonpost.com/archive/politics /1977/11/05/helms-fined-2000-term-suspended/cdb385bd-d4a0–45e0 -a838–8feb4200fbb9/.

4. Anthony Marro, "Helms is Fined $2,000 and Given Two-Year Suspended Prison Term," *New York Times*, November 5, 1977, p. 1, https://www.nytimes.com/1977/11 /05/archives/helms-is-fined-2000-and-given-twoyear-suspended-prison-term-us .html.

5. "Helms Fined $2,000, Term Suspended."

6. Ibid.

7. Donnie Radcliffe, "Cynthia Helms and the Caprices of Power," *Washington Post*, March 1, 1981.

8. Gregory Craig, interview with the author, October 23, 2020.

9. "Helms Is Fined $2,000 and Given Two-Year Suspended Prison Term"; *ABC News*,

November 4, 1977, Vanderbilt Television News Archive, Vanderbilt University https://tvnews.vanderbilt.edu/.

10. *A Look Over My Shoulder*, 445–46.

EPILOGUE

1. Helms Deposition, *Howard Hunt Jr. v. Liberty Lobby Inc.*
2. Letter, EHH to WFB, February 15, 1978, WFBP.
3. Santiago Morales, interview with the author, July 24, 2021.
4. John M. Broder, "Clinton Offers His Apologies to Guatemala," *New York Times*, March 11, 1990, p. 1.
5. "DCI John McCone and the Assassination of President John F. Kennedy," 8.
6. Final Report of the Select Committee on Assassinations, U.S. House of Representatives, Ninety-Fifth Congress, Second Session, Summary of Findings and Recommentations (Washington, D.C. U.S. Government Printing Office, 1979,) 3.
7. *A Look Over My Shoulder*, 229.
8. Letter, Richard Nixon to Richard Helms, October 24, 1983, RHP.
9. *Legacy of Ashes*, 503.
10. Mark Platte and Danielle E. Fouquette, "Richard Nixon,: 1913–1994 : Guest List Covered Wide Spectrum: Audience: Longtime allies, a few ex-enemies and representatives from 86 nations attended," *Los Angeles Times,* April 28, 1994, p. 1.
11. [Redacted] Trailblazer Awards, CIA, Intellipedia, https://documents.theblackvault.com/documents/intellipedia/intellipedia-trailblazeraward.pdf.

SOURCE MATERIAL

COLLECTIONS

Cuban Heritage Collection, University of Miami

Harry S. Truman Library and Museum, Independence, Missouri

Howard H. Baker Jr. Papers, Betsey B. Creekmore Special Collections and University Archives, the University of Tennessee, Knoxville, Tennessee (HBP)

John Davis Lodge Papers, Hoover Institution, Stanford, California

John F. Kennedy Presidential Library and Museum, Boston, Massachusetts

John F. Kennedy Assassination Records Collection, National Archives, College Park, Maryland (NARA/JFK)

Lyndon Baines Johnson Library, Austin, Texas

Richard Helms Papers, Booth Family Center for Special Collections, Georgetown University Library, Washington, D.C. (RHP)

Richard Nixon Presidential Library and Museum, Yorba Linda, California

Records of the House Un-American Activities Committee, U.S. Congress, Washington, D.C.

William F. Buckley, Jr., Papers, Manuscripts, and Archives, Yale University Library (WFBP)

BIBLIOGRAPHY

Alsop, Stewart. *The Center: People and Power in Political Washington* (New York: Harper & Row, 1968).

Anderson, Jon Lee. *Che: A Revolutionary Life* (New York: Grove Press, 1997).

Anderson, Scott. *The Quiet Americans: Four Spies at the Dawn of the Cold War—a Tragedy in Three Acts* (New York: Doubleday, 2020).

Bell, Griffin B., with Ronald J. Ostrow. *Taking Care of the Law* (New York: William Morrow & Company, 1982).

Ben-Veniste, Richard, and George Frampton. *Stonewall: The Real Story of the Watergate Prosecution* (New York: Simon & Schuster, 1977).

Bonachea, Rolando E., and Nelson Valdes. *Introduction to Revolutionary Struggle 1947–1958*, Volume I of the Selected Works of Fidel Castro (Cambridge, MA: The MIT Press, 1974).

Bower, Tom. *The Perfect English Spy: Sir Dick White and the Secret War 1935–90* (New York: St. Martin's Press, 1995).

Cirules, Enrique. *The Mafia in Havana: A Caribbean Mob Story* (Melbourne: Ocean Press, 2004).

Colhoun, Jack. *Gangsterismo: The United States, Cuba, and the Mafia 1933–1966* (New York: OR Books, 2013).

Colby, William, and Peter Forbath. *Honorable Men: My Life in the CIA* (New York: Simon & Schuster, 1978).

Colson, Charles. *Born Again* (New York: Bantam, 1976).

Dean, John. *Blind Ambition* (New York: Simon & Schuster, 1976).

Demery, Monique Brinson. *Finding the Dragon Lady: The Mystery of Vietnam's Madame Nhu* (New York: Public Affairs, 2013).

Dohrenwend, Bruce P., Nick Turse, Thomas J. Yager, and Melanie M. Wall. *Surviving Vietnam: Psychological Consequences for U.S. Veterans* (New York: Oxford University Press, 2019).

Ehrlichman, John. *Washington Behind Closed Doors: The Company* (New York: Pocket Books, 1977).

Escalante, Fabián. *The Secret War: CIA Covert Operations Against Cuba 1959–62.* (Melbourne: Ocean Press, 1995).

—— *Executive Action: 634 Ways to Kill Fidel Castro* (Melbourne: Ocean Press, 2006).

Feldstein, Mark. *Poisoning the Press: Richard Nixon, Jack Anderson, and the Rise of Washington's Scandal Culture* (New York: Farrar, Straus and Giroux, 2010).

Fonzi, Gaeton. *The Last Investigation* (New York: Thunder's Mouth Press, 1993).

Ford, Harold P. *William E. Colby as Director of Central Intelligence* (Langley, VA: Central Intelligence Agency, 1993).

Frank, Jeffrey. *Ike and Dick: Portrait of a Strange Political Marriage* (New York: Simon & Schuster, 2013).

Gray, L. Patrick with Ed Gray. *In Nixon's Web: A Year in the Crosshairs of Watergate* (New York: Times Books, 2008).

Grose, Peter. *Gentleman Spy* (Boston: Houghton Mifflin, 1994).

Halberstam, David. *The Best and the Brightest* (New York: Random House, 1973).

Haldeman, H. R. *The Haldeman Diaries: Inside the Nixon White House* (New York: G. P. Putnam's Sons, 1994).

—— with Joseph DiMona. *The Ends of Power* (New York: Times Books, 1978).

Hamburg, Eric, editor. *Nixon: An Oliver Stone Film* (New York: Hyperion, 1995).

Hathaway, Robert M., and Russell Jack Smith. *Richard Helms as Director of Central Intelligence 1966–1973* (Washington, D.C.: Center for the Study of Intelligence, 1993).

Helms, Cynthia, with Chris Black. *An Intriguing Life: A Memoir of War, Washington, and Marriage to an American Spymaster* (Lanham, MD: Rowman & Littlefield Publishers, 2013).

Helms, Richard, with William Hood. *A Look Over My Shoulder: A Life in the Central Intelligence Agency* (New York: Random House, 2003).

Herken, Gregg. *The Georgetown Set: Friends and Rivals in Cold War Washington* (New York: Alfred A. Knopf, 2014).

Hougan, Jim. *Secret Agenda* (New York: Ballantine Books, 1984).

—— *Spooks: The Haunting of America: The Private Use of Secret Agents* (New York: William Morrow and Company, 1978).

Hunt, E. Howard. *Give Us This Day.* (New Rochelle, NY: Arlington House, 1973).

—— *Undercover: Memoirs of an American Secret Agent.* (London: W. H. Allen, 1975).

—— with Greg Aunapu. *American Spy: My Secret History in the CIA, Watergate, and Beyond* (Hoboken, NJ: John Wiley & Sons, 2007).

Johnson, Loch A. *A Season of Inquiry Revisited: The Church Committee Confronts America's Spy Agencies* (Lawrence, KS: University Press of Kansas, 2015).

Kaiser, David. *The Road to Dallas: The Assassination of John F. Kennedy* (Cambridge, MA: Harvard University Press, 2007).

Karalekas, Anne. *History of the Central Intelligence Agency* (Laguna Hills, CA: Aegean Park Press, 1977).

Kinzer, Stephen. *Poisoner in Chief: Sidney Gottlieb and the CIA Search for Mind Control* (New York: Henry Holt and Company, 2019).

Kissinger, Henry. *White House Years* (Boston: Little, Brown and Company, 1979).

Kornbluh, Peter. *The Pinochet File: A Declassified Dossier on Atrocity and Accountability* (New York: New Press, 2003).

Kutler, Stanley I. *The Wars of Watergate: The Last Crisis of Richard Nixon* (New York: W. W. Norton & Company, 1990).

Li, Victor. *Nixon in New York: How Wall Street Helped Richard Nixon Win the White House* (Vancouver, Canada: Fairleigh Dickinson University Press, 2018).

Liddy, G. Gordon. *Will: The Autobiography of G. Gordon Liddy* (New York: St. Martin's Press, 1991).

Llovio-Menéndez, José Luis. *Insider: My Hidden Life as a Revolutionary in Cuba*, translated by Edith Grossman (Toronto: Bantam Books, 1988).

Lukas, J. Anthony. *Nightmare: The Underside of the Nixon Years* (New York: Penguin, 1988).

Magruder, Jeb Stuart. *An American Life: One Man's Road to Watergate* (New York: Atheneum, 1974).

Mailer, Norman. *The Armies of the Night: History as a Novel, the Novel as History* (New York: Signet, 1968).

Marchetti, Victor, and John D. Marks. *The CIA and the Cult of Intelligence* (New York: Laurel, 1983).

Mazo, Earl. *Richard Nixon: A Personal and Political Portrait* (New York: Avon Books, 1960).

McCord, James. *A Piece of Tape* (Rockville, MD: Washington Media Services Ltd., 1974).

McKnight, Gerald D. *Breach of Trust: How the Warren Commission Failed the Nation and Why* (Lawrence, KS: University Press of Kansas, 2005).

Meyer, Cord. *Facing Reality: From World Federalism to the CIA* (New York: Harper & Row, 1980).

Nichter, Luke. *The Last Brahmin: Henry Cabot Lodge and the Making of the Cold War* (New Haven, CT: Yale University Press, 2020).

Nixon, Richard. *RN: The Memoirs of Richard Nixon* (New York: Touchstone, 1979).

—— *Six Crises* (New York: Touchstone, 1990).

Olmsted, Kathryn S. *Challenging the Secret Government: The Post-Watergate Investigations of the CIA and FBI* (Chapel Hill and London: University of North Carolina Press, 1996).

O'Sullivan, Shane. *Dirty Tricks: Nixon, Watergate, and the CIA* (New York: Hot Books, 2018).

Parker, Matthew. *Goldeneye: Where Bond Was Born: Ian Fleming's Jamaica* (New York: Pegasus Books, 2015).

Phillips, David Atlee. *The Night Watch: 25 Years of Peculiar Service* (New York: Atheneum, 1975).

Powers, Thomas. *The Man Who Kept the Secrets* (New York: Simon & Schuster, 1979).

Prados, John. *Lost Crusader: The Secret Wars of CIA Director William Colby* (New York: Oxford University Press, 2003).

—— *Family Jewels: The CIA, Secrecy, and Presidential Power* (Austin, TX: University of Texas Press, 2013).

Rabe, Stephen G. *Eisenhower and Latin America: The Foreign Policy of Anti-Communism* (Chapel Hill, NC: University of North Carolina Press, 1988).

Reeves, Richard. *Nixon: Alone in the White House* (New York: Simon & Schuster, 2001).

Riebling, Mark. *Wedge: The Secret War Between the FBI and CIA* (New York: Alfred A. Knopf, 1994).

Rosen, James. *Strong Man: John Mitchell and the Secrets of Watergate* (New York: Doubleday, 2008).

Russo, Gus. *The Outfit: The Role of Chicago's Underworld in the Shaping of Modern America* (New York: Bloomsbury, 2001).

St. John, David. *On Hazardous Duty* (New York: New American Library, 1965).

—— *Festival of Spies* (New York: New American Library, 1966).

—— *One of Our Agents Is Missing* (New York: New American Library, 1967).

Schlesinger, Arthur M. Jr. *Robert Kennedy and His Times* (New York: Ballantine Books, 1978).

—— *Journals: 1952–2000* (New York: Penguin Press, 2007).

Schorr, Daniel. *Staying Tuned: A Life in Journalism* (New York: Pocket Books, 2001).

Sheehan, Neil. *A Bright Shining Lie: John Paul Vann and America in Vietnam* (New York: Vintage Books, 1989).

Smith, Joseph B. *Portrait of a Cold Warrior: Second Thoughts of a Top CIA Spy* (New York: G. P. Putnam's Sons, 1976).

Stockton, Bayard. *Flawed Patriot: The Rise and Fall of CIA Legend Bill Harvey* (Washington, D.C.: Potomac Books, 2006).

Strober, Gerald S., and Deborah Hart Strober. *Nixon: An Oral History of His Presidency* (New York: Harper Perennial, 1996).

Suchliki, Jaime. *University Students and Revolution in Cuba* (Coral Cables, FL: University of Miami Press, 1969).

Summers, Anthony, with Robbyn Swan. *The Arrogance of Power: The Secret Life of Richard Nixon* (New York: Viking, 2000).

Talbot, David. *Brothers: The Hidden History of the Kennedy Years* (New York: Free Press, 2007).

—— *The Devil's Chessboard: Allen Dulles, the CIA, and the Rise of America's Secret Government* (New York: HarperCollins, 2015).

Thomas, Evan. *The Very Best Men* (New York: Simon & Schuster, 2006).

Thomas, Hugh. *The Cuban Revolution* (New York: Harper & Row, 1977).

Thompson, Fred D. *At That Point in Time* (New York: New York Times Books, 1975).

Weiner, Tim. *Legacy of Ashes: The History of the CIA* (New York: Doubleday, 2007).

Whipple, Chris. *The Spymasters: How the CIA Directors Shape History and the Future* (New York: Scribner, 2020).

Wills, Garry. *Nixon Agonistes: The Crisis of the Self-Made Man* (Boston: Houghton Mifflin, 1970).

Wine-Banks, Jill. *The Watergate Girl: My Fight for Truth and Justice Against a Criminal President* (New York: Henry Holt and Company, 2020).

Wise, David, and Thomas B. Ross. *The Invisible Government* (New York: Bantam Books, 1965).

Woodward, Bob, and Carl Bernstein. *All the President's Men* (New York: Simon & Schuster, 2014).

—— *The Final Days* (New York: Simon & Schuster, 1976).

Zito Valdez, Miriam. *Asalto* (Havana, Cuba: Casa Editora Abril, 1998).

INDEX

ABM. *See* anti-ballistic missile systems

Agnew, Spiro ("Ted"), 97–98

Albert, Carl, 228

Alch, Gerald, 189, 203–4, 207–8

Alessandri, Jorge, 127, 129

Allende, Salvador, 127–33, 156–57, 213, 236, 245

Alsop, Joe, 138

Alsop, Stewart, 36, 119

AMBIDDY-1. *See* Artime, Manuel

AMC-LATTER-1. *See* Barker, Bernard

American Civil Liberties Union, 207

AMHINT-2. *See* Salvat, Juan Manuel

AMLASH, 42–43, 45–46, 52, 58–59, 69–70, 79–80, 87, 130, 135, 155, 197, 238, 244, 246, 266

AMSNAP-3. *See* Martinez, Rolando

AMSPELL, 37–38, 55–59, 67

Anderson, Jack, 135–37, 154, 159–61, 179

Anderson, Stephen, 171

Angleton, James, 30, 59, 64–66, 125, 219, 237–38

anti-ballistic missile systems (ABM), 107–8

Anti-Ballistic Missile Treaty, 174

antiwar movement, 89, 96, 106, 111, 115–16, 118, 134, 142, 162, 221, 257

Arbenz, Jacobo, 17, 23

Artime, Manuel ("Manolo"), 27, 42, 79–80, 113, 197, 202

Bachrach, Judy, 102

Baker, Howard Henry, Jr., 5–6, 149, 157, 174, 176, 209, 224, 227, 229–30, 233, 253, 267

Baldwin, Alfred, 166, 170, 175, 195, 204

Barker, Bernard ("Macho"), 2–3, 140–41, 162, 164–65, 169–70, 172–73, 181, 196–97, 202, 204

Batista, Fulgencio, 10–11, 21–22

Bay of Pigs, 27, 29, 63, 91–92, 113, 120–21, 140, 151–54, 173, 179, 266

Belin, David, 243–45

Bell, Griffin, 254, 258

Bennett, Donald, 124–25

Bennett, Robert, 122, 166, 188–89

Ben-Veniste, Richard, 221–22, 229

Bernstein, Carl, 4, 56, 234
Bissell, Richard, 20, 26, 29, 32, 244
Bittman, William, 187, 203
Black Panther Party, 116, 124
black-bag jobs, 125, 156–57, 255
blackmail, 32–33, 85, 136–37, 162, 179,
    200, 204, 207, 220, 253, 267
Blanco Rico, Antonio, 10–11, 18, 21
Bludhorn, Charles, 163
Bobst, Elemr, 39
Broe, Bill, 86, 131
Brookings Institution, 144
Brown, Pat, 35
Brugioni, Dino, 241
Buckley, William F., 16, 74, 76, 90, 92,
    113, 188, 202, 265
Bundy, McGeorge, 26, 110
burn bags, 160
Bush, George H. W., 248
Butterfield, Alex, 144, 225
Byrne, Matthew, 217

Cabell, Charles, 28
Caddy, Douglas, 163
Cambodia, 116–17, 119, 123, 134
Camp David, 198–200, 204
le Carré, John, 135
Carter, Jimmy, 253, 258–59
Castro, Fidel, 3, 10, 12, 21, 28, 40, 57, 81,
    91–92, 113, 154, 164, 249, 266
    assassination plans against, 23–24, 26,
        33–34, 42–44, 46, 69–70, 79, 84–86,
        135–37, 179, 239, 243–44
    CIA and, 23, 58
    Oswald and, 55–56
Castro, Raul, 22, 81
Caulfield, Jack, 205, 208
Central Intelligence Agency (CIA), 1–2,
    4–5, 7, 13–16, 33, 62–63, 130,
    196, 211, 266. See also Bay of
    Pigs; Directorio Revolucionario
    Estudiantil
    Anderson, J., surveillance by, 160–61
    antiwar movement and, 89
    Baker appendix on, 233
    Cambodia and, 117

Castro assassination plans, 23–24, 33–34,
    45–46, 58, 69–70, 135–37
Chile and, 130–33
Counterintelligence Staff, 64, 66, 69,
    87, 241
Cuba and, 3, 23, 29–30, 32–34, 37,
    43–44
Directorate of Intelligence, 78, 107
Directorate of Plans, 15–17, 20, 29, 63,
    266
Domestic Contacts Division, 32, 59, 74,
    85, 213
domestic covert operations, 141–42
Family Jewels report, 219–20, 237, 250,
    258
Foreign Broadcast Information Service,
    80
Historical Intelligence Collection, 120
Intelligence Evaluation Committee and,
    125–26
JFK and, 29, 86, 266–67
JFK assassination and, 54–60
Mafia and, 137, 154, 253
McCord and, 203–5
Mexico City station, 27, 57
Miami station, 22, 55, 163, 170
Mullen Company and, 188–89, 194
New York Times story on, 237–39
Nixon, R., and, 111–12, 238–39
Office of Security, 17, 47–48, 92–93,
    121, 147, 159, 176, 203, 229
Operations Group, 74
organized crime contacts, 32–33
Oswald and, 54–57, 69–70
post-Watergate power, 265–66
Security Command Center, 89
Security Research Service, 120–21
Security Research Staff, 159, 161, 175,
    203–4, 237
Special Investigations Group, 64–65
Technical Services Division, 24,
    148–49, 172, 233
Truman on, 62–63, 70, 213
Vietnam and, 49, 78, 105, 117–18
Watergate break-ins and, 170, 181–82,
    186

Central Office for South Vietnam
    (COSVN), 117–18
Chennault, Anna, 94–95, 97, 99, 101, 103,
    144
Chiang Kai-Shek, 68, 94
Chile, 127–33, 139, 153, 155–56, 198, 213,
    236, 245, 251, 254, 258, 266
Chilean Embassy break-in, 156, 181, 218
China, 73, 142
Chou En-lai, 142
Chung, Connie, 223–24
Church, Frank, 67, 248–50
Church Committee, 67, 248–50, 253, 267
CIA. *See* Central Intelligence Agency
CI/SIG. *See* Special Investigations Group
Civil Air Transport, 41
civil rights movement, 231
Civiletti, Benjamin, 254, 261
Cline, Ray, 95, 239
Clinton, Bill, 257, 266
COINTELPRO, 116
Colby, William, 88, 90, 171–72, 219–20,
    236–38, 248, 250, 258
"The Cold War Comes Home" (St. George),
    227
Colson, Charles, 90, 113, 115, 143, 146,
    150, 173, 198, 252
Committee for a Free Cuba, 122
Committee to Re-elect the President, 158,
    171, 188–89, 193, 200
Conein, Lou, 147, 150
Connally, John, 53, 241
COSVN. *See* Central Office for South
    Vietnam
"Countering Critics of the Warren
    Commission" (Broe), 86–87
Cox, Archibald, 221, 225–26, 228
Craig, Gregory, 257–60
Cronkite, Walter, 94
Cuba, 9–12, 18, 51, 91, 139, 173, 266
    CIA and, 3, 23, 29–30, 32–34, 37,
        43–44
    JFK and, 25–26, 29–30, 35–36, 39–41,
        51–52, 113
    LBJ and, 79
    revolution in, 21–23

Cuban Missile Crisis, 35–36
Cuban Student Directorate, 55
Cubans for Nixon, 113
Cubela, Rolando, 9–10, 21–22, 42–46, 52,
    69, 79–81, 87, 130, 238, 245, 266
Cushing, Dick, 17–18
Cushing, Nancy, 17–18
Cushman, Robert, 23, 105, 109, 147–48,
    172, 209, 212

Dash, Sam, 229
Davis, Martin, 163
Dean, John, 144, 176–77, 181–82,
    186–87, 192, 208–9, 217, 220–21
Defense Intelligence Agency, 124
"Definition of Internal Security Threat-
    Foreign" (CIA), 125
DeLoach, Cartha, 87
Democratic National Committee, 164,
    167, 169, 189, 209
desegregation, 45
Diem, Bui, 95, 147, 150–53, 155, 173,
    193
Diem, Ngo Dinh, 48–50
Directorio Revolucionario, 10–11,
    21–22
Directorio Revolucionario Estudiantil
    (DRE), 36–39, 55–57, 65, 67
Dobrynin, Anatoly, 110
Dodd, Christopher, 66, 69
Domestic Contacts Division, 32
domestic covert operations, 141
domestic radicals, 123–24
domestic spying, 106, 115–16, 120
DRE. *See* Directorio Revolucionario
    Estudiantil
Dulles, Allen W., 13, 15, 20, 29, 63, 68,
    70, 83, 90, 104, 185
Dunlevy, Elizabeth, 189, 210, 230
Duran, Silvia, 57–58

Earman, John, 86–87, 135
Echeverría, José Antonio, 10, 21, 43, 167,
    214, 266
Edwards, Augustín, 129, 213
Egerter, Betty, 65

Ehrlichman, John, 2, 112–13, 143, 147, 149–52, 160–61, 163, 173–74, 178, 199, 208, 221, 223, 230
  Hunt, E. H., and, 182–83
  recordings of conversations with, 225–26
Eisenhower, Dwight, 13, 15, 17, 20, 27–28, 31
Ellsberg, Daniel, 140–41, 144, 146–48, 157, 172, 182–83, 185, 193, 204, 217, 220
Ervin, Sam, 5, 209, 220, 224, 229
Esterline, Jake, 19, 32, 163, 170
Evans, Frederick, 190

Fair Play for Cuba Committee, 55–56, 92, 122
Family Jewels report, 219–20, 237, 250, 258
FBI, 177, 196, 209
  Counterintelligence Program, 116
  Internal Security Division, 125
  JFK assassination and, 64
  Oswald and, 65
  Watergate investigation, 181–82, 186, 190
Federacion de Estudiantil Universitaria (FEU), 10
Felt, Mark, 220
Fensterwald, Bernard, 215–16, 227
FEU. See Federacion de Estudiantil Universitaria
Fielding, Lewis, 148–49, 157, 172, 183, 198, 212, 217
FitzGerald, Desmond, 46, 52, 55, 61, 78, 238
FitzGerald, Frances, 78, 252
Fleming, Ian, 14–15, 26, 74–75, 99
Ford, Gerald, 235–39, 243, 248, 251
Foreign Broadcast Information Service, 80
Foreign Intelligence Surveillance Act, 265
40 Committee, 245
Frederick Praeger Publishing Company, 32
Frente Revolucionario Democrático, 26
Friar's Club case, 136, 253
Frost, David, 33–34, 254–56
Fulbright, J. William, 210–13, 218, 227
Furbershaw, Miriam, 158–59

Garay, Jaime Melgoza, 128
Garrison, Jim, 85, 241
de Gaulle, Charles, 39, 46–47
Gayler, Noel, 124–25, 141
Gaynor, Paul, 93, 120–21, 159, 175, 203, 207–8
Gelb, Leslie, 144
Gemstone, 162
Giancana, Sam, 24, 33, 44, 96, 136, 253
"Give Us This Day" (Hunt, E. H.), 91, 113, 120–21
Gleason, Penny, 170
Goldwater, Barry, 71, 234
González, Virgilio, 165, 169–70, 197
Goutiere, Dorothy Wetzel de, 16–17
Graham, Katharine, 74, 224
Graham, Ronald, 99
Gray, L. Patrick, 3, 177, 179–80, 182–83, 186–87, 209, 222, 224
Groden, Robert, 242
Guatemala, 17, 23, 27–28, 266
Guevara, Ernesto ("Che"), 21–22, 81, 130
Guin Diaz, Ramon, 79
Gunn, Edward, 24, 52, 164

Haig, Alexander, 131, 133, 160, 196
Haldeman, H. R. ("Bob"), 2–3, 47, 98–99, 102–4, 109, 111, 113, 124, 144, 150, 171, 173–74, 177–79, 181, 185, 187, 196, 199, 221, 225–26, 229, 255
Halperin, Morton, 100–101, 109, 250
Hampton, Fred, 116
Harvey, William King, 33–34, 136, 253
Heckscher, Henry, 79, 130
Helms, Cynthia, 46, 90, 103–4, 111, 135, 137, 140, 163, 170, 172, 191, 214, 234–35, 251–53, 262
Helms, Dennis, 90
Helms, Julia, 48, 77
Helms, Richard, 1, 3, 5–8, 12–16, 18–20, 27, 37–38, 42, 63, 73, 83, 99, 115, 141–42, 151, 157, 190, 228, 263
  ambassador nomination, 1, 199–200, 209–12
  on AMLASH, 43
  Anderson, J., surveillance and, 160–61

antiwar movement and, 89, 106, 115–16
appointment to director of Central
    Intelligence, 81–82
assassination plans and, 33–34, 44–46,
    69
Chile and, 129, 131, 133, 245, 251, 254
Church Committee and, 67, 248–50
on CIA and Watergate break-in, 176,
    178–79
Cuba and, 23, 32, 40, 51–52, 78–79,
    243–44
Cubela and, 43–44
death of, 268
defense team, 257–59
as Deputy Director of Plans, 29, 63
as Directorate of Plans chief of
    operations, 16–17
domestic covert operations and, 106, 141
DRE and, 57
Family Jewels report and, 250
Hunt, E. H., and, 48, 74–77, 121–22,
    145, 149–50, 163, 173, 182–83, 210,
    212, 218, 229, 264–65
Intelligence Evaluation Committee and,
    124–26
Iran ambassadorship, 214, 222, 227,
    234–35, 252
JFK assassination and, 54–55, 59, 64,
    66, 267
June 23 meeting and, 3–4, 179–81, 186,
    221–22, 232–33, 255
Mafia and, 85, 87–88
Maheu and, 33
Mansfield request and, 210
McCord, J., and, 158, 170, 174, 208, 221
New York Times CIA story and, 238–39
Nixon, R., and, 98–99, 104–6, 109, 123,
    125, 138–39, 152–55, 167, 177–78,
    193–94, 198–200
notification of Watergate arrests, 169–71,
    227
NSC and, 100–101, 104, 106
Oswald and, 64–66, 70
plea deal, 259–62
prosecution decisions against, 214,
    250–51, 254–55, 258

RFK and, 54, 60, 85–86
Rockefeller Commission and, 243–47
"State of the Agency" address, 183–85
testimony on Watergate, 223–25,
    228–30
Three Days of the Condor filming and,
    236
Vietnam and, 48, 50, 78, 88, 90, 95,
    105, 117–19, 193
Warren Commission and, 68–70,
    86–87, 267
Hersh, Seymour, 237
Ho Chi Minh, 72, 109
Hoa, Nguyen Loc, 68
Hood, William, 65–66
Hoover, J. Edgar, 15, 54, 64, 116, 124–26,
    141, 177
House Armed Services Committee, 182,
    220
House Judiciary Committee, 7, 228,
    232–34
House Select Committee on Assassinations,
    69, 267
Houston, Larry, 163, 189, 194, 208
Hughes, Howard, 122, 136, 164
Hughes, Tom, 135
Hughes Tool Company, 122
Humphrey, Hubert, 95–96
Hunt, David, 202
Hunt, Dorothy, 47–48, 90, 122, 172, 187,
    196, 200–202
Hunt, Everette Howard, 2–4, 15–19,
    23–24, 27–28, 32, 42, 47–48, 74, 99,
    113, 119, 123, 145, 161–67, 169–73,
    177–79, 185, 187–89, 192–98, 204,
    207–8, 216–21, 224, 227–30, 239,
    243, 247, 251, 255, 266
Bay of Pigs memoir, 91–92, 120–21
blackmail and, 220
cables forged by, 150–52
CIA assistance to, 148–49, 172, 233
death of wife, 201–2
Ehrlichman and, 182–83
Ellsberg and, 146
feelings of abandonment, 197–98
guilty plea, 208

Hunt, Everette Howard (*continued*)
  Helms, R., and, 48, 73–77, 121–22, 145,
    149–50, 163, 173, 182–83, 210, 212,
    218, 229, 264–65
  Nixon, R., and, 147–48
  novel writing, 74–77, 90–93, 119, 163,
    202
  pay-off to, 200
  Plumbers and, 146–47
  recruiting by, 140–41
  retirement from CIA, 76–77
  sentencing, 216
  Watergate arrests and, 170, 172
Hunt, St. John, 170, 187, 201
Huston, Tom, 116, 124, 126
Huston Plan, 124–26, 145, 220–21,
  233

Information Council of the Americas
  (INCA), 56
Intelligence Evaluation Committee,
  124–25
Iran, 214, 222, 227, 234–35, 252
Iran-Contra affair, 265
Israel, McCord and, 197–98

Jackson State shooting, 118
Jaworsky, Leon, 226, 228, 232
JCS. *See* Joint Chiefs of Staff
Jenkins, Carl, 79–80
Jessup, Peter, 149, 157, 219
JFK. *See* Kennedy, John F.
Joannides, George, 38, 55, 57, 67
Johnson, Lyndon (LBJ), 62, 64, 66–67,
  71–73, 78–79, 81, 84–85, 87–90,
  94–97, 153–54
Joint Chiefs of Staff (JCS), 40, 138, 160
  destruction of transcripts, 235–36
Juan Pedro, 9, 11
June 23 meeting, 3–4, 179–81, 186,
  221–22, 232–33, 255
Justice Department, 111, 136, 161, 176–77,
  190, 197, 217, 236–37
  Helms, R., prosecution and, 214, 250–51,
    254–55, 258
  plea deal offered by, 259, 261

Karamessines, Tom, 2–3, 32, 48, 57–60,
  75–76, 102, 120, 123, 129–32, 141,
  148, 157, 161, 163, 173, 204, 212
Katzenbach, Nicholas, 64
Kendall, Donald, 68, 129
Kennedy, Edward ("Ted"), 113, 147,
  151–52
Kennedy, Jacqueline, 30, 53, 60
Kennedy, John F. (JFK), 24–25, 28–30,
  62, 185
  assassination of, 53–60, 64–67, 69–70,
    84–85, 137, 240–43, 246, 266–67
  Cuba and, 25–26, 29–30, 35–36, 39–41,
    51–52, 113
  Hunt, E. H., on, 91
  Nixon, R., and, 39–40, 153
  Vietnam and, 49–50, 150–51
Kennedy, Joseph, 24
Kennedy, Robert, 30, 33–34, 39, 44–45,
  52, 54, 60, 79, 84–86, 92, 96, 238,
  241
Kent State University shooting, 118
Keyes, Paul, 97
Khrushchev, Nikita, 13, 35–36
King, Martin Luther, 95
Kissinger, Henry, 97, 100–101, 104–6,
  108–11, 117–19, 128–29, 131–33,
  142, 144, 159–60, 177, 183, 193, 196,
  234, 236, 248, 268
Kleindienst, Richard, 194, 209, 221
Korry, Edward, 251

Laird, Melvin, 101, 108, 118, 142
Lansky, Meyer ("Little Man"), 10–12, 22
Lanuza, Jose Antonio, 55–56
Laos, 72, 105, 138
Laugh-In (television show), 96–97
LBJ. *See* Johnson, Lyndon
Levi, Edward, 251
Liddy, Gordon, 146, 148, 150, 157,
  161–62, 164–67, 169–71, 175, 177,
  185, 187, 192, 200, 204, 207, 267
LINGUAL program, 141–42, 155, 193,
  219, 237–38
Linowitz, Sol, 157
Lodge, Henry Cabot, 49–51, 151

Lon Nol, 116–17
Long, Edward, 85
Long Committee, 136
Lorenz, Marita, 24
Luciano, Charles ("Lucky"), 11
Lukoskie, Martin, 122, 188

Madame Nhu, 48–50, 151
Madman Theory, 109–10
Mafia, 11, 24, 85, 87–88, 135, 137, 154,
    179, 220, 253
Magruder, Jeb, 166, 171, 176, 195
Maheu, Robert, 15, 24, 32–33, 44, 122,
    136–37, 154, 177, 253, 267
Mailer, Norman, 89–90
Mansfield, Mike, 209–10, 229
Mao Zedong, 73
Marchetti, Victor, 161, 177, 203
Martin, Dick, 96
Martin, Laura, 264
Martínez, Rolando, 2–3, 42, 140–41, 157,
    163, 165, 169, 172, 194, 197, 212
Maury, John, 211
McCarthy, Eugene, 74, 83
McCarthy, Joe, 25, 251
McClelland, Robert, 53–54
McCone, John, 29, 34, 37, 39–40, 44,
    49, 54, 63–64, 66, 68–69, 73, 129,
    135–36, 155, 185, 209
McCord, James, 2–5, 30, 89, 107, 121,
    158–59, 164–66, 176, 185, 188–91,
    193, 195–98, 200–202, 207–8,
    211–12, 215–17, 221, 228–29
  arrest of, 169–71
  back-channel communication by, 203–5,
    208, 219
  Chung interview with, 223–24
  Watergate Memoir, 174–75
McCord, Ruth, 170, 174–75, 212
McDonald, J. Kenneth, 85
McGovern, George, 157, 166, 173, 192, 267
McGuire, Phyllis, 33, 96
McKelvie, Cynthia, 77, 99
McKelvie, Roderick, 111, 191
McNamara, Robert, 50, 110
Mertz, John, 30

Meyer, Cord, 102, 135, 163, 238
Minh, Duong Van, 49–50
"missiles in caves" story, 36–37
Mitchell, John, 109, 111–12, 114–15,
    125–26, 136–37, 141–44, 154, 162,
    166, 176–77, 200
MKULTRA, 120, 220
Mohrenschildt, George de, 59
Moore, J. Walton, 59
Moorer, Tom, 138–39
Morales, Santiago, 81, 266
Morgan, Edward, 84–85, 136
Mossadegh, Mohammad, 252
Movimiento de Recuperación
    Revolucionaria (Movement for the
    Recovery of the Revolution/MRR), 27
Mullen, Robert, 121, 166
Mullen Company, 121–23, 141, 163,
    166–67, 170, 188–89, 194–95, 204,
    210, 212, 233

Nasser, Gamal Abdel, 12–13
National Intelligence Estimates, 48, 108
National Photographic Interpretation
    Center, 241
National Security Act, 62, 185, 211, 219,
    265
National Security Agency, 95, 124, 149
National Security Council (NSC),
    100–101, 104, 106, 113, 159–60
Nedzi, Lucien, 227, 229
New York Times, 237–39
Nhu, Ngo Dinh, 49–50, 151
Nixon, Donald, 112
Nixon, Pat, 31, 71, 82
Nixon, Richard, 1–3, 6, 8, 10, 12–15,
    19–20, 30–31, 38, 70, 81–82, 143,
    159, 231, 248, 263, 265
  California governor campaign, 35–36
  Cambodia and, 117, 119, 123
  Chennault file and, 144
  Chile and, 128–29, 131
  China and, 73, 142
  CIA and, 111–12, 238–39
  Cuba and, 23–25, 139, 173
  death of, 267

Nixon, Richard (*continued*)
  domestic radicals and, 123–24
  Ellsberg and, 147
  Frost and, 254–56
  Guatemala and, 17
  Helms, R., and, 98–99, 104–6, 109,
      123, 125, 138–39, 152–55, 167,
      177–78, 193–94, 198–200
  Hoover and, 141
  Hunt, E. H., and, 147–48
  impeachment investigation, 228, 232–34
  inauguration, 101–2
  JFK assassination and, 54, 60, 153
  JFK criticized by, 39–40
  Langley visit, 106–7
  Laugh-In appearance, 97
  LBJ and, 67
  at Mudge Rose, 46–47
  NSC and, 100
  pardon of, 236, 252
  political dirt sought by, 151
  presidential race of 1964 and, 71
  recording devices ordered by, 138, 173
  recordings sought from, 225–26, 232–33
  reelection campaign, 192, 195
  resignation, 235
  resignations requested by, 196
  transcripts released by, 232
  Vietnam and, 50–51, 68, 72, 94, 98,
      109–10, 117–19, 134–35, 150, 193, 206
  Vietnam War and, 7
  Watergate and, 171, 177–78
Nixon, Tricia, 231–32
North Vietnam, 72, 78, 94–95, 98, 109–10,
      117, 206–7, 243
NSC. *See* National Security Council
Nuñez, Orlando, 141

Obama, Barack, 257, 266
Ober, Richard, 89, 112, 125
O'Brien, Larry, 164–67, 192, 195
O'Connell, James, 136
Office of Strategic Services (OSS), 13, 17, 62
O'Leary, Jerry, 36–37
Oliver, Spencer, 165–66, 192, 195
Olson, Frank, 4–5

O'Malley, Francis, 122–23
Onassis, Aristotle, 15, 136
Operation CHAOS, 89, 112, 115–16, 120,
      125–26, 142, 155, 193, 219, 237–38
Operation Northwoods, 40–41, 59, 267
Operation Zapata, 3, 23–27, 140
Osborn, Howard, 89, 92, 147–48, 160,
      170, 172, 176, 189–90, 203, 237
OSS. *See* Office of Strategic Services
Oswald, Lee Harvey, 54–57, 61, 64–66,
      68–70, 84, 86–87, 91–92, 137, 267

Paar, Jack, 39
Paris Peace Accords, 207
Parker, Barrington, 260–62
Parkinson, Kenneth, 200
Patman, Wright, 193
Pawley, William, 41–42
Pearson, Drew, 84, 86, 136, 154, 159, 179
Pennington, Cecil Harold, 190
Pennington, Lee, 175–76, 190, 204, 212,
      223, 229
Pennington ruse, 190, 230
Pentagon Papers, 140, 144, 153, 217
Percy, Chuck, 134, 211
Pérez Jiménez, Marco, 19
Peter Ward novels, 74–77, 90–93, 119, 163,
      202
Pforzheimer, Walter, 75–76, 120, 228
Phillips, David, 18, 23, 26, 28, 36–37, 39,
      42, 78, 129–30, 132, 186, 199
Phoenix Program, 88
A Piece of Tape (McCord, J.), 174
Pinochet, Augusto, 266
plausible deniability, 70, 150, 176
Plumbers, 146–47, 150, 160, 162, 164, 185
Powers, Thomas, 45–46, 87, 95, 97, 245
Prados, John, 218, 237–38, 248
Project Mudhen, 160

Raborn, William, 73
Radford, Charles, 160
Ratliff, Rob Roy, 149, 157, 219
Reagan, Ronald, 96, 265–67
Redford, Robert, 236
"Restless Youth" (Helms), 106

Richard, John, 228
Richardson, Elliot, 221, 226
Rivera, Geraldo, 240–43
Robarge, David, 41, 64
Robert Mullen Company. *See* Mullen Company
Rocha, Luis Fernandez, 37–39, 55–57
Rockefeller, Nelson, 96–97
Rockefeller Commission, 210, 238–39, 243–47
Rogers, William, 109, 116, 118, 209
Roman, Jane, 65, 241
Rosen, James, 126, 161, 245
Ross, Thomas, 74
Rosselli, Johnny, 24, 32–34, 84–85, 88, 136–37, 154, 177, 253, 267
Rostow, Walt, 98
Rowan, Dan, 33, 96
Ruby, Jack, 61
Rusk, Dean, 78, 80
Russell, Lou, 215
Ryan, Pat, 13

Salvat, Juan Manuel, 39, 55
Sanchez, Nestor, 38, 45, 52, 58, 79–80, 87, 102, 245
Sayle, Edward, 175, 190
Schlatter, George, 97
Schlesinger, Arthur, 30, 35
Schlesinger, James R., 218–20, 248
Schlesinger, Richard, 59
Schneider, René, 127–32, 213, 236, 245–46, 251, 259, 266–68
Schorr, Daniel, 239, 246
Scott, Hugh, 134, 234
Scott, Win, 57
Scowcroft, Brent, 214
Select Committee on Presidential Campaign Activities in 1979 (Senate Watergate Committee), 1, 4–7, 165, 171, 216, 223, 229, 253
report of, 232–33
Senate Armed Services Committee, 74, 182, 220
Senate Foreign Relations Committee, 210, 217, 227, 261

Senate Intelligence Committee, 266
Senate Select Committee on Intelligence Activities, 67, 248
Senate Watergate Committee. *See* Select Committee on Presidential Campaign Activities in 1979
Servicio Inteligencia de Militaria (SIM), 10
Sforza, Tony, 43, 130–32
Shackley, Ted, 32, 55–56, 182
Shaw, Clay, 85, 154, 241
Sheehan, Neil, 88, 117, 119, 143
Shields, Julia, 13
Shultz, George, 178
Sihanouk, Norodom (Prince), 116–17
Silbert, Earl, 161–62, 189–90, 194, 198, 204, 221
SIM. *See* Servicio Inteligencia de Militaria
Sirica, John, 207, 215–16, 220, 225
Six Crises (Nixon, R.), 31
Six-Day War, 88
Smith, Merriman, 53
Smith, Walter Bedell, 185
South Vietnam, 48–50, 68, 72, 95, 150, 193
Soviet Union
  Cuba nuclear missile deployment by, 35–36
  Oswald and, 55–56, 62, 65, 68–69, 87
  SS-9 missile, 107–8
  strategic arms limitations talks and, 109
Special Investigations Group (CI/SIG), 64–65
SRS. *See* Security Research Service
St. George, Andrew, 156–57, 227
Sternfield, Lawrence, 163, 182
Stevens, Michael, 164–65, 202
Stone, Oliver, 199–200
strategic arms limitations talks, 109
Sturgis, Frank, 3, 22, 24, 42, 156–57, 162, 165, 169–70, 197, 227, 243, 247
Sullivan, William C., 125
Sulzberger, Cyrus, 74, 92
Swenson, Harold, 45–46
Symington, Stuart, 211, 213, 227, 229–30, 251, 258

Taiwan, 68, 94
Tepedino, Carlos, 43–44
Tet Offensive, 94–95
Thieu, Nguyen Van, 95, 97, 150, 193, 244
Thompson, Fred, 4, 224, 229–30
Three Days of the Condor (film), 236
303 Committee, 51
Trujillo, Rafael, 151, 239
Truman, Harry, 62–63, 70, 185, 213, 266
truth tapes, 56
26th of July Movement, 10, 21–22
2506 Brigade, 27, 29

United Flight 553 crash, 201

Valenti, Jack, 90–92, 163, 229
Valenzuela, Camilo, 131–32
Vasaly, Lou, 175
Veciana, Antonio, 39
Venezuela, 19–20, 51
Ventura, Esteban, 9–10
Viaux, Roberto, 130–32, 213, 236, 245
Vidal, Gore, 16, 30, 77
Viet Cong, 68, 72, 78, 88, 206
Vietnam War, 7, 72, 78, 88–90, 94, 98,
    105, 109–10, 117–19, 243–44
  bombing escalation, 193, 206
  opposition to, 134, 139
  Paris Peace Accords, 207

Wagner, Karl, 148, 172, 182
Walker & Company, 121
Walters, Vernon ("Dick"), 4, 167,
    177–82, 186–87, 196, 221–22

Waltz Group, 134–35, 191
Warren, Earl, 67–68, 84, 87
Warren Commission, 64, 66–70, 85–86,
    137, 242–43, 267
Watergate burglars, 166, 169, 186, 197,
    200, 203, 207–8, 216, 224
Watergate office complex, 164, 172, 176,
    185
Watson, Marvin, 87
Weather Underground, 124
Weathermen, 116
Wells, Ida, ("Maxie"), 166, 169, 192
Weybright, Victor, 74
Whitten, John, 33, 57, 59, 70, 253
Wilkinson, Mary Louise, 56
Williams, Edward, 189, 251, 254, 257–58,
    260–62
Wills, Garry, 71, 102–3
Wine-Volner, Jill, 226
wiretapping, 125, 141, 165–66, 176,
    191–93, 195, 197, 233
Wise, David, 74
Wisner, Frank, 12–13, 16, 20, 76,
    137
Woods, Rose Mary, 12, 31, 71, 82,
    102–3, 168, 232, 234, 267
  recordings transcribed by, 225–26
Woodward, Bob, 4, 170, 172, 188, 220,
    234, 252

Young, David, 146, 148, 157

Zapruder, Abraham, 240–41, 243,
    246–47